The Autobiography
of a Seventeenth-Century
Venetian Rabbi

The Autobiography of a Seventeenth-Century Venetian Rabbi

~

Leon Modena's
Life of Judah

(1571-16 48)

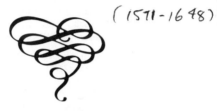

TRANSLATED AND EDITED BY

Mark R. Cohen

WITH INTRODUCTORY ESSAYS BY
Mark R. Cohen and Theodore K. Rabb,
Howard E. Adelman, and
Natalie Zemon Davis

AND HISTORICAL NOTES BY
Howard E. Adelman and
Benjamin C. I. Ravid

Princeton University Press
Princeton, New Jersey

Copyright ©1988 by Princeton University Press
Published by Princeton University Press, 41 William Street,
Princeton, New Jersey 08540
In the United Kingdom: Princeton University Press, Guildford,
Surrey

All Rights Reserved

Library of Congress Cataloging-in-Publication Data
Modena, Leone, 1571–1648.
The autobiography of a seventeenth-century Venetian rabbi.
Translation of: Ḥaye Yehudah.
Bibliography: p.
Includes index.
1. Modena, Leone, 1571–1648. 2. Rabbis—Italy—Venice—
Biography. 3. Venice (Italy)—Biography. 4. Jews—Italy—
Venice—History. 5. Venice (Italy)—Ethnic relations. I. Cohen,
Mark R., 1943– . II. Title. III. Title: Leon Modena's Life of
Judah. IV. Title: Life of Judah.
BM755.M546A3 1988 296′.092′4 [B] 88-4190
ISBN 0-691-05529-7 ISBN 0-691-00824-8 (pbk.)

Publication of this book has been aided by the Whitney Darrow
Fund of Princeton University Press

This book has been composed in Linotron Bembo type

FRONTISPIECE: Portrait of Leon Modena, detail enlarged
from the title page of the 1638 Venice edition of his
Historia de' riti hebraici.

To Hanan and Tamar
and to the students in
History/Near Eastern Studies 442

"I thought that it would be of value to . . . the fruit
of my loins, and to their descendants, and to my students . . ."
—from *The Life of Judah*

Contents

Illustrations

The translator-editor and publishers are grateful to the following for permission to use photographs and copyright material: the librarian of the Jewish Theological Seminary Library for the frontispiece and figures 8 and 10; Allen Lane-Penguin Books Ltd. for figure 1; the World Monuments Fund (formerly the International Fund for Monuments) for figure 14; Biblioteca Ambrosiana, Milan for figures 3, 4, 6, 9, 11, 12, and 18; the Comunità Israelitica di Venezia for figures 5 and 7.

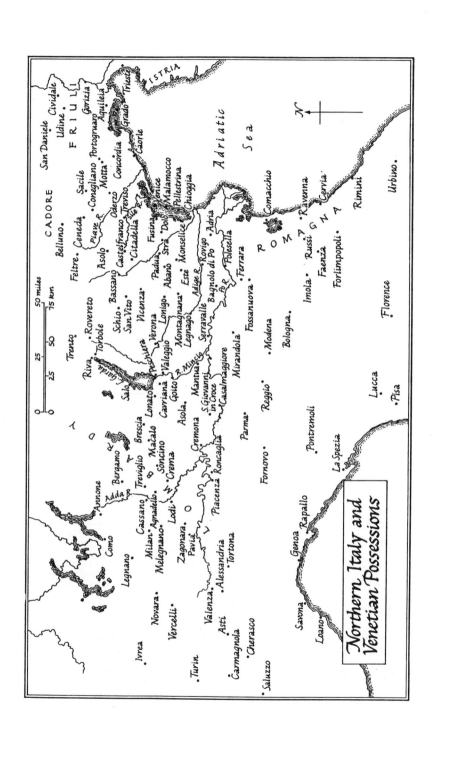

Northern Italy and Venetian Possessions

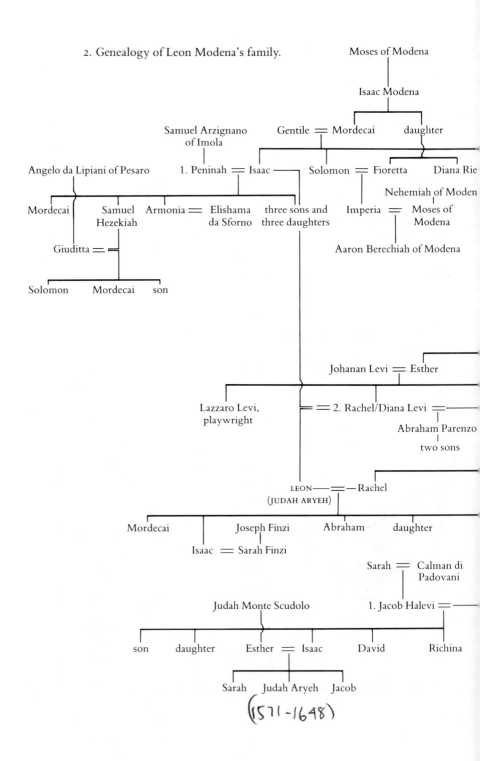

2. Genealogy of Leon Modena's family.

Moses of Modena

Isaac Modena

Samuel Arzignano of Imola

Gentile = Mordecai   daughter

Angelo da Lipiani of Pesaro   1. Peninah = Isaac   Solomon = Fioretta   Diana Rie

Nehemiah of Moden

Mordecai   Samuel   Armonia = Elishama   three sons and   Imperia = Moses of
             Hezekiah   da Sforno   three daughters   Modena

Giuditta =   Aaron Berechiah of Modena

Solomon   Mordecai   son

Johanan Levi = Esther

Lazzaro Levi,   = 2. Rachel/Diana Levi =
playwright   Abraham Parenzo

two sons

LEON——=—Rachel
(JUDAH ARYEH)

Mordecai   Joseph Finzi   Abraham   daughter

Isaac = Sarah Finzi

Sarah = Calman di
        Padovani

Judah Monte Scudolo   1. Jacob Halevi =—

son   daughter   Esther = Isaac   David   Richina

Sarah   Judah Aryeh   Jacob

(1571-1648)

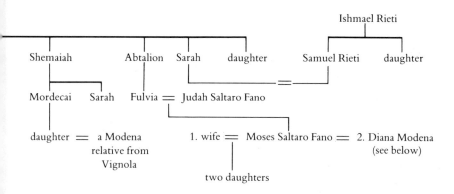

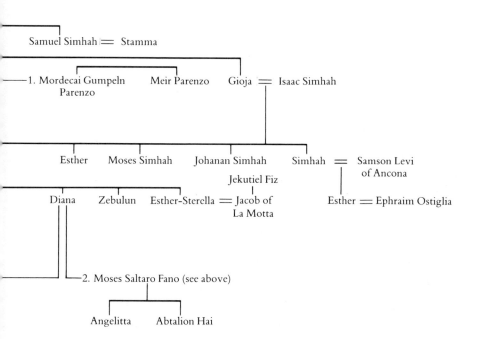

Ishmael Rieti

Shemaiah   Abtalion Sarah   daughter   Samuel Rieti   daughter

Mordecai Sarah Fulvia = Judah Saltaro Fano

daughter = a Modena   1. wife = Moses Saltaro Fano = 2. Diana Modena
relative from   (see below)
Vignola

two daughters

Samuel Simhah = Stamma

1. Mordecai Gumpeln   Meir Parenzo   Gioja = Isaac Simhah
Parenzo

Esther   Moses Simhah   Johanan Simhah   Simhah = Samson Levi
                            Jekutiel Fiz   of Ancona

Diana   Zebulun   Esther-Sterella = Jacob of   Esther = Ephraim Ostiglia
                               La Motta

2. Moses Saltaro Fano (see above)

Angelitta   Abtalion Hai

Preface

IN THE SPRING of 1980 Natalie Zemon Davis, Theodore K. Rabb, and I collaborated to design and teach an undergraduate seminar at Princeton on the Jews in early modern Europe from the comparative perspective of early modern European and Jewish history. Our syllabus included readings in Jewish primary sources in English translation, touching on several important problems in the economic and social history of the sixteenth, seventeenth, and eighteenth centuries. Wishing to devote a session to the genre of autobiography and self-presentation, we decided at my suggestion to assign an autobiography that had intrigued me ever since I had read it for the first time while preparing my study of the book on Jewish rites, *Historia de' riti hebraici*, by that fascinating figure of the seventeenth-century Venetian ghetto, Leon Modena (1571–1648).[1] The work we chose was the latter's well-known Hebrew autobiography, *Hayyei yehudah* (The Life of Judah), published by Abraham Kahana in 1911. For the seminar we relied on a tentative English translation of the Kahana text prepared under my supervision by a Princeton senior, Brenda Bodenheimer.

Subsequently, Davis, Rabb, and I decided that because only excerpts of this autobiography, so important for both Jewish and general history, had been published in English,[2] it ought to be made available in its entirety to the English reading public. Accordingly, I undertook to prepare a translation based directly on the original manuscript, which Kahana had not been able to locate.[3] Davis and Rabb undertook to contribute introductory material that would give the comparative perspective. And I invited two specialists on

[1] Mark R. Cohen, "Leone da Modena's *Riti*: A Seventeenth-Century Plea for Social Toleration of Jews," *JSS* 34 (1972): 287–321.

[2] Leo W. Schwarz, *Memoirs of My People* (Philadelphia, 1960), pp. 75–83; Jacob R. Marcus, *The Jew in the Medieval World* (repr. Cleveland, 1960), pp. 406–408; Curt Leviant, *Masterpieces of Hebrew Literature* (New York, 1969), pp. 543–550 (reproducing the section translated in Schwarz).

[3] As stated in his introduction, Kahana thought that the manuscript had been donated about 1883 to the Brera Library in Milan; actually (see below) it was located in the Ambrosiana Library there.

Jewish Venice, Benjamin Ravid of Brandeis University and Howard Adelman—then engaged with a dissertation at Brandeis on
Leon Modena and now on the faculty of Smith College—to pool
their scholarly resources and compile historical notes for the edition.

The manuscript of *Hayyei yehudah* first came to the attention of
Jewish scholars in the nineteenth century. Several of them quoted
or paraphrased parts of it in their writings.[4] One was Moses Soave,
who copied it in its entirety in 1857 and then published an Italian
summary of its contents in twenty installments in *Il Corriere israe-
litico* (1863–1865). Kahana, unable to locate the original manuscript, used the handwritten Hebrew transcription by Soave for his
edition of *Hayyei yehudah*.

The whereabouts of the manuscript were unknown until the
1960s, when Nehemya Allony and Ephraim Kupfer rediscovered it
among a cache of uncataloged Hebrew manuscripts in the Biblioteca Ambrosiana in Milan.[5] (Folio numbers are given in the translation in brackets, marked "MS," and all mentions of specific passages in the autobiography are cross-referenced by these folio
numbers.) Allony and Kupfer judged Kahana's printed text to be
generally faithful to the original, though "with mistakes in a few
places." My own study of the manuscript, however, initially from

---

[4] Samuel D. Luzzatto briefly summarized the manuscript for his friend, Solomon L.
Rapoport, in his letter to him dated April 18, 1834, published in *Iggerot shadal (S. D.
Luzzatto's hebräische Briefe)*, ed. Eisig Graber, 2 (Przemyśl, 1882), no. 96, pp. 288–293.
Hayyim J. Michael, who died in 1846 while compiling a dictionary of Jewish scholars,
selected details from the manuscript for his entry on Modena, and his short summary
appeared in his posthumously published work, *Or ha-hayyim* (Frankfurt am Main,
1891), pp. 439–444. In his introduction to *Behinat ha-kabbalah* (Gorizia, 1852), a study of
the controversial book *Kol sakhal*, attributed by many to Modena, and of Modena's incomplete response to it entitled *Sha'agat aryeh*, Isaac Samuel Reggio summarized Modena's life on the basis of a copy of *Hayyei yehudah* made from the autograph manuscript.
From the same copy, Abraham Geiger quoted some sections of the autobiography and
summarized others in *Leon da Modena: Rabbiner zu Venedig und seine Stellung zur Kabbalah, zum Thalmud, und zum Christenthume* (Breslau, 1856), Hebrew section, fols. 15a–
17b.
[5] Nehemya Allony and Ephraim Kupfer, "Kitvei-yad 'ivriyim nosafim be-ambrosi-
anah be-milano she-lo nikhlelu bi-reshimat bernheimer," *Areshet* 4 (1965–1966): 234–
235, 257. The manuscript (shelfmark X 119 sup.) is described in Aldo Luzzatto and Luisa
Mortara Ottolenghi, *Hebraica Ambrosiana*: Part I, *Catalogue of Undescribed Hebrew Manuscripts in the Ambrosiana Library* (Milan, 1972), pp. 81–82. Several later manuscripts of
Hayyei yehudah exist in European libraries. I read one of them (Oxford MS 1234.11) and
found it to be full of mistakes.

microfilm and later at the Biblioteca Ambrosiana itself, revealed many mistakes and also omissions in the Kahana text. Equally important, examination of the manuscript disclosed interesting features that tell much about Modena's manner of writing and sense of self. Finally, access to the manuscript has made it possible to verify for the first time the assumption held by nearly all previous observers that it is, indeed, the author's autograph. A full discussion of these matters has been reserved for excursus 2, "Who Wrote the Ambrosiana Manuscript of *Hayyei yehudah?*"

The new Hebrew edition of the autobiography published by Daniel Carpi in 1985[6] (page numbers are given in the translation in brackets and marked "C"), with its accurate transcription of the Ambrosiana manuscript, obviated the need for the full critical apparatus originally planned for this volume. Most of the references in the textual notes to manuscript readings and other paleographical aspects relate to characteristic features of the manuscript or to the meaning of specific words or passages.

The Translation

The translation of Modena's autobiography strives to be as literal as possible, conveying straightforwardly the facts and episodes recounted by the author in the Hebrew original. Of necesssity, missing from the English rendition is a sense of the literary flavor of the author's prose. Modena took pride in his ability as a writer of letters and an author of published works, and he paid careful attention to style. This fact can be ascertained, for instance, from the handwritten drafts of some of his letters and responsa that still survive, from his professional activity as a writing teacher, and from notes on stylistic rules that he made in preparation for an epistolographic manual he planned to write.[7] Even though Modena never intended

---

[6] *Sefer hayyei yehudah le-r. yehudah aryeh mi-modena ish venetziah*, ed. Daniel Carpi (Tel Aviv, 1985). Carpi's view on the copyist of the manuscript, which differs from the one held here, is discussed in excursus 2. Carpi mentioned his theory in the introduction to his companion edition of Modena's grandson Isaac min Haleviim's autobiography, *Meddabber tahpukhot* (Tel Aviv, 1985), p. 22, and his view was earlier reported by Yacob Boksenboim in the introduction to his new edition of Modena's Hebrew correspondence, *Iggerot rabbi yehudah aryeh mi-modena* (Tel Aviv, 1984), pp. 4–5.

[7] The character of Modena's rough drafts is discussed by Boksenboim in *Iggerot*, pp. 1–3; for Modena's notes on stylistic rules, see ibid., pp. 343–344.

Hayyei yehudah to be published, it seems clear from the text that he tried hard to make what was essentially a prosaic narrative interesting from a literary point of view. As elsewhere in his works, Modena's writing of the autobiography may have gone through stages, beginning with rough ideas and ending with polished prose. Certain features of the Ambrosiana manuscript discussed in the second excursus suggest, in fact, that Modena may even have written out drafts of some sections of the autobiography before transcribing them into the manuscript in their present form.

One very creative feature of Modena's Hebrew style that comes across only imperfectly in the translation is his skillful use of biblical allusions. Like many other Hebrew authors, especially in premodern times, Modena enjoyed taking a fragment of a biblical verse, well known to the reader in its scriptural or rabbinic context, and applying it in a fresh and linguistically catchy manner in a new context.[8] An example from early in the autobiography will illustrate a simple type of such adaptation. Modena writes about a dispute between his father and his paternal uncles. This quarrel lasted more than thirty-two years and, he says, diminished the family's potential business profits: "ve-'im hayu la-ahadim hayah beineihem 'osher yoter mi-me'ah elef" (had they united, together they would have had wealth in excess of one hundred thousand). The translation "had they united" does less than justice to the allusion here. The phrase "ve-'im hayu la-ahadim" is borrowed from part of a verse in Ezekiel (37:17), "ve-hayu la-ahadim be-yadekha" (and they shall become one in your hand). In Ezekiel, a group of sticks "become one" in the prophet's hand, symbolizing God's messianic promise to gather all the dispersed children of Israel and reunite them in their land under King David. Modena intended the reader of his autobiography to recall the passage in Ezekiel and admire his original and clever use of this reference in a new, rather mundane, context.

In more involved examples of this creative adaptation of biblical verses, Modena ingeniously altered words in order to convey entirely new meanings while retaining an echo of the original. Thus, in a passage describing his daughter Diana's first husband, Jacob

---

[8] Some of the stylistic rules Modena included among the notes for his book on letter writing refer to this literary device; see previous note.

Halevi, Modena changed the words in Exodus 4:36, "hatan damim la-mulot" (a bridegroom of blood because of the circumcision) to "hatan tamim le-maʿalot" (a son-in-law of perfect virtues). Interestingly, either the copyist Soave or the editor of the first printed edition, Kahana, failing to understand the pun, transcribed incorrectly "hatan damim le-maʿalot," thus obliterating Modena's artful adaptation.

In a translation it is very difficult to convey these sorts of literary devices. The reader interested in studying this aspect of Modena's style more thoroughly should consult the new Hebrew edition of *Hayyei yehudah* by Carpi. In the textual notes to this translation I have supplied biblical references selectively, with special attention to passages containing adaptations of or wordplay on biblical texts.

Like most other Hebrew works of its period, Modena's is peppered with abbreviations. For the most part I have translated them as if they had been written out in full in the original, for example "of blessed memory" for *z-l*, the abbreviation for *zikhrono li-vera-khah*. The frequently used abbreviation *alef-alef* for *adoni avi*, "my master, my father," has been rendered somewhat freely as "my revered father." For dates rendered according to the Jewish *anno mundi* system, Modena recorded the year sometimes with and sometimes without the letter *h* (*heʾ*), the fifth letter of the Hebrew alphabet, which stands for the millennium 5(000). In the latter instance I placed the number 5 in brackets.

Far too many events take place on *r-h, rosh hodesh,* for all of them actually to have occurred on "the first day of the month," namely, the new moon. I have preserved the ambiguity of the original by translating *rosh hodesh* "at the beginning of the month," except, of course, when the day of the week is also given and it corresponds to the day of *rosh hodesh*. The phrase "leil biʾat yom X," which Modena employs quite often, is rendered "the night of the arrival of [day] X," in order to capture the reality of Jewish calendrical reckoning, which regards a day as beginning the previous night in accordance with the verse in the biblical Creation story, "and it was evening, and it was morning" (Genesis 1:5 etc.).

In the original, names of people are almost invariably preceded by some designation. Women are called *marat*; men are called *r* for *rabbenu*. I have left these words, "mistress" and "master," respectively, untranslated, because they are not proper titles. Only when a genuine title is involved have I rendered it in the text. Thus *m-h-r-r* (morenu ha-rav rabbenu) along with its variants (e.g., *k-m-h-r-r*, kevod morenu ha-rav rabbenu), the official designation of a scholar who had been ordained rabbi, is translated "Rabbi," and the abbreviation *h-h-r (he-haver)* is rendered *haver*, the title formally accorded to students who had not yet attained rabbinical rank.

The rendition of Italian family names poses something of a problem. Did Jews called *mi-x*, "of *X*," in Hebrew go by the name "*da [or di] X*" in Italian? The mistake regarding the name "Leon da Modena" that has perpetuated itself in publication after publication provides a case in point. In the autobiography (fol. 5a), Modena, who in Hebrew was known as Yehudah Aryeh *mi-modena*, states explicitly that he signed his name in Italian "Leon Modena *da Venezia*," as he was not a resident of Modena at all. Rather, he relates, that was the Italian city in which his ancestors had settled after migrating from France. His grandfather had moved from Modena to Bologna, and Leon himself had been born and later settled permanently in Venice. Interestingly, the only place in the autobiography that he writes "*da Modena*" (fol. 35b) is the exception that proves the rule, for in that instance he is copying in Hebrew transcription a reference to himself in Italian in a book by Manasseh ben Israel.

In general, therefore, Hebrew toponymic names in the autobiography have been treated in the translation as simple family names (Mordecai Modena, Moses Fano, etc.), unless the preposition "of" occurs in the text in the form of the Hebrew transcription of the Italian *da* or *di* (two examples: fols. 6a and 14a) or it is known from other sources or seems implicit from the context in the autobiography that the person actually lived in the place (two examples: fols. 4b [see historical note] and 24b). For Italian personal names that vary in the vernacular sources as regards the use of single or double consonant (e.g., Grasin/Grassin), the spelling with double consonant has been adopted for the sake of consistency.

A somewhat simplified system of Hebrew transliteration has been employed, omitting the underdot that in more scientific transliterations distinguishes *het* from *he'* and *tet* from *tav*, rendering *tzadi* by *tz*, and using *v* for both *vet* and *vav*. All Hebrew words in titles and extracted phrases have been rendered in lowercase letters (including proper nouns) because Hebrew does not distinguish between capital and lowercase letters. The symbols ' and ' represent *alef* and *'ayin*, respectively. Wherever a Hebrew transcription of an Italian word reflects the Venetian dialect by dropping a final vowel, that spelling has been retained in the translation (as in Leon for Leone, Francolin for Francolino, *camin* for *camino*).

Finally, for converting dates from the Jewish calendar to the Gregorian, use was made of Eduard Mahler's *Handbuch der jüdischen Chronologie* (Leipzig, 1916).

A Collaborative Edition

This edition of *The Life of Judah* is a collaborative effort of Jewish and general historians, and the introductory essays and historical notes are meant to demonstrate its value for both Jewish studies and European history as a whole. The first introductory essay, entitled "The Significance of Leon Modena's Autobiography for Early Modern Jewish and General European History," coauthored by myself and Theodore Rabb, provides a sketch of some of the fascinating features of Jewish social life in sixteenth- and early seventeenth-century Italy reflected in the autobiography and suggests ways in which this and other sources about the Jews might be studied comparatively with beneficial results. Howard Adelman's introductory essay, "Leon Modena: The Autobiography and the Man," draws on an intimate knowledge of the man's biography and works to present a fresh overview of his life and to lay the groundwork for a new assessment of this very important figure of early modern Jewish history. Natalie Davis's illuminating essay, "Fame and Secrecy: Leon Modena's *Life* as an Early Modern Autobiography," places the work within the context of European autobiography, both Christian and Jewish, and shows just how fruitful a comparative study of Jewish autobiography can be. The historical notes compiled by Howard Adelman and Benjamin Ravid, on the basis of primary information in Jewish literary sources and in the Venetian archives as well as on the latest research on Venice, illuminate the author's life and place him within the wider context of Venetian and Italian Jewish history at the end of the sixteenth century and during the first half of the seventeenth. (Words or passages in the text annotated in the historical notes are indicated by a superscript letter.) Benjamin Ravid's essay, "The Venetian Ghetto in Historical Perspective" (excursus 1), presents a succinct and up-to-date description of the setting in which Leon Modena lived.

We hope that this collaborative work will serve students and teachers alike by providing a worthy addition to the small library of Jewish autobiographies from the early modern period that have already been translated, in whole or in part, into English, including the popular memoirs of Glückel of Hameln, the oft-cited autobiography of Solomon Maimon, the memoirs of Ber of Bolechow, the memoirs of David Reuveni, and the handy autobiographical excerpts (including one from *Hayyei yehudah*) in Leo W. Schwarz's *Memoirs of My People*. These works, as well as many other Hebrew ones less accessible to the general reader—such as the memoirs of Josel of Rosheim, the autobiographical sections of Abraham Yagel's *Gei'hizzayon*, and the memoirs of Leon Modena's younger contemporaries, Yom Tov Lippman Heller (*Megillat eivah*, represented by a short excerpt in Schwarz's *Memoirs of My People*), Asher Halevi (a brief excerpt from which can be found in English translation in Jacob R. Marcus's *The Jew in the Medieval World*), and Modena's own grandson Isaac min Haleviim—offer promising opportunities for studying the social history of the Jews within the context of early modern European history and, as Natalie Davis's essay suggests, for investigating the genre of Jewish autobiography from a comparative perspective.

Princeton, New Jersey   Mark R. Cohen
Eve of Rosh Hashanah 5748
September 23, 1987

Acknowledgments

WITH MANY collaborators come many acknowledgments. I am grateful to the keepers of the manuscript collections of the Biblioteca Ambrosiana in Milan for their assistance during my visit there in July 1983 to work on the *Hayyei yehudah* manuscript, and, in particular, to the library's knowledgeable Hebrew manuscripts bibliographer, Don Pier Francesco Fumagalli, who was also kind enough to answer additional questions about the manuscript by mail. Princeton University's Committee on Research in the Humanities and Social Sciences provided grants to subsidize my trip to Milan and to assist with some of the technical aspects of preparing this book for publication. The Committee on Aid to Faculty Scholarship of Smith College provided assistance to collaborator Howard Adelman. Abraham David of the Institute for Microfilmed Hebrew Manuscripts of the Jewish National and University Library, Jerusalem, helped locate manuscripts to be consulted for the historical notes. John G. Graiff of the William A. Neilson Library at Smith College assisted in obtaining interlibrary loans of books needed to check references in the historical notes. Many insights of Marvin Fox, rendered as a member of Howard Adelman's dissertation committee (together with Benjamin Ravid and myself), have found their way into this volume, particularly in the historical notes. Reuven Bonfil of the Hebrew University helped me understand and hence properly translate several difficult passages in the autobiography. Conversations in Jerusalem with Yacob Boksenboim, the editor of Modena's Hebrew letters, about aspects of Modena's writings gave me additional insights. The constructive criticisms of David Ruderman of Yale University, one of the readers of our manuscript for Princeton University Press, helped make the book a better one. A number of other scholars made helpful comments about specific portions of the work, and their contributions are acknowledged at the appropriate places. The beautiful original photographs of scenes of Jewish Venice that grace this book are the work of photographer Benjamin Hertzberg and his wife Lilian.

I wish also to thank collaborators Howard Adelman and Benjamin Ravid for carefully reading my drafts of the translation and textual notes and suggesting numerous valuable changes. It would not have been possible to complete the project were it not for the enthusiasm, cooperation, and continued advice and counsel of all four of my collaborators, from each of whom I have learned much, not only about the subject at hand but also about how rewarding a collaborative project can be. Thanks are due, too, to our Princeton editor, Joanna Hitchcock, whose enthusiasm for the project from beginning to end was a continual source of encouragement, and to H. Abigail Bok, whose astute copy-editing helped bring unity to a complex book of multiple authorship. For their assistance with the typing of components of the manuscript I thank Grace Edelman, Judy Gross, and Dorothy Rothbard. Finally, I thank my wife, Ilene, who saw the worthiness of publishing Leon Modena's autobiography in an English translation years ago and never ceased to encourage me through the countless stages of revision.

NATALIE DAVIS's introductory essay to this volume was published in an Italian translation in *Quaderni Storici* n.s. 64 (1987): 39–60, and excursus I was published by Benjamin Ravid in a slightly different version in *Brandeis Review* 5 (Spring 1986): 11–14.

Abbreviations

AJSR	*Association for Jewish Studies Review*
ASV	Archivio di Stato di Venezia
BL	British Library
B.T.	Babylonian Talmud
CI	*Il Corriere israelitico*
EI	*L'Educatore israelitica*
EJ	*Encyclopaedia Judaica*
ENA	Elkan Nathan Adler Collection of Manuscripts
HUCA	*Hebrew Union College Annual*
JBA	*Jewish Book Annual*
JE	*Jewish Encyclopedia*
JQR	*Jewish Quarterly Review*
JSS	*Jewish Social Studies*
JTSA	Jewish Theological Seminary of America
KS	*Kiryat Sefer*
MGWJ	*Monatsschrift für Geschichte und Wissenschaft des Judentums*
n.s.	new series
Or.	Oriental Collection
o.s.	old series
PAAJR	*Proceedings of the American Academy for Jewish Research*
REJ	*Revue des études juives*
RMI	*La Rassegna mensile di Israel*
TJHSE	*Transactions of the Jewish Historical Society of England*
VI	*Il Vessilo israelitico*
ZHB	*Zeitschrift für Hebräische Bibliographie*

Currency Equivalents

1 lira	=	20 soldi
1 ducat	=	6 lire 4 soldi
1 ducat	=	124 soldi
1 ducat	=	6.2 lire
1 ducat	=	1 florin = 1 scudo

Introductory Essays

The Significance of Leon Modena's Autobiography for Early Modern Jewish and General European History

MARK R. COHEN AND
THEODORE K. RABB

LEON MODENA began writing his autobiography two months after the death of his eldest son, Mordecai, on November 7, 1617, though he had first conceived of the idea of writing his life story more than twenty-four years earlier, wishing "to bequeath it as a gift for my firstborn son, the apple of my eye, the root of my heart." Too late for that, he sought solace in his bereavement by relating the events of his life for the benefit of his other children, his descendants through them, and his students.

Between January 1618 and 1622, Modena compiled a history of his family from the migration of his paternal forebears from France to Italy to the brutal murder of his youngest son Zebulun in the latter year. In the years following that shocking event, Modena returned to his autobiography at irregular intervals (not every six months as he had originally planned), filling in the continuing saga of his life and family. He continued to add to his chronicle until just a few weeks before his death on March 21, 1648.

Though essentially the story of one man's life within his family,[1] *The Life of Judah* also opens a window on northern Italian Jewish life in general in the sixteenth and seventeenth centuries. Tucked into this intimate autobiography is a wealth of fascinating detail that sheds much light on the economic, social, and cultural realities of the age in which the author lived.

Modena's ancestors belonged to that familiar group of Ashkenazic (known in Italian as Tedeschi) moneylenders who, during the later Middle Ages, abandoned the increasingly inhospitable lands of northern Europe to establish new homes in the credit-hungry

---

[1] On Modena's life and achievements, see Howard Adelman's introductory essay, "Leon Modena: The Autobiography and the Man."

3

cities of northern Italy. They were awarded residential and money-lending privileges in the city of Modena, where, he claims, "they were the first to establish a pawnshop." One member of the family, a contemporary of Leon's, retained all the "privileges" confirmed over the generations by the gentile rulers of that city. Moneylending continued to be the economic mainstay of young Modena's family in its moves from place to place in northern Italy during the latter part of the sixteenth century; Modena's father left behind "notes of credit worth thousands of gold pieces" when the family was forced to leave Bologna in 1569 "because of the oppressive expulsion decreed by Pope Pius V."

By the end of the sixteenth century, when Modena was a young man, commerce, especially of a maritime nature, had become well entrenched alongside Ashkenazic moneylending. It was cultivated mainly by Sephardim—whether arrived in Italy directly from the Iberian Peninsula or indirectly via some intermediate port of call, primarily in the Levant—who knew how to take advantage of the possibilities offered by the far-flung Iberian diaspora. On the occasion of his marriage in 1590 to a cousin living in Venice, Modena could note with pride the presence of "Levantine Jews, who at that time abounded in important persons." This wedding took place just one year after the Levantine Jewish merchants and Marrano émigrés from the Iberian Peninsula (called by the Venetian government "Ponentine Jews") had received their first charter regularizing their status in Venice. Twice in his life Modena missed the opportunity to enter commerce—once in partnership with a Sephardi named Solomon Navarro, who let him down. A career in trade might have made his life considerably easier, but doubtless he would have been less productive as a scholar.

In fact, the autobiography graphically documents the vicissitudes of a Jewish family, typical of many others at that time, not blessed by great inherited wealth. Our autobiographer's father became impoverished when Leon was still very young and died without leaving any material legacy. Modena was left to seek his livelihood mainly in such unlucrative occupations as teacher, preacher, scribe, and rabbi. In one place he tells us: "I earned these [ducats] by using my pen, my tongue, and my wits." The reader, assaulted by the recounting of poverty, attendant debts, and other hardships, develops a certain sympathy for the suffering writer who, time and again, resorts to the gambling table in hopes of staving off economic disaster, if only temporarily, and perhaps also of gaining some diversion from his tribulations.

The autobiography offers glimpses of the physical, social, and cultural realities of the Venetian ghetto;[2] it is a confined existence, crammed into multistoried, multifamily dwellings. Generations of vertical expansion within the ghetto's limited space sought to accommodate a population growing from both natural increase and immigration. Modena writes during the plague of 1630–1631: "Above and below me and on all sides, left and right, people have taken ill and died." Newcomers, lacking a well-established family dwelling, were frequently forced to move from place to place within the ghetto; hence the peregrinations of the Modena family from apartment to apartment.

Despite the physical segregation of the Italian Jews in the seventeenth century, there persisted a rich cultural life that exhibited tastes and interests acquired during the Renaissance—that time of intense interaction between Jews and their Christian surroundings in Italy. Witness Modena's brief description of his youthful course of study, which included "a little instruction in playing an instrument, in singing, in dancing, in writing, and in Latin"; or his eulogy for his favorite son-in-law, Jacob Halevi, whose "profession was dancing," that is, a dance teacher. On and off during his own lifetime, Modena drew income from such secular pursuits as "music," "Italian sonnets," "writing comedies," and "directing them," and lists one of his comic plays, a pastoral called *Rachel and Jacob*, in the "bibliography" recorded in his autobiography.

Although the ghetto imposed a physical barrier between Jews and Christians, members of the two groups continued to have frequent contact even after the erection of its walls and gates. As the autobiography shows, the ghetto gates were open during the daylight hours, and people moved in and out freely. Indeed, a venture outside the ghetto—whether to shop for books, to work in the printshop of Christians, to gamble, to visit gentile friends, to give

---

[2] On the origins of the ghetto in which Modena lived and on the historical significance of the "ghetto" in Jewish history, in general, see excursus 1, "The Venetian Ghetto in Historical Perspective," by Benjamin Ravid.

instruction to gentile students, to appear in court at St. Mark's—is such a commonplace that Modena takes it for granted without special comment. He describes a walk via the Rialto to Campo San Cassiano only because of a mishap on the way—he narrowly escapes being crushed to death by a falling chimney.

Also, conversely, there is frequent mention of the flow of Christians into the ghetto compound, curious gentiles who find much to fascinate them in this teeming Jewish quarter. Not the least of the attractions are the sermons of the ghetto's most popular preacher, Rabbi Leon Modena. He boasts, "I preached in the synagogue of the Sephardim. . . . In attendance were the brother of the king of France, who was accompanied by some French noblemen and by five of the most important Christian preachers who gave sermons that Pentecost. God put such learned words into my mouth that all were very pleased, including many other Christians who were present." Modena, like so many other learned Italian Jews during and after the Renaissance, had extensive relations with Christians, as students, admirers, correspondents, and interlocutors.

Through the interstices of this personal and family portrait there are glimpses of the religious atmosphere in this still premodern Jewish society. Everywhere in the autobiography the presence of God is to be felt. He is thanked and praised. His blessings are invoked. His mercy is sought. And when the writer suffers, he states, "I do not know why God continues to treat me so roughly." By Modena's time, kabbalistic mysticism had permeated Italian Jewish religiosity, and its adherents frequently appeared in his life: the noted Menahem Azariah Fano, who circumcised him; childhood tutors, including members of the eminent Basola family; and his son-in-law, Jacob Halevi. Modena knew the Kabbalah well. Ultimately, he came to oppose it, as we learn from the autobiography's account of the origins of his antikabbalistic treatise, *Ari nohem*.

The life cycle of births, marriages, and above all confessions, elegies, burials, and mourning—the religious rites surrounding death—emerges as well in the autobiographical narrative, which has no shortage of deaths to report. We read of life in the synagogue—services, study sessions, and, because Modena excelled in it, the all-important sermons—and of the extrasynagogal religious and charitable activity of the various Jewish confraternities, which by the seventeenth century existed in large numbers. On and off Modena supplemented his income by preaching and teaching for the Ashkenazic Torah Study Society. He even compiled a confessional for use by the burial confraternity known as the Gemilut Hasadim Society (Society for Good Deeds). And he contributed a poem to a book for the Shomerim La-boker Society, a group, influenced by Kabbalah, that rose early each morning to hold penitential vigils.

Alongside synagogue, confraternity, and expressions of faith in the supreme being, the autobiography provides a healthy dose of what is known as "popular religion." Modena's life, like that of many of his Jewish contemporaries, attests to the characteristic modus vivendi in Judaism between certain types of popular magic or superstition and "official" rabbinic religion. Bibliomancy—seeking an omen by asking a child what biblical verse he had learned that day in school—is a favored device when trouble looms. The same Rabbi Leon Modena who preaches, teaches, and issues responsa also writes, teaches, and traffics in amulets and engages in dream divination. Astrology is a commonplace for him: children are born "under a propitious star," and he lives with the firm conviction that "the heavens [are] battling against us."

He has his horoscope foretold "by four astrologers, two Jews and two Christians," then rues having done it, nervously contemplating its prediction that he will die two years hence. As if to cancel the horoscope after the fact, he dons his cap as rabbi and exponent of "official" Judaism and acknowledges that engaging in the very act runs counter to the belief in God's omnipotence. "So here I am today, pained on account of the past and anxious about the future. But God will do as he pleases." Finally, the autobiography unabashedly presents Jews (often along with Christians) engaged in the popular pastime of alchemy. Modena's uncle Shemaiah "became attracted to alchemy"; Modena himself pursues the magical art; his son Mordecai sets up an alchemy laboratory in the ghetto, only to fall ill and die from exposure to the fumes produced by the chemicals.

One is struck by the preoccupation, characteristic of the wider society as well, with illness and death. Graphic descriptions of symptoms abound: "All through that summer I was ill with pains in my stomach"; "everyone said that nothing was wrong except for a little diarrhea"; "he . . . took to his bed, sick and in a crazed state. He lasted only five days, with a persistent burning fever"; and so on. Smallpox was a distressing fact of life. Modena had caught the illness as a child; his own sons contracted it in an outbreak of 1596 during which "more than seventy boys and girls in our holy community died within six months," though, fortunately for him, his own survived; and he lost an infant grandson to the disease. Mentioned, too, is the mental illness of his wife that dominated his later life, and his own bouts of depression, which cast a shadow over his personal life time and time again.

There is also, of course, the scourge of plague. Particularly noteworthy for the additional light it sheds on general Italian history is Modena's eyewitness account of the devastating plague of 1630–1631. He offers, for instance, a glimpse of the quarantine procedure in Venice—goods suspected of being contaminated are sequestered in the Lazzaretto. And he recounts the harsh economic consequences of the pestilence: "An unprecedented rise in prices has been the worst blow of all, causing many Jews in these communities to become impoverished, the rich becoming middling and the middling poor, and no one taking pity any longer on the poor, for there is no money."

Related to illness and death is the attitude about medicine. Modena greatly respects the medical profession, the Jewish practitioners of which were much admired during the Renaissance and after. He relates that his own grandfather had been "a great, distinguished physician, having been awarded the medical diploma while Emperor Charles V was still in Bologna." Like others of his time, Modena combines admiration for the healing skills of trained physicians with a belief in the efficacy of folk medicine. As his son Mordecai lies on his deathbed, Modena tries everything, "but could not find a remedy." Then he has "eleven doctors, Jewish and Christian, consulting about his malady, some during personal visits and others through correspondence." Finally, when all else fails, he accedes in his desperation to his son's request for the suspect "remedies" of the very same priest who had introduced him to the alchemy that was to cause his death.

The life of the Jewish family figures prominently in the text, epitomized by Modena's closeness to his son, Mordecai. Modena's reverence for his ancestors is apparent. The very opening of the text proclaims his lineage, and he then waxes eloquent about several of his forebears. Marriages take place—of course, arranged by parents—along with the all-important assembling of a dowry, a burden that caused the nearly perpetually penurious writer anxiety on more than one occasion. Women in the family appear frequently—to be sure, mostly in their roles as wife and childbearer. But there is also Aunt Fioretta, "a woman very learned in Torah and Talmud," and Modena's mother courageously riding "like a man" from Montagnana to Ferrara and Venice to plead for her husband's release from debtor's prison. Modena writes with concern about his daughter Diana, whose second husband mistreated her (although the evils wrought by the man are left to the reader's imagination). There is even a glimpse of a woman's romantic love for her intended groom in what must be the most poignant scene in the autobiography, and indeed in the Hebrew literature of the period. Modena arrives in Venice to wed his beautiful cousin Esther, with whom he had been matched by his mother and aunt and of whom he had dreamed "using prayer without conjuration, in order to see the woman intended as my mate." He finds her confined to bed and near death. "On the day she died, she summoned me and embraced and kissed me. She said, 'I know that this is bold behavior, but God knows that during the one year of our engagement we did not touch each other even with our little fingers. Now, at the time of death, the rights of the dying are mine.' "

In addition to the saddening death of the young, the autobiography is peppered with festive weddings and the joyous birth of children. In evidence are the warm feelings of husbands for wives, of parents for children—even stepchildren—and parental hopes for children's futures. Parents visit married children even in other cities, and the reverse is also true. Particularly absorbing in this text is the relationship of Modena with his three sons, each of whom led a life that caused his father grief. In Modena's own words, "one died"—his eldest and favorite, Mordecai, poisoned by alchemical experiments; "one was murdered"—the impetuous youngest son, Zebulun, killed by his Jewish gang friends; "and one lives in exile"—Isaac, the errant middle son, whom the father several times actually encouraged to stay away from home, hoping that God might "instill in his heart the right path, so that he will no longer disgrace my name wherever he goes."

Similarly gripping is the relationship of Modena and his wife. Sister of his intended bride, she had been forced upon him as a substitute immediately after Esther's death in order, in his mother's words, "to perpetuate the kinship and to give comfort to the mother and father of the young woman." Modena had in later years to endure his wife's sickly constitution and, late in life, a form of mental derangement that nearly drove him mad at a time that his own health was rapidly deteriorating.

Fascinating, too, is the incidence of crime, violence, and punishment in the autobiography. One of the precocious young Modena's teachers is killed by a highway robber; the perpetrator is apprehended, imprisoned, and executed. The aforementioned Uncle Shemaiah loses his life as a result of his attraction to alchemy when "a certain gentile . . . enticed him to take all the silver and gold from the pawnshop . . . claiming that they would melt it down and increase its value many times over. But there he thrust a sword into Shemaiah's belly, killing him, and stole all the silver and gold and ran off." This criminal, too, is caught red-handed; his punishment is to have his body quartered. Modena's grandson is jailed for two months for violating a prohibition against printing by Jews, an episode that includes interesting details about the varying degrees of darkness imposed on prisoners in Venetian cells.

In the most heartrending and tragic episode of violence in the autobiography, Modena's son Zebulun is ambushed and brutally murdered by a gang of Jews to which he belonged. Modena actually witnessed the killing: "Just as I arrived . . . they came out of hiding, pretending that they wanted to beat up someone else. The bastard called to him and said, 'Come down, for your friends are in a fight; come to their aid!' On the run, the impetuous one came down, passing me by without my recognizing him. As soon as he emerged they surrounded him and struck him on the head, bruising him without drawing blood. Then they stabbed him in the throat with a sword or a spear, so that he fled, shouting, 'Father, Father, I am dying!' " One suspects that the father carried a burden of guilt for failing to come to the aid of his son in that hour of desperate need; he seems, however, to have found some solace in the fact that the perpetrators were punished by the authorities.

In 1636 and 1637, as a result of a crime committed by two Jews who received stolen goods and hid them in the ghetto, the threat of expulsion—according to Modena—hung over the entire Jewish community of Venice. Crisis led to crisis. Dog ate dog as one incriminated Jew implicated two others who had informed against him, accusing them of having bribed some Christian officials. Modena's own name surfaced during the investigation of the bribery charge, and "even though I was innocent of any transgression, it was a time of anger and wrath, with punishments and arrests being made for every slight suspicion. So I left for Padua and stayed there for ten days like someone in hiding." The terror subsided only after sentence was handed down: a particularly harsh and unprecedented banishment that extended to relatives of the guilty parties. One of Modena's sons-in-law was among the convicted.

The near expulsion of the Jews from Venice in 1637 is testimony to the tenuous nature of Jewish collective security in Italy. Modena keenly sensed this hazard, correctly perceiving that it was a manifestation of the less tolerant post-Renaissance times in which he lived. He writes, "The outcry against and contempt for all Jews on the part of everyone in the city—noblemen, citizens, and commoners—increased as usual. For when one individual committed a crime, they would grow angry at the entire community, calling us a band of thieves and [saying] that every kind of crime is concealed in the ghetto. Ever since then, they [the Jews] have been the object of scorn and hatred, instead of, as formerly, being loved by all."

In this atmosphere of communal uncertainty and insecurity, the individual, too, had to be on guard lest an offense against Christendom, real or trumped up, threaten his personal status. An especially sensitive area was that of the dissemination of ideas through the printed medium. Modena's experience with his *Historia de' riti hebraici* exemplifies the general situation. In 1614 and 1615 he wrote "at the request of an English nobleman, who intended to give it to the king of England," a small treatise in Italian on Jewish rites and beliefs. "When I wrote it I was not careful about not writing things contrary to the Inquisition, because it was only in manuscript and was meant to be read by people who were not of the pope's sect." Twenty years later he was convinced by Jacques Gaffarel, the French Catholic mystic and Hebraist, to have the manuscript published in France. In April 1637, hearing by mail that the Frenchman had, indeed, printed the book in Paris and still trembling from the panic of the previous year in the Venetian Jewish community, Modena began to fret that some of the statements in the book might be construed as anti-Christian. "I said to myself, 'When this book is seen in Rome, it will become a stumbling block for all the Jews and for me, in particular.' " And so, to protect himself, he volunteered a copy of the manuscript (having not yet seen the book printed in Paris) to the Inquisitor for evaluation and, after receiving the latter's objections, republished it in Venice omitting the objectionable items.

The episodes of 1636 and 1637, told at such length and with such vivid detail in the autobiography, combine with the more fleeting vignettes of economic, social, and cultural life scattered throughout the text to make it an extremely valuable source for Jewish social history in the early modern period. But its importance ought not to be viewed narrowly. The Jews were not isolated from trends and forces that defined life in society as a whole. Despite their residential separation in ghettos they were very much a part of the world at large, interacting with their environment on all levels, from the highest to the lowest (as the seamier episodes in Modena's autobiography so graphically show). And even though they often exhibited distinctive behavior and specifically Jewish modes of response to the forces acting upon them, their experience, as the next section of this essay argues, deserves to be incorporated into the broader picture of early modern European history.[3]

IF WE MOVE beyond the importance of Modena's autobiography for Jewish history we can uncover further interpretive dimensions, and perhaps additional levels of significance, by viewing the book in the broader context of current work on early modern European

---

[3] For a discussion that incorporates *The Life of Judah* into the broader picture of European autobiographical literature of the sixteenth and seventeenth centuries, see Natalie Davis's introductory essay, "Fame and Secrecy: Leon Modena's *Life* as an Early Modern Autobiography."

history. In particular, the significant new historical methods and topics that have transformed the broader field in the past few decades raise questions about the larger rethinkings of Jewish history that may now be possible. How should the revolution that has overtaken the discipline—and especially studies of early modern Europe—affect the treatment of Jewish materials? The changes have been wholesale. New approaches, especially the techniques of historical demography, statistical analysis, and psychohistory, as well as borrowings from the methods of other disciplines (notably anthropology) have fundamentally shifted both the nature and the goals of historical research. New problems are being raised, new kinds of sources are being used, and new subjects are being opened for investigation. Yet very few historians have made general use of Jewish materials in this fashion, even for comparative purposes, and within Jewish history itself the new approaches have been but rarely applied.[4]

The most obvious, in view of the Jews' minority status, would be a consideration of their experience in the light of recent studies of other "pariah" groups—how they came to be defined thus, how they were set apart, and how they and their hosts viewed themselves and one another. In this respect, Jews were not very different, socially or intellectually, from the Quakers or other minority groups that have given theorists such as Max Weber the materials for studies of "castes" and similar distinct groupings. Because from this perspective Jews were just like other minorities in, for example, developing entrepreneurial skills or finding themselves excluded from a variety of activities (such as most branches of general education) and having to develop their own alternatives, it may be interesting to see whether their situation will usually confirm or amend well-established conclusions about the role of "pariah" groups. In particular, to give but one example from the text at hand, the anecdotal evidence in Modena's autobiography of an easy interaction between Jews and Christians raises questions about the supposedly rigid separation between ghettoized Jew and host society in early modern Europe.

[4] Good examples of these first steps are: Todd M. Endelman, *The Jews of Georgian England, 1714–1830: Tradition and Change in a Liberal Society* (Philadelphia, 1979); and Jonathan Israel, *European Jewry in the Age of Mercantilism, 1550–1750* (Oxford, 1985).

Another potential reevaluation arises from the long recognized association of Jews with early capitalist activity. Excluded from most rural pursuits, except in Poland, they had perforce to seek other means of livelihood. The resulting pressures helped shape the experience of early modern Jews and in many ways defined their role in western society, as Modena's Venetian contemporary, Simone Luzzatto, recognized when he made economic advantage a central part of his apologetic appeal for the preservation of Jewish residential rights in Venice, and as Manasseh ben Israel of Amsterdam emphasized when presenting to Cromwell the case for the readmission of his coreligionists to England.[5]

A cursory look at the topic in light of recent general research in economic history is most suggestive. It becomes clear, for example, that—like most successful early capitalists—Jews found their métier in high-risk areas that others shunned, such as the highly dangerous trade in jewels. Moreover, the profound mistrust of partners and agents that is all too apparent in the sources—for example, in Glückel of Hameln's memoirs—gave an edge to the sense of taking chances for high rewards that was essential to the creation of new economic forms. From the larger European perspective, it is apparent that, by their willingness to assume these risks and by their creation of networks of coreligionist agents, bankers, and contacts throughout the continent and the Levant, the Jews were providing crucial oil for the machine of capitalism in its earliest days, when distant but uniform business linkages were only slowly being put into place. Indeed, these vital advances in the solidity and sophistication of international trade are nowhere more clearly displayed than in the careers of those Sephardic and Marrano entrepreneurs (like Joseph Pardo and Solomon Navarro) who appear occasionally in Modena's autobiography and more regularly in other Jewish sources of the early modern period. Neither of the essential commercial processes they embodied—the growth of high-risk enterprise and the development of dense international commercial

---

[5] See Benjamin C. I. Ravid, *Economics and Toleration in Seventeenth Century Venice: The Background and Context of the Discorso of Simone Luzzatto* (Jerusalem, 1978) and " 'How Profitable the Nation of the Jewes Are': The *Humble Addresses* of Menasseh ben Israel and the *Discorso* of Simone Luzzatto," in *Mystics, Philosophers, and Politicians: Essays in Jewish Intellectual History in Honor of Alexander Altmann,* ed. Jehuda Reinharz and Daniel Swetschinski (Durham, N.C., 1982), pp. 159–180.

networks—has been fully described by an economic historian, but when they receive the attention they deserve they will have impact on history both Jewish and general.

Equally revealing can be the consideration of social relations, about which—as Modena's work indicates—the Jewish autobiographical literature has much to say. In a community without the huge gaps in wealth and status that were characteristic of the Christian world, and with a unique respect for learning, an alternative—and perhaps subtler—set of distinctions was necessary for the Jews. Rich and poor, powerful and powerless, lived in close proximity. In addition, all were linked by a universal male literacy (another subject that has received new treatment by historians in recent years) that was without parallel in Europe or elsewhere—a literacy reflected, for instance, in Modena's recounting of his many publishing ventures, most of which implied a wide Jewish readership. The pervasive commitment to charity, another remarkable feature of the Jewish community that was visible at all levels, from Sabbath meals to burial societies, may have derived from this tighter social structure, from patterns of literacy, from segregation and vulnerability, or from a respect for biblical teachings. Whatever the reason, though, the contrasts with the outside world were striking and seem to be an ideal object of comparative research. The results would be as likely to illuminate the practices of the larger society (currently being restudied with new vigor) as of the Jews, but there is as yet little indication of the issues being posed in quite this fashion. Research into literacy, for example, may be a very active field, but the ideas it suggests for analyzing Jewish evidence have yet to be followed up as a means of understanding both literacy in general and this one unusual case in particular. And there are equally promising opportunities in the study of migration, where the problems of internal control faced by the young European settlements in the New World seem to have had a distant echo in the new communities that had to be established in both eastern and western Europe by Jews expelled from Spain and elsewhere. Again, the research seems likely to be revealing, but it has yet to be started.

The history of the family offers similar opportunities. None of the new specialties that have arisen during the past thirty years has had a larger body of adherents or a wider influence. A bibliography published in 1980 listed some 6,200 books and articles on the subject, nearly all of them published since 1950.[6] Yet this spate of activity has included the history of the Jews only tangentially. As a result, it is difficult to assess either the extraordinary structures one finds in the Jewish family or their implications for the topic in general. What, for example, is one to make of the singularly early marriage age of both males and females? The kind of detailed research into registers and family histories that will be necessary to establish exact figures has not been done, but less precise forms of evidence suggest that weddings took place as much as ten years earlier than among Christian contemporaries. The usual explanation of the so-called western marriage pattern has been economic: young people married so late because they could not afford to set up their own households until parents died or passed on an inheritance. Yet here was an even poorer society that ignored this constraint and found an answer to the economic problem by allowing the young couple to live with the parents of one of them for a stipulated period, while the husband either pursued religious studies or learned a trade to support an independent household. This solution may have contributed to the tensions and mistrust characteristic of Jewish family entrepreneurship, but it also created a striking contrast to the standard western relationship, where the old couple moved in with the young, thus losing independence and accepting subordination. Yet this kind of accommodation was not the only one reached by Jewish families. There are also instances of the custom, common in the larger society, whereby the young took in parents who could no longer support themselves, not to mention cases of married children returning to their original home in times of stress. We can see examples of these varied patterns in Glückel of Hameln's memoirs and in Modena's autobiography, but considerable research will have to be done before we can assess the Jewish case in its full comparative perspective. Did Jews have a greater concern for chastity? A greater respect for age? Or should the causes be sought, again, in the vulnerability of the community? Such questions, though they can be raised tantalizingly by applying the issues of general research

[6] Gerald L. Soliday, ed., *History of the Family and Kinship: A Select International Bibliography* (Millwood, N.Y., 1980).

to Jewish history, cannot be answered until the evidence of the latter is fully absorbed—to the advantage of both—into the former.

Rituals—under which term one can include popular religion, magic, festivities, and worship—are another of the major new interests of historians, often informed by the outlook and methods of anthropologists. This area may yet prove to be the liveliest, even if often the most elusive, of the potential cross-fertilizations, because the parallels seem almost self-evident. The fascination with astrology, alchemy, and other forms of magic that we encounter in Modena's autobiography; Purim as a form of carnival, with its celebration of "the world turned upside down"; the nature of death, burial, and marriage rituals; the tales of the Baal Shem Tov; the possibilities of comparing Hasidism and the Protestant Reformation, with the Vilna Gaon taking on something of a Counter-Reformation position on worship and the nature of belief; all are examples of the type of comparative research that holds enormous promise. And here again Modena's autobiography is suggestive, for the comfortable relationship in Judaism between "popular" and "official" religion that his book reveals stands in sharp contrast to the more differentiated relationship that is apparent in the Christian world.

That there is an extraordinarily rich body of evidence available for these studies cannot be doubted. The Jews were a significant and coherent community living in western Europe but behaving differently from their neighbors in many respects. The questions general historians ask may well have to be modified when they are applied to, or tested against, the abundant but neglected materials that this community has left behind; and the results may well change not only what we know about Jewish history but also what has been concluded about the development of western society in this period. Comfortable assumptions about such matters as the beginnings of capitalism or average age at marriage may have to be revised, and the stimulus is likely to extend throughout economic and social history.

Nevertheless, amidst all of these fruitful possibilities, none seems to hold more promise than the unexpected and revealing treasure trove that one encounters in the small but vivid corpus of Jewish autobiographies from the early modern period. Not only do they impinge on the full range of topics just discussed, but they contrast so markedly with contemporary Christian equivalents that they seem almost a different genre. This is a subject that will be discussed more fully below, in Natalie Davis's introductory essay. But here it should be noted that Modena's work—now presented for the first time in its entirety in an English translation—is likely to demonstrate to social historians, not only of Venice but also of seventeenth-century Europe, how useful this and other types of Jewish source materials can be both for comparative study and for the light they cast on the broader society. If the autobiography turns out to be as suggestive as we hope, it should encourage the publication of other texts and should also stimulate further cross-cultural comparisons. And if some of the topics outlined above do attract the research they deserve, all historians will benefit from the reciprocal illumination of Jewish and general early modern history.

Leon Modena: The
Autobiography and the Man

HOWARD E. ADELMAN

An Overview of the Life
of Leon Modena

LEON MODENA's autobiography tells a partial story. Essentially a private family chronicle, it concentrates on the author's children, relatives, and—only selectively—his own life and writings.[1] He does not relate in full such things as his professional accomplishments, his role in communal controversies, or his relations with significant figures, both Jewish and Christian, outside his family, but only refers to them briefly in passing. Modena was more concerned with documenting his intimate personal reactions to events that had an impact on him, especially when the result was unpleasant or negative. Important achievements in his life would be described in his letters, responsa, and polemics or would be mentioned in community records, but often they would not appear in the autobiography in any detail, if at all. At the same time, there are places in the autobiography in which Modena consciously tempers his description of events so that he or members of his family would appear in the best possible light.[2] Thus, for a study of Leon Modena's life, the autobiography can serve only as a frame. To reconstruct a more complete biography—one that will allow for a balanced assessment of the man—one must take cognizance of other writings, which fill in many of its gaps and show the true extent of the author's public activities and, with that, his true place in Jewish history.

Leon Modena was born in 1571 into two important Italian Jewish families known for their scholarship and wealth.[3] His father came

---

[1] See *The Life of Judah*, fol. 4a. On the Jewish family at this time, see Jacob Katz, "Family, Kinship, and Marriage in the Sixteenth to Eighteenth Centuries," *Journal of Jewish Sociology* 1 (1959): 4–22 and idem, *Tradition and Crisis: Jewish Society at the End of the Middle Ages* (New York, 1961), pp. 135–156.

[2] For example, see historical notes to fol. 6a.   [3] See *The Life of Judah*, fols. 4b–6b.

from an old French Jewish family that had left its native land probably as a result of one of the expulsions of the fourteenth century.[4]
His paternal forebears settled first in Viterbo and then in Modena,
a toponymic his family retained even after moving to Bologna and
later Ferrara.[5] His mother came from an Ashkenazic family that had
resettled in Italy.[6] Leon himself was born in Venice, but from the
time he was about eight months old, throughout most of his youth,
his branch of the family lived in Ferrara, Cologna da Veneto, and
Montagnana. At an early age Modena demonstrated his skills as a
precocious student and talented preacher. In addition to all
branches of traditional Jewish knowledge, he also made progress in
poetry, letter writing, voice, music, dancing, and Latin.[7] At the age
of ten, under the influence of an uncle who had once spoken in
Latin to the pope in defense of the Talmud, Modena began to show
an interest in religious polemics.[8]

Modena's entry into adolescence was distinguished by the production of some outstanding and unusual literary creations, including a rabbinic responsum on Jewish prayer,[9] a translation of parts
of Lodovico Ariosto's *Orlando furioso*,[10] a macaronic poem, *Kinah
shemor*, which had the same sound and conveys the same idea in
both Hebrew and Italian, and a pastoral dialogue on gambling.[11]
During this time also his family's fortunes declined, a fact that he
emphasized not only in his autobiography but also in other writings,[12] and he had to turn to teaching and writing to earn a living.[13]

For the years 1584 to 1588, between his thirteenth and seventeenth years, Modena recorded few of his activities in his autobiography.[14] By way of contrast, his letters show that while living in

---

[4] See ibid., fol. 4b.　[5] See ibid., fol. 5a.　[6] See ibid., fol. 6b.　[7] See ibid., fols. 7a–8b.

[8] See his introductory letter to Abner of Burgos, *Sefer alfonso*, Parma 2440 (De Rossi
533), fol. 1a–b, partially quoted in Isaac Reggio, *Behinat ha-kabbalah* (Gorizia, 1852), pp.
xiii–xv.

[9] *Ziknei yehudah*, ed. Shlomo Simonsohn (Jerusalem, 1956), no. 1.

[10] Ariosto (1474–1533) was the court poet of Ferrara, and his house was near the Giara
district where young Modena's family had lived from 1572 to 1577; see *The Divan of Leo
de Modena*, ed. Simon Bernstein (Philadelphia, 1932), no. 1 and *The Life of Judah*, fol. 7a.
For another Hebrew translation of Ariosto, see JTSA 0584, fol. 369b and Max Berenblut, "A Comparative Study of Judaeo-Italian Translations of Isaiah" (Ph.D. diss., Columbia University, 1949), p. 10.

[11] See *The Life of Judah*, fols. 8b and 20a.

[12] For example, see *The Life of Judah*, fols. 7b and 8b and Modena's *Midbar yehudah*
(Venice, 1602), fol. 4a.

[13] See *The Life of Judah*, fol. 9b.　[14] See ibid., fols. 8b–9b.

Montagnana during those years, he maintained a lively correspondence with other young men from small northern Italian
towns who had intellectual and social needs similar to his own.[15]
Many of them, like Modena, traveled to Venice from time to time.
Modena's missives show him exchanging with his correspondents
news, books, and recent scholarly insights presented at various
houses of study. In these letters Modena wrote that, with few peers
in Montagnana, he found life there painfully boring. One of his
most interesting writings from this period is a letter in which the
first and last word of each line is the same, and these words, which
appeared in a column at each margin, form a biblical verse.[16] During his adolescence, Modena was already able to write letters of
professional quality, which were used by others as their own.[17] Also
during this period he began the study of Kabbalah.[18] The young
Modena also wrote poetry, much of it dwelling on his illnesses and
dreams, and he even composed his own epitaph.[19]

At the age of nineteen, in 1590, Modena went to Venice, where
he married his cousin Rachel Simhah shortly after the death of his
originally intended mate, her sister Esther.[20] At the time of his wedding, Modena was invested with the title of *haver*, which marked
the first step on the way to rabbinic ordination.[21] This academic rite
of passage introduced him to the Venetian rabbis, with whom he
remained in contact following his return to Montagnana.[22]

In 1592, at the age of twenty-one, Modena moved with his wife
and year-old son Mordecai to Venice, bent on a rabbinic career in

---

[15] These friends included Jacob Katz (Kohen-Tzedek) of Este, Asher Clerli of Venice, Gershon Cohen of Cologna, and his half-brother Abraham Parenzo in Ancona; see Yacob Boksenboim, *Iggerot rabbi yehudah aryeh mi-modena* (Tel Aviv, 1984), nos. 2, 3, 4, 6, 10, 11, 12, 18; also *Divan*, no. 90.

[16] Deuteronomy 33:1. BL Or. 5396, fol. 15a, a feature not preserved in Boksenboim, *Iggerot*, no. 1.

[17] Simon Bernstein, "The Letters of Rabbi Mahalalel Halelujah," *HUCA* 7 (1930): 527, 529; cf. Boksenboim, *Iggerot*, nos. 10, 137.

[18] Leon Modena, *Ari nohem*, ed. Nehemiah Libowitz (Jerusalem, 1929), p. 6.

[19] *Divan*, nos. 14, 15, 16; 5; 4, 18; Boksenboim, *Iggerot*, nos. 5, 6.

[20] See *The Life of Judah*, fols. 9b–10b.   [21] See historical notes to fol. 10b.

[22] In a letter to the Venetian rabbi Solomon Sforno, Modena asked about an elegy he had written on the death of Pope Sixtus V on August 27, 1590. He was not sure whether it was appropriate to say "may peace be upon him" (*'alav ha-shalom*) for the pope, even though he had been good to the Jews; see Boksenboim, *Iggerot*, no. 15. Modena also represented Samuel Judah Katzenellenbogen's rabbinic interests in Montagnana; see Boksenboim, *Iggerot*, no. 138.

that city.[23] The Venetian Jewish lay leaders, however, constantly challenging the authority of the rabbis, were then in the process of raising the minimum age for rabbinical ordination.[24] His plans foiled, the young man had to eke out a living for many years until he was ordained a rabbi shortly before his fortieth birthday.[25]

Letters Modena wrote soon after his arrival in Venice show that he was depressed and was having great difficulty adjusting to life there: "My heart cries out for the past, is startled by the present, and is terrified of the future."[26] Gradually, however, he found sources of income and influence. He taught,[27] composed letters for students,[28] and was soon called upon to preach regularly in Italian, as was the custom, at several of the synagogues and schools during Sabbath services and at midweek lectures.[29] He also earned money composing poetry for occasions such as births, weddings, funerals, and tombstones. Modena's poetic skill brought him prominence far beyond the gates of the ghetto. What was to become his most profitable poem, though it is not even mentioned in the autobiography, is a case in point. On September 17, 1601, Maria de Medici, the wife of Henry IV, the king of France, gave birth to a son, the later Louis XIII. As part of the Venetian celebration in the infant's honor, Modena wrote and published a poem in Hebrew and Italian.[30] To augment his sparse earnings, he also turned to gambling, a popular form of entertainment in Venice. Indeed, he gambled intermittently, despite his own better judgment and with both Jews and Christians, for the rest of his life.[31]

During the early years in Venice, when Modena could not yet

---

[23] See *The Life of Judah*, fol. 11b.

[24] For example, see Boksenboim, *Iggerot*, nos. 27, 33, 62, 139, 204; *Divan*, nos. 64, 66; *Ziknei*, no. 80, pp. 191–198; Reuven Bonfil, *Ha-rabbanut be-italiah bi-tekufat ha-renasans* (Jerusalem, 1979), pp. 41–42.

[25] See historical notes to fol. 15a.

[26] Boksenboim, *Iggerot*, no. 22; see also nos. 17, 23, 25.   [27] Ibid., no. 26.

[28] Ibid., nos. 135, 142, 295, 297, 299, 323, 324, 327; perhaps Modena was also the ubiquitous letter-writing teacher mentioned in these letters.

[29] See *The Life of Judah*, fols. 11b–12a; Boksenboim, *Iggerot*, nos. 18, 26, 36.

[30] On this poem, later republished in Hebrew, Italian, and Latin, see Isaac min Haleviim, introduction to *Magen ve-herev*, in *Ma'amar magen ve-tzinnah*, ed. Abraham Geiger (Breslau, 1856), fol. 11a; *Divan*, no. 56; Ludwig Blau, "Plantavits Lehrer im Rabbinischen," *ZHB* 11 (1907): 113–121; Jean Plantavit de la Pause, *Bibliotheca rabbinica* (Lodève, 1645), p. 588, no. 323. The Italian text of the poem, "Alle Feste, anzi a' sacri, anch'io presente," is only available in Plantavit.

[31] See *The Life of Judah*, fol. 12a; for other examples, see, e.g., fols. 13a and 18a.

function as a rabbinic authority in matters of religious law, civil disputes, communal strife, or excommunications, he nonetheless gained some rabbinic experience as a legal clerk for the Venetian rabbinate, which included such prominent figures as Samuel Judah Katzenellenbogen,[32] Benzion Zarfati,[33] Avigdor Cividal,[34] Leib Saraval,[35] and Joseph Pardo.[36] In this way Modena learned at first hand about the issues facing the Venetian rabbis and was able to add his voice, albeit not his name, to their rulings.

Another source of income and outlet for Modena's creativity was his involvement in Jewish publishing in Venice as a proofreader and jobber who communicated with authors and arranged for the type fonts, the size of the book, and the nature of the paper, as well as the proofreading, binding, and distribution.[37] He also composed dedicatory poems for books. His first such poem, in fact his first literary creation to appear in print, was published in 1593 in the book *Tevat noah* by the Christian Marco Marini.[38] As with his service to the rabbinate, Modena's work in publishing constituted a source of both pride and frustration.[39] In the 1590s the Hebrew printing business in Venice was showing signs of depression, and there was not enough work for a young aspirant to a career in that profession. Moreover, as he wrote in a letter, he would much rather have been preparing his own books for publication.[40] About this time, too, Modena began to develop a disdain for teaching.[41]

By 1603, following his thirtieth birthday, Modena's family, after the death of several infants, had reached its full size, with three sons

[32] See historical notes to fol. 10b and Boksenboim, *Iggerot*, nos. 27, 139, 210, 211, 212, 233, 262; cf. nos. 33, 35, 90, 138; Ludwig (Judah Leib) Blau, *Kitvei ha-rav yehudah aryeh mi-modena* (Budapest, 1905, 1906; Strasbourg, 1907), nos. 95, 138.

[33] See historical notes to fol. 11b and Boksenboim, *Iggerot*, no. 198; cf. nos. 52, 62, 65, 66, 69, 71, 74.

[34] See historical notes to fol. 10b and Boksenboim, *Iggerot*, nos. 198, 220, 265.

[35] See historical notes to fol. 15a and Boksenboim, *Iggerot*, nos. 198, 212; cf. nos. 51, 97, 102, 103, 107, 108, 139, 165, 166, 260, 263.

[36] See historical notes to fol. 13b and Boksenboim, *Iggerot*, nos. 185, 186, 202, 245; cf. nos. 169, 269; also Blau, *Kitvei*, nos. 81, 152, 153.

[37] Boksenboim, *Iggerot*, nos. 28–31.

[38] *Divan*, no. 47, see also nos. 21, 22, 24, 25. For a complete list of Modena's dedicatory poems, see *The Life of Judah*, fol. 20a; cf. Isaac min Haleviim, *Medabber tahpukhot*, ed. Daniel Carpi (Tel Aviv, 1985), p. 72.

[39] On Modena's frustration at this time, see Boksenboim, *Iggerot*, nos. 36, 35.

[40] Boksenboim, *Iggerot*, no. 33. Between 1594 and 1596 di Gara issued Modena's first two books, *Sur mera'* and *Sod yesharim*, see *The Life of Judah*, fol. 20a.

[41] Boksenboim, *Iggerot*, no. 29,

and two daughters.[42] For a decade, with six other mouths to feed and limited opportunities for further professional development in Venice, Modena regularly sought work outside the city, usually departing for that purpose on a trip at the end of the summer before the Jewish High Holidays.[43] In August 1604, he went alone to work as a teacher in Ferrara.[44] His situation there must have looked most promising, however, because he soon sent for his family, and he ended up living in Ferrara for three years. There he served the family of Joseph Zalman, a wealthy Jew, as private tutor, and the Jewish community at large as preacher, teacher of advanced students, and rabbinical authority in matters of Jewish religious and civil law.[45] In one of his books Modena indicated that the Zalman family treated him with much respect, more like a brother than an employee, and that if he lived to be a thousand he would not forget their kind treatment.[46] The relationship that Modena developed with the Zalman family was presumably the kind that he sought each time he left Venice.

In Ferrara Modena came into his own in several areas, a fact that is not expressed in his autobiography. Three accomplishments of his Ferrara period are entirely omitted in *The Life of Judah*. Unmentioned is a successful presentation he made on Jewish moneylending before the papal legate, Cardinal Orzario Spinola, which may have been crucial in reestablishing that privilege for Ferraran Jews.[47] Passed over in silence is his siding with most of the rabbis of northern Italy and his own relatives against the rabbis of Venice in a major and continuing controversy that had erupted in 1589 over the

---

[42] See *The Life of Judah*, fols. 10b–14a.

[43] See, for instance, his correspondence concerning a teaching position in a talmudic academy that was to be opened in Conegliano, and, perhaps, the mention of a trip to Padua; Boksenboim, *Iggerot*, nos. 42, 43; see also *The Life of Judah*, fol. 13b.

[44] See *The Life of Judah*, fol. 14a.

[45] Modena made a list of the rabbinic decisions he issued in Ferrara. Most of these decisions involved mundane matters such as when to go to the mikveh (ritual bath), the condition of the slaughtering knife, the wearing of tefillin (phylacteries), the recitation of certain blessings, and many other matters about which Modena claimed he had offered no innovative responses; Ancona, Comunità Israelitica, MS 7, fols. 8b–10b.

[46] Leon Modena, *Lev ha-aryeh* (Venice, 1612), fol. 4a; (Vilna, 1886), fol. 2a.

[47] Leon Modena, *Diffesa da quello che scrive Fra' Sisto Sanese nella sua Bibliotheca de precetti da talmudisti a hebrei contra christiani*, "Attacchi contro il Talmud di Fra Sisto da Siena e la riposta, finora inedita, di Leon Modena, rabbino in Venezia," ed. Clemente Ancona, in *Bollettino dell'Istituto di storia della società e dello stato veneziano* 5–6 (1963–1964): 297–323.

religious acceptability of a ritual bath in nearby Rovigo.[48] Modena does not relate in his autobiography that he also supported a major musical performance in Ferrara that took place in the synagogue on Friday evening, the 15th of Av.[49] In fact, so great was Modena's enthusiasm for synagogue music that he refrained from making his position on the ritual bath in Rovigo public in hopes that the rabbis of Venice would endorse his views on this other, aesthetic, matter. Yet despite Modena's accomplishments in Ferrara and the fact that his annual income of 260 ducats was one and a half times what he had been making in Venice,[50] Modena greatly missed the city of his birth.[51]

Accordingly, he returned to Venice in 1607 and lived there, teaching and writing letters, until 1609.[52] Although these events are unrecorded in his autobiography, while in Venice during the summer and autumn of 1608 Modena held important meetings with Protestants, many of whom were English. Two unrelated developments—the resumption in 1603 after a forty-five-year hiatus of diplomatic relations between England and Venice, and James I's authorization in 1604 of a new Bible translation—may have led a few English Christians to seek Hebrew instruction in Venice, in the absence of professing Jews in their country. Modena knew Henry Wotton (1568–1639), the English ambassador to Venice;[53] William Bedell (1577–1644), Wotton's chaplain, provost of Trinity College in Dublin, later a Protestant bishop in Ireland, and translator of the

---

[48] For Modena's views on this controversy, see Boksenboim, *Iggerot*, nos. 25, 58, 60, 62, 64, 65, 66, 67, 72, 73, 75, 77, 78, 211, 272. On the controversy itself, see Ludwig Blau, *Leo Modenas Briefe und Schriftstücke* (Strasbourg, 1907), pp. 127–137; Isaiah Sonne, "Ha-bedutah ʿal devar ha-sefer *Milhamot ha-shem* be-ʾinyan ha-mikveh me-rovigo," *KS* 11 (1935): 360–364; Abraham Yaari, "Teʿudah lo nodaʿat be-ʾinyan pulmus ha-mikveh be-rovigo," *Sinai* 36 (1954): 367–374. This controversy generated three large collections of responsa, many of which Modena had read before they were published: *Mashbit milhamot* (Venice, 1606); *Mikveh yisrael* (Venice, 1607); and *Palgei mayim* (Venice, 1608).

[49] It was perhaps the first musical celebration of this ancient Jewish holiday, which is also observed with song and dance festivals today in the State of Israel.

[50] In a letter he wrote "ha-sekhar veha-peras, peras ve-hetzi" (cf. Avot 1:3). Thus in Venice his income had been 175 ducats a year at the most. In addition, he wrote that food cost much less in Ferrara than in Venice. Boksenboim, *Iggerot*, no. 46, interprets the phrase to mean that Modena was making only three-quarters of what he had been making in Venice.

[51] Boksenboim, *Iggerot*, nos. 64, 71, 72, 73, 74.

[52] Boksenboim, *Iggerot*, nos. 33, 317.

[53] On Wotton, see *Ziknei*, no. 32; Cecil Roth, "Leone da Modena and England," *TJHSE* 11 (1924–1927): 206–207.

Bible into Gaelic;[54] Samuel Slade (1568–1612), an Oxford graduate, vicar, and bibliophile; and perhaps Thomas Coryat (1577–1617), whose travelogue, *Coryat's Crudities*, describes an encounter in Venice with an unnamed rabbi who could easily have been Modena.[55] Modena also corresponded from Venice with David Farar of Amsterdam, who consulted him about his disputations with Hugh Broughton (1549–1612), an English Hebraist and dissenter.

Many of the Christians with whom Modena associated in Venice during these years, such as Wotton and Bedell, were also friends of Fra Paolo Sarpi (1552–1623), the Venetian leader in the controversy with the papacy that culminated in the papal interdict imposed on Venice in 1606. Sarpi—who lived near the ghetto and whose years in Venice coincided with those of Modena—regularly attended gatherings where Jews were present, which was among the reasons given by Pope Clement VIII (1592–1605) for refusing to grant Sarpi a bishopric. Nevertheless, the only piece of evidence that shows some sort of relationship between Modena and Sarpi is that when Modena acquired a copy of Sarpi's *Istoria del Concilio Tridentino* (History of the Council of Trent), he copied sections from it and referred to Sarpi as "my" friar.[56]

After a brief jaunt to Reggio and his first trip to the family's ancestral Italian hometown of Modena,[57] in 1609 Leon Modena relocated once again, this time to Florence for a year. As in the case of his selective treatment of his stay in Ferrara, again in the autobiography Modena reports only his complaints and ignores his many accomplishments during this important period of his life.[58] Letters Modena wrote from Florence show him actively engaged in a wide variety of communal and intellectual matters. He corresponded with the rabbis of other cities, including Simone Luzzatto of Venice, on legal matters, with authors who sent him poetry to evaluate,

[54] On Bedell, see Gilbert Burnet, *The Life of William Bedell, D.D.* (Dublin, 1736); E. S. Shuckburgh, *Two Biographies of William Bedell* (Cambridge, 1902); Cecil Roth, "Leone da Modena and His English Correspondents," *TJHSE* 17 (1951–1952): 41.

[55] Thomas Coryat, *Coryat's Crudities* (London, 1611), pp. 231–237; (Glasgow, 1905), pp. 370–376; partially excerpted in Roth, "Leone da Modena and England," pp. 217–223.

[56] Ancona 7, fol. 63a. On Sarpi, see Alexander Robertson, *Fra Paolo Sarpi* (London, 1894); William Bouwsma, *Venice and the Defense of Republican Liberty: Renaissance Values in the Age of the Counter Reformation* (Berkeley, 1968), pp. 358–370; Gaetano Cozzi, "Società veneziana, società ebraica," in his *Gli Ebrei e Venezia* (Milan, 1987), pp. 333–374.

[57] See *The Life of Judah*, fol. 5a and *Ari nohem*, p. 49. [58] See *The Life of Judah*, fol. 15a.

with young students regarding their marriage plans, with the leaders of a society for the ransoming of Jewish captives, with a Christian Hebraist interested in kabbalistic literature, and with his late half-brother's sons, Mordecai and Solomon Modena.[59] In Florence Modena served as he had in Ferrara as a rabbinic authority on Jewish law.[60] But he was not entirely comfortable in this role, and he felt obliged to explain his decisions to important rabbinic authorities.[61] His most distinguished student in Florence was the French Catholic Jean Plantavit de la Pause (1576–1651), to whom he taught Hebrew, Bible, and rabbinics.[62] Three times a week Modena taught a monk who served as a teacher in the court of the duke.[63] While in Florence, Modena also considered going to Rome, but apparently he never visited that city.[64]

Finally, in 1609, when he was almost thirty-nine years old, Modena received his rabbinical ordination from the rabbis of Venice—a fact that is not recorded in his autobiography—and soon he returned from Florence to his beloved birthplace, endowed for the first time with the authority to issue rabbinic responsa there in his own name.[65] In Venice he attained enough prestige to be appointed cantor for the Italian synagogue. Like other salaried officials of that synagogue, the cantor also needed to be reelected by a two-thirds majority of the voting members of the board. The minutes book of the congregation shows Modena to be so highly regarded a public servant that he served on the board of the synagogue with voting rights, a privilege denied other salaried officials. Characteristically, however, his cantorial work at the Italian synagogue, which constitutes so significant a mark of the respect he had achieved, is barely mentioned in the autobiography.[66]

Serving as cantor required Modena to attend synagogue every

[59] Boksenboim, *Iggerot*, nos. 95–104, 145, 152, and pp. 362–366.   [60] *Ziknei*, no. 23.

[61] Meir Benayahu, *Ha-yehasim she-bein yehudei yavan liyhudei italiah* (Tel Aviv, 1980), pp. 162–168, 321–323; Isaac Yodlov, "Pesak din shel rabbanei venetziah mi-shenat [5]379," *Sinai* 84 (1979): 166–172; Boksenboim, *Iggerot*, nos. 91–98.

[62] See historical notes to fols. 35b–36a; Blau, "Plantavits Lehrer," pp. 113–121.

[63] Boksenboim, *Iggerot*, no. 104; on the study of Hebrew by Christian kabbalists near Florence at this time, see Kenneth Stow, "Conversion, Christian Hebraism, and Hebrew Prayer in the Sixteenth Century," *HUCA* 47 (1976): 222–224.

[64] Leon Modena, *Tefillot yesharim* (Venice, 1642), introduction, cited in Nehemiah Libowitz, *R. yehudah aryeh mi-modena* (New York, 1901), pp. 121–122.

[65] Boksenboim, *Iggerot*, nos. 102, 103.

[66] Reference to Modena's position of cantor appears only in the list of his twenty-six activities, see *The Life of Judah*, fol. 28b.

evening, morning, and afternoon, to lead the service, to recite prayers for the sick and the dead, to preach every Sabbath morning before the Torah was removed from the ark to be read, and to teach two or three laws after it was read and returned to the ark Mondays and Thursdays. Modena also served as secretary for the congregation, though his total salary of about twenty ducats a year constituted only a small percentage of a yearly income necessary to make ends meet.[67] Modena also preached regularly each week in three or four locations before a combined audience of three hundred to six hundred people. His sermons came to be discussed as far away as Prague.[68] At this time he also began to issue rabbinic decisions in Venice.

Modena presented many of his views about preaching, including his formula for a successful sermon, in a responsum on the question of whether it was permissible on the Sabbath to have a gentile carry and turn over an hourglass filled with sand to time a sermon. He felt that to be a successful preacher and to encourage people to attend sermons, they must not be too long. If the congregation wanted a half-hour sermon, he would preach for twenty minutes. He wrote that if he merited praise for his sermons, it was because of their brevity alone and that this is how he taught his students to preach. Updating his advice in a postscript, he expressed his willingness to reduce the length of sermons even more. If the congregation wanted a half-hour sermon, his students should preach for just fifteen minutes, because congregants had grown less patient than before. He related that in every important community of Italy in which he had preached, the only complaints about his sermons he had ever received were that they were too long and never that they were too short.[69] He viewed the preacher as a public servant with responsibilities toward the congregation, which included

[67] The Italian congregation's minutes book, which Modena himself kept, and its expense ledger, in which Modena signed a statement each time he was paid (see figure 10), are still extant, JTSA 8594 and 8593; Riccardo Pacifici, "I Regolamenti della scuola italiana a Venezia nel secolo XVII," *RMI* 5 (1930): 392–401. On Modena and the cantorate, see Haleviim, *Medabber*, p. 49, 64; idem, introduction to *Magen ve-herev*, fol. 11a–b; *Ziknei*, nos. 53, 107, 127.

[68] *Ziknei*, no. 22.

[69] Indeed, to control the enthusiasm of a preacher, Modena viewed the hourglass as a necessity and was even willing to override certain customs against carrying on the Sabbath by a gentile for the benefit of the sermon; see *Ziknei*, no. 82.

moral guidance as well as explaining the traditional texts. For this service, he claimed, he was paid and respected.[70]

In Venice, Modena's prestige continued to grow, though he reported few of his accomplishments in his autobiography. His opinions were sought by Christians and Jews alike. In 1611 Jean Plantavit de la Pause offered him the chair of oriental languages in Paris, presumably on the condition that he convert to Christianity.[71] In 1614, an English lord, probably Henry Wotton, commissioned him to write a description of Jewish practices for King James I of England. The resulting *Vita, riti, e costumi de gl' Hebrei—In brevissimo compendio ma amplamento raccolti & descritti*, which was not published until 1637 as *Historia de gli riti hebraici* and again in 1638 as *Historia de' riti hebraici*, had the distinction of being the first description of Jewish ritual by a Jew written for a gentile audience in the vernacular and of becoming a major source of information for Christians about Judaism for many generations to come.[72] During his early years as a rabbi in Venice Modena also wrote some important and interesting responsa on contemporary Jewish cultural and legal issues, such as going about bareheaded and playing tennis or traveling in a boat on the Sabbath.[73] Showing their confidence in his intellectual gifts, Jewish leaders called on Modena to respond to the growing number of Jews, particularly former Marranos in the major port cities of Venice, Amsterdam, and Hamburg, who had begun challenging rabbinic tradition and authority.[74]

In the midst of this flurry of satisfying involvement in important issues of Jewish life, both at home and abroad, came the traumatizing death of Modena's eldest son Mordecai at the end of the year 1617.[75] This loss, which receives much attention in the autobiography, devastated Modena, though it did not prevent him from

[70] *Ziknei*, Introduction.

[71] Cecil Roth, "Leone da Modena and the Christian Hebraists," in *Jewish Studies in Memory of Israel Abrahams* (New York, 1927), pp. 388–389, 394.

[72] On the *Riti*, see *The Life of Judah*, fols. 20a, 25a, 35b–36a. The first title is from a manuscript copy of the *Riti* presented by Modena to William Boswell in September 1628, available in St. John's College Library, Cambridge, L. 19.

[73] *Ziknei*, nos. 22, 21, and 90, respectively; see also Isaac Rivkind, "Teshuvat ha-rav yehudah aryeh modena 'al gillui ha-rosh," *Sefer ha-yovel li-khevod levi ginzberg li-mele'at lo shiv'im shanah* (New York, 1946), pp. 401–423.

[74] *Ziknei*, nos. 16, 24, 33, 35, 41, 54, 75, 77, 80, 86, 94; *Divan*, nos. 64, 66; Boksenboim, *Iggerot*, nos. 33, 146, 147, 209.

[75] See *The Life of Judah*, fols. 16b–17a.

continuing his professional activities. Unreported in the autobiography is the fact that his influence continued to grow among some of the most talented Jewish medical students at the nearby University of Padua, many of whom became important intellectual leaders of the Jews.[76] He continued to ordain candidates for the degrees of *haver* and rabbi, to approve the decisions of other rabbis, and to authorize books for publication, and he was considered the leading preacher in Venice. At this time, also unreported in the autobiography, Modena began to serve as the chief official translator of Hebrew documents for the Venetian government. He was elected secretary of the Fraterna di Maritar Donzelle della Natione degli Hebrei Tedesca di Venezia, the Ashkenazic society for dowering brides, another aspect of his life not reported in the autobiography.[77] In 1618, on the title page of a book for which he had written a poem, he was described as a gaon and an excellent, well-known, honored, and brilliant preacher who worked daily at the publishing house on the books of others.[78] By 1620, Modena signed his name third in order among the Venetian rabbis, after Isaac Gershon and Moses Cohen Porto, indicating that he was gaining in seniority.[79]

In 1622, at the age of fifty-one, Modena's life was again struck by tragedy when his youngest son, Zebulun, was murdered by a gang of Jews. With his only remaining son, Isaac, wandering abroad, Modena now immersed himself even more in his work.[80]

Modena's stature in Venice continued to increase during the

[76] These students, who pursued rabbinic and scientific studies, included Joseph Solomon Delmedigo of Crete (see his *Sefer elim* [Amsterdam, 1629]); David Hayyim Luria (*Divan*, nos. 79, 263 and *Ziknei*, p. 191); Moses Uziel (*Divan*, no. 78); Joseph ben Yedidiah Urbino of Rovigo (*Ziknei*, p. 191); and Joseph Hamitz (see historical notes to fol. 20a, at item s). For a description of Jewish medical students in Padua, see David Ruderman, "The Impact of Science on Jewish Culture and Society in Venice (with Special Reference to Jewish Graduates of Padua's Medical School)," in *Gli Ebrei e Venezia*, pp. 417–448.
[77] Leon Modena, *Tzori la-nefesh* (Venice, 1619), fol. 2a. On Modena's work as the chief official translator, "il primo traduttore officiale di documenti ebraici," see Leone di Mosè Luzzatto, "All'Illustre Dr. M. Steinschneider in Berlino," *VI* 31 (1883): 252–255; Haleviim, *Medabber*, pp. 74, 91. On Modena's work as scribe, see *Regolatione della Fraterna di Maritar Donzelle della Natione degli Hebrei tedesca di Venezia*, ASV Scuole Piccole e Suffragi, b. 733, fols. 47a–64a (258b–240b). For this work his salary began at four ducats a year and was soon raised to six.
[78] Gedaliah ben Solomon, *'Etz shatul*, see historical notes to fol. 20a, item q.
[79] Mordecai ben Abraham Jaffe, *Sefer levushim*, see historical notes to fol. 20a, item o.
[80] See *The Life of Judah*, fols. 18b–19b.

1620s. At the Italian synagogue, where he was cantor, he developed a series of ordinances to establish its finances and the order of its prayers.[81] At the Ashkenazic and Sephardic synagogues he was appointed the main preacher.[82] A good deal of Modena's boasting in his autobiography concerns his accomplishments in this domain. Thus, he reports as one of his most memorable experiences the occasion on which the brother of the king of France, Gaston, duc d'Orléans, accompanied by an entourage of nobility and clergy, attended one of his sermons in the synagogue of the Sephardim. Afterward (probably between 1629 and 1631), he adds, Henri, duc de Rohan (1572–1638), the erstwhile leader of the French Huguenots and at that time commander in chief of the Venetian military, along with his companion Henri, duc de Candale, also attended a sermon of his.[83] His rank among the Venetian rabbis reached a new pinnacle by 1627, when he began signing his name before all the others on ordinances and book copyrights.[84]

During the summer of 1628, Modena became director of the Accademia degl'Impediti, a music academy in the ghetto composed of Jewish musicians—a professional accomplishment only briefly alluded to in the autobiography.[85] One of the first choral performances of the Jewish worship service and of some of the Psalms was given under Modena's direction at the Sephardic synagogue on Simhat Torah. The Christian nobility of Venice flocked to this spectacular event, and the authorities had to intervene to control the crowds.[86]

This success was short-lived. In the summer of 1629 an epidemic broke out that claimed more than one hundred Jewish lives during the following seven months. Among the victims was Modena's beloved son-in-law Jacob Halevi, husband of his daughter Diana.[87] Further, about this time relations between Modena and the lay lead-

---

[81] JTSA 8594, pp. 1, 2, 12, 13, 14; Pacifici, "I Regolamenti," pp. 392–401.

[82] See *The Life of Judah*, fol. 20b.   [83] See ibid., fol. 21b and historical notes.

[84] Joseph Yedidiah ben Benjamin Yekutiel Carmi, *Kenaf renanim* (Venice, 1626), last page (unnumbered); see historical notes to fol. 20a. On the importance of signing first, see Haleviim, *Medabber*, p. 81.

[85] See *The Life of Judah*, fol. 28b.

[86] Israel Adler, "The Rise of Art Music in the Italian Ghetto," in *Jewish Medieval and Renaissance Studies*, ed. Alexander Altmann (Cambridge, Mass., 1967), pp. 348–349; Cecil Roth, "L'Accademia musicale del ghetto veneziano," *RMI* 3 (1928): 160–162.

[87] See *The Life of Judah*, fol. 21b and historical notes.

ers of the Jewish community became strained when the latter tried
to ban gambling. Even though Modena was not frequenting the
gaming table at this time, he published a Hebrew pamphlet in the
form of a rabbinic responsum in which he questioned whether
gambling was a sin according to traditional Jewish belief and chal-
lenged the lay leaders' authority to issue such a ban without rabbinic approval.[88] But even the rabbis of Venice, on whose behalf he
argued, opposed Modena's views.[89] In frustration, Modena may
even have taken his case to the secular government of Venice.[90]
Nevertheless, despite the coolness of the rabbis toward his views
on gambling, in several responsa on other subjects Modena indicated that the rabbis of Venice were working together with him and
saw him as their leader.[91]

The epidemic of 1629 was followed in 1630 and 1631 by the outbreak of a major plague that caused enormous human devastation
in Venice.[92] During the plague, Modena worked frantically, as if it
were the last thing he would write, to prepare *Ziknei yehudah*, a
collection of his rabbinic decisions and letters. In the midst of the
pestilence, on December 26, 1631, following a practice common
among the Jews of Venice,[93] Modena desposited a will with a
Christian notary.[94] Although the practice was contrary to Jewish
law, he made his daughter Diana his executrix, feeling this step to
be necessary because his son Isaac refused to return to Venice from
Livorno.[95] But he survived the plague, and new opportunities soon
came his way, including the chance to meet numerous prominent
Christians, many of whom sought Modena's instruction. Among

[88] *Ziknei*, no. 78; and see *The Life of Judah*, fol. 22a and historical notes.
[89] Haleviim, *Medabber*, p. 41; Jacob Leveit Halevi, *She'elot u-teshuvot* (Venice, 1632),
no. 26; *Ziknei*, nos. 79, 122.
[90] This interpretation is based on the potentially damaging translations of Jewish communal records presented by Modena to the Venetian government, probably made in his
role as official translator of Hebrew documents; see Benjamin Ravid, "Ripublikah nifredet mi-kol shilton aher: ha-otonomiah ha-yehudit bi-venetziah ba-me'ah ha-sheva'-es-
reh ve-tirgum sefer ha-gadol," *Hagut u-ma'aseh: sefer zikkaron le-shim'on rawidowicz*, ed.
Abraham Greenbaum and Alfred Ivry (Tel Aviv, 1983), pp. 53–76.
[91] For example, *Ziknei*, no. 69.
[92] See *The Life of Judah*, fols. 22a–23a and historical notes.
[93] Carla Boccato, "Testamenti di israeliti nel fondo del notaio veneziano Pietro Brac-
chi seniore (secolo XVII)," *RMI* 42 (1976): 281–297.
[94] Clemente Ancona, "L'Inventario dei beni di Leon da Modena," *Bollettino dell'Istituto
di storia della società e dello stato veneziano* 10 (1967): 256–267.
[95] See *The Life of Judah*, fol. 22b.

them were Jacques Gaffarel,[96] Louis Iselin,[97] Gabriel Naudé,[98] Andreas Colvius,[99] Giovanni Vislingio,[100] and Vincenzo Noghera.[101] Modena also enjoyed lucrative private teaching and preaching jobs in the Venetian Jewish community.[102] Modena now had the responsibility of raising his orphaned grandson Isaac min Haleviim as his own son, because his daughter Diana had remarried and moved out of Venice.[103] In 1634, as he wrote in his autobiography, Modena had to endure the arrest and imprisonment of this fourteen-year-old grandson as a result of trying, contrary to the law, to print *Beit yehudah*, Modena's midrashic anthology and commentary.[104] In the same year Modena felt that old age had finally overtaken him, and he began to prepare once again for his death by writing a Hebrew testament, a proposal for his burial, and the text of his tombstone. These important personal matters he recorded in his autobiography.[105]

So, too, Modena described in his autobiography the following events, which caused his life to take another turn for the worse. As noted in the Cohen–Rabb introductory essay, in the spring of 1636, when Modena was almost sixty-five, a major scandal broke out in Venice. Indirectly implicated, Modena experienced a period of great anxiety, which lasted more than a year. His distress was exacerbated when he learned in 1637 that his manuscript on the Jewish rites, which two years earlier he had given with permission to publish to Jacques Gaffarel, who was then in Italy seeking to acquire works for Cardinal Richelieu's library,[106] had been published by Gaffarel in Paris. His anxiety stemmed from the fact that he had

---

[96] See ibid., fol. 25a, and historical notes.   [97] See ibid., fol. 24a.

[98] Gaffarel's Latin letter to Modena of March 31, 1637, published in most editions of the *Riti*, mentions their relationship. On Naudé, a bibliographer, librarian, physician, and historian who worked for Cardinal Francesco Barberini and Cardinal Giulio Mazarin, see Natalie Davis's introductory essay, n. 38, and the book by Jack Clarke, *Gabriel Naudé, 1600–1653*, cited there.

[99] François Secret, "Notes sur les hebraisants chrétiens," *REJ* 124 (1965): 157–159.

[100] A prominent professor at Padua; see Boksenboim, *Iggerot*, p. 347 and frontispiece.

[101] A theologian in Bologna; see ibid., p. 347 and frontispiece. Many other Christian associates of Modena's are mentioned throughout his works; see Roth, "Leone da Modena and the Christian Hebraists," pp. 384–401 and *Divan*, nos. 55, 175, 51.

[102] Modena only mentioned these postions in his autobiography after he lost them in 1638: see *The Life of Judah*, fol. 25a. From the information given there, it appears that his annual income was about 150 ducats.

[103] See ibid., fol. 23a.   [104] See ibid., fols. 23a–24a.   [105] See ibid., fol. 38a–b.

[106] On Gaffarel, see historical notes to fol. 25a.

not considered what might be offensive to the Catholic Italian inquisitors in the manuscript he had originally composed for an English Protestant audience. In addition to Modena's account in his autobiography of this traumatic period in his life, fascinating
documentary material about both these events, including the precipitous appearance by Modena before the Venetian Inquisition, is
to be found in the Venetian inquisitorial archives and those of the
Council of Ten.[107]

This crisis passed, but Modena's distress did not. He and his wife
had become sick,[108] and their only daughter who remained in Venice was not getting along with her husband.[109] His son Isaac was
now in Brazil.[110] Modena lost two major jobs, teaching and preaching, and half of his income.[111] Shortly thereafter, in a new controversy with the government over the authority of the rabbis to excommunicate, the Venetian rabbis, including Modena, were all
arrested.[112] Modena's troubles intensified in 1640 when his grandson married and moved out of the house, leaving Modena and his
wife alone to quarrel incessantly.[113] Now his gambling debts became greater than ever. He had been developing an asthmatic condition that soon made it difficult for him to appear in public and
prevented him from climbing stairs.[114] As a result of this infirmity,
he and his wife had to move a number of times during these troubled years in search of a suitable apartment in the ghetto.[115] To sus-
tain himself and his wife, Modena had to rely on gifts. One such
gift was 150 ducats from Claude Mallier, M. de Houssay, the former French ambassador to Venice, in gratitude for receiving a copy
of the poem Modena had written in 1601 in honor of the birth of
Louis XIII; this windfall is not recorded in the autobiography. He
also had to rely on the proceeds from pawning or selling much of
his library.[116]

Throughout the final decade of his life, when crises loomed

---

[107] See *The Life of Judah*, fols. 24b–25b. The archival findings, some of them previously unpublished, are discussed in detail in the historical notes.
[108] See ibid., fols. 25a ff.   [109] See ibid., fol. 26a.   [110] See ibid.
[111] See ibid., fol. 26a.   [112] See ibid., fol. 26b.   [113] See ibid., fol. 27a.
[114] See ibid., fols. 26a, 27a.   [115] See ibid., fols. 27a ff.
[116] Boksenboim, *Iggerot*, nos. 129, 194. Now that he was old, the Italian synagogue
wanted to honor as well as help him by adding another six ducats to his salary so that he
could hire an assistant to teach the Sabbath, Monday, and Thursday lessons; JTSA 8594,
p. 13. On the poem for Louis XIII, see above, note 30, and historical notes to fol. 28a.

large, Modena managed to continue the activities that had endeared him to the Jews of Venice, including those by which he had made his mark in Italian Hebrew literature. He wrote letters, composed poems, preached, taught, and published popular books. He prepared, though he never published, serious writings on controversial topics such as the validity of rabbinic authority in the Jewish community,[117] the Kabbalah,[118] and Christianity.[119] He also served as secretary for religious and communal organizations;[120] officiated as cantor; and issued rabbinic decisions and copyrights, still signing ahead of all the other rabbis of Venice.[121]

The last addition to the autobiography, penned on February 24, 1648, apparently represents Modena's final written words.[122] Two weeks later, on March 7, his wife Rachel died; the characteristically brief entry in the official necrology of Jews in the record book of the Venetian Ministry of Health relates that "Rachel, wife of Rabbi Leon da Modena, died at the age of about seventy-eight, of fever and catarrh, after four months, Ghetto Nuovo."[123] Two weeks later, on Saturday, March 21, Modena himself passed away; the official entry in the records of the Ministry of Health, three entries after that of Rachel, relates that "Rabbi Leon Modena died at the age of about seventy-seven, of fever and catarrh, after four months, Ghetto Nuovo."[124]

[117] See *The Life of Judah*, fol. 26b, and historical notes.
[118] See ibid., fols. 24a, 26b; *Ziknei*, no. 131.   [119] See *The Life of Judah*, fol. 37b.
[120] These included Fraterna di Maritar Donzelle (the Society for the Dowering of Brides), see Moise Soave, "Vita di Giuda Arie Modena," *CI* 2 (1863): 288, and 'Ozer Dallim (the Society for Helping the Poor), JTSA 8468.
[121] *Devar shemuel*, ed. Samuel Aboab (Venice, 1702), no. 19, fols. 7a–8b, the week of January 16, 1644. An original copy of this responsum, signed by Modena and fourteen of his colleagues, is available in the library of the Talmud Torah in Livorno (no. 18.193) and is photoreproduced in Carlo Bernheimer, *Paleografia ebraica* (Florence, 1924), pp. 105–106, 169. For information on Modena's literary contribution, see historical notes, especially to fol. 20a–b.
[122] See *The Life of Judah*, fols. 34a and 37b.
[123] "È morto Rachel moglie de Rabi Lion da Modena d'anni 78 in circa, da febbre et cattaro mesi 4—Ghetto Nuovo"; see also Luzzatto, "All'Illustre Dr. M. Steinschneider," p. 254.
[124] "È morto Rabi Leon Modena d'anni 77 in circa da febbre et cattaro mesi 4—Ghetto Nuovo," ASV, Provveditori alla Sanità, busta 19, Necrologio ebrei, Reg. 996. His death was also recorded in a register kept by the Jewish community: "È morto l'eccelsamente Rabbi Leon da Modena, d'anni 77 in circa, amalato mesi quattro in circa, di febre et catarro in Getto novo," Comunità israelitica di Venezia, Registro dei morti dal 23 Settembre 1627 al 5 Novembre 1653; see Carla Boccato, "Ebrei veneziani nelle registrazioni dei provveditori," *RMI* 50 (1984): 16–17.

The night of Modena's death, twenty-eight members of the board of the Italian synagogue met to discuss a proposal that, in view of his service to the congregation and of his reputation as their cantor and teacher, they would ask each member to donate the equivalent of one-half of his yearly seat rental to defray the cost of the boat to take Modena's remains to the cemetery on the Lido, to pay for the torches following the coffin, and to finance the lighting of the synagogue during the nights on which the eulogies were to be delivered.[125] Although according to the will of 1634, recorded on the final page of the notebook containing his autobiography, Modena had wanted only his grandson to eulogize him at his funeral, the congregation apparently expected a lengthy period of speeches. The proposal was passed by a vote of twenty to eight.[126]

During the week following Modena's death, in recognition of his great merits, the board of the Society for Helping the Poor elected his grandson Isaac min Haleviim his successor as secretary.[127] Shortly afterward Isaac was elected to fill his grandfather's position at the Italian synagogue as well, also out of respect for the merits of the deceased.[128]

On April 3, 1648, Modena's daughter Diana brought the Venetian notary Andrea Calzavara an itemized and appraised inventory of her late father's possessions. The items were divided into three categories: clothing and household effects, appraised by Gershom (Grassin) the son of Solomon Alpron and Aaron the son of Judah Volterra; Hebrew books, appraised by Isaac Nizza; and books in other languages, appraised by Moses Luzzatto. According to a passage at the beginning of the inventory, all this property was to go to Diana Modena to satisfy that which was owed her, in accordance with the written instructions made by Modena on December 26, 1631 and the document drawn up by the Officio del Mobile on March 31, 1648. The total value of all the items was 158 ducats and 2 lire, divided roughly into 96 ducats for household items, 49 for Hebrew books, and 13 for other books.

The list presented to the notary was so detailed that it allows us to reconstruct the Modena apartment and wardrobe and to paint a

[125] These funeral customs are described in Modena's own *Riti*, 5.8.3 and 5.9.5.
[126] JTSA 8594, p. 71; see also Luzzatto, "All'Illustre Dr. M. Steinschneider," p. 253.
[127] JTSA 8468, p. 21.   [128] JTSA 8594, pp. 59, 63.

picture of his final days. The few possessions that he and his wife had owned were almost all old and torn. Nevertheless, touches of taste and comfort also appear, including hides stamped with gold to decorate walls, pictures, velvet pillows, three women's hat-boxes, plenty of comforters, and the usual linens, coats, handker-chiefs, shirts, dresses, chairs, tables, desks, and other utensils.[129] Diana shared these possessions with her sister Esther.[130] Several years later, however, Modena's errant son Isaac returned to Venice from Brazil, where he had been living under Dutch rule since the 1630s and from which he had probably had to flee after the Portu-guese reconquest in 1654.[131] Discovering that his father's property had reverted to his sisters rather than to him, the only surviving son, Isaac harassed the two women and made life very difficult for them, even taking his case before the Venetian courts. Esther and Diana had to sell all of their worldly possessions to defend them-selves against their brother, at a cost of fifty ducats.[132] Sadly, sudden impoverishment and family grief, so much a part of Leon Modena's life, seem to have been his legacy to his children after his death.

Nevertheless, Modena's legacy to his generation transcended the bickering of his family. He was mourned in at least three poetic elegies written for prominent Jewish leaders who died during that period. The first was by Isaac Shabbetai Rafael della Rocca, a con-temporary Hebrew poet, who mourned him as a leading rabbinic authority, teacher, preacher, and printer. This eulogy is the first available source to call Modena the head of the yeshiva, *resh metivta*, though this should probably be understood as an honorific rather than as an actual title.[133] Yom Tov Valvasson (1617–1690), a signif-icant poet, mourned Modena as a great scholar, a good preacher, and a mighty one who would be assured a place in the highest heav-ens and the Garden of Eden.[134] And Jacob Frances (1615–1667), a major poet of the period, included Modena in an elegy he wrote in late 1648 or early 1649. He cited Modena's death as an example of

[129] Ancona, "Inventario," pp. 256–267. On Isaac Nizza, see the historical notes to fol. 37a.

[130] Haleviim, *Medabber*, p. 90.   [131] See *The Life of Judah*, fol. 26a.

[132] Haleviim, *Medabber*, p. 90.

[133] David Kaufmann, "Ein Elegie Isaac Shabbatai Rafael della Rocca's auf Leon und Elia da Modena," *ZHB* 2 (1897): 97–99.

[134] David Kaufmann, "Echogedichte," *ZHB* 1 (1896): 145; on Valvasson, see Hale-viim, *Medabber*, pp. 82–83.

the loss of Venice's adornments, which left her naked and exposed. Frances wrote that no sermons could be compared to Modena's.[135]

Toward a New Assessment
of Leon Modena

As Modena's unpublished manuscripts, including his autobiography, were rediscovered during the nineteenth century, Jewish writers, unaware of his positive achievements during his lifetime and possessing little information about the complexities of Venetian Jewish life, were unable to place these literary remains in proper perspective and arrive at a just assessment of the man.[136] His writings, especially the book *Ari nohem* challenging the authenticity of the Kabbalah, were viewed as attacks on rabbinic Judaism. Moreover, certain works allegedly by Sephardic opponents of rabbinic Judaism and Modena's polemical treatises against them—the most famous of which were called, respectively, *Kol sakhal* and *Sha'agat aryeh*—were considered to have been simply a cover for Modena's own heretical views. As the details of his autobiography became known, especially the revelations concerning his gambling, most Jewish writers tried to argue that Modena was not a traditional Jew but rather a hypocrite and a heretic who had developed a program designed to undermine rabbinic Judaism. By contrast, the early proponents of Reform Judaism looked to Modena as one of their precursors and used him to prove that traditional rabbis of the past could have harbored "liberal" opinions. In the same tendentious spirit, those who wished to vitiate the Reform appropriation of Modena as a model looked to his gambling to damage his reputation and undermine his suitability as an exemplar for the Reform movement. Especially outspoken in his charges against Modena's integrity was the nineteenth-century scholar Samuel David Luz-

[135] Jacob Frances, "Kinah 'al arba'ah anshei venetziah," in *Kol shirei ya'akov frances*, ed. Peninah Naveh (Jerusalem, 1969), pp. 517, 520.

[136] For a complete discussion of all the assessments of Leon Modena in Jewish historiography, see the prolegomenon to my 1985 Brandeis University dissertation, "Success and Failure in the Seventeenth Century Ghetto of Venice: The Life and Thought of Leon Modena, 1571–1648," pp. 1–184. These findings are summarized in my article, "New Light on the Life and Writings of Leon Modena," in *Approaches to Judaism in Medieval Times*, ed. David Blumenthal, 2 (Chico, Calif., 1985), pp. 109–122.

zatto: "That rabbi was a hater of the sages of the Mishnah and the Talmud more than the Karaites. He was more Reform than Geiger. This was 220 years ago! And in Italy!!"[137] Such biased views of Modena gradually became accepted in the canons of Jewish history. To this day there is hardly a work dealing with the period that does not include mention of Modena as a gambler, a deviant, a free-thinker, or someone racked by contradictions. Trying to make sense of these complexities, some recent historians have sought simply to find in Modena the personification of the Renaissance Jew or the "first modern rabbi."[138]

None of these assessments does justice to the man. The interpretation that views Modena as the quintessential Renaissance Jew fails to take into account the fact that in Italy the Renaissance was over by the time he lived. While Modena cherished and cultivated many of the cultural values that had informed Jewish intellectual life during the earlier period and he is therefore mentioned quite rightly in standard works on Jewish society during the Renaissance, any evaluation of his life must take cognizance of the significant changes for Jews that had been taking place in Counter-Reformation Italy since the middle of the sixteenth century. To see Modena, though, as the "first modern rabbi" is to miss the point that he spent much of his adult life defending traditional medieval rabbinic authority over the Jewish community against aspects of incipient modernity, such as the attempts by the Jewish laity and the officials of the Venetian state to limit the rabbis' coercive powers. Indeed, it may be more apt to view Modena as one of the last medieval rabbis and the period in which he lived as the earliest beginnings of the modern period for the Jews, when individual Jews would gradually have more direct relationships with the secular authorities and allegiance to the Jewish community, and the rabbis' powers would be based on greater voluntary cooperation.

Further, an assessment of Modena must come to grips with his

---

[137] Samuel Luzzatto, *Iggerot shadal*, ed. Eisig Graeber (Przemyśl, 1882), no. 401, p. 980. Luzzatto also accused Modena of doing a poor job of proofreading the rabbinic Bible of 1616/1617; Samuel Luzzatto, "Literarisch-historische Mittheilungen," *Israelitische Annalen* 3 (January 1, 1841): 6, note 4. But according to the autobiography, which Luzzatto had read, Modena had not done the proofreading of this work himself; see *The Life of Judah*, fol. 16a.

[138] Roth, "Leone da Modena and the Christian Hebraists," p. 384.

acceptance of the superstitions and folk beliefs that appear so regularly in his autobiography: alchemy,[139] amulets,[140] fortune telling,[141] bibliomancy,[142] dream divination,[143] astrology,[144] omens,[145] and name changing.[146] Modena also dealt in amulets and remedies. Two of the twenty-six activities he lists in his autobiography involve teaching these occult practices.[147] The notes at the end of his autobiography indicate that Modena carefully followed the commerce in amulets and may himself have conducted traffic in them with a Frenchman in 1637 and again in 1639. As with so many other important aspects of Modena's life, only a small part of this activity appears in the autobiography. In his letters he mentions his trade in amulets much more explicitly.[148] During the plague of 1630 and 1631 he sold amulets that contained a prayer based on a divine name, which he said he had learned in a dream in which he had seen prophets. According to Modena's grandson Isaac min Haleviim, Modena claimed that every house to which he had affixed this amulet remained untouched by the plague.[149] Elsewhere Modena admitted that several collections of magic and remedies had passed through his hands.[150] Modena may have composed amulets encased in copper for Christians, who used them for help in achieving sexual satisfaction.[151] Modena seems to have left his grandson Isaac min Haleviim a collection of thirteen occult books and manuscripts, all but two of which were in Hebrew—assuming he was the Isaac Levi, a preacher and rabbi at the Italian synagogue, whose

[139] On alchemy, see *The Life of Judah*, fols. 5b, 9b, 14a, 15b, 16a, 34b.
[140] On amulets, see ibid., fols. 22b, 28b, 34b.
[141] On fortune telling, see ibid., fol. 16b.
[142] On bibliomancy, see ibid., fols. 5a, 7b, 12a.
[143] On dream divination, see ibid., fols. 9b, 11a, 13a, 16b, 17a, 17b.
[144] On astrology, see ibid., fols. 8b, 9b, 10b, 16b, 18b, 19b.
[145] On omens, see ibid., fols. 6b, 14b, 27b.
[146] On name changing, see ibid., fol. 6b; cf. 10b–11a.
[148] Boksenboim, *Iggerot*, no. 54.   [147] See ibid., fol. 28b.
[149] Isaac wrote that he had seen the name and had remembered it, but did not want to write it because, although he himself was an expert in amulets and secrets, he did not desire to use them; introduction to *Magen ve-herev*, fol. 11b.
[150] *Ari nohem*, p. 76.
[151] This information about Modena is found in a handwritten note on the title page of *Belil hamitz* (Venice, 1623) at JTSA. Gershom Scholem, *Sabbatai Sevi*, trans. R. J. Zwi Werblowsky (Princeton, 1973), p. 745, read the date of this note as 1620 and identified the handwriting as Modena's; the date of 1630 is equally possible and the hand is likely not Modena's. Because this information was placed so close to Modena's name on the title page it is likely that it was about him and not by him.

possession of this inheritance and whose reported activities as a diviner and as a worshiper of demons caused him to be investigated by the Venetian Inquisition in 1661.[152]

Be that as it may, Modena's enthusiasm for some forms of magic and astrology in no way contradicts his position as a rabbinic leader or even as an enlightened man, as some have argued. His avid interest in theurgic beliefs and practices conforms with a general proclivity in the wider society and with what seems also to have been a growing preoccupation among some Jewish intellectuals of the late Renaissance.[153]

Similarly, attempts to discredit Modena's sincerity by citing the compulsive gambling that he so candidly disclosed in his autobiography places all too much emphasis on a habit he shared with numerous contemporaries, both Jewish and Christian. The following observation, recorded in about 1626 by Immanuel Aboab, an Italian rabbi of Marrano origins and author of the *Nomologia*, well describes the extent of the phenomenon: "I have seen in Italy many places where the gentlemen come together in 'conversation of play' (as they call it) for their diversions; and I have seen some persons broken and reduced to poverty by the games of cards, dice, and tables. . . . How many houses have we seen ruined, how many fortunes lost, through love of gambling."[154]

Moreover, any assessment of Modena's obsessive gambling must take into consideration his strained financial circumstances. His annual income does not seem to have increased beyond the 175–260 ducats he made during his early years in Venice and Ferrara and may indeed have been less, though it is hard to reconstruct the total picture. In 1625 his teaching salary from the Ashkenazic Torah

---

[152] Brian Pullan, *The Jews of Europe and the Inquisition of Venice, 1550–1670* (Totowa, N.J., 1983), p. 90. The identification of Isaac Levi with Isaac min Haleviim is assumed by Carpi, in *Medabber*, p. 12, n. 17.

[153] Moshe Idel, "The Magical and Neoplatonic Interpretations of the Kabbalah in the Renaissance," in *Jewish Thought in the Sixteenth Century*, ed. Bernard Cooperman (Cambridge, Mass., 1983), pp. 186–242 and David Ruderman, "On Stretching the Permissible: The Place of Magic in Judaism According to a Sixteenth-Century Jewish Physician," to appear in the proceedings of the the the conference on Jewish societies in transformation in the sixteenth and seventeenth centuries, The Van Leer Jerusalem Institute, January 6–8, 1986.

[154] Cecil Roth, "Immanuel Aboab's Proselytization of Marranos," *JQR* n.s. 23 (1932–1933): 138–139 and reprinted in his *Gleanings: Essays in Jewish History, Letters, and Art* (New York, 1967), pp. 169–170.

Study Society was at least 72 ducats a year.[155] At the Italian synagogue he always earned about 22 ducats a year, not including the donations he received for officiating at special events.[156] In the 1630s Modena held a teaching job that paid 6 ducats a month and a preaching job for which he earned an unspecified amount. When he lost these sources of income he reported that he was left with half of what he needed to meet his expenses.[157] Modena was capable of enhancing his earnings by writing and could have earned even more by working at publishing houses or by taking on more teaching. His grandson Isaac min Haleviim wrote that Modena made 3,000 ducats during his life from his writings; averaged on an annual basis, this would mean an additional 50–60 ducats a year.[158] Thus Modena's income appears to be similar to that of a master mason who earned about 120 ducats a year in Venice.[159] This picture of a man struggling to maintain a position in the lower middle class is also confirmed by what he was paying for rent: in late 1623 Modena reported in a letter that he paid 44 ducats a year in rent.[160] Christian rents for small houses ranged from 8 to 40 ducats, and slightly larger houses ran from 40 to 60.[161] According to a memorandum of 1632/1633, empty apartments in the ghetto were available at rents of between 60 and 70 ducats a year,[162] while a Levantine Jewish merchant was said to have rented a fine house for more than 80 ducats per annum.[163] This estimation of Modena's lower-middle-class socioeconomic status is confirmed by the dowries of between 650 and 1,000 ducats he was just barely able to provide for his daughters.[164] These figures are substantially lower than some Jewish dowries, which ran as high as 12,000 ducats, a sum typical of middle-class Christians and nowhere near the 20,000–60,000 ducats often spent by the nobility. At the same time, they are con-

---

[155] See *The Life of Judah*, fol. 21a.   [156] JTSA 8593, fols. 21b, 22a; 8594, p. 13.

[157] See *The Life of Judah*, fol. 26a.

[158] Haleviim, introduction to *Magen ve-herev*, fol. 11a.

[159] Pullan, *The Jews of Europe*, pp. 76–77.   [160] Boksenboim, *Iggerot*, no. 121.

[161] Paul Grendler, *The Roman Inquisition and the Venetian Press, 1540–1605* (Princeton, 1977), p. 18.

[162] Benjamin Ravid, "The Establishment of the Ghetto Nuovissimo of Venice," to appear in the memorial volume for Umberto Cassuto.

[163] Pullan, *The Jews of Europe*, p. 196.

[164] See *The Life of Judah*, fols. 15b, 18a.

siderably higher than the 10–18 ducats typically spent on dowries by the poor in Venice.[165] Thus it is likely that Modena pursued gambling in part because he was looking for a way to increase his income.

Modena also pursued gambling for reasons other than financial gain; the stakes for which he played were enough to ruin him but not enough to raise his socioeconomic status in a significant way. With great insight into his own psychological circumstances, Modena once preached that the transition from wealth to poverty may require strengths and skills that an upbringing in an affluent family did not provide. He noted that a person who had been poor from birth might have a better idea how to make do with less and how to endure bad times than one who had been accustomed to comforts all his life.[166] Born into and reared as the child of a prosperous family, not only did Modena have to endure witnessing his father's financial deterioration, but he also had to live with the fact that he was unable to reverse the family's misfortunes. At the gambling table he tried to make up for the deficiencies he felt in his position in life and his abilities. Whether he won or lost, he could do it in a big way.

For whatever reasons Modena gambled, his habit does not seem to have affected his ability to serve the Jewish community or to carry out the functions of a rabbi. Once—ironically, during a period of abstention from gambling in the summer of 1617—Modena had to defend himself against the charge made by Hakham Isaac Uziel of Amsterdam that he gambled better than he wrote. Modena responded that the opposite was true: his monetary losses from gambling had only been in multiples of fifty, while his profits from writing letters and from publishing compositions ran into the hundreds. To the charge of having acted foolishly, he replied that among the traditional 365 negative commandments he could not find a single prohibition against gambling.[167]

---

[165] Pullan, *The Jews of Europe*, pp. 196, 238; Grendler, *The Roman Inquisition*, p. 18.

[166] *Midbar yehudah*, fol. 34a; Ellis Rivkin, "The Sermons of Leone da Modena," *HUCA* 23.2 (1950–1951): 298.

[167] Boksenboim, *Iggerot*, no. 146. In much of the literature on Jewish gambling, it is regularly stated erroneously that the aforementioned ordinance against gambling was made by the rabbis of Venice, was passed during the plague and enacted in 1631, forbade

By focusing attention on Modena's presumed deviations from the norms of traditional Jewish society, assessments of the man often lose sight of his phenomenal intellectual accomplishments. Modena mastered an enormous number of disciplines. They included, of course, traditional rabbinic scholarship: the Babylonian and Palestinian Talmuds, midrashic literature, medieval compendiums of laws, legends, and Bible commentary, and all of the responsa; the Hebrew Bible; Hebrew and Aramaic grammar and style; Hebrew poetry; medieval Jewish philosophy, kabbalistic and antikabbalistic literature; polemical treatises, sermons,[168] and Hebrew letters, both published and in manuscript; and Jewish historical writing. Modena's writings show that he was particularly well read in the Jewish literature of medieval Christian Spain and Renaissance Italy as well as that of the contemporary Ottoman Empire, including Palestine, and of Poland. Apart from rabbinic scholarship, Modena studied Karaite literature. In addition to Jewish literature, Modena was well versed in non-Jewish books, Christian and pagan, including ancient philosophy, the Vulgate, the New Testament, works on Latin and Italian grammar and style, Italian poetry, Christian scholastic literature, works on science, and Renaissance belles lettres.

Modena's contribution to Jewish communal life must be measured against the opportunities available for rabbis in Venice. Rabbinical influence in Venice was much less dominant than that of the professional rabbinate that developed in other parts of Italy and the world. Venetian rabbis were not appointed by the community and

---

all gambling, was directed against Modena, caused him to be excommunicated, and provoked his immediate reaction. Modena is also often viewed as a youthful opponent of gambling who later turned to lead the Jewish gamblers of Venice and who worked in the Jewish community to support his habit. None of these assertions is true.

[168] A manuscript Modena purchased in 1595, the first he ever bought, reveals much about the way he prepared his sermons. It was an unbound collection of sermons from 1557, which at first he thought to be a work by one of the Provençals from Mantua. Although he was wrong, he found satisfying innovations in this book and was able to use them in his own sermons. Modena's lengthy inscription on the cover shows his confidence in his position as a writer and preacher and assumes that future generations would care about the circumstances under which he had obtained the book. It also indicates his integrity as a writer and speaker. He wrote that when he used ideas from this book or any other work, he would always give proper credit. Modena called this manuscript *Miknat kesef*, meaning "purchased by money," of which he obviously had enough in 1595 to buy a manuscript; JTSA Rabbinics 172 (Halberstam 457); Libowitz, *R. yehudah aryeh mi-modena*, p. 114.

did not receive any salary. Rather, they were called upon when needed to render a rabbinic decision and were paid for each service they provided. Out of necessity, to support their families they sought other positions outside the rabbinate: cantor, scribe, teacher within the Jewish community, merchant, pawnbroker, musician, or proofreader for Christian printers of Hebrew books. Moreover, many magistracies within the Venetian government, influenced by the harsh attitudes of the Counter-Reformation papacy and the strong sentiment in Venice against judicial autonomy for any religious community—including the Jews[169]—were ready to enforce the restrictions on rabbinical prerogatives such as excommunication.[170] Also, since 1548, Jews had been forbidden to publish or to print books, so Jewish books had to be published by Christians and were subjected to rigorous prepublication censorship by the church, the state, and the Jewish community. Particularly difficult for rabbis were prohibitions against publishing or even owning the Talmud and Italian translations of the Bible.[171]

Yet Modena desperately defended ideas of Venetian rabbinic grandeur even when the other rabbis would not support him, as happened during the controversy over the ban on gambling. Unfortunately, in addition to clinging to a distorted notion of rabbinic authority, he also desperately held onto similar notions about his own family. He felt the need to preserve the powers inherent in the positions of husband and father, but he did so without taking into consideration the needs of his wife or his children. To maintain his delusions concerning his leadership role in family matters, he was willing to send a young son away from home and allow him to remain abroad for a long time. Similarly, later in life he let his feud with his son-in-law Moses Saltaro Fano cast a shadow over all family events. He showed little concern that his wife slipped farther

[169] On the issues surrounding the papal interdict of Venice, see Bouwsma, *Venice and the Defense of Republican Liberty*; Grendler, *The Roman Inquisition*, pp. 29–30, 202–204, 206, 211, 218, 222–224, 252.

[170] ASV, Inquisitorato agli ebrei, busta 39, "Scomuniche abbolite dal Magistrato Eccell. del Cattaveri"; Vittore Colorni, *Legge ebraica e leggi locali* (Milano, 1945), pp. 335–338, 371–374. This proposal was not accepted, but it indicates substantial opposition to rabbinic autonomy.

[171] Benjamin Ravid, "The Prohibition Against Jewish Printing and Publishing in Venice and the Difficulties of Leone Modena," in *Studies in Medieval Jewish History and Literature*, ed. Isadore Twersky (Cambridge, Mass., 1979), pp. 135–153.

from sanity as he constantly berated her for slights she showed him during difficult periods: "After she recovered [from the gout], her feet and hands remained immobilized, but not her tongue, and her words were as cutting as a sword. All day long she would not be silent."[172] His anger was not reserved for members of his family. He also showered harsh invectives on colleagues on several occasions when he felt that he had been wronged by them.[173]

One of the ironies of Modena's legacy is that the very intimate nature of many of the writings he left to posterity has created a misleading impression about his personality and character. Had Modena not kept records of his gambling and his troublesome relations with family members in his autobiography and letters, his life and character would never have been subjected to the intense and sometimes tendentious scrutiny of modern historians.

Left to stand on their own, Modena's writings demonstrate his highly developed skills as an author, educator, preacher, and popularizer of the Jewish religion and rabbinic literature. The most significant products of Modena's literary work, for which he is best remembered, are his polemical writings involving Christianity, heretical views about rabbinic Judaism, and Jewish mysticism. His central concern in all three areas was the defense of rabbinic Judaism against attacks that originated in Christian circles and which had become increasingly widespread owing to the emergence of the published book as a factor in intellectual life during the sixteenth century. Modena, who worked regularly for Christian publishers of Hebrew writings and who was sought out by Jews and Christians because of his interest in books, was well able to gauge their power to promulgate ideas that had once been peripheral. Formerly, the study of esoteric subjects by Jews and Christians had been limited by many factors, such as restrictions imposed by religious authorities and the high cost of rare manuscripts. But as technological advances were made in book publication at this time, access to these materials became much easier. Gradually Modena

---

[172] See *The Life of Judah*, fol. 28a.

[173] For examples of Modena's writing in his most irate state, see Boksenboim, *Iggerot*, nos. 143–144, 156–157, 161, 163. For an interesting example of how a colleague responded to such a letter, see the letter by Samuel Aboab from November 1647 in Meir Benayahu, "Yedi'ot 'al hadpasat sefarim ve-hafatzatam be-italiah," *Sinai* 17 (1954): 159–179.

came to realize that even the publication of the Zohar was a threat to traditional Judaism, so he turned against it.[174]

An assessment of Modena must also take into consideration the standards by which he judged his own work. Fortunately the many lists Modena meticulously compiled during his lifetime reveal those aspects of his life he deemed important. They include the "bibliography" of his published and unpublished writings in his autobiography, which he continually updated,[175] along with lists of the people he had ordained as rabbis and *haverim*,[176] some of his distinguished students,[177] Hebrew books (possibly all of which he had himself owned),[178] writers against Kabbalah,[179] and aspects of his professional work.[180]

This last list, incorporated into his autobiography, includes twenty-six items and is often cited in assessments of Modena as proof of his instability. But the list is really to be evaluated differently. First, Modena held down most of the jobs simultaneously throughout his entire life and did not flit from one to another. Second, they are not really twenty-six different occupations. Many of the entries are really subspecialties of the professions of rabbi, teacher, and author. For example, "Jewish pupils" and "Gentile pupils" are aspects of teaching; "Preaching," "Cantorial work," and "Secretary for societies" constitute aspects of his position at the Italian synagogue; "Decisions [of Jewish law]," "Judging," "Yeshiva,"[181] "[Conferring] diplomas of 'rabbi' and 'haver,' " and "Drawing up contracts" are all rabbinic duties; "Poems for weddings and gravestones," "Italian sonnets," "Writing comedies" fall under the category of author's work; "Printing my writings," "Proofreading for print," and "Commercial brokerage" were aspects of his employment at the Hebrew printing companies of Venice; and "Translating," "Matchmaking," and "Music" were jobs that he did from time to time.

---

[174] See historical notes to fol. 26b and the literature cited there.
[175] See *The Life of Judah*, fol. 20a.   [176] *Ziknei*, p. 189.
[177] Boksenboim, *Iggerot*, pp. 346–347 and frontispiece.   [178] Ancona 7, fols. 2b–4b.
[179] Ancona 7, fol. 13b.   [180] See *The Life of Judah*, fol. 28b.
[181] It is not clear from the available sources whether references to a yeshiva in Modena's writings indicate a judicial or an educational institution or whether there was a *rosh yeshivah* in Venice during his lifetime; see above, note 91; also *The Life of Judah*, fol. 24a, and historical notes to fols. 10b and 24a. His grandson regularly uses the title in connection with Simone Luzzatto.

Apart from these lists, we find Modena occasionally assessing his accomplishments more explicitly. In a letter to Samuel Archivolti, one of the major influences on his intellectual development, Modena—then a young man and at the beginning of his career in 1602—candidly tried to evaluate his own sermons in the context of the development of Jewish preaching. He was conscious of the influence of both traditional Jewish sermons and contemporary secular models on his homiletic style. He wrote to Archivolti that he believed he had employed rhetorical devices that he had not seen Jewish preachers use previously. He was also proud of the stylistic balance he had achieved between Christian and Jewish models, between the refined secular, philosophical sermons of Judah Moscato (1532–1590), a Jewish preacher from the Italian Renaissance, and the works of many "simple" Levantine and Ashkenazic preachers.[182] The two dedicatory poems he placed at the beginning of his collection of sermons, *Midbar yehudah*, published in 1602, reflect his sense of himself as a transitional figure on a continuum of three generations of Jewish preaching. The first poem was by his teacher, Archivolti, representing the previous generation, and the other was by Azariah Figo (1579–1647), his own former student and a promising young preacher of the upcoming generation.

If Modena saw himself early in life as making a significant contribution to the progressive development of Jewish homiletics, by the time his career had ended he was less confident that he had been successful in influencing his fellow Jews. Assessing his own writings a few months before his death in his will of 1647–1648 (written at the end of the autobiography), Modena wrote: "In a different generation their renown would be great and they would be more pleasing than many others."[183] His grandson Isaac min Haleviim, too, sensed that Modena's writings were not widely appreciated by his Jewish contemporaries and that "he was better known among the Christians than among us, beloved and adored for his wisdom and his modesty in the eyes of the cardinals, dukes, priests, emis-

[182] Boksenboim, *Iggerot*, no. 40.

[183] See *The Life of Judah*, fol. 37a; Reuven Bonfil, "Cultura e mistica a Venezia nel Cinquecento," in *Gli Ebrei e Venezia*, pp. 469–506; idem, "The Historian's Perception of the Jews in the Italian Renaissance: Towards a Reappraisal," *REJ* 143 (1984): 59–82; G. Sermonetta, "Aspetti del pensiero moderno nell'ebraismo italiano tra Rinascimento e età barocca," in *Italia Judaica*, 2 (Rome, 1986), pp. 17–35; *Ziknei*, p. 21.

saries of kings and princes of every people and language and since him there has not been another like him."[184] Indeed, it took a Christian to express the appreciation that Modena would have wished to have received from a fellow Jew. In a letter to John Selden, Sir William Boswell wrote of Modena's aspirations as "with what confidence he speaks of atteyning immortality &c. . . ." and then added, "all which, meethink, well become him."[185] Modena still awaits the appreciation he deserves in modern Jewish historiography.

[184] Haleviim, introduction to *Magen ve-herev*, fol. 11a.
[185] Roth, "Leone da Modena and His English Correspondents," p. 39.

Fame and Secrecy:
Leon Modena's *Life* as an Early
Modern Autobiography

NATALIE ZEMON DAVIS

Leon Modena was a child in Italy in 1575 when the polymath Girolamo Cardano put the finishing touches on his *Book of My Life*, and in 1580 when Michel de Montaigne brought out the first edition of his *Essais*, that "incessant" study of himself. By the time Montaigne's work had appeared in its first complete Italian edition in 1633, Modena, then a rabbi of Venice, had already written many pages of his own *Life*; when Cardano's *De propria vita liber* had its first printed edition in 1643, the septuagenarian Modena was complaining bitterly in his manuscript of the miseries of old age.[1] Leon's *Life of Judah*, as he called it, is thus situated within the flowering of Renaissance autobiography, and it adds much to our notion of what was possible in the seventeenth-century presentation of the self. There is confession, a choice autobiographical mode, but in the Jewish life to distinctive ends; there is a quest for fame, but in the rabbi's life, ever in tension with a catalog of woes; and there is a contrast between the intimate life and the public persona

I AM GRATEFUL to Mark Cohen for assistance with the Hebrew texts used in this essay and want to acknowledge the contribution made to my thinking about Jewish autobiography by our joint seminar at Princeton University on the Jews in early modern Europe. An excellent seminar paper on gambling by Howard Jacobson opened the comparison between Leon Modena and Girolamo Cardano, which is carried in other directions in my essay. I also want to thank Reuven Bonfil, Lorraine Daston, Moshe Greenberg, Stephen Greenblatt, and Geoffrey Hartman for helpful reactions to the argument of this essay.

[1] Girolamo Cardano, *De propria vita liber* (Paris, 1643), republished in his *Opera omnia*, ed. Charles Spon, 1 (Lyons, 1663), pp. 1–54. It is available in English as *The Book of My Life (De vita propria liber)*, trans. Jean Stoner (New York, 1962). Michel de Montaigne, *Essais*, 2.6, in *Oeuvres complètes de Montaigne*, ed. Albert Thibaudet and Maurice Rat (Paris, 1962), p. 358. Selections from Montaigne's *Essais* appeared in Italian in Ferrara, 1590; a complete Italian translation by Marco Ginammi was published in Venice, 1633: *Saggi di Michel sig. di Montagna, overo Discorsi naturali, politici e morali*. For a study of Montaigne's *Essais* as autobiography, see James Olney, *Metaphors of Self: The Meaning of Autobiography* (Princeton, 1972), chap. 2.

somewhat unusual even among Modena's expressive coreligionists.

European autobiography of the sixteenth and seventeenth centuries was fed by many currents,[2] two of which we will consider here. The religious exploration of the self that Augustine had established in his *Confessions* continued to inspire writers and readers as it had in the medieval period. The *Vida* of Teresa of Ávila is the most celebrated of the Catholic conversion stories, but there are others written by clerics and layfolk alike. Protestant autobiography from the early decades of the Reformation always included an account of how one was freed from papist shackles and discovered the truth of the Gospel. Subsequent Presbyterian Lives in England might document the author's sinfulness or search his or her experience for signs of election.[3]

Another major impulse behind self-description among Christians was concern for one's family—for recording its history, its triumphs and disasters, and its recipes for living, and for passing these on with the patrimony to the next generation. In the Middle Ages a ducal family might appoint a learned clerk to compose its

[2] Among many publications on early modern autobiography, see Karl J. Weintraub, *The Value of the Individual: Self and Circumstance in Autobiography* (Chicago, 1978); Paul Delany, *British Autobiography in the Seventeenth Century* (London and New York, 1969); and Gilbert Schrenck, "Aspects de l'écriture autobiographique au XVIᵉ siècle: Agrippa d'Aubigné et *Sa Vie à ses enfants*," *Nouvelle Revue du seizième siècle* 3 (1985): 33–51. For an important overview of the field and a valuable select bibliography, see James Olney, ed., *Autobiography: Essays Theoretical and Critical* (Princeton, 1980). The writings of Philippe Lejeune (*L'Autobiographie en France* [Paris, 1971] and *Le Pacte autobiographique* [Paris, 1975]) are very suggestive, even though, like Schrenck and others, I do not agree that writing about the self before 1760 is the "prehistory" of autobiography. Georges May, *L'Autobiographie* (Paris, 1979) is also a valuable introduction, with some examples chosen from the early modern period. For the Middle Ages, there is the classic work of Georg Misch, *Geschichte der Autobiographie*, 4 vols. in 8 (Bern and Frankfurt, 1949–1969); vols. 2, 3, and 4, pt. 1 are on the medieval period; vol. 4, pt. 2 covers the Renaissance to the eighteenth century. See also Paul Zumthor, "Autobiography in the Middle Ages?" *Genre* 6.1 (March 1973): 29–48. Jewish autobiography of the early modern period has not yet been integrated into the historical and theoretical literature.

[3] T. C. Price Zimmerman, "Confession and Autobiography in the Early Renaissance," in *Renaissance Studies in Honor of Hans Baron*, ed. Anthony Molho and John A. Tedeschi (Dekalb, Ill., 1971), pp. 119–140. Teresa of Ávila, *Libro de la vida*, published in her *Obras* (Salamanca, 1588); English translation by E. Allison Peers: *The Autobiography of St. Teresa of Ávila* (New York, 1960). An example of a Reformation autobiography with a conversion as a central thread is Thomas Platter's *Lebensbeschreibung*, published by Alfred Hartmann (Basel, 1944) and in French translation by Marie Helmer, *Autobiographie*, Cahiers des annales 22 (Paris, 1964). See also Delany, *British Autobiography*, chaps. 3–6.

history, but by the late fourteenth century Florentine merchants were doing it themselves, expanding their account books with family events and other news. By the sixteenth century *ricordanze* or *livres de raison* were being kept in many French households, those of country gentlemen, city lawyers, and merchants, and even of prosperous artisans. Sometimes these were spare, confined to births, marriages, illnesses, and deaths, bound in with account books or books of hours or Bibles; other times they were shaped memoirs and personal history, composed at intervals or all at once toward the end of one's days.[4] For instance, the Florentine historian and political figure Francesco Guicciardini wrote memoirs of his ancestors "to the glory of our house" and to serve as examples of virtue and vice for descendants, as well as a book of *ricordanze* about himself. The French Protestant captain, poet, and historian Théodore Agrippa d'Aubigné (1551–1630) composed his *Life* at the request of his children, so he said; he wanted to lay bare "in paternal privacy" his honorable actions and his faults. These would be more useful than the Lives of the emperors or the great. Like Guicciardini, he instructed them never to let anyone outside the family read the manuscript.[5]

One school of interpretation, going back to Jacob Burckhardt's *Civilization of the Renaissance*, has seen this attachment to family as detracting from the exploration of the self. "In the Middle Ages," Burckhardt wrote, "both sides of human consciousness—that which was turned within as that which was turned without—lay dreaming or half awake. . . . Man was conscious of himself only as

---

[4] Georges Duby, *The Knight, the Lady, and the Priest: The Making of Modern Marriage in Medieval France* (New York, 1983), chaps. 12–13. Gene Brucker, "Introduction: Florentine Diaries and Diarists," in his *Two Memoirs of Renaissance Florence: The Diaries of Buonaccorso Pitti and Gregorio Dati*, trans. Julia Martines (New York, 1967), pp. 9–18. I have given an introduction to and further bibliography on the writing of French family histories in "Ghosts, Kin, and Progeny: Some Features of Family Life in Early Modern France," in *The Family*, ed. Alice Rossi, Jerome Kagan, and Tamara K. Hareven (New York, 1978), pp. 87–114.

[5] Francesco Guicciardini, "Memorie di famiglia" and "Ricordanze," in *Scritti autobiografici e rari*, ed. Roberto Palmarocchi (Bari, 1936), pp. 1–99. Théodore Agrippa d'Aubigné, "Sa Vie à ses enfants" in *Oeuvres complètes*, ed. E. Réaume and F. de Caussade, 6 vols. (Paris, 1873–1892), vol. 1, pp. 3–113; at p. 4: "J'ay encores à vous ordonner qu'il n'y ait que deux copies de ce livre: vous accordants d'estre de leur gardiens et que vous n'en laissiés aller aucune hors de la maison. Si vous y faillez, vostre desobeissance sera chatiee par vos envieux, qui esleveront en risee les merveilles de Dieu en mes delivrances et vous feront cuire vostre curieuse vanité."

a member of a race, people, party, family or corporation—only through some general category." The preceding examples suggest that, on the contrary, certain forms of embeddedness and most especially in the family could assist in consciousness of self. Not only were kinfolk imagined as the audience for which the life was recorded, but also playing oneself off against different relatives— helpless brothers or rebellious sons—was a major part of self-revelation.[6]

Even in those Renaissance texts in which male writers were strongly concerned to show how particular were their qualities, the placing of the self in a family field was important to the story. Girolamo Cardano was not sure whether the readers of his *Life* would be kinfolk, students, or strangers; the literary models he mentioned were ancient ones, such as Marcus Aurelius; he devoted whole chapters to his appearance, tastes, habits, and feelings. Nonetheless, his self-portrait was partly established by measuring himself against his father, whose vocation of law he rejected for medicine and whose mathematical talents he surpassed; and his anxiety about his own reputation was more than matched in the *Life* by his "great discouragements" about his sons, one executed for poisoning his wife, the other a wastrel.[7] And Montaigne, who claimed that he was the first to communicate himself to others "not as a grammarian or a poet or a jurist" but "by [his] universal being," still compared himself with his father in height, appearance, agility, temperament, record keeping, and building activities, and thought that his adult self was in part a fulfillment of his father's design.[8]

The relation of embeddedness to the exploration of the self provides an interesting perspective on Jewish autobiography in early modern Europe. Identification as a Jew was concrete and omnipresent, filtering experience as ghetto gates filtered people and the laws of kashrut separated food. Still, it did not efface distinctive

[6] Jacob Burckhardt, *The Civilization of the Renaissance in Italy*, trans. S.G.C. Middlemore (Oxford, 1945), p. 81. I have given further discussion to embeddedness and its relation to self-exploration in "Boundaries and the Sense of Self in Sixteenth-Century France," in *Reconstructing Individualism: Autonomy, Individuality, and the Self in Western Thought*, ed. Thomas Heller, Morton Sosna, and David Wellbery (Stanford, 1986), pp. 53–63, 333–335.

[7] Cardano, *Book of My Life*, prologue, chaps. 5, 6, 8, 21, 31; chap. 10, pp. 40–41; and chap. 30, p. 108.

[8] Montaigne, *Essais*, 1.35, p. 221; 2.17, p. 625; 3.9, pp. 928–929; 3.13, p. 1079.

family memories, which sorted Jews out within the often unpredictable life of their own communities. Genealogies were contrived and remembered, and passed on through expulsions and migrations. In the late eleventh century a Jew living in Calabria used "family documents and traditions" to trace his ancestors back to Titus's destruction of the Temple and left an account of their doings in Italy and Egypt for the past two hundred years. Isaac Abravanel, writing from Naples after his expulsion from Portugal and Castile, insisted that his ancestors were all "worthy leaders," descended from King David.[9] Leon Modena's family had a written genealogy that went back five hundred years to when his father's ancestors had lived in France. Although it had slipped from his cousin's possession, Modena reconstructed part of it in his *Life*, recording the Italian movements of his ancestors and the "tradition," learned from his father, that "this family has always combined Torah with stature, riches with honor, and great wealth with charitableness." Meanwhile in Alsace, Modena's younger contemporary, the teacher, trader, and scribe Asher Halevi, was writing down his paternal genealogy back to his great-grandfather, an exile from Spain.[10]

These genealogies and family pasts are a frame for Jewish life history, and they may be a more common form of self-expression in early modern Europe than has previously been thought.[11] The

[9] Ahimaaz ben Paltiel, *Sepher Yuhasin* (Book of Genealogies), trans. and excerpted by Leo W. Schwarz, *Memoirs of My People Through a Thousand Years* (Philadelphia, 1960), pp. 3–14; full English translation by Marcus Salzman (New York, 1924). Isaac Abravanel, preface to his *Commentaries on the Former Prophets*, published in Hebrew in Pesaro, 1511–1512 and trans. and excerpted by Schwarz, ibid., pp. 43–47.

[10] See *The Life of Judah*, fol. 4b. Asher Halevi, *Die Memoiren des Ascher Levy aus Reichshofen im Elsass (1598–1635)*, trans. M. Ginsburger and published with the Hebrew text (Berlin, 1913), pp. 67–69. (I am grateful to Paula Hyman for calling Halevi's autobiography to my attention.) In the late seventeenth century a Bohemian Jew opened his *Book of Remembrances*, "I can trace my family tree for four generations. I learned from my grandfather Jacob that his father, Abraham Halevi, had come to Bohemia from Poland as a young man." Alexander Marx, "A Seventeenth-Century Autobiography: A Picture of Jewish Life in Bohemia and Moravia," in his *Studies in Jewish History and Booklore* (New York, 1944), p. 183.

[11] For an introduction to Jewish autobiography, see the entry on "Biographies and Autobiographies" in *EJ*, vol. 4, cols. 1009–1015. Arnaldo Momigliano has written a fascinating essay on the twelfth-century autobiography of a Jewish convert to Christianity, Judas Levi, alias Hermannus, and has included information and bibliography on the autobiography of the contemporary convert to Judaism, Obadiah ("A Medieval Jewish Autobiography," in *Settimo Contributo alla storia degli studi classici e del mondo antico*

known examples do not indicate that the author considered such composition unusual for a Jew to undertake, nor do they resort to the biblical Nehemiah or the unlikely Josephus as a legitimating model:[12] not Modena, who was quick to note his pioneering in other of his writings ("No one to this day has written a book on that subject," he said of his work on place memorization); and not the German Glückel of Hameln, who as a late seventeenth-century woman writing her first and only book might have been expected to reflect on the novelty of her genre.[13] As Christian parents were adding their lives to a family history and using them to help shape the future, so Jewish parents may have been increasingly doing the same thing in manuscripts still undiscovered or forever lost to our eyes.

The setting for the Jewish autobiographies may be somewhat different from the Christian ones, however. They were not ordi-

---

[Rome, 1984], pp. 321–340). Alan Mintz has done a study of major importance for the modern period in "Guenzburg, Lilienblum, and the Shape of Haskalah Autobiography," *AJSR* 4 (1979): 71–110. David G. Roskies is currently undertaking a study of forms of Jewish autobiography. In Israel, studies are forthcoming by Israel J. Yuval on medieval German Jewish autobiography and by Moshe Idel on an autobiographical fragment by Johanan Alemanno.

[12] On Nehemiah as autobiography, see *EJ*, vol. 4, p. 1010. The *Life of Josephus Flavius* was available in Latin printed editions by the early sixteenth century, along with his *Jewish War* and *Jewish Antiquities* (for example, the British Library has editions of these works published together in Paris in 1511, Basel in 1554, and Lyons in 1566). Josephus's defense of his efforts to urge the Jews to surrender during Titus's destruction of the Second Temple and his collaboration with the Romans would not have recommended his *Life* as a model for later Jewish autobiography even for those who read the text. An anonymous chronicle of the destruction of Jerusalem circulated among the Jews in the medieval and early modern period under the title *Sefer yosippon*; it was believed to have been written by Josephus "for internal Jewish consumption" and took a very different view of events from those given in the *Jewish War* (Yosef H. Yerushalmi, *Zakhor: Jewish History and Jewish Memory* [Seattle and London, 1982], pp. 34–35). *Yosippon* did not contain a "Jewish" version of the *Life*, however.

[13] See *The Life of Judah*, fol. 20a. The autobiography of Glückel of Hameln (1646–1724) was written in Yiddish and first published in that language by David Kaufmann as *Die Memoiren der Glückel von Hameln* (Frankfurt am Main, 1896). A new Yiddish edition is being prepared in Israel by Chava Turniansky. A German translation was made by Bertha Pappenheim (*Die Memoiren der Glückel von Hameln* [Vienna, 1910]), and an abridged version was published in German by Alfred Feilchenfeld (*Denkwürdigkeiten der Glückel von Hameln* [Berlin, 1913]). Two editions exist in English: *The Memoirs of Glückel of Hameln*, trans. Marvin Lowenthal, intro. Robert Rosen (New York, 1977) and *The Life of Glückel of Hameln, 1646–1724 Written by Herself*, trans. Beth-Zion Abrahams (New York, 1963). The Lowenthal translation is based on the Feilchenfeld German edition and is even further truncated to make it "tighter" (p. xii). The Abrahams translation is based on the original Yiddish edition and is the one used here. Glückel of Hameln, *Life*, p. 2.

narily appended to or bound in with Holy Scripture or prayer books; indeed Jewish law prohibited any such desecration. (The parchment New Testament binding later added to Asher Halevi's *Book of Recollections* was presumably for camouflage.)[14] Neither do they appear to be a mere expansion from account books, like the *ricordanze* or *livres de raison*. The events recorded by the Sienese Jew Giuseppe in his family's account book from 1625 to 1633 concerned personal quarrels and litigation about promises, purchases, and payments instead of being steps in a whole life history.[15] Perhaps the account book seemed too precarious a genre from which to develop a Jewish life: the pawnshop might be closed at any moment, the leased house withdrawn. The memoirs needed to be connected with a surer patrimony.

What played this role was the Jewish ethical will, encouraging, as did the genealogy, the writing about the self. (Indeed, nineteenth-century autobiographies from the Jewish Enlightenment still employed some of the conventions of the ethical will.)[16] From the twelfth century on, Jewish wills had sometimes included, along with the disposition of the inheritance and the prescriptions for burial, pages of moral injunctions and rules for the children. Such testaments were still being composed in the seventeenth century, not only by learned men but by merchant women like Pesselé Ries

[14] Halevi, *Memoiren*, p. 5. According to the *Magen avraham*, a seventeenth-century commentary on the Jewish law code Shulhan Arukh, one should not insert quires into holy books or write one's accounts in them or try one's pen on them (Shulhan Arukh, *Orah hayyim*, para. 154, citing the thirteenth-century *Sefer hasidim*). This prohibition could be ignored, as in a Hebrew prayerbook from Alsace that included a note on attacks on the Jews in 1475/1476 (J. Kracauer, "Rabbi Joselmann de Rosheim," *REJ* 16 [1888]: 85–86, 95–96). But on the whole Jews seem to have thought the holiness lost by breaking the prohibition was greater than the holiness gained by locating one's personal or family news on a sacred book.

[15] Cecil Roth, "The Memoirs of a Siennese [sic] Jew (1625–1633)," *HUCA* 5 (1928): 353–402. Giuseppe's *ricordanze* are in the blank pages of a Hebrew business ledger kept from 1562 to 1567 by Jacob ben Eleazar Modena of Siena, perhaps Giuseppe's ancestor. Giuseppe's entries are in Italian, each one beginning "Ricordo," with occasional words in Hebrew.

[16] On the Jewish ethical will, see Israel Abrahams, ed., *Hebrew Ethical Wills*, foreword by Judah Goldin (Philadelphia, 1976). On the use of conventions of the ethical will in the nineteenth century, see Mintz, "Haskalah Autobiography," pp. 76–77, 100. Christian wills of the sixteenth and seventeenth centuries might include various formulas of devotion to the Lord and (in the Catholic case) to Mary and other saints, and might include prescriptions about future activities of the children, but moral teachings and rules for living are not part of the testament.

of Berlin, whose will was praised by Glückel of Hameln.[17] Indeed, with reversal of fortune so common among Jewish traders and leaders and with ownership of real estate unlikely, the ethical bequest might loom larger than the economic one: "I have nothing to bequeath to you of worldly possessions," said Leon Modena's ruined father to him on his deathbed, "except that you always remember to fear the Lord thy God and to honor his creatures."[18]

These ethical commands and practical regimens are partway to self-portrait, as Judah Goldin has astutely noted. Here one must speak as "I";[19] one must reflect on oneself to another. In addition, there was the general confession expected of every Jew on the deathbed.[20] The next step was deciding to write "all." "I have made up my mind," said Asher Halevi, "to record indelibly, for the preservation of the good and the bad, everything that has befallen me."[21] And Modena opened *The Life of Judah*;

I have desired in the depths of my soul to set down in writing all the incidents that happened to me from my beginnings until the end of my life, so that I shall not die, but live. I thought that it would be of value to my sons, the fruit of my loins, and to their descendants, and to my students, who are called sons, just as it is a great pleasure to me to be able to know the lives of my ancestors, forebears, teachers, and all other important and beloved people.

Modena wrote his first and second wills at the end of the manuscript; his *Life* has subsumed the ethical instruction.[22]

Like Christians, Jews might start writing their autobiographies

---

[17] Glückel of Hameln, *Life*, p. 92.

[18] *The Life of Judah*, fol. 11a.

[19] Goldin, foreword, *Hebrew Ethical Wills*, p. 18. On the use of "I" in medieval Christian literature, see Zumthor, "Autobiography."

[20] Leon Modena, *The History of the Rites, Customes, and Manner of Life of the Present Jews, Throughout the World*, trans. Edmund Chilmead (London, 1650), pp. 230–231: "When any one thinketh he shall die, he then desireth, that Ten, or more Persons may be called unto him; among which, there is to be one *Rabbine*: yet sometimes they do not desire to have so great a Company called. When they are all met together, that are sent for, the sick Man begins to say that *Generall Confession* before spoken of. . . . If he have any desire to confer Privately with the *Rabbine*, or ask his Counsel about anything, or commit any Secret to his trust, he hath liberty to do so." Both men and women made these deathbed confessions, as can be seen from *The Life of Judah*, fols. 10a, 12b, 37a and Glückel of Hameln, *Life*, p. 21. All other personal confession was private, made only to God (Modena, *Rites*, p. 228).

[21] Halevi, *Memoiren*, p. 9.

[22] *The Life of Judah*, fols. 4a, 35b–38b.

at different phases of the life cycle. Asher Halevi seems to have started his *Recollections* as a young man, but was already planning to leave space for his children's doings at the end of his manuscript. Glückel of Hameln composed the first part of her *Life* "to banish the melancholy thoughts which came to [her] during many sleepless nights" after her husband's death; the second part she wrote years later after she had remarried and lost her second husband. Modena had wanted to start his *Life*, so he claims, after his first child Mordecai was born; he turned to it only at forty-seven in his immense grief following Mordecai's death and added the rest from time to time over the next thirty years.[23] In all three cases, their descendants realized at least one of the goals of the writers: they kept their manuscripts and presumably talked among themselves of the lessons of the *Life*.[24]

What those lessons consisted of depended in part on what the authors had chosen to disclose—what they had selected from "all the incidents"—and what interpretation they had given to their experiences. In Modena's case, the *Life* is a combination of confession, of lament for his calamities, and of celebration of his achievements in preaching and writing.

As for confession, Modena referred often to his "sins" in the plural, but he admitted only to gambling, an action much condemned by Jewish law in its compulsive form and freely allowed only at Hanukkah, Purim, and certain other feast days.[25] He began to play games of chance one Hanukkah when he was twenty-three and re-

[23] Halevi, *Memoiren*, p. 9; Glückel of Hameln, *Life*, pp. 2, 149; *The Life of Judah*, fol. 4a–b. A late seventeenth-century autobiography of Bohemian origin was written when the author was still a young man in his twenties (Marx, "A Seventeenth-Century Autobiography," p. 196).

[24] Halevi's *Recollections* were kept by his brother-in-law, Jonah Cohen, who added notes at the end (*Memoiren*, pp. 69–71). Glückel of Hameln's *Life* was copied by her son Moses Hameln, Rabbi of Baiersdorf, and other copies remained in the family (*Life*, p. xv; *Memoirs*, p. xi). The Vienna, 1910 edition was also a family affair, for the translator, Bertha Pappenheim, was a descendant of Glückel (see note 13 above). *The Life of Judah* stayed with Modena's descendants for some time and was doubtless part of the inspiration for the autobiography *Medabber tahpukhot* composed by his grandson Isaac min Haleviim, some two decades or so after Modena's death (ed. Daniel Carpi [Tel Aviv, 1985]).

[25] Leo Landman, "Jewish Attitudes Toward Gambling," *JQR* n.s. 57 (1966–1967): 298–310; 58 (1967–1968): 34–62 (p. 42 on the permitted times for games of chance). See also I. Abrahams, "Samuel Portaleone's Proposed Restrictions on Games of Chance," *JQR* o.s. 5 (1893): 505–515.

turned to it at intervals throughout his long life, almost always losing (or so he reported it), gambling away daughters' dowries and
family support and going heavily into debt. He explained it at first
as Satan's tricks and the compulsion of the stars; but later in the *Life*
it became part of himself, "the sin of Judah."

He also made sense of it by the way he ordered the gambling
episodes in his narrative: they follow after some turn in the wheel
of fortune, as in 1620 when, after the death of his son Mordecai, "I
returned out of great anxiety to the enemy . . . playing games of
chance." Here Modena is playing with the argument of his youthful
publication *Turn from Evil*, a dialogue on gambling between Eldad
and Medad. Modena uses the criteria of the studious Eldad to dub
himself a sinner for gambling, but it is the argument of the gambler
Medad that guides the placement of games of chance in the autobiography:

For [the gambler, says Medad] has learnt the lesson by daily experience at
the card-table, that when he thought to win, he lost; that it was a matter
of ups and downs; and so he comes to understand clearly that there is no
such thing with us mortals as constant and permanent possessions. Hence,
should any calamity overtake him, he will "bless God for the evil as for
the good," and even though it might involve the absolute loss of his
money, he will simply say to himself, "What can I do? Let me imagine I
lost it at play."

These are not the ups and downs of Machiavelli's Fortuna, to be
mastered as humans can. Gambling threads through Modena's autobiography, a sin that underscores the unpredictable elements in
the *Life*.[26]

Similarly, gambling plays a dual role in regard to the claims to
genuineness in Modena's autobiography. By Jewish law, as Eldad
reminds Medad, the gambler is disqualified to serve as judge or
witness. What kind of witness, then, can Modena be to his own
deeds? Medad counters that there is no better test for human character than the way the gambler reveals himself at play—better than
by his spending, better even than by his writing. *The Life of Judah*

---

[26] *The Life of Judah*, fols. 12a, 13a, 27b, 17b. Leon Modena, *Sur mera'*, in *The Targum to "The Song of Songs"; The Book of the Apple; The Ten Jewish Martyrs; A Dialogue on Games of Chance*, trans. Hermann Gollancz (London, 1908), p. 204. Niccolò Machiavelli, *The Prince*, trans. George Bull (Harmondsworth, 1961), chap. 25: "How far human af-fairs are governed by fortune, and how fortune can be opposed."

tells of gambling and of writing both; can it not, then, be counted on to reveal its author?[27]

As for Modena's calamities, they are foreshadowed from the first page: "Few and evil have been the days of the years of my life."[28] Even his birth was ill-omened, as he entered the world rump first right after an earthquake. His miseries he classified in three ways. There was the agony of the loss of his sons, which he blamed not on God but on himself: "It is punishment for my sins and transgressions that of my three sons one died, one was murdered, and one lives in exile." He cast himself as Job, finding each day accursed. There was the intense fear of persecution at the hands of Christian authorities, as in 1637, when he imagined (as it turned out quite needlessly) that the Paris publication of his *Historia de' riti hebraici* would bring the Inquisition down on his head and on other Jews as well. There was the bitter disappointment of the ills of old age and especially of his wife's suddenly starting to quarrel with him "for no reason, when I had committed no wrong" (one wonders whether his daughters agreed if and when they read the manuscript after his death).[29]

Balancing this story of an accursed life is the story of Modena's achievements. They, too, begin early, as he pictures himself at two and a half—the Jewish prodigy—reciting Scripture in the synagogue. He grew up to become a preacher (in Italian) so celebrated that "all the congregations gave great praise and thanks" and Catholic friars and foreign notables crowded into the Great Synagogue to hear him. And he grew up to publish books on so many subjects in Hebrew and Italian that he believed he could count on "everlasting reputation." The list of his writings he inserted into the autobiography just after his terrifying description of the murder of his son Zebulun before his eyes by Jewish enemies. His books, at least, are "a source of great comfort"; through them his "name will never be blotted out among the Jews or in the world at large."[30]

How can we relate this construction of a life to contemporary Christian autobiography and to Jewish representation of the self?

[27] *Sur mera'*, pp. 193–194, 196, 203.
[28] *The Life of Judah*, fol. 4a and note 1. The quotation is from Jacob's speech to Pharaoh.
[29] Ibid., fols. 21b, 26a, 25a–b, 27a.
[30] Ibid., fols. 7a, 11b, 21b, 23b, 20a.

On the whole it fits well with one of the great autobiographical strategies identified by the critic William L. Howarth, that of autobiography as oratory (as contrasted with autobiography as drama or as poetry).[31] The writer both persuades by his or her life and relives its lessons. Great expert in rhetorical skills,[32] Modena shaped much of his narrative to such didactic purposes.

Howarth's category of autobiography as oratory includes but is not confined to those patterned after Augustine, which makes it helpful in thinking about Modena's *Life*. The rabbi's account of his insatiable gambling lacks one element ordinarily present in Christian confessional autobiography of the medieval and early modern period, namely, a definitive conversion. Even though the Christians retain their capacity to sin throughout their days, the life leads up to a conversion: Teresa of Ávila finally dominates her flesh and her imagination; a Puritan finally understands the need for true repentance. Modena's life is not told as a development; he knows gambling is a sin from the start. The years are strewn with broken vows; and though he applies Job's laments to himself, he does not go through Job's change of heart. He does change his mind about a few things, as when he moderates his belief in astrology and makes a negative remark about his early interest in alchemy,[33] but most of the time he presents his life as a repetition of motifs.

[31] William L. Howarth, "Some Principles of Autobiography," in *Autobiography: Essays Theoretical and Critical*, pp. 88–95.

[32] Not only was Modena a celebrated preacher whose sermons were published and widely appreciated for their "pleasant words and clear language" (*The Life of Judah*, fol. 20a), but several of his other publications concerned rhetorical matters, such as his book on place memorization, *Lev ha-aryeh* (ibid., fol. 20a, and historical notes to fol. 15b), his book on letter writing (ibid., fol. 20a, and historical notes to 20a), and his Italian–Hebrew dictionary, *Novo dittionario hebraico et italiano* (Venice, 1612). On Modena's preaching techniques, see Howard Adelman's introductory essay.

[33] *The Life of Judah*, fols. 16b, 22b, 14a, 16a and historical notes to fol. 14a. Modena did not make explicit that his attitude toward Kabbalah had cooled over the years, as Howard Adelman and Benjamin Ravid point out (historical notes to fol. 20a). As *The Life of Judah* does not stress spiritual transformation, so it does not stress intellectual transformation. Cf. the presentation of intellectual growth in the *Life* of Giambattista Vico, written in 1725–1731 (*The Autobiography of Giambattista Vico*, trans. Max H. Fisch and Thomas G. Bergin [Ithaca, N.Y., 1944]) and in the eighteenth-century autobiography of Solomon Maimon, discussed below at note 58. The brief *Autobiography* of the scholar Joseph Scaliger, 1540–1609 (ed. George W. Robinson [Cambridge, Mass., 1927], pp. 29–33), documents his early growth in learning, but not his change in views. See also Anthony Grafton, "Close Encounters of the Learned Kind: Joseph Scaliger's *Table Talk*," *The American Scholar* 57 (1988): forthcoming.

Is this way of describing one's spiritual life characteristic of other Jewish autobiography from the sixteenth and seventeenth centuries? For a Marrano like Uriel da Costa, certainly not, for his *Exemplar humanae vitae* of 1640 was built around his conversion to the faith of his Jewish ancestors and his subsequent disenchantment with rabbinical Judaism.[34] Likewise for Glückel of Hameln during the few years in which she believed that Sabbatai Zevi might be the Messiah, for she saw that time of joy and penance as a special moment, even though it came to naught. But the rest of her life she portrayed as imbued with a continuous sense of her sins, a continuous experience of God's power, and a continuous fear of the unpredictable. The decisions she described as significant concerned remarriage and the resolution of her dilemma about living with her children in her old age.[35] The Jewish spiritual life seems more likely to have been interpreted as a constant trial than as a pilgrimage.

As for Leon Modena's quest for fame in this world, it is very much like that of other learned men and artists of his day. To be sure, Modena would never have gone so far in his *Life* as Montaigne did in "De l'Affection des peres aux enfans" and ask whether Augustine would have rather buried his writings, "from which our religion receives such fruit," or his children (Montaigne speculates that Augustine would have chosen to bury the children), but then few contemporary Christian fathers would have set up such a choice either.[36]

Where Modena's *Life* may differ from Christian autobiography is in the character of the interplay among achievements, sins, and

---

[34] Uriel da Costa, *Exemplar humanae vitae* (1640), published by Philippe van Limborch in *De veritate religionis christianae: Amica collatio cum erudito judaeo* (Gouda, 1687), pp. 346–354 and reprinted in Latin with a Portuguese translation in Uriel da Costa, *Três Escritos*, ed. A. Moreira de Sá (Lisbon, 1963), pp. 36–69. Schwarz gives an English translation, based on the Limborch version, in *Memoirs of My People*, pp. 84–94.

[35] Glückel of Hameln, *Life*, pp. 45–46 and books 6–7.

[36] The classical statement of the desire for fame in the Renaissance is, of course, in Burckhardt, *Civilization of the Renaissance*, pp. 87–93; a recent major study of the quest for fame is Leo Braudy, *The Frenzy of Renown: Fame and Its History* (New York and Oxford, 1986), especially pp. 25–361 on the Renaissance and seventeenth century. Montaigne, *Essais*, 2.8, pp. 364–383, "De l'Affection des peres aux enfans." I have treated this theme more fully in "A Renaissance Text to the Historian's Eye: The Gifts of Montaigne," *Journal of Medieval and Renaissance Studies* 15 (1985): 47–56. For a sensitive treatment of the issue of fame in Montaigne, see Steven Rendall, "Montaigne Under the Sign of *Fama*," *Yale French Studies* 66 (1984): 137–159. For Montaigne's reservations about fame, see *Essais*, 2.16, pp. 601–614, "De la Gloire."

calamities. Montaigne's self-exploration is unbound by such categories, the relation between his enormous sense of loss at the death of his friend La Boétie and his writing of his *Essais* too complex to be weighed in account. The voyage of "De la Vanité" (3.9) is through a more densely populated mental landscape than Modena's, with stopping places such as autonomy that the rabbi does not mark. Benvenuto Cellini's *Life*, by contrast, is simpler in structure than Modena's, for it moves dramatically from artistic creation to narrow escape to revenge without moral assessment.[37]

It is Cardano's *Vita* that lends itself readily for comparison with Modena's *Life*, for it has some of the same motifs: pride in his many books on varied subjects, despair about his sons, and admissions of his "vices," one of which was gambling. Indeed, it is conceivable that Modena read Cardano's *Vita* when it was published in 1643 (he had connections with its editor, Gabriel Naudé) and that it had some influence on the organization of the late pages of his own manuscript, where like Cardano he adopted a topical treatment of "Miseries of my heart in brief" and of citations of his work by other scholars.[38] Nonetheless, the overall moral economy of the two

[37] Montaigne, *Essais*, 1.28, pp. 181–193, "De l'Amitié." Among many treatments of the relation between Montaigne's loss of La Boétie and the writing of his *Essais*, see Donald Frame, *Montaigne: A Biography* (New York, 1965); Richard Regosin, *The Matter of My Book: Montaigne's Essais as the Book of the Self* (Berkeley, 1977); and François Rigolot, "Montaigne's Purloined Letters," *Yale French Studies* 64 (1983): 145–166; Barry Weller, "The Rhetoric of Friendship in Montaigne's *Essais*," *New Literary History* 9 (1977–1978): 503–523. For an important discussion of Montaigne's "De la Vanité" (3.9, pp. 922–980), see Jean Starobinski, *Montaigne in Motion*, trans. Arthur Goldhammer (Chicago, 1985), chap. 3. *The Life of Benvenuto Cellini*, trans. John Addington Symonds (London, 4th ed., 1896). Howarth, "Principles of Autobiography," pp. 98–104.

[38] Bibliophile, librarian, and independent thinker on religious and political subjects, Gabriel Naudé had acquired the manuscript of Cardano's *Vita* during his stay in Italy from 1631 to 1641 under the patronage of the Cardinal Gianfrancesco de' Conti Guidi da Bagno (Gabriel Naudé, *Vita Cardani ac de eodem iudicium* in Cardano, *Opera omnia*, vol. 1, fol. iia; Jack A. Clarke, *Gabriel Naudé, 1600–1653* [Hamden, Conn., 1970], chap. 3). Modena had both direct and indirect connections with Naudé. The indirect ones were through Jacques Gaffarel, prior of Saint-Gilles, Hebraist and scholar of religious customs, to whom around 1634–1635 Modena gave a copy of his *Riti hebraici* for eventual publication in Paris (*The Life of Judah*, fol. 25a and historical notes to 25a). Gaffarel was a longtime friend of Naudé, and while in Venice in 1633 was in correspondence with him (Gabriel Naudé, *La Bibliographie politique* [Paris, 1642], dedication to Jacques Gaffarel, pp. 3–6; this book was written at Gaffarel's request and was first published in Venice in 1633). But Modena also had direct connections with Naudé, so we learn from Gaffarel's prefatory letter to the *Riti* in the spring of 1637: "you had been before informed" (he says to Modena) "by our Learned Countryman Naudaeus that I had already, in a just Volume, written . . . concerning the Observation of Dreams" (*Rites*, trans.

Lives is different. Cardano's book is made up of many small parallels, his virtues and vices, his friends and his enemies, his honors and dishonors, and the like. His sense of sin is weak—he even brags a little about his "shrewdness" and "skill" in games of chance—and his chapter on "Religion and Piety" celebrates God's gifts to him more than it does God's awesome majesty.[39] The wins and losses of Modena's *Life* are much starker, the relationship of books, sorrow, and sin the central line of the narrative.

In short, Cardano's glory and complaints delimited a secular sphere within the large Christian universe of meaning, while Modena's were still closely tied to God's tangled relations with his chosen people. In an impressive book on *Jewish History and Jewish Memory*, Yosef H. Yerushalmi has emphasized the persistence of liturgical and ritual forms of remembering in the spate of Jewish historical writing that followed the Spanish expulsion.[40] Every historical experience was ultimately interpreted as part of the sufferings of exile, either punishment for the sins of the Jewish people or a test of their faith, as Abraham was tested by the command to sacrifice Isaac. I think we can see a similar process at work in Jewish autobiographical writing of the sixteenth and seventeenth centuries, and specifically in *The Life of Judah*, in which the distinctive details of person and family are organized in terms of the collective

---

Chilmead [1650], fol. B1a). That Modena might have heard about the publication of Cardano's *Vita* by Naudé in 1643 and acquired the book itself is not unlikely. Modena's "Miseries of my heart in brief" on fols. 34b–35a of his manuscript seem to be a topical rethinking of his life about 1645, the date of the last entry. He had previously used the topical mode only for the list of his books. Here items are added—such as a cryptic reference to what may be homoerotic activity between his son Mordecai and other men—that are not treated earlier in the *Life*. Fols. 35b–36a of the manuscript then turn to evidence of "what fame I have had," citing Selden and others. Cf. Cardano, *Vita*, chap. 30: "Pericula et casus, et de insidiis multiplicibus, variis et assiduis" ("Perils, Accidents, and Manifold, Diverse, and Persistent Treacheries," *Book of My Life*) and chap. 48: "Testimonia clarorum Vivorum de me" ("Testimony of Illustrious Men Concerning Me"). Of course, the similarity between Modena and Cardano could be accidental. If Modena took some of his inspiration from the learned Christian gambler Cardano, however, it makes all the more significant the difference in spirit between the two *Lives*. For an early seventeenth-century Jewish scholar definitely familiar with and influenced by Cardano's scientific writings, see David Ruderman's discussion of Abraham Yagel in "Three Contemporary Perceptions of a Polish Wunderkind of the Seventeenth Century," *AJSR* 4 (1979): 156–159.

[39] Cardano, *Vita*, chap. 13: "Mores, et anima vitia et errores"; *Book of My Life*, chap. 13, pp. 54–55; chap. 22, pp. 78–80.
[40] Yerushalmi, *Zakhor*, chaps. 1–2.

model of suffering as a punishment or a test and the expression of feeling is deepened by biblical language. And the other elements of the historical model are here too: Torah and survival. In Modena's initial plan for his funeral, foreseen in a dream, he wanted his books to be present, piled on top of his coffin, while the cantors were to chant Psalm 25, "His soul shall abide in prosperity and his seed shall inherit the land." In this image, like those of his birth and the wunderkind reciting Scripture, the collective and the particular come together: Modena had gambled away his family's inheritance, but he had furthered Torah through his preaching and writing, and chances were that his seed would survive through his grandson Isaac.[41]

Modena's funeral plan also had a warning in it: care must be taken lest someone lay hands on his manuscripts.[42] His worry calls up a last trait of his *Life*, which was, of course, included among those texts to be protected from gentile and most Jewish eyes: the strong contrast it suggests between secret life and public life, between different representations of the same person. Christian autobiographies varied enormously in the way they mediated between the intimate life and the public life, the variation involving both their definition of the secret and whom they wanted to hear their secrets. Teresa of Ávila put her personal torments and her known convent reforms all together in a work published a few years after her death; the holy life was to be transparent to every reader. By contrast, in 1639 a Presbyterian settler in Bermuda,

[41] *The Life of Judah*, fol. 38a. On the collective model of the wunderkind, see Ruderman, "Three Contemporary Perceptions," pp. 149–153. Glückel of Hameln's *Life* has the same structure: her sufferings are the loss of her first husband and of some of her children and the bankruptcy of her second husband; her sins are not fully specified, but include her unwillingness to accept her fate and lamenting too much, and they are connected with her suffering ("we were sinful in sorrowing so much" over the death of daughter Mattie [p. 73]; "this is because of my sins and I shall always mourn" the death of husband Chaim [p. 110]); her achievements are her Jewish progeny and her book describing a Jewish life. Lucette Valensi has noted the same cultural shaping of autobiographical accounts today among the Jews of the ancient community of Jerba in Tunisia, though with the loss of the messianic hope: "The Jews of Jerba situate their identity at the very heart of sacred history. . . . The first experience of writing in the first person, just as the oral recounting of a life, re-establishes ties with the legacy of the religious tradition, with the perception of a collective destiny, the refuge of the book, the recurring theme of exile. But the exile is now without redemption . . . only mourning remains" ("From Sacred History to Historical Memory and Back: The Jewish Past," *History and Anthropology* [special issue entitled *Between History and Memory*] 2 [October 1986]: 291, 303).

[42] *The Life of Judah*, fol. 38a.

Richard Norwood, recorded half a century of his life with such private attention to sexual guilt, nightmares, and visits from Satan that a modern reader comments on the difference between the hysterical Norwood of the *Journal* and the stable Norwood of "external evidence." "In everyday life he was a successful colonist who was quite moderate in the outward practice of his religion."[43] Montaigne's *Essais* made the knotty relation between the public and the private a central theme, while Cardano's manuscript *Vita* seems written with the intention of erasing the distinction between the secret and the open. Unlike those who wrote of their own lives as they thought they ought to be and not as they were, Cardano's book was to be "a sincere narrative" (*sincera narratio*). He portrayed himself in all his settings—as a physician attending the archbishop of St. Andrews in Scotland, as a man accused of "abusing boys," as an extemporaneous lecturer.[44] He wanted to give a single representation of a many-sided man.

Modena in his *Life* listed his many ways of making a living ("trying without success," he added), but did not show himself fully in all his public roles. As Howard Adelman and Benjamin Ravid document in the historical notes in this volume, during months in which Modena described all his doings as "worthless," he was in fact busily teaching the laws at the synagogue, instructing pupils, and preaching.[45] This is, of course, part of the literary strategy of Modena's autobiography. Leon entitled his manuscript *The Life of Judah*, the Hebrew name given him at his circumcision. The secret agony of the gambling rabbi might go beyond sons to students and to "others who know me"—it was already familiar to his fellow gamblers, creditors, and patrons—but it was not for the general Jewish public, let alone for gentile eyes. Especially not for Christian eyes were other Jewish secrets that Modena tells here about the ghetto, about how it feels to be part of a community in which all are blamed for the crime of one, about how it feels to be

[43] Teresa's *Libro de la vida* was written "by herself at the command of her confessor" (*Autobiography*, p. 65). Written between 1561 and 1565, it remained in manuscript until 1588, two years after her death, when her *Obras* were published at Salamanca by Fray Luis de León. *The Journal of Richard Norwood* is described and discussed by Delany, *British Autobiography*, pp. 57–62.

[44] Cardano, *Vita*, chap. 13, p. 10; chap. 40, p. 32; chap. 30, p. 20; chap. 12, p. 9; *Book of My Life*, pp. 49 ("straightforward narrative" for *sincera narratio*), 177, 108–111, 44.

[45] *The Life of Judah*, fols. 28b, 15b; historical notes to fol. 15b.

turned from "being loved by all" to being "the object of scorn and hatred."[46]

Nothing demonstrates as well this inner character of Modena's *Life* as the contrast with his *History of the Rites, Customes and Manner of the Present Jews Throughout the World*, composed in Italian in 1614–1615 for King James I of England and published in Paris in 1637 and in Venice in 1638.[47] Archrhetorician, he claims he writes "forgetting I am a Jew, fancying myself a simple and neutral relater."[48] In fact, he never forgets his goal for a moment in his text, which (as Mark Cohen has shown)[49] was to present the Jews in a way acceptable to gentiles, as nonsuperstitious, benevolent, moderate, and modest. No word of games of chance here, not even on the allowed holidays of Hanukkah, Purim, and the new moon; no word of the hatred and passion of the ghetto in his picture of "this Nation . . . very full of Pitie and Compassion toward all people in want whatsoever"; no sense from the description of "their" mourning customs—he refers to the Jews as "they," not "we"—of how Modena would burst out, "My bowels, my bowels. I writhe in pain" for the loss of a son whose illness had begun even while he was writing the *Riti*.[50]

---

[46] Ibid., fols. 13b, 21a, 22b, 24b. It is not at all clear whether Modena intended his daughters to read his *Life* or whether they had sufficient Hebrew to do so. Modena praised his aunt Fioretta as "a woman very learned in Torah and Talmud" but never says whether he taught his daughters Diana and Esther to read Hebrew. In any case, they must have learned of the autobiography after he died, for Modena made his grandson Isaac, the son of Diana, his literary executor, and the manuscript passed into his hands.

[47] Ibid., fol. 25a–b, and historical notes to that folio.

[48] The Italian phrase in Modena's preface is "Nello scriver, in verità, che mi sono scordato d'esser Hebreo, figurandomi semplice, e neutrale relatore" (*Historia de' riti hebraici: Vita e osservance degl' Hebrei di questi tempi* [Venice, 1638], proemio). Interestingly enough, when the work was translated into English by Edmund Chilmead he mistranslated the phrase as "And, in my Writing, I have kept myself exactly to the Truth, remembering myself to be a *Jew*, and have therefore taken upon Mee the Person of a Plain, Neutral *Relater* only" (*Rites*, trans. Chilmead [1650], fol. C5b).

[49] Mark R. Cohen, "Leone da Modena's *Riti*: A Seventeenth-Century Plea for Social Toleration of Jews," *JSS* 34 (1972): 287–321.

[50] *Rites*, trans. Chilmead (1650), pp. 121, 161–167, 50–55, 239–242; *The Life of Judah*, fol. 17a. For a treatment of grief and mourning in Christian autobiography of the fifteenth century in Italy, see Richard C. Trexler, *Public Life in Renaissance Florence* (New York, 1980), pp. 172–185 (on the mourning of merchant Giovanni Morelli for his son Alberto); and George W. McClure, "The Art of Mourning: Autobiographical Writings on the Loss of a Son in Italian Humanist Thought (1400–1461)," *Renaissance Quarterly* 39 (1986): 440–475. Modena's recurrent mourning in *The Life of Judah* differs from both the ritual mourning of the merchant Morelli and the rhetorical consolation of the humanists.

These Jewish secrets were quite well kept, except perhaps from those Christians who were regular habitués of the ghetto. If Shakespeare had lived to read the *Riti*, he might have pondered the rabbi of Venice who had reservations about taking usury from Christians,[51] but *The Life of Judah*, hidden from gentiles, is discrepant from Shylock on almost every page: a Jew who chances his money with thriftless abandon, who cries for revenge against Jewish slayers of his son, who basks in Christian admiration, and who invokes against Christian scorn not merely a common humanity, as does Shylock, but an ancient lineage and learning.[52]

This sense of a protected inner space points to a distinctive Jewish construction of the Renaissance contrast of inside/outside. Christian writers, in their frequent meditation on masking and dissimulation, usually assumed the inside/outside contrast to apply to the individual and to be bad but inevitable in a society of advancement and preferment. One told one's secrets to oneself, to one's confessor (if one was a Catholic), to one's immediate family perhaps, but beyond them the world was unsafe. The transcending of this predicament is one of the great gifts of Montaigne's *Essais*.[53] In the Jewish case, the *inside* was defined not only as the individual and his or her family, but also as the wider Jewish community. In the historical circumstances of the exile, the contrast was often necessary and not always bad. Some secrets it was dangerous to let out to Christians; better to drown them in the noisemaking against the

---

[51] *Rites*, trans. Chilmead (1650), pp. 73–77 for Modena's opinion that the Deuteronomic permission "Unto a Stranger thou mayst lend upon Usury" (23:20) applied only to the Seven Nations of Canaan and not to "those Nations, among whom they are at this Present dispersed." The Jews "allege it to be Lawful" now because they have no other way to make a living. See discussion of this text and rabbinical reaction to it in Cohen, "Leone da Modena's *Riti*," pp. 310–311.

[52] Cf. William Shakespeare, *The Merchant of Venice*, especially I:3 and III:1. For Christians who did frequent the ghetto of Venice, see Brian Pullan, *The Jews of Europe and the Inquisition of Venice, 1550–1670* (Totowa, N.J., 1983), pp. 160–167.

[53] On Montaigne's condemnation of lying and false appearance and his ultimate means of reconciling himself to appearances while telling the truth about himself in his book, see Starobinski, *Montaigne in Motion*. On Renaissance concern about masking, see Natalie Z. Davis, *The Return of Martin Guerre* (Cambridge, Mass., 1983), especially chaps. 4, 6, 10, and the poem of the French man of letters Guillaume de La Perrière in regard to an emblem about masks. Whereas in classical times, masks were worn only for special occasions, now they are used all the time: "Chacun veult feindre et colorer sa ruse. / Trahison gist souz beau et doux langage. / Merveille n'est si tout le monde abuse. / Car chacun tend à faulser son visage." *Le Theatre des bons engins* (Lyons, 1549), emblem 5.

wicked oppressor Haman at Purim. Some secrets it was imprudent to let out: certain rabbis were critical of Jewish scholars who taught Hebrew and Kabbalah to Christians, as no good could come from it.[54]

That the inner/outer contrast is found so acutely in Modena is surely a product of his experience of moving between the two worlds, using the Italian language, motifs, and genres and being listened to seriously by Christians. But it can also be found, if less explicitly, in the *Recollections* of Asher Halevi, who sometimes mediated between the Jews of Alsace and the civil authorities, and in the *Life* of the merchant Glückel of Hameln, who traded with Christians and drew her moral tales from both Jewish and Christian sources.[55] How might this contrast feed the process of self-exploration? It offered a range of situations that could be described to others in Hebrew or Yiddish with frankness and with a vehemence of personal feeling that went beyond biblical borrowings; possibly, too, it offered a double perspective from which to regard the self. Not that one literally reported everything about the inside to the insiders: Modena did not elaborate on the quarrels with his wife or on a cryptic reference in "Miseries of my heart" to his son Mordecai "with Raphael Spira . . . and afterward, until his death, with the Morisco."[56] But Asher Halevi could tell his descendants that he had a nocturnal emission on Yom Kippur night (an omen of premature death) and went to his wife's bed and wept with her. And the *Book of Remembrances* by a would-be Jewish scholar and trader of Bohemian origin took the step, unusual in any sixteenth- or seventeenth-century autobiography, of blaming his parents for his failures: the neglect of his father and stepmother had brought him to his mid-

---

[54] D. Kaufmann, "Elia Menachem Chalfan on Jews Teaching Hebrew to Non-Jews," *JQR* o.s. 9 (1897): 500–508 and Moshe Idel, "Particularism and Universalism in Kabbalah: 1480–1650," a paper given at the conference on Jewish societies in transformation in the sixteenth and seventeenth centuries, The Van Leer Jerusalem Institute, January 6–8, 1986.

[55] Halevi, *Memoiren*, p. 60. Glückel of Hameln, *Life*, pp. 114–126 for the business activities of Glückel after the death of her first husband. She does not give the names of any Christians with whom she did business, but it is clear from her activities selling stockings, seed pearls, and other items and from her attendance at fairs at Leipzig, Brunswick, and Frankfurt an der Oder that some of her clients must have been gentiles. Moral tales with non-Jewish motifs are found on pp. 10–11 (Alexander), 52–53 (Charlemagne), 93–94, and 153–156 of her *Life*.

[56] *The Life of Judah*, fol. 34b.

twenties "devoid of wisdom and intelligence, without sons and spouse."[57] If early modern Jewish autobiography was sustained by the recurring application of the Jewish myth of exile, suffering, and survival to the individual life, it could move to surprising discovery, generated by the contrast between outer and secret worlds.

Because they were rarely published except in snippets in learned Hebrew prefaces or in the unusual case of the Latin apologia for Uriel da Costa, Jewish autobiographies remained a genre for relatives and familiars until the late eighteenth century. In 1792, when the Berlin philosopher Solomon Maimon published his *Lebensgeschichte* in German, the Jewish Life was given a very different shape.[58] In it there is a full conversion from village Jewish genius to outrageous participant in the mixed city salon; intimate yearnings and Jewish secrets are revealed in print, and both Christianity and Judaism are found wanting; the comic mood has taken over from the lamentation, even when things go wrong. Maimon's autobiography owes much to Enlightenment experiences and models, but it was also nourished by some of the traditions of rhetoric and self-exploration that the reader will meet in Leon Modena's *Life of Judah*.

[57] Halevi, *Memoiren*, p. 49. Marx, "A Seventeenth-Century Autobiography," p. 196.

[58] *Salomon Maimon's Lebensgeschichte. Von ihm selbst geschrieben und herausgegeben von K. P. Moritz. In zwei Theilen* (Berlin, 1792–1793). An English translation was made by J. Clark Murray and published in 1888; it was reissued as *The Autobiography of Solomon Maimon, with an Essay on Maimon's Philosophy* by Hugo Berman (London, 1954). A condensation of Murray's translation in *Solomon Maimon: An Autobiography*, ed. Moses Hadas (New York, 1967).

חיי יהודה

3. Title page of the manuscript of *Hayyei yehudah*.

The Life of Judah

אלה תולדות יהודה אריה, בן השוע איש אמונים
כמ"ה יצחק ז"ל, בן הגאון הרופא כמהר"ר מרדכי ז"ל,
בן הותיק כמ' יצחק ז"ל, בן הקצין כמ"ה משה ז"ל,
ממודינא :

מעט ורעים היו ימי שני חיי בעה"ז

4. First page of the manuscript of *Hayyei yehudah*.

[MS 4a/ א , C 31] With God's help may we do this successfully, amen.

THIS IS the life story of Judah Aryeh,[a] son of the noble and trust-worthy Isaac[b] of blessed memory, son of the gaon and physician, Rabbi Mordecai[c] of blessed memory, son of the venerable Isaac of blessed memory, son of the wealthy Moses[d] of blessed memory, Modena:[1]

"Few and evil have been the days of the years of my life"[2]
in this world.

Inasmuch as the King's [God's] word has power[3] to remove man from this world on the day of his death—after which all is forgotten[4]—for more than twenty-four years I have desired in the depths of my soul to set down in writing all the incidents that happened to me from my beginnings until the end of my life, so that I shall not die, but live.[5] I thought that it would be of value to my sons, the fruit of my loins, and to their descendants, and to my students, who are called sons,[6] just as it is a great pleasure to me to be able to know the lives of my ancestors, forebears, teachers, and all other important and beloved people.

In particular, I longed to bequeath it as a gift to my firstborn son, the apple of my eye, the root of my heart, whose bright countenance was similar to mine, a man of wisdom, Mordecai of blessed memory, who was known as Angelo.[e] All my thoughts were of him. I was proud of him, and he was the source of all my joy. But for those twenty-four years up to the present I did not succeed in writing this down as a memoir in a book.[7] Now that God has taken away my joy,[8]—it being two months since God took him away,

---

[1] This word, *mi-modena*, is written on a separate line and centered below the list of Leon Modena's forebears. Apparently he meant to convey that this was the family name and that it applied to all the above-named ancestors. On the problem of Italian family names, see the preface to this volume, near the end of the subsection on the translation.
[2] Genesis 47:9.   [3] Ecclesiastes 8:4.   [4] Ecclesiastes 2:16.
[5] Psalm 118:17. As is common in Jewish texts, Modena gave only the beginning of the biblical verse, understanding that his readers (in this case, the descendants for whom he was writing this account of his life) would know the continuation, "and declare the works of the Lord."
[6] This expression, which Modena repeated regularly later in his life, is based loosely on Sifrei Deuteronomy par. 34, ed. L. Finkelstein (New York, 1969), p. 61.
[7] Exodus 17:14.   [8] Adaptation of Genesis 30:23.

leaving me desolate and faint all day long[9]—my soul has refused to be comforted,[10] for I will go to my grave mourning for my son,[11] waiting for death[12] as for a solemnly appointed time.[13]

And so, at the age of forty-seven, an old man, full of disquietude,[14] I resolved, in the month of Tevet 5378 [December 29, 1617–January 26, 1618] to begin and to finish, God willing, giving an account of all the essential as well as of the incidental happenings in my life. Should my children or [C 32] children's children or students or others who know me look at it, they will see[15] the woes that befell me.[16] From the moment I entered the world [MS 4b/ ב] I had neither tranquility nor quiet nor rest, and then disquietude came upon me,[17f] namely, disquietude over my son Mordecai[g] of blessed memory. I await death, which does not come.[18]

Subsequently, from year to year, at six-month intervals, I shall add to this account what new happens to me.[h] After that will come my will[i] concerning my body, soul, and literary remains—and God will do what is proper in his eyes.[19]

I RECEIVED the tradition from my father, my teacher of blessed memory, that our ancestors came from France.[j] In his house there was a family tree[k] going back more than five hundred years, which had been found among the writings of my grandfather, the gaon of blessed memory. From my uncle, Rabbi Solomon[l] Modena of blessed memory, it had passed to his daughter's son, my kinsman Rabbi Aaron,[20m] the son of Moses of Modena, may God his Rock protect him and grant him long life, who lives at present in Modena.[n] He told me that it had left his possession, and although I have searched for it thoroughly I have so far been unable to obtain it.

Nonetheless, I know that it is so, from tradition passed on by my

---

[9] Lamentations 1:13.   [10] Psalm 77:3.
[11] Genesis 37:35.   [12] Job 3:21.   [13] Lamentations 2:22.   [14] Adaptation of Job 14:1.
[15] The phrase "giving an account of all the essential" and the words "look at it, they will see," interwoven with the narrative here, form a play on Psalm 22:18.
[16] Lamentations 5:1.   [17] Job 3:26.   [18] Job 3:21.
[19] Modena left a space equivalent to about three lines before beginning the next paragraph, thus clearly separating his introduction from the autobiography proper.
[20] In the manuscript there is a marginal gloss at this point: "author of *Ma'avar yabbok* and *Me'irei ha-shahar*." This gloss is not in Modena's handwriting. In the Kahana edition the phrase is integrated into the text, thus creating for the editor the problem (see his edition, page 10 note 4) that *Ma'avar yabbok* was not printed until several years after 1618, the year in which Modena wrote this first section of *Hayyei yehudah*.

elders, that this family has always combined Torah with stature, riches with honor, and great wealth with charitableness.[21] He [Rabbi Aaron] told me that after our forebears left France, they dwelled for a long time in Viterbo,[o] and then came to Modena, where they acquired property and became fruitful and multiplied.[22] Because they were the first to establish a pawnshop there[p] and become wealthy, they took their name from that city. To this day, control over the cemetery there is in the hands of my aforementioned kinsman Moses, because our first forebears in the city purchased it for their own use. The first house they acquired in Modena is still in the possession of Moses, and I have seen it. In some places therein is found our crest[q] in marble, the figure of a leopard[23] standing on its two hind legs [C 33] with a palm branch in its paw. Moses told me that it [the crest] has been in our family for more than five hundred years. He also has in his possession in writing the privileges of all those who ruled Modena—popes, emperors, dukes, and the like[r]—who confirmed it.

Apparently, in the days of Isaac, the grandfather of my revered father of blessed memory [MS 5a/ג], they moved to Bologna,[s] though they continued to keep their house and pawnshop in Modena. And there, too, they became great and prospered,[24] yet retained the name Modena. As for me, because I was born and grew up in Venice, and have lived in its environs,[25] and have been in Modena only during the past ten years and but two or three times,[t] I sign my name in Italian, "Leon Modena da Venezia,"[u] and not "da Modena." For that city has become our byname instead of our toponym, and as such you will find it in my printed Italian writings.

For that reason, my grandfather, the gaon Rabbi Mordecai[v] of blessed memory, who was a great Torah scholar, also lived in Bologna. He had been ordained by the gaons of his city, and I now possess his certificates of ordination. Several years earlier he had begun a work similar to the Beit Yosef of the gaon Caro[w] of blessed memory. He also composed many rabbinic explanations, legal rulings, and other treatises,[x] most of which are in the possession of the

---

[21] Proverbs 8:18. [22] Genesis 47:27.
[23] The word for leopard (*namer*) was written by Modena above the word for lion (*aryeh*).
[24] Jeremiah 5:27. [25] Ezekiel 5:5.

aforementioned Rabbi Aaron of Modena. He was also a great, distinguished physician, having been awarded the medical diploma while Emperor Charles V[y] was still in Bologna. At that time, he was made a *Cavalier di Speron d'Oro*[26]—Knight of the Golden Spur—by him, for thus did the emperor do to all those who received the medical diploma while he was there,[z] whether Christian or Jew. He was honored by all the people of his city and was known throughout Italy. You will find him mentioned favorably among the gaons of his generation in the book *Shalshelet ha-kabbalah*[a] by Rabbi Gedaliah Yahya of blessed memory, in [the entries for] the generation of Rabbi Joseph ibn Gikatiliya.

He [my grandfather] passed away at the age of fifty [C 34] in the year [5]290[1] [1529/1530], when the mule he was riding kicked up its leg [threw him], and the other doctors in the city, out of jealousy, bribed the expert physician treating him to put poison on the bandages and kill him. On the day of his death, he summoned my revered father of blessed memory, who was a little boy at the time, and said: "Recite for me your verse from the Bible."[b] He responded, "O House of Jacob, go forth in the light of the Lord."[2] He [my grandfather] then said, "If it be so, then I must depart." He immediately summoned [MS 5b/ ד] the teacher who lived in his house, Isaac Gallico[c] of blessed memory, as well as his wife, my grandmother Gentile of blessed memory, a woman of great valor, whom I met in Ferrara during my childhood and who died at the age of ninety-four. Through a scribe, he [my grandfather] made his will, designating those two individuals as guardians of his estate, for he left four male children.[d] The eldest was my revered father Isaac of blessed memory, aged nine; the second, Rabbi Solomon of blessed memory; the third, Shemaiah of blessed memory; and the fourth, Rabbi Abtalion of blessed memory, eighteen months old at the time.[e]

Rabbi Solomon[f] grew up to be very learned in Torah and in wisdom. I once kissed his hands in Ferrara, in the month he died—the

---

[26] Written in Hebrew letters and reflecting the dropping of the final vowel in the Venetian dialect.

[1] For the number 290, Modena wrote *tz-r* (*tz* = 90, *r* = 200), reversing the normal order for this date, *r-tz* (200–90), in order to allude to the expression *tzar li*, "I am distressed."

[2] Isaiah 2:5.

month of Av in the year 5340 [July–August 1580]—while I was still studying there. He left a daughter named Imperia, who was married to Moses, the father of the aforementioned Rabbi Aaron of Modena. Rabbi Solomon's wife was Fioretta[g] of blessed memory, a woman very learned in Torah and Talmud, as was her sister Diana, mother of the Rieti children of Mantua. Both of them were the daughters of the sister of my grandfather of blessed memory. Fioretta went to the Holy Land at the end of her life, and when she passed through Venice,[h] I conversed with her and found her very expert in Torah. She died when she reached the border of the Land of Israel and was buried there next to the border.[3]

Shemaiah lived in Modena, managing the pawnshop there. But he became attracted to alchemy.[i] A certain gentile deceived him by showing him a deceptive increase. He enticed him to take all the silver and gold from the pawnshop and brought him to a certain room, [C 35] claiming that they would melt it down and increase its value many times over. But there he thrust a sword into Shemaiah's belly, killing him, and stole all the silver and gold and ran off. This happened the night of the burning of leaven [before Passover]. The next day, people sensed that something had happened and found him and buried him. Three days later the murderer was seized with all the silver and gold—nothing was missing—and he was quartered. Shemaiah left a son and a daughter: Mordecai of blessed memory—who died in Ferrara in [5]372 [1611/1612],[4] leaving an only daughter, who is now married to one of our Modena kinsmen from Vignola[j]—and Sarah, [MS 6a/ ה] who died without children.[5]

Rabbi Abtalion[k] of blessed memory excelled in knowledge of Torah, Gemara, and secular subjects; there was no one like him in his generation. After he settled in Ferrara, his fame spread throughout the land.[6] Rabbi Azariah de Rossi of blessed memory praises him many times in his book *Me'or 'einayim*,[l] as can be seen. Indeed, most of that book is "flour ground between the millstones" of my aforementioned uncle Rabbi A[btalion]. In his youth he con-

---

[3] Numbers 22:36.
[4] Modena at first wrote sh-'-', numerically equivalent to 371, then corrected the date to sh-'-b, 372.
[5] The phrase could also mean "without sons."   [6] Psalm 19:5.

jured Elijah the prophet, who revealed himself to him. In the year [5]341 [1580/1581] he went on behalf of the Italian communities to Pope Gregory XIII[m] concerning the false accusations against Hebrew books and spoke to him several times. Once, in particular, he spoke before the pope and some cardinals for more than two hours in Latin, in defense of the Gemara. He returned thence with great honor, for he achieved all that he had sought. He died in Ferrara at the age of eighty-two, in the year [5]371 [1611], may he repose in honor. I delivered a proper eulogy for him in public here in Venice during the week in which the biblical portion Ekev is read.[7] He left a daughter, married to the sage, Rabbi Judah Fano, commonly known as Saltaro.[n] Her name is Fulvia, and she has children and grandchildren. [C 36]

My revered father of blessed memory grew up to be wise in Torah and practical matters. At the age of seventeen[o] he began to work in the pawnshop and in commerce. He emerged from guardianship[8p] and became so successful that at the age of thirty, when the brothers wanted to divide their father's estate, he showed that it had more than doubled. Despite this, the quarrel between the brothers continued[q] for more than thirty-two years, for their hearts were divided;[9] had they united,[10] together they would have had wealth in excess of one hundred thousand.[r]

Although, as I have mentioned, he no longer devoted himself to studying past the age of seventeen, he always remained learned and wise from the knowledge that he had obtained during his youth. He could answer[s] any of the questions addressed to the sages of our generation. He married Peninah, the daughter of Samuel Arzignano of Imola, and she bore him five sons and four daughters. His eldest son was named Mordecai. He grew up to be very wise and understanding and passed away at the age of twenty-four. My revered father of blessed memory always [MS 6b/ ו] recalled him with words of praise and mourned over him. The others also died: only Samuel Hezekiah[t] of blessed memory and Armonia, who was the wife of Elishama da Sforno of blessed memory, outlived my

---

[7] During the week beginning on the 20th of Av (Saturday, July 30, 1611).
[8] Cf. Tosefta Ketubbot 9:3. See historical note p.
[9] Hosea 10:2.   [10] Ezekiel 37:17; cf. Preface, p. xviii.

revered father of blessed memory. I will speak of them again in their proper place.

Because of the oppressive expulsion decreed by Pope Pius V in 532-[11u] my revered father journeyed from Bologna, leaving behind his possessions[12]—a house, a mansion, and notes of credit worth thousands of gold pieces. He took what he had in hand[13] and came to live in Ferrara.

My revered father's wife Peninah died in the year [5]329 [1568/1569], and in the same year, on the holiday of Shavuot [May 22–23, 1569], he married Rachel, the daughter of Johanan Halevi[v] of blessed memory, from Apulia,[w] but from a family of Ashkenazim. She was at that time the widow of Mordecai, known as Gumpeln Parenzo, the brother of Meir Parenzo, who is mentioned by name in several printed books.[x] She had one son by that Mordecai, [C 37] named Abraham,[y] who was nine years old at the time. Previously my father had asked the sage Rabbi Abraham Rovigo,[z] who was well versed in several kinds of wisdom, whether he would succeed if he married that woman. He replied that with her my father would not be successful in material matters, and that if he married her, he should change her name. So he changed her name to Diana.

Diana became pregnant in 5331 [late 1570], at which time a huge and severe earthquake struck Ferrara,[a] the likes of which had not been known in all the lands, all of which is related in the book *Me'or 'einayim* by the aforementioned sage de Rossi.[b] My revered father and the members of his household fled for their lives to Venice.[c]

While they were still there, on Monday the 28th day of Nisan— corresponding to the 23d day of April [5]331 [1571]—between the eighteenth and nineteenth hours [noon to 1:00 P.M.],[14] I, the bitter and impetuous,[15] was born. I would almost, like Job and Jere-

---

[11] The manuscript reads *h-sh-k* (*h* = 5[000], *sh* = 300, *k* = 20) followed by a lacuna of two dots where another letter, representing a number between one and nine, belongs. Apparently the exact year of his family's departure from Bologna had slipped Modena's mind. There is a mark in the margin at this point. It may have been put there by the author to remind himself to fill in the missing letter (year). See historical note u.

[12] Cf. Exodus 9:21.   [13] Exodus 32:14.

[14] In counting the hours of the day here and throughout the autobiography as well as in his *Riti* (e.g., 3.1.13), Modena follows the Jewish practice of starting the day at sunset, standardized at 6:00 P.M.

[15] Habbakuk 1:6.

miah,[16] curse that day. For why did I go out [of the womb] to witness toil, anger,[17] strife, and trouble—only evil[18] continually?

My mother experienced great difficulty in childbirth.[19] I was
born in the breech position,[d] my buttocks turned around facing
outward, so that calamities turned upon me[20] even at the beginning.
At the end of eight days, with great rejoicing, I was circumcised by
the gaon and noted kabbalist, Rabbi Menahem Azariah Fano,[e] may
the All-Merciful preserve him and bless him. My revered father and
Sarah, the daughter of my uncle Shemaiah, served as my godparents.[f] I was named Judah Aryeh, may God have mercy on my soul
and may the troubles of my life be expiation for my sins and trans-
gresssions. Amen.

[MS 7a/ ג] My family remained in Venice for about eight months
and then set out to return to Ferrara.[g] While they were on the way
to Francolin, near Ferrara, as they disembarked from the boat, I
was handed over to a gentile porter, [C 38] who ran off, clasping
me to his chest. When they realized that I was missing, Samson
Meshullam of blessed memory, my revered father's [pawnshop]
manager,[h] chased after him for about two miles; he caught him and
took me, giving him many fisticuffs, and brought me back to my
parents.

So we came to Ferrara and settled down there. My revered father
of blessed memory bought a nice mansion in Ferrara in the section
called La Giara.[i] He had already arranged a match for my [half-]
brother Samuel with the daughter of Corinaldo, who was known
as Panetto[j]—Little Bread—of blessed memory. But afterward, because he was going in bad ways,[k] they broke the engagement.

I began to learn the alphabet from a certain so-and-so, who was
called Hazanetto[l]—Little Cantor—and after that from Isaac Supino,
and after that from Rabbi Azriel Basola, the son of the gaon Rabbi
Moses[m] of blessed memory. And even though it is written in Scripture: "Let another man praise you rather than your own mouth,"[21]
now that this is no longer praise, for people say about me "when
you were young you were like a grown man; now that you are old

---

[16] Job 3:3; Jeremiah 20:14.   [17] Jeremiah 20:18.
[18] Genesis 6:5. The words *rak ra*ʿ, "only evil," are reversed in the manuscript.
[19] Cf. Genesis 35:16.
[20] Job 30:15.   [21] Proverbs 27:2.

you are like a very small child"[22]—I really showed promise in my studies from the very beginning. At the age of two and a half I recited the Haftarah[n] in the synagogue, and at the age of three I recognized my Creator[o] and the value of learning and wisdom and was able to translate the weekly Torah portion [from Hebrew into Italian] and understand it. Thus I progressed from stage to stage, as I will relate.

illui
———
prodigy

One day, while walking in the garden at twilight,[23] I fell from a rock and pierced the palm of my hand, and was sick for some days. I was also troubled by worms, and a certain woman gave me mineral oil to drink, from which I passed out and almost remained permanently unconscious. Soon after that I contracted smallpox.[24] All these things that happened to me before the age of four I remember as if they happened only yesterday.[25] And the thoughts I had then are still with me today.

[C 39] In the year 5335 [1574/1575] we left Ferrara and moved to Cologna,[p] a small village belonging to Venice, to engage in money-lending in a pawnshop. My revered father took great pains to construct a ritual bath inside his house for the women to make their ritual ablutions, by drawing the proper kind of water into the house; and at the end of 5336 [summer 1576] he pronounced it ritually fit for use.[q] On that day I had been learning the chapter of the Mishnah beginning "One whose dead [is laid out]"[r] with Rabbi Gershon Cohen,[r] who is now the head of a yeshiva in Poland but who at the time was a boy [MS 7b/ ח] like me. When our teacher left, the two of us went to the ritual bath to play,[2] as young boys do.[3] I fell into the bath, which was full to the brim.[4] The other boy fled screaming, and when the members of the household heard him they ran with my revered father and my mother searching here and

[22] Cf. B.T. Baba Kamma 92b.

[23] Genesis 3:8. Commentary in Bereshit Rabbah gives "evening" as one possible meanings of *le-ruah ha-yom* in that verse. Possibly the accident happened as it was turning dark.

[24] Italian word *varole*, written in Hebrew letters and reflecting a Venetian dialectical form of the modern Italian word, *vaiòlo*.

[25] See 2 Samuel 15:20.

[1] Berakhot 3:1. Modena took the title of this chapter as an omen of what was to happen to him next.

[2] The Hebrew here, *lishok*, can be taken to mean "to play games of chance." The first explicit reference to gambling in the autobiography occurs later, fol. 9a.

[3] Cf. 2 Samuel 2:14.   [4] Joshua 3:15.

there for me, for they did not know where I had fallen. Meanwhile an hour passed, with me holding on with my hands to one side of the rim of the bath, until the people in the house arrived. Then a servant girlˢ threw herself into the water and pulled me out, and they carried me to a room laid out on a bed like one deadˢ from fright.

There in Cologna took place the wedding of my [half-]brother Samuel to Giuditta, the daughter of Angelo da Lipiani of Pesaro, with a banquet and celebration.⁶ At the table I recited words of Torah that my teacher had taught me, and those who heard it marveled. My teacher then was Rabbi Malachi Gallicoᵗ of blessed memory, a rabbi, physician, and kabbalist.

Around that time a certain Christian named Priamo was severely beaten and injured. A discussion about whether he would die took place in the presence of my revered father and my teacher and some people and guests in our house, and I jumped up and said, "He will surely die, for there is an explicit scriptual reference to this—'Their fruit (*piryamo*) shalt thou destroy from the earth.' "⁷ At that, they all had a good laugh and said of me, "The young pumpkin is known by its young shoot."⁸ᵘ

In the month of Elul, at the end of the year [5]338 [August–September 1578], we left Cologna and moved to Montagnana,ᵛ a village five miles away. My revered father set up a synagogue there in his house in order to pray to God, and it exists to this day, in the house of Zerah Halevi,ʷ may God his Rock protect him and grant him long life. [He did so] because for many years [C 40] the local men had not prayed in a prayer quorum (*minyan*) on account of quarrels among them. But we put everything back in order.

In the year 5339 [1578/1579] the constellations began to war against us with a strong hand and an outstretched arm.⁹ In the month of Nisan [March–April 1579], at the request of Cardinal Alvise d'Este, my revered father of blessed memory was thrown into prisonˣ because of a debt of fifteen hundred scudiʸ that had already been repaid. He sat there for about six months, and even after his

---

⁵ The omen fulfilled! See above.   ⁶ Esther 9:19.

⁷ Hebrew: "piryamo me-eretz te'abbed" (Psalm 21:11). The word for "their fruit" (*piryamo*) can also be vocalized *priamo*. Hence the clever wordplay.

⁸ B.T. Berakhot 48a.   ⁹ Deuteronomy 4:34.

release they distrained all our money for three years at the request of Alvise Mocenigo,[z] who was supposed to have collected it from the aforementioned cardinal. The expenditure for claims and counterclaims was great, and no one gained, but rather everyone lost and squandered money. My mother of blessed memory girded her loins like a man and rode to Ferrara and to Venice in order to speak with noblemen and judges of the land. From that time on we became impoverished, for in three years that false accusation caused us damage amounting to more than eight thousand ducats, as well as much anxiety.

[MS 8a/ ט] At that time Rabbi Malachi left us, and my teacher for one year was Rabbi Eliakim Macerata[a] of blessed memory, a kabbalist and a godly man. A short time later Rabbi Malachi was killed on the road to Piedmont by an attendant in charge of the horses who wanted to steal his money. But because the attendant stole and put on Rabbi Malachi's red cloak,[10] the Jew from whose home the latter had departed sensed what had happened. They put the attendant in prison and executed him; may God avenge his [Rabbi Malachi's] blood.

In the month of Nisan 5340 [March–April 1580] my revered father sent me to Ferrara, to the home of his nephew[b] Mordecai Modena,[c] so that I could be taught books and wisdom, and I was there for one year. For four months I studied with Rabbi Jehiel Tardiolo,[d] may God his Rock protect him and grant him long life, and for eight months with Rabbi Hezekiah Finzi,[e] may God his Rock protect him and grant him long life.

[C 41] It was Rabbi Hezekiah's custom that every Sabbath,[11] all of the students studying Alfasi[f] would prepare a discourse of their own on the weekly Torah portion. On the Sabbath day he would gather a prayer quorum (minyan) in the house of study, and one of the boys would preach before them. When my turn came it was the weekly portion Terumah.[12] I chose as the topic the verse "gold and silver and copper"[13] and the rabbinic saying, "Rabbi Simon the son of Gamaliel says 'On three things the world stands: on Torah, on

---

[10] Italian word *camisola*, written in Hebrew letters and reflecting a Venetian dialectical form of the modern Italian word *camiciòla*.

[11] Isaiah 66:23.   [12] Exodus 25–27; 8th of Adar (Saturday, February 11, 1581).

[13] Exodus 25:3.

worship, and on kind deeds.' "[14] I made the three things, "gold, [silver, and copper]" allude to "Torah, [worship, and kind deeds]," saying that these are what God desires from man, and that through them he causes his Divine Presence to dwell among the Jews. When I had finished, Rabbi Hezekiah remarked to two old men who were present, "I am certain that this boy will become a preacher to the Jews, for from his manner it is clear that he will be fruitful in preaching."[g] Years later, in 5365, 5366, and 5367 [1604–1607], when I was preaching in the Great Synagogue every Sabbath at the bidding of the holy congregation, he always came to my sermons. And when people praised my words, he would say, "Twenty-five years ago I prophesied that he would become a good preacher to his people."

I also had a little instruction in playing an instrument, in singing, in dancing, in writing, and in Latin.[h] But on account of two of Mordecai's maidservants who hated me and embittered my life[15] by their wickedness—may their Master forgive them—I returned home at the end of a year.

In Iyyar 5341 [April–May 1581] my revered father of blessed memory sent me to Padua, to the home of Rabbi Samuel Archivolti[i] of blessed memory, to board at his table and study Torah under him. From him I learned the art of poetry and the language of letter writing. He loved me dearly from then until the day of his death, for he used to say that I was one of the students to whom he had given birth in his own image and likeness[16] in wisdom. I lived there an entire year, and then my revered father of blessed memory summoned me home.

[MS 8b/ ' , C 42] Because my parents wanted to keep me with them at home, God provided us, in Nisan 5342 [March–April 1582], with a young Italian who had just come back from Safed. His name was Moses, the son of Benjamin della Rocca,[j] the son of the daughter of the gaon Rabbi Moses Basola, a man of knowledge and understanding. Moses was content to dwell with the man,[17] and I acquired a useful teacher from whom I learned much.

About this time,[k] in order to quiet my [half-]brother Samuel of blessed memory, who all his life had been treading an evil path of

[14] Mishnah Avot 1:2. [15] Cf. Exodus 1:14.
[16] Cf. Genesis 5:3. [17] Cf. Exodus 2:21.

wastefulness and loss,[1] my revered father agreed to divide [his es-
tate] with him as if with a brother; and he gave him half of all he
possessed in goods, riches, notes of credit, and money, which
amounted to about four thousand ducats,[m] as his share. And Samuel went off and established for himself a home.

At the end of two years, in Iyyar 5344 [April–May 1584], the
aforementioned Rabbi Moses della Rocca left us and went to Cyprus, where he married. And while he was still in his youthful
prime, he was called to the heavenly academy. When the bad news
reached me[18] I wrote elegies for him, in particular one octet [which
makes sense in both] Hebrew and Italian. It is entitled "Kinah Shemor,"[n] and it is printed in my book *Midbar yehudah*.[o] I was then
thirteen years of age. All the poets saw it and praised it;[19] to this
day it is a marvel to both Christian and Jewish sages.

From then on I ceased studying with a regular teacher, but rather
studied on my own. I was not even in a large city where friends
could have helped me support my studies. Alas, I lived through[20]
my best learning years without a teacher or master.[p]

My revered father began sending me from time to time to Ferrara
in order to oversee matters regarding notes remaining to be collected there, which were managed by Samson Meshullam of
blessed memory. But I would just go in and out, walking around
doing nothing.

In the month of Tishre 5347 [September–October 1586] it came
to pass that Isaac was old, and his eyes were dim, so that he could
not see,[21] that is to say, the eyes of my revered father of blessed
memory grew dim, and for about six months he was blind, grop-
ing in darkness.[22] After many medicines, everyone said that there
was no more hope. Nevertheless, he did not cease praying to God
day and night, until eventually God heard his voice and inspired a
certain physician to give him plain water [C 43] to put in his eyes,
whereupon he regained his strength and his sight. This latter miracle was even greater because before it he had had to read with eye-
glasses,[23] while afterward he read and saw everything without them
for the five additional years that he lived.

---

[18] 1 Samuel 2:24.   [19] Cf. Song of Songs 6:9.   [20] Adaptation of Psalm 120:5.
[21] Cf. Genesis 27:1.   [22] Deuteronomy 28:29.
[23] Hebrew *battei ʿeinayim*, literally, "eyeholders."

During this time, we were becoming poorer and poorer. We were eating but not earning because my revered father was terrified on account of the constellations that fought against him. His heart would not stir him up[24] to make a decision to journey from a place where he fared badly and go to another,[25] or to do anything similar.

[MS 9a/ אי] My [half-]brother, my mother's son Abraham Parenzo, mentioned previously, who had grown up in the house of my revered father, had in his youth been enticed by bad company to play games of chance[q] and had lost much of his own and of my revered father's money. Yet, my father had always treated him only with kindness and goodness, as a father shows compassion for a son.[1] When, therefore, about this time, my [half-]brother realized that he had been doing evil, he moved to Ancona, where many families of my mother's kinsmen lived, may her memory be a blessing. They liked him, for he was handsome, good-looking, and bright. So they gave him a wife and guided him on the proper path.[2] He, too, repented and turned to the straight path; he ceased to be destructive and evil, and was loved and esteemed by all the Christian merchants of the city and by the entire Jewish community. He became successful and earned a great deal of money, and his losses were offset by his gains.[3]

Several times he wrote to my revered father that the time had come for him to repay the latter for all the good he had done him. He entreated my father to move there near him, saying that it would be good for him and that he would show me the ways of commerce, for he loved me greatly and would have been our savior.[4] He pleaded with my revered father very much, but the latter did not wish to hear of it, for he saw nothing but evil continually[5] and had lost all hope. Then he sent there goods and linen and silk articles, as well as some synagogue appurtenances, and agreed to send Judah on before him.[6]

That year, a severe plague struck the holy community of Ancona, and many householders perished. Two of my [half-]brother's sons died, as well as two of his wife's brothers, both of whom were

---

[24] Exodus 36:2.   [25] Cf. B.T. Baba Metzia 75b.   [1] Psalm 103:13.   [2] Psalm 27:11.
[3] Mishnah Avot 5:11.   [4] Adaptation of Psalm 80:3.   [5] Genesis 6:5.
[6] Cf. Genesis 46:28. Modena made a mark above the word "Judah" to indicate the play on his name.

married and had children. In the month of Iyyar 5378 [read: 5348, April–May 1588] I set out on the road from Montagnana to Ancona. When I reached Venice[r] I heard that my [half-]brother's mother-in-law had also died, and that his wife was very ill. I made a stormy passage by water[7] and reached Ancona at the beginning of the month of Sivan 5348 [began May 27, 1588], where I discovered that God had relented and had cured my [half-]brother's wife. He was very bitter on account of all the hardships that had befallen him. [C 44] But when he saw me he was very happy and was a bit comforted. He respected me very much, and I was also esteemed in the eyes of the people of the city.

On the day after the holiday of Shavuot [June 3, 1588], he felt sick in his head and took to his bed, as if it were nothing serious. But from day to day his illness became graver, and nobody knew what it could be. From the time he took to his bed he said that he would surely die, and he related dreams that he saw. Flies would come to his bed [MS 9b/ בי] and he would say, "These are the flies of death."[8] Finally he went mad, and after fifteen days, on the night of the Holy Sabbath, the 23d of Sivan, corresponding to June 18, 5348 [1588],[9] at dawn, he expired and was gathered to his ancestors at the age of twenty-eight. The entire Jewish community honored him in his death with sermons and elegies, and all wept for him, for he had been popular with all his kinsmen[10] and acquaintances. I composed elegies for him,[s] in rhyme with an echo, and they are included among my poems and letters.

Afterward I was left dumbfounded and forlorn, for the heavens were battling against us. Alone and without any Jewish companions, I boarded a boat and went to Venice, and from there home to Montagnana. The mouth cannot describe the pain and sadness that enveloped my mother with trembling,[11] for she had loved him [Abraham] deeply and never forgot him until the day she died. My revered father of blessed memory also wept over him like a son. Truly, from then on all glory was gone from our house, and our

---

[7] Cf. Isaiah 43:16. [8] Ecclesiastes 10:1.

[9] The date in the manuscript, 5378 (h-sh-ʿ-h) is an error that conceivably could have resulted from a slip of the pen. In the margin someone wrote the correction, 5348 (h-sh-m-h).

[10] Adaptation of Esther 10:3. [11] Cf. Ezekiel 26:16.

hope and support were lost.[12] I foresaw from that day on that it had been determined by the constellations that I would not see any good.

At the beginning of the month of Tammuz 5349 [began June 15, 1589], in order not to remain idle, I began to give lessons in Torah to the son of Manasseh Levi of blessed memory and to Joseph the son of Zerah Halevi, may God his Rock protect him and grant him long life. I continued in this profession until 5372 [1611/1612]ᵗ in spite of myself,[13] because it did not seem fitting to me.ᵘ

After thisᵛ my mother spoke to me each day, saying, "If you would heed my command and comfort me in my troubles you would take as your wife my niece, namely, Esther—the daughter of my mother's sister Gioja,[14] the wife of Isaac Simhah, may God his Rock protect him and grant him long life—for she seems fitting to me. I will thereby create a marital tie within my family[15] and peace will reign in our house." And so she requested of my revered father of blessed memory in every conversation. She wrote to her sister about it, and she gave her answer.[16] And so the matter stood.

Anyhow, I had engaged in dream divination,ʷ using prayer without conjuration, in order to see the woman intended as my mate. In my dream, an old man [C 45] held my hand and led me to a certain wall upon which was drawn a portrait covered with a curtain. When he drew aside the veil[17] I saw a portrait of my cousin, Esther, as well as the color of her garment. While I was still gazing at the image, it changed, and another one, which I could not clearly make out, replaced it. In the morning I reported the dream to my revered father of blessed memory and to my mother, but they did not believe it.

Then, in the month of Elul 5349 [August–September, 1589] my mother of blessed memory and I arrived in [MS 10a/ גֹ] Venice on our way to Ancona to retrieve property and goods that had been in the hands of my [half-]brother of blessed memory, because his wife had seized them and we had not seen even a shoelace of it. Afterward we changed our mind about going on and lingered in Venice;ˣ and while there, my mother and her sister and the relatives again

---

¹² Cf. Ezekiel 19:5.   ¹³ Adaptation of Jeremiah 32:31.
¹⁴ Someone wrote the name "Gioja" in Roman letters in the margin of the text.
¹⁵ Adaptation of Leviticus 10:3.   ¹⁶ Cf. Judges 5:29.   ¹⁷ Exodus 34:34.

discussed the match. We completed the marriage agreement, shook hands, and made the symbolic acquisition[y] with great rejoicing. I pointed out to my mother that she [Esther] was wearing clothes of the same color and ornamentation that I had described more than a year previously[z] when I had seen her in my dream. She was truly a beautiful woman,[18] and wise, too. I said that "finds" and not "found" applied to me.[19]

When the wedding date, which was the 13th of Sivan 5350 [June 15, 1590], approached, I wrote to my revered father, who was then in Bologna,[a] so that he would come. I also invited my friends and relatives,[b] and we all traveled to Venice immediately after Shavuot, rejoicing and lighthearted. When we arrived there, we found the bride confined to her bed, and everyone said that nothing was wrong except for a little diarrhea and that she would soon recover. Her illness grew worse from day to day, however, until she lay near death. Yet her heart was like that of a lion,[20] and she was not afraid.

On the day she died, she summoned me and embraced and kissed me. She said, "I know that this is bold behavior, but God knows that during the one year of our engagement we did not touch each other even with our little fingers.[c] Now, at the time of death, the rights of the dying are mine. I was not allowed to become your wife, but what can I do, for thus it is decreed in heaven. May God's will be done."

Then she requested that a sage be summoned so that she could make confession. When he arrived she recited the confessional prayer and asked for the blessing of her parents and my mother. On the night of the Holy Sabbath, the 21st of Sivan 5350 [June 22, 1590]—almost on the night that my [half-]brother of blessed memory had died—at the hour of the entry of the Sabbath bride, my own bride departed from this life of vanity for eternal life and passed away. The weeping on the part of all who knew her, both within and outside her family,[21] was great. May she rest in peace.

[18] Song of Songs 1:8.

[19] That is to say, the biblical verse "He who finds a wife finds goodness" (Proverbs 18:22) and not the verse "A woman more bitter than death I have found" (Ecclesiastes 7:25). The allusion is based on B.T. Berakhot 8a.

[20] 2 Samuel 17:10, apparently with the double meaning that she was of one heart with her intended groom, Judah Aryeh ("the lion").

[21] Adaptation of Genesis 6:14.

Immediately after her burial, all the relatives set upon me and my mother, saying, "Behold, her younger sister is as good as she. Why forfeit the opportunity to perpetuate the kinship and to give comfort to the mother and father of the young woman?" They entreated me to the point of embarrassment[22] to take her sister [MS 10b/ ר׳] Rachel to wife. [C 46] I wrote to my revered father,[d] who answered me as he had always done in this matter, and these were his words: "Do as you like, for the choice is yours. Today or tomorrow I will be taken from you, and you and your children will be left with her.[23] For this reason, understand well what lies before you, and act to the best of the ability granted you by God."[24]

In order to please my mother, as well as the dead girl, who had hinted at it in her words, I agreed to marry the aforementioned Rachel. Immediately we wrote up the agreement and were married on Friday the 5th of Tammuz 5350 [July 6, 1590],[25c] under a favorable star. On that Sabbath, Rabbi Solomon Sforno[f] gave a beautiful sermon on the Torah portion Korah[1] in the Italian synagogue.[g] By the authority of the three gaons,[h] Rabbi J[udah] Katzenellenbogen[i] of blessed memory, Rabbi Jacob Cohen,[j] and Rabbi Avigdor Cividal[k] of blessed memory, who were present there along with all the gaons of the city, including Levantine Jews, who at that time abounded in important persons,[l] he [Rabbi Sforno] decreed that I should be granted the title of *haver*.[m] I responded with "ten [C 47] words"[2] of explanation of the mishnaic dictum, "Find yourself a teacher (*rav*) (and acquire for yourself an associate [*haver*]),"[3] which pleased the hearers very much. Then we returned home to Montagnana.

That summer and the following year there was severe drought and great famine, and we earned nothing, while spending and losing much. From Sivan 5351 [May–June 1591] through the summer we were oppressed on account of the reopening of the false accusations of Cardinal d'Este.[n] My revered father became very frightened, could not calm down,[4] and became very ill. My mother and

---

[22] 2 Kings 2:17.   [23] Adaptation of 2 Kings 2:10 and 1 Samuel 28:19.
[24] Adaptation of Ezra 7:9.   [25] See historical note.   [1] Numbers 16–18.
[2] This expression, taken from Mishnah Avot 5:1, means "briefly."
[3] Mishnah Avot 1:6. In accordance with standard practice in citing familiar texts (see above, fol. 4a, note 4), Modena wrote only the first half of this rabbinic saying.
[4] Cf. Job 3:26.

my wife and I also took sick, and we remained so all summer long. Disease did not leave our house until the month of Tevet [December 1591–January 1592].

My wife became pregnant, and on Monday, the 20th of Elul, corresponding to September 9, at the end of the year [5]351 [1591], in the twenty-first hour [3:00 P.M.], she gave birth to a son. We were all sick in our beds,[5] my wife most of all. But eight days later we had become a little stronger, and Benjamin Katz[o] of Este of blessed memory, an excellent circumciser, circumcised the boy. My revered father of blessed memory and my mother of blessed memory served as his godparents.

My revered father of blessed memory did not want me to name him Mordecai, saying that he had had a wise and pleasant son by that name who had died at the age of twenty-four. But out of love for the name of my grandfather, the gaon of blessed memory, who as mentioned had been a great man, I said, "I will not fear," [MS 11a/וט] and named him Mordecai. Alas, woe is me on account of my misfortune,[6] for at the age of twenty-six he was snatched away.[7] And Mordecai went out,[8] taking my heart with him and abandoning me in the valley of agony and the depths of despair.

Shortly thereafter, a righteous man was no more,[9] for my revered father of blessed memory had just regained his strength and was healthy and robust when, in the month of Kislev 5352 [November–December 1591], he again took to his bed, sick and in a crazed state. He lasted only five days, with a persistent burning fever. After confessing before God in the presence of ten men, he blessed me with his hands and said to me, "I have nothing to bequeath to you[p] of worldly possessions except that you always remember to fear the Lord thy God and to honor his creatures. May God bless you and keep you." Then, during the night of the arrival of Friday, at the tenth hour [4:00 A.M.], on the 20th day of Kislev, corresponding to December 6, 5352 [1591], he passed away, departing from the tribulations of this angry world that he had borne all the seventy-two years of his life, especially fifteen of them,[q] [C 48] during which he accepted his tribulations in humility and in

---

[5] Psalm 41:4. [6] Cf. Jeremiah 10:19. [7] Adaptation of Genesis 37:33.
[8] Esther 8:15. [9] Adaptation of Psalm 37:10.

good spirit, out of love and with patience, like every righteous man who fears God and turns away from evil.

Father

This is how he looked: he was of average height, with a strong, slender body, and for the most part healthy. He had a dark complexion and a short beard. He was wise in practical matters and in Torah, which he had learned in his childhood, and careful about observing the details of commandments and customs of administering his household. He loved his neighbors, was close to his relatives, and loved his wife, whom he honored more than himself. He was neither wasteful nor stingy, but was watchful concerning his money. Yet he did not shut his hand in time of need. He was generous in giving charity, did not like playing games of chance, and was trustworthy in his business dealings.

Because the day of his death was short[r] and it was raining heavily and the roads were in disrepair, I was unable to bring him to be buried in Padua, as had been his wish. I chose rather to lay his body and soul to rest immediately and spare him the beating of the dead by demons (if it really exists).[10] So, on that Friday I buried him there in Montagnana,[t] and a year later I placed a tombstone[u] on his grave with the following epitaph: "Leader and noble, honest, righteous man, known to all, full of understanding. The sun of his generation, his light has gone out, the venerable Isaac, a man of Modena."

About a month after his death he appeared to me in a dream, or so it seemed to me, for I knew that he was dead. Several times during his life he had spoken to me about the reward and punishment of the soul after death, the gist of his words having been that a certain Sephardi had said at the time of the latter's death: "Now I will know what a soul is"—meaning that it is impossible to know this until after death. So I asked him [in my dream], "Tell me, please, honored scholar, what is the state of your soul, and what is it like for you in that other world?" He answered me, "I[11] [MS 11b/ יי] eat well and drink well there." I then said, "But how can this be? Did not the sages of blessed memory say that 'in the world to

---

[10] The parentheses are in the manuscript.

[11] The word _ani_, "I," the last word on page 15 (Hebrew pagination; fol. 11a) of Modena's autograph manuscript, is repeated at the top of page 16 (Hebrew pagination; fol. 11b). This is evidently a case of dittography.

come there is no eating and no drinking, etc.?' "[12] He replied, "If you want this fool to seem wise in your eyes, look at the end of the saying—'instead, the righteous sit . . . and enjoy . . . as it is written in Scripture:[13] And they beheld God and ate and drank.' "

After this, I spent about a year wavering between a decision to stay [C 49] in Montagnana or to move away. Finally, I decided to move, but the diabolical Solomon Navarro, a Sephardi from Ferrara, deceived me by saying that he would come to live there [in Montagnana] and go into partnership with me in commerce. So I rented a dwelling for him, but he kept me dangling for more than four months laying out money,[v] and in the end changed his mind. At that point I made up my mind and left Montagnana with all the members of my household and came to Venice.[w] I arrived there on Friday, the 15th of Kislev[x] 5353 [November 20, 1592], and took an apartment directly underneath that of my father-in-law[y] of blessed memory. My first employment, which commenced at the beginning of the month of Tevet 5353 [began December 6, 1592], was giving lessons to young boys. My first pupil was Abraham the son of Meir Luzzatto,[z] may they both rest in peace.

The Sabbath of Consolation 5353 [Saturday, August 14, 1593] was the first time that I preached a sermon in the Great Synagogue before a large audience,[a] to the glory of the King of the king of kings,[14] the Holy One, blessed be he. Many great and venerable sages were present, and the crowd was so large that the synagogue could not hold them. The sermon is printed in my collection of sermons, *Midbar yehudah*.[b] God granted that I so pleased all my hearers that in Iyyar 5354 [April–May 1594], when the wealthy Kalonymos Belgrado[c] of blessed memory established an academy in the "garden,"[d] I was the first preacher there.[e]

For the past twenty-five years,[f] praised be God, I have, as is known, consistently maintained a good reputation throughout the land because of my sermons. And even though for more [C 50] than twenty years I have continuously taught Bible and rabbinic texts each weekday evening and morning and have preached in three or four places each Sabbath, this holy community has not grown tired of me, nor has it had its fill[15] of my sermons. Rather,

---

[12] B.T. Berakhot 17a.   [13] Exodus 24:11.
[14] Adaptation of and play on Proverbs 14:28.   [15] Ecclesiastes 1:8.

every day they seem new in people's eyes. Even many esteemed friars, priests, and noblemen come to listen.[g] And through God's mercy (may it be to God's honor and that of Judaism and not mine)[16] they praise, glorify, and laud. If only[17] my revered father of blessed memory had been allowed to hear me, his pain would have been turned into pleasure,[18] for above all he had longed for me to be fruitful in the art of preaching. But I did not succeed in winning recognition in it during his lifetime. My mother, however, heard and was happy;[19] thanks be to God, for both man's thoughts and the ability to express them well come from him.[20] He gave me this gift for the good of the many (rather than for my personal glorification), may his name be praised forever.

[MS 12a/ רי] My wife became pregnant again and gave birth on the night of the arrival of Thursday, the 2d of Heshvan, which fell on October 28, 5354 [1593]. At approximately the sixth hour of the night [midnight] her labor pains began, and she gave birth to a boy.[21] Jacob, the son of Meir[h] of blessed memory, circumcised him, and my father-in-law and mother-in-law of blessed memory served as his godparents with much gladness and rejoicing. I named him Isaac, may God his Rock protect him and grant him long life, after my righteous, revered father of blessed memory, may God favor him and bless him. Amen.

About fifteen days after giving birth, my wife took sick with a persistent fever that lasted approximately twenty days. Afterward, on the 25th of Adar [March 17, 1594], she fell into bed, and it was discovered that she had petechiae.[i] Her illness worsened, and she lost consciousness, reaching the gates of death. The doctors said there was no longer any hope. On Wednesday, the 6th of Nisan 5354,[22] she came so close to expiring that preparations were already

---

[16] The parentheses are in the manuscript.

[17] Modena first wrote *ve-lule'*, "had not," then corrected the word to *ve-lu*, "if only," by crossing out the final two letters. Notwithstanding Carpi's observation (p. 50 n. 23) that these two words were used interchangeably in Modena's time, actually in the autobiography the form *lule'/lulei* is reserved for the negative (see examples in Carpi edition, pp. 59 line 2; 62 line 19; 87 line 9; 110 line 2). Hence the correction is very probably that of the author, not of someone else.

[18] Adaptation of and play on Psalm 41:3 and Job 18:10.   [19] Adaptation of Job 29:11.

[20] Adaptation of Proverbs 16:1.   [21] Adaptation of Isaiah 66:7.

[22] The 6th of Nisan 5354 fell on Sunday, March 27. Probably Modena meant to write "Friday the 4th of Nisan" but slipped and reversed the Hebrew letters *v* (= 6 for the

being made for her burial, and I wept copiously for her. Then I asked a certain boy, "Recite your verse from Scripture for me." He answered with the verse: "In order that your days may be long . . . ,"[23] whereupon I offered many prayers. God granted my plea; her sickness began to abate, and she was healed.[24] But, because the milk had left [C 51] her breasts, I gave the boy Isaac to a Jewish wet nurse,[25] the wife of Ephraim, an expert in the preparation of herbs, for about eight months and at considerable expense.

At the beginning of the year [5]355 [began September 15, 1594], I went to Montagnana with my mother and teacher, and with my son Mordecai to travel around.[j] After my safe return I began to teach in the house of Eliakim Cohen Panarotti,[k] may God his Rock protect him and grant him long life; that is to say, I boarded at my own table and gave lessons in his house; I had about twenty-three pupils.

During Hanukkah of the year 5355 [December 7–14, 1594], Satan fooled me into playing games of chance,[ll] causing me no small amount of damage, for I lost about one hundred ducats.

On Thursday, the 6th of Nisan, which fell on March 16, 5355 [1595], between the fourteenth and fifteenth hour of the day [8:00–9:00 A.M.], my wife bore a son, our third conceived child. The aforementioned Jacob son of Meir circumcised him, and his godparents were my wife's uncle and aunt, Samuel Simhah and his wife Stamma. In deference to my mother, I named him Abraham after her son Abraham Parenzo of blessed memory.

A year later, on the 7th of Second Adar 5356 [March 7, 1596], the boy became ill with smallpox[z] during an outbreak in which more than seventy boys and girls in our holy community died within six months, and he returned to the Lord who had given him [to us]. My other two sons were also ill with that disease and were in great danger, but God graciously spared them for me, may he be blessed forever.

---

sixth day of the week, namely, Friday) and *d* (= 4 for the fourth day of the month), as suggested already in note 59 on page 26 of the Kahana edition. The 4th of Nisan fell on Friday, March 25.

[23] Deuteronomy 11:21.

[24] The word is written with metathesis of two letters, *p* and *alef*. There are two dots above the *alef* and one dot above the *p*, doubtless indicating the required correction.

[25] Exodus 2:7.   [1] Adaptation of Genesis 21:6.   [z] See fol. 7a, n. 24.

[MS 12b/ **נ׳**] After that, my wife, may she be blessed above all women of the house, gave birth to a daughter in the Cividale house in the Ghetto Nuovo,ᵐ where I had moved in Tammuz [5]356 [June 1596]. It was twilight on the Sunday of Hanukkah, which fell on the New Moon of Tevet [C 52] 5357 [December 22, 1596], but I did not have a chance to name her, because after seventeen days she returned to her Father's house in her newborn state,[3] expired, and died.ⁿ

On the 10th of Shevat [January 30, 1597], I heard behind me a loud voice[4] announcing the news that my [half-]sister Armonia had died in Modena. I had never seen her face or known her.

To add to my sorrow and pain, my mother, who was so happy when my deeds and especially my sermons were publicly acclaimed,[5] and especially the day of Shavuot [May 23, 1597] when I preached and she heard me and was happy,[6] became sick with an intestinal disease on the next day, which was the same day on which my [half-]brother, her son Abraham Parenzo of blessed memory, had become sick. Her illness lasted twenty-nine days, with diarrhea and a mild fever. But because of my sins her time was up and her end was near, at the age of almost sixty-one. On Friday the 4th of Tammuz 5357 [June 20, 1597], the illness became more severe, and signs of death appeared. At about the nineteenth hour [1:00 P.M.], after several confessions and prayers, and while she was in full possession of her faculties, I lost Rachel,[7] who was called Diana, may she rest in peace. She was buried here in Veniceᵒ as the Sabbath bride approached, near the graves of her father, her mother, and her brothers, may she rest in honor. I placed a gravestone at the head of her grave, with the following epitaph:ᵖ "On the fourth of Tammuz [in the year] hinted at by the word *hater*,[8] Rachel, who is Diana, died. The gracious wife of Isaac of Modena, she attained honor.[9] Blessed is he who causes death and resurrection."

---

[3] Adaptation of Leviticus 22:13 and Numbers 30:4. Here, of course, "Father" refers to God.

[4] Cf. Ezekiel 3:12.   [5] Adaptation of Proverbs 31:31.   [6] Job 29:11.

[7] Cf. Genesis 35:19.

[8] Hebrew: *s-v-n-'* (*sone'*), with an abbreviation mark before the final letter, signifying that the letters are also to be read as the date 357 (*s* = 300, *v* = 6, *n* = 50, ' = 1). The normal way of writing this date is *s-n-z* (*z* = 7).

[9] Adaptation of Proverbs 11:16.

During the intermediate days of the holiday of Sukkot [September 28–October 1, 1597] I traveled to Cento^q because I was considering moving there to live with Paciotto Revere.^r I stayed there and in Ferrara and Mantua for about twenty days. When I returned here to Venice on the 6th of Heshvan [5]358 [October 18, 1597], I changed my mind about the move,^s for at that time the duke of [C 53] Ferrara^t died, and those districts were in danger of war.^u I congratulated myself on not going, for, shortly thereafter, the aforementioned Paciotto was murdered, may God avenge his blood.

Nevertheless, while I was away [from Venice], several of my pupils left me, and for that whole year my income was limited. But he who feeds all creatures did not desert me or abandon me. With God's help, I supported the members of my household with honor through my writings and compositions.^v

[MS 13a/ יט] It's a girl! May she live[10] a long life under a favorable constellation. Amen. On Friday the 4th of Nisan 5358 [April 10, 1598], at about the eighteenth hour of the day [noon], in the week of the Torah portion that contains the verse "And when a woman gives birth . . . ,"[11] my wife bore me a daughter. Before that, on the night of the 13th of Second Adar^w [Friday night, March 20, 1598], which was the night of the Holy Sabbath, as I slumbered in bed,[12] I had dreamed that my mother, may she rest in peace, came to me, saying, "Very soon, you will be with me." Patiently I responded and asked her when this would happen. She answered, "During the final days of the upcoming Passover holiday." Then I awoke, stricken with anxiety.[13] I related my dream to Rabbi Solomon Sforno of blessed memory, who interpreted it to me as meaning that my wife would give birth to a daughter and that I would name her after my mother, may she rest in peace. And it came to pass that, as he had interpreted it to me, so it happened,[14] as mentioned

---

[10] The exclamation is conveyed in the manuscript by an enlarged letter *b* in the word *bat*, "girl," identical with the enlarged *b* that opens the autobiography itself. The expression "It's a girl! May she live," paraphrasing Exodus 1:16, where Pharaoh orders the Hebrew midwives to kill all Hebrew male children but to allow newborn daughters to live ("if it is a girl, let her live"), is given a different twist here. Sixteen months earlier Modena and his wife had lost a newborn daughter after seventeen days, as mentioned earlier. Here he expresses hope that this one will survive. She did!

[11] Leviticus 12:5, in the Torah portion Tazria, which was read that year during the week ending on Saturday the 5th of Nisan (April 11, 1598).

[12] Adaptation of Job 33:15.   [13] Adaptation of Genesis 41:7–8.   [14] Genesis 41:13.

above. To make the dream come completely true, on the last day of Passover I summoned ten men and the cantor, and the latter blessed her as I gave her the name Diana, which my mother of blessed memory had received when hers was changed. I could not call her Rachel, because that was the name of my wife, may she be blessed above all women of the house.

At the beginning of the month of Elul [began September 2, 1598], at the end of [5]358, I moved back into the home of Gutzeln[x] Panarotti my kinsman, may God his Rock protect him and grant him long life, to teach his children and board at his table.[y] And I moved into the [C 54] Spagnoletto[z] home.

During Hanukkah [December 23–30, 1598], "Satan"[15] duped me into playing games of chance, and by the following Shavuot [May 30–31, 1599] I lost more than three hundred ducats.[a] But from then until the eve of Hanukkah [5]361 [evening of November 30, 1600], I watched myself carefully, devoting myself to my teaching for eighteen months, and paid all my debts.[b] Then that same friar misled me into the secret company[16] [of players of games of chance] and caused me to lose much money.

At the beginning of the month of Iyyar [5]361 [Thursday, May 3, 1601] I began to preach in the house of study of the Ashkenazic Torah Study Society,[c] may God their Rock protect them and grant them long life. That week I began to explain the Proverbs of Solomon[d] and succeeded in giving a perfect interpretation of it,[17] with God's help.

My wife became pregnant and gave birth to a son on Tuesday the 29th of Nisan, which was Calends[18] of May [5]361 [1601], at approximately nineteen and a half hours [1:30 P.M.]. With rejoicing and a merry heart I brought him into the covenant of the holy sign.[e] Meshullam Halevi, the son of Asher of the Meshullam family— distant relatives of my mother's family—circumcised him. His

---

[15] The manuscript has *h-s-t-n (ha-satan)* with an abbreviation mark before the final letter signifying that the letters are also to be read as the date 5359 (*h* = 5[000], *s* = 300, *n* = 50, *t* = 9), which corresponds to 1598/1599. Hanukkah falls in December. The normal order of the letters for this date is *h-s-n-t*.

[16] Allusion to Jeremiah 15:17.

[17] Modena plays here on the assonance of the words *Mishlei shelomo* (Proverbs of Solomon) and *m-sh-l-m*, which is probably to be vocalized *mushlam*, "perfect."

[18] The Hebrew letter *k* in the manuscript is the abbreviation of *kalini* (Calends, the first day of the Roman month). Tuesday the 29th of Nisan fell, indeed, on May 1.

godparents were Moses Simhah of blessed memory and his wife. I named him Zebulun, may God his Rock protect him and grant him long life, because all my life I had wondered why this name was not used by many Jews, as it represents one of God's twelve holy tribes. I wanted to establish the name of that righteous man among the Jews. In addition, he [Zebulun] was born in Venice, a city on the coast—and it is written in Scripture: "Zebulun shall dwell at the shore of the sea"[19]—and during the reign of Doge Marin Grimani,[f] so that the Christians called him Marin.[g] May God raise him to fear and serve him; [MS 13b/ ב] may he make his end be better than his beginning; and when he grows old, may he not turn away from the correct path. Amen.

[C 55] On Tuesday the 10th of Tammuz [5]361 [July 10, 1601], the sage, Rabbi Joseph Pardo,[h] may God his Rock protect him and grant him long life, became inspired to employ me[i] to produce a commentary on the Torah, which would be compiled from all authors who were in print up to that time. I began with twenty-seven authors,[j] choosing from among them only the type of comment that explicated the plain meaning of the text[k] and was therefore suitable for every householder. In truth, had I completed it, it would have been an impressive and beautiful work.[l] But I only did the portions Bereshit, Pinhas, Mattot, and Mas'ei,[m] for I did not refrain from playing games of chance. When Rabbi Pardo saw that I was not devoting myself to the task, he took it away from me and did not wish to see it finished.[n]

Having left the Panarotti house in the month of Tammuz [5]361 [July 1601] and begun to board at my own table in my own house with a few students,[o] I carried on in this way until the month of Iyyar[20] [5]362 [April–May 1602]. That Iyyar I won about five hundred ducats in the company of Solomon son of Eliakim Panarotti, but after the holiday of Shavuot they returned the same way they had come, and more of them as well, until finally I lost everything. My students left me, and I remained alone and idle.[p]

Accordingly, in the month of Tammuz [5]362 [June–July 1602] I girded up my loins to print a few of my sermons. I took the notes that I had and put them together, and each day, as I wrote [the

---

[19] Genesis 49:13.   [20] The month, Iyyar, was added above the line.

sermons out], they were printed, until, with the help of God, praised be he, I had compiled from twenty-one of them the book *Midbar yehudah*,[q] part one. The book has already been widely distributed among the Jews,[r] praise God. I still have in my possession more than four hundred sermons, in addition to commentaries on the Torah and many anthologies.[s]

[C 56] Back at the end of the month of Nisan [5]362 [ended April 21, 1602] I had received the news of the death in Rome of my older [half-]brother Samuel Hezekiah of blessed memory. He was the son of my revered father by his first wife, Peninah, of blessed memory. During his life he squandered and threw to the winds thousands of gold dinars. Although my revered father had divided his wealth with him in the year [5]343 [1582/1583], and he had received more than three thousand ducats in cash and goods, within two years nothing remained in his hands. He went to live in Pesaro, where he taught children. There he lost his firstborn son. Finally he went to live and teach in Rome, and there he died, leaving two sons. The first was named Solomon and the second was named Mordecai. They are married and live in Rome, where they go about their business honestly.[t]

In the month of Elul [August–September 1602], near the completion of the printing of my aforementioned book, I punctured my foot on a piece of iron and spent about fifteen days in bed. When I recovered, I went to Ancona[u] and returned home on the eve of Yom Kippur [5]363 [September 24, 1602].

[MS 14a/ כא] During the winter of the year 5363 [1602/1603], I was without students[v] and pursued the vanity of the craft of alchemy,[w] into which the physician, the *haver* Abraham di Cammeo[x] of Rome, then a young man and here with his father, enticed me. On this, too, I spent much money.

After the holiday of Passover [ended April 3, 1603], I settled down with a few students. The sons of Manasseh Calimani[y] were the best among them. The elder was named Simhah, a boy pure of mind, astoundingly bright, and handsome. He died at the age of six,[z] after I had left Venice for Ferrara.[a]

On Sunday the 24th of Elul, which was August 31, [5]363 [1603], my wife gave birth to a daughter at approximately the twenty-first hour [3:00 P.M.]. I named her Esther, may she be blessed above all women of the house, after my mother's mother and my wife's sister, my first betrothed, of blessed memory. May she grow up to be married and have children, and may my own eyes see this.[21] Amen.

During the entire year 5364 [1603/1604], I lived in poverty and distress,[b] and did not turn away from the evil of playing games of chance. Finally, at the end of the year, at the end of Elul [ended September 24, 1604], I went to Ferrara.[c] There I contracted [C 57] to stay and teach the sons and grandsons of the wealthy Joseph Zalman[d] of blessed memory in his house. After a month I brought my wife and children[e] to live there. Only Zebulun remained in Venice, for my in-laws and my brother-in-law Moses[22] of blessed memory would not let him go.

There I was received with great affection and was honored and welcome in that household like a lord benefactor.[23] Unbelievable as it is to tell, that entire holy community, great and humble alike, loves me dearly to this day. They appointed me their regular Sabbath preacher in the Great Synagogue[f] and loved and praised my words. Some young men organized an academy and [study] society, and to fill my pockets, I would teach them each weekday, and on the Sabbath [give them] words of Torah and a sermon. In this way I accumulated more than 260 scudi a year. I boarded at the table of the aforementioned Zalman, but despite this, I was overcome by depression[g] and did not live there willingly, due to my great longing and love for Venice, the city of my birth.

On the 24th of Av 5365 [August 8, 1605], my brother-in-law Moses Simhah of blessed memory passed away at the age of about thirty-three. When the news reached my ears, my heart turned over inside of me,[24] for he was upright and well liked by all, [MS 14b/ כב] sociable, knew how to play songs, dance, and conduct business, and possessed wisdom and a knowledge of books. My wife, may she be blessed above all women of the house, was deeply pained, for she had been his favorite sister. I composed an elegy for him, which is engraved as an epitaph on his tombstone here in Venice. These are the words: "A man lifted up from his people, good

[21] 1 Kings 1:48.
[22] This person is Moses Simhah, whose death is reported below.
[23] Italian word *patrono*, spelled *patron* in Hebrew transcription, reflecting the dropping of the final vowel in the Venetian dialect.
[24] Lamentations 1:20.

and pleasant to God and man, snuffed out in midlife, may he be bound here to be sacrificed like a lamb. His name was Moses son of Isaac of the family Simhah; he departed on the 24th of Av in the year 'may others arise like Moses.' "[25]

Because the air in Ferrara bothered my son Mordecai[h] of blessed memory, I had sent him, too, to the house of my father-in-law of blessed memory in Venice. In physical appearance and personal characteristics no two people were as alike as that son of mine and my brother-in-law, and because of this I always feared in my heart[i] that he would be short-lived like him, as, because of my sins, did come to pass.

At the end of the month of Av 5366 [ended September 2, 1606], the wealthy Joseph Zalman of blessed memory passed away[j] after a two-day illness. If before I had longed to leave Ferrara, my yearning [C 58] became greater after his death. He had loved me like a son, and though I also loved his sons, the eldest of them, Johanan of blessed memory, did not get along very well with people. Therefore, I intended to move back to Venice.[j] I did not succeed in implementing this plan, however, until Adar 5367 [February–March 1607], when I departed with all the members of my household. I came to Venice and set up an apartment and a school on the top floor of the house belonging to the family dal Osto, the Levites, may God their Rock protect them and grant them long life. I took on students and also resumed preaching in the "garden"[k] and in the house of study of the Torah Study Society,[l] may God their Rock protect them and grant them long life. And as the Lord is my shepherd nothing was wanting.[2]

In the month of Heshvan 5368 [October–November 1607], I went to live in the house of a very unpleasant person, my wife's relative Moses Copio,[m] may his name be blotted out,[3n] in order to teach his son Abraham Copio, a chip off the old block, and four

---

[25] Modena placed a mark above the word ke-mosheh, "like Moses," to indicate that its numerical value (365) should be computed to arrive at the year of death, namely, 5365. To show the paronomasia of the words, kemo seh, "like a lamb," and ke-mosheh, "like Moses," Modena set them off by writing them between the lines.

[1] Lamentations 5:17.　[2] Adaptation of Psalm 23:1.

[3] In the manuscript, the abbreviation y-sh for yimah shemo, "may his name be blotted out," is found in the margin, but immediately following Moses Copio's name, which comes at the end of a line. The addition was apparently an afterthought. The ink, which has turned reddish brown on the page as a result of oxidation of its iron content, came

other students, and to board at his table. And because no one could live cooped up with such a wild person,[4] the following Tammuz [June–July 1608] I left his house and, with students, set up a school in my apartment, which was located in the Ghetto Vecchio on an upper floor of the house belonging to the Treves family.[o]

Meanwhile, because my son Isaac, may God his Rock protect him and grant him long life, was behaving improperly with childish escapades,[5] I sent him to Patras in Morea.[p] For about thirteen years [C 59] he wandered around the Levant. During most of this time he lived in Zante,[q] working very hard to make a living. He did earn money and would have accumulated something had not he, too, been tempted by the vanity of playing games of chance. Ultimately he returned home after those years empty-handed.

[MS 15a/ כג] In the month of Heshvan 5369 [September–October 1608] I moved into the Ghetto Nuovo, on the ground floor of the house belonging to Zanvil of Udine, may God his Rock protect him and grant him long life. There I had many pupils throughout the winter. But I did what the angel messengers said to Sarah in answer to her denial [namely, played games of chance][6] until my behavior became so wild that I agreed to go and live away from Venice. Through correspondence I contracted to go to Florence, to preach and to teach students for an annual salary of 220 ducatoni,[r] paid by the community.

And so I left for Montagnana, where I spent Passover [April 19–26, 1609]. Afterward I proceeded to Ferrara and from there to Florence. On the way I was accompanied by several Christians and by two young Jewish men. Near Loiano, which is between Bologna and Florence, while I was conversing with a certain friar, an incident took place when the mule upon which I was riding kicked and struck him on the leg. Saying that I did this, they gathered up against me and struck me—one friend of the friar with his fists in

from a different batch from that used in the body of the text up to this point, which was of higher quality and hence still retains its original black color. See historical note n.

[4] Cf. B.T. Ketubbot 72a.

[5] There may be wordplay intended. The Hebrew ma'aseh na'arut, "childish escapades," can also be vocalized ma'aseh na'arot, "escapades with young girls."

[6] A clever allusion to Genesis 18:15, lo ki tzahakt, "no, but you did laugh." The verb tzahak, like the verbal noun tzehok throughout Modena's autobiography and in contemporaneous Hebrew generally, is taken in the postbiblical sense of "play" (like the verb sahak), and alludes to playing games of chance.

the ribs, and a certain young man from Modena with a strap in the face and in my right eye. So I arrived in Florence at the beginning of the month of Iyyar [began May 5, 1609], smitten by priests and afflicted.[7s] I was welcomed into the home of Abraham Todesco of blessed memory, and I recuperated there. I stayed in his house for a month, honored and esteemed, until my wife and children arrived on the eve of the holiday of Shavuot [June 7, 1609]. After the holiday I settled into my house, teaching and preaching.

That summer I was sick for about a month with a boil at the base of my throat.[t] I was also afflicted on my left hand. On the High Holidays [September 29–October 8, 1609] I quarreled with the aforementioned Abraham and some other members [C 60] of the community.[u] In addition, the air bothered my eyes and my wife's, and we constantly longed for and yearned to return to Venice.[v] Finally, after Passover [ended April 15, 1610], almost exactly one year to the day since my arrival in Florence, I departed and came back to Venice.

I arrived in Venice at the beginning of the month of Iyyar 5370 [began April 24, 1610] and negotiated with the members of the Ashkenazic Torah Study Society, may God their Rock protect them and grant them long life, and contracted to teach their students and to preach. A month later my wife and children arrived from Florence. I secured lodgings in a small house belonging to Joseph Cohen Roman of blessed memory, and reconciled myself to that heavy load of teaching[w] and preaching in order to stand at the threshold of the city of my desires.

At the beginning of the month of Tammuz [began June 22, 1610] I sent my dear son of blessed memory to San[8] Vito[9x] to the home of Leb Romanin, may God his Rock protect him and grant him long life, to teach his grandsons. He stayed there for eight months and saw the fruits of his teaching, for he preached there every Sabbath. I still possess his original interpretations, which, however, on

---

[7] Adaptation of Isaiah 53:4.

[8] In the manuscript the word San is represented by the Hebrew letter ʿayin, which follows s (samekh) in the alphabet, evidently because of Jewish reluctance to say or write that word. Modena did not follow this taboo consistently. See fol. 16a, where "San" is abbreviated with a Hebrew s in the phrase "Church of San Geremia."

[9] Transliterated with Hebrew d in place of t. See also fol. 24b, note 21, and fol. 25a, note 23.

account of my anguish, I do not read, though I know that they contain much knowledge. At the beginning of the month of Nisan 5371 [began March 15, 1611], I brought him home in order to assist me in teaching the boys of the Torah Study Society school. [MS 15b/ כד][10] Shortly thereafter, the members of the society agreed to give him full responsibility for the students, leaving me to preach on the Sabbaths and teach the public on weekdays. He was successful in all his endeavors.

In the month of Tammuz 5371 [June–July 1611] I arranged a match for my daughter Diana, may she be blessed above all women of the house, with the *haver* Jacob Levi,[y] may God his Rock protect him and grant him long life, the son of the one called Calman di Padovani of blessed memory. I pledged to him 450 ducats in cash and 200 ducats worth of clothing, relying on heaven's mercy[z] [to provide the dowry].

[C 61] In the month of Av [July 1611] my revered uncle, the gaon Rabbi Abtalion of Modena of blessed memory, died in Ferrara at the age of eighty-two, and I delivered a proper eulogy for him.[a] He left a daughter, as I mentioned before.

During the entire period of my daughter's engagement, which lasted for more than two years, I pursued the vanity of playing games of chance, and all my doings were worthless.[b]

In the month of Iyyar 5372 [May 1612] I completed the printing[c] of my works *Galut yehudah*[d] and *Lev ha-aryeh*.[e] The lord, patriarch of Aquileia, Ermolao Barbaro,[f] accepted with appreciation the dedication that I had composed for him in the book and gave me a gift of twenty-five scudi, even though he was a righteous man who was very thrifty with his money.[11] I distributed copies in Venice, Padua, Verona, Mantua, Modena, and the Italian provinces, and realized about 250 ducats, but much of it I lost and squandered.

The date set for my daughter Diana's wedding approached, and at the beginning of the month of Elul 5373 [began August 18, 1613], we were in a great dither trying to come up with what was

[10] Beginning at the top of fol. 15b, Hebrew page 24 (*kaf dalet*), and for the next five folios, Modena employed a batch of ink of poorer quality, which in time turned reddish brown on the page and contrasts with the black color of the better ink used up to this point in the journal.
[11] Modena's sarcasm is based on the Talmud, B. T. Sotah 12a, where it is stated that the righteous are cautious with their money.

needed for her dowry. Finally, with my son Mordecai of blessed memory and after much trouble and grief, we collected what I had pledged to give her. On the 6th day of Heshvan 5374 [October 21, 1613], her wedding took place with rejoicing, praise God. At that time, the title of *haver* was bestowed upon my son-in-law, the aforementioned Jacob, [C 62] and he established a home. While he honestly pursues his profession as dance and music teacher,[g] he has not neglected his Torah studies and, in fact, does well at them. He is both a good preacher and a good scholar. He fathered a son who died at the age of eight months, and after that a daughter who died, too, at ten months of age.[12h] May God be with him and bless him.

In Kislev 5374 [November–December 1613] I resumed doing evil by playing games of chance, and from then on only evil surrounded me.

On the 10th of Tishre[i] 5375 [September 13, 1614] my son Mordecai of blessed memory went away as a result of the vexations of a certain wicked and sinful man, and gave up teaching the students of the society. Upon his return in the month of Kislev [November–December 1614] he began to engage in the craft of alchemy with the priest Joseph Grillo, a very learned man. He worked at it assiduously and became so adept that all the venerable practitioners marveled at what such a lad knew. Finally, in the month of Iyyar [April–May 1615], he arranged a place in the Ghetto Vecchio [MS 16a/ כה] and with his own hands made[13] all the preparations needed for the craft. There he repeated an experiment that he had learned to do in the house of the priest, which was to make ten ounces of pure silver from nine ounces of lead and one of silver. This I saw done by him twice and examined it and sold the silver myself for six and a half lire per ounce.[j] It stood the test of the *coppella*,[k] and I knew that it was real.[l] Even though the process required great work and labor and took two and one-half months each time, in the end

---

[12] Manuscript has the masculine form, *ben*, rather than the expected *bat* in the expression, "of age." Possibly Modena slipped up under the influence of the word *ben* in the phrase, "ben h [= 8] hodashim" (at the age of eight months), which he had just written.

[13] Hebrew: "u-miyado ʿasah." The catchword at the bottom of the previous page differs from the first words at the top of folio 16a. It says "and with his own hands prepared" (u-miyado hekhin). Apparently Modena decided in the course of writing (or perhaps recopying; see excursus 2) this sentence to replace the word "prepared" with a synonym ("made," ʿasah) for stylistic reasons, not wanting to write "prepared all the preparations" (hekhin kol ha-hakhanot).

it could have yielded a profit of about a thousand ducats a year. And this is not vanity, for I also wasted my life trying to understand things such as these, and I would not have deluded myself had not sin caused me.

On the holiday of Sukkot 5376 [October 15–23, 1615], much blood from Mordecai's head suddenly started flowing out of his mouth, and from then on he ceased to engage in that craft because he was told that possibly the vapors and smoke from the arsenic and salts that go into it had done harm to his head. He remained like this for two years until his death, limiting himself to some light activities.

[C 63] On the 9th of Heshvan 5377 [October 20, 1616] the erudite sage, my beloved friend Rabbi Solomon Shemaiah Sforno of blessed memory, passed away. I delivered the eulogy for him in the Great Synagogue[m] and exhorted the congregation to take up a collection to marry off one of the daughters he had left behind. I praised him so warmly in that eulogy that God made me please the audience, and they contributed about five hundred ducats. It was amazing to Jews and even Christians, whose preachers, on their days of penitence, would say in order to inspire their audiences to give charity: "Did not one Jew in the ghetto raise five hundred ducats with one sermon to marry off a young girl?" When I was in the Church of San Geremia,[n] the preacher said that and pointed me out with his finger.

God immediately rewarded me, for I tried together with Abraham Haver Tov,[o] may God his Rock protect him and grant him long life, to find someone to print an edition of the Bible with commentaries (*Mikra gedolah*).[p] My son Mordecai of blessed memory traveled to several Italian Jewish communities in order to solicit subscribers who would commit themselves to buying copies. Through his diligence, he obtained about four hundred subscribers,[q] and returned in success.[14] Then, at last, I reached a decision on who would print it, and, after brokerage and the cost of having it proofread, I earned close to five hundred ducats, all of which, after the death of my aforementioned son, became dissipated on account of the calamities that befell me.[15]

---

[14] 2 Chronicles 31:21.   [15] Adaptation of Psalm 73:19.

Nevertheless,[16] I did not cease to be the beneficiary of divine inspiration because, measure for measure, I was immediately sent the very amount I had induced to be given as charity to marry off my own daughter. [MS 16b/ כב] So, if I was clever, it was for my own benefit.[17]

On the night of the 13th of Tevet 5377 [December 21, 1616] I had a dream in which I saw a man standing before me, and many people were saying to me, "Do you see that man? He is a prophet, and the spirit of God is in him." So I approached him and said, "Master, as they tell me you are a prophet, please tell me when I shall die and how much longer [C 64] I shall live." The man immediately answered, "Four years and seven months," whereupon I awoke. In the morning I composed a poem as a reminder, in the style of a poem that A[zariah] de Rossi of blessed memory had composed, having had it revealed to him in a dream that later was fulfilled, and which is written [i.e., copied] from his hand in [a copy of] his book that is in my possession:[r] "While resting on my bed, on the night of the 13th of Tevet 5377, I dreamed of a prophet, who foretold my end. Another four years and seven months, in Tammuz or Av[18] [5]381, I'll go to my resting place."[19]

I will not refrain from telling you here that from my youth I had had a passionate desire to learn from the astrologers, on the basis of my birth date, what would happen to me during the days of my life and how many they would be. I had seen the horoscope that a certain man named Alessandro Bivago[s] had compiled for my revered father of blessed memory in Bologna when he was seventeen. He told him everything that would happen to him year by year,

---

[16] This next passage is a difficult one. It seems to mean: despite the loss of the five hundred ducats, I was still rewarded by God measure for measure and received myself the same sum of money I had induced others to contribute toward the dowry of the daughter of Rabbi Solomon Shemaiah Sforno, a sum—five hundred ducats—that turned out to be the very amount I later needed to dower my daughter Esther (fol. 18a). Thus, by being "clever" with the sermon that yielded five hundred ducats for Rabbi Sforno, I was actually being "clever" for myself.

[17] Adaptation of Proverbs 9:12.

[18] Modena first wrote "Av or . . ." then crossed it out and substituted "Tammuz or Av."

[19] Rhymes in Hebrew. As before (fol. 14b), to show the rhyme, Modena wrote the last word of the second stich (*rivtzi*, "my resting place") between the lines, at the left margin, lining it up with the rhyme word *kitzi*, "my end."

and not one word failed to come true.[20] He said that he would live seventy-two and one-half years, and it turned out to be seventy-two and two months. From that time on, I yearned for something like it. A horoscope was compiled for me by four astrologers, two Jews and two Christians, and to this day, on account of my sins, what they wrote has proved accurate.[21] The time of my death is predicted for the age of fifty-two, approximately, and I am fifty now.[t] Palmistry also indicates that it will occur about the age of fifty.

I now regret having undertaken that endeavor, for man's only proper way is to be pure before God, and he should not make such inquiries. So here I am today, pained on account of the past and anxious about the future. But God will do as he pleases. My only prayer to him is that he should not take me away before I repent of my sins. Ever since I was born I have had no joy, that I should worry about lacking it; neither have I seen any good in this world, that I should have difficulty leaving it. These, my final days, are burdensome. May the Creator be praised for everything forever. If the time or any other[22] that has been decreed for me according to the aforementioned persons should pass, I will write of that fact further on. But if their words prove to be true, one of the readers should write it here below.

[MS 17a/ כז , C 65] My bowels, my bowels. I writhe in pain. The chambers of my heart moan within me[23] as I come to tell with two-fold brokenheartedness[24] about the death of my son Mordecai of blessed memory. After the holiday of Sukkot 5376 [ended October 16, 1615], when he first began to bleed from his mouth, it recurred, at first once a month, after that once a week, and then from Passover [5]377 [began April 30, 1617] on, every day. I tried frantically to cure him, but could not find a remedy. I saw no sign of benefit in any of the many medicines that I gave him. Finally, in the month of Elul [September 1617], his illness grew worse. I had eleven doctors, Jewish and Christian, consulting about his malady, some during personal visits and others through correspondence. He wished very much for the remedies of the aforementioned priest Grillo,

---

[20] 1 Kings 8:56.   [21] Adaptation of Psalm 19:10.   [22] Cf. B.T. Megillah 2a.
[23] Adaptation of Jeremiah 4:19.   [24] Adaptation of Jeremiah 17:18.

having seen an example of his treatment of others. But, as it differed from the ways of all the other doctors, I was afraid to treat him accordingly. Only close to his death, to satisfy his wishes, did I allow him to take them.

About that time I dreamed that he said to me, "I have taken a house for myself outside the ghetto."u I responded, "Show me where, so that I may come and find you." He answered, "I do not want to tell you, for I do not want you to come to find me." Meanwhile, bedridden, he continued to wane.

On the Sabbath of Repentance [5]378 [October 7, 1617] he got up from his bed to come hear two of my sermons. That evening he returned to his bed and began to run a fever, the likes of which he had never previously known. Finally, on the night of the arrival of Tuesday the 9th of Heshvan 5378v [November 7, 1617], his appointed time drew near, and he confessed his sins and recited many psalms and confessional prayers. He lay dying for about three hours, and then, about the ninth hour [3:00 A.M.], his soul returned to the Lord who had given it to him.

Truthfully, were it not for the maxim of the talmudic sages of blessed memory, "Just as the Holy One, blessed be he, gives the righteous the strength to accept their reward, so he gives strength to the wicked to accept their punishment,"25 I could not possibly live with the pain and sorrow that have seized me from then until now. Not a day passes that [his death] is not fresh to me, as if his corpse were lying before me. The saying, "It is decreed that the dead should be forgotten by the heart,"1 does not apply to me, for it is today three years since his death,2 and wherever [C 66] I turn he is there before me.

He was an average-looking man, slender and not fat, with a hairy body. His face was not pale, but he had a small, rounded beard. He pleased all who saw him, and was wise in all worldly matters, as well as in the advice he gave when anyone asked him about matters divine. He preached well in public, delivering sermons in Florence,

---

25 Cf. B.T. Sanhedrin 100b.   1 Cf. B.T. Pesahim 54b.

2 Modena wrote this section of the autobiography just after his fiftieth birthday, which fell on April 19, 1621 (see fols. 16b and 18b). This was three years and five months after his son Mordecai's death in November 1617, the event that had caused him to begin to compile his autobiograpy.

Mantua, Ferrara, and Venice. He was neither a happy nor a sad person, and got along well with people. None surpassed him in respect for parents. We were like two brothers, for he was twenty-six years and two months old [at his death], [MS 17b/ כה] and I was forty-six and a half. Alas for me, I lost him, and I do not even know how to count his praises.

Later on it was reported to me in Ferrara, as he had related it, that one year before his death he told a certain woman how he had asked in a dream to be shown the woman decreed to become his wife and was shown a coffin covered in black.

I thought that my son Zebulun, may God his Rock protect him and grant him long life, would bring me consolation, but to this day his ways have not been straight, and he adds trouble and sorrow to my pain. May God guide him in the path of his commandments, so that he may console me before I die.

Following the death of the apple of my eye and root of my heart, I returned out of great anxiety to the enemy that always drove me out of the world—namely, playing games of chance—from which I had abstained for two years in order to please my aforementioned son. Until Passover 5380 [began April 19, 1620], I compounded the evil day after day.

I cannot neglect recording a remarkable fact. The erudite scholar Rabbi S[olomon] Sh[emaiah] Sforno of blessed memory, mentioned before, had been deeply attached to my charming son of blessed memory. He recognized that he was intelligent, understanding, and wise in all matters. Likewise, he [my son] of blessed memory loved that scholar with all his heart, for he was like "a city in which everything is found,"[3] encompassing everything there was to be said about wisdom. The two of them were always intimate conversationalists.[4] Now it came to pass that the aforementioned scholar died during the night of the arrival of Tuesday[5] the 9th of Heshvan [5]377, in a room in a dwelling belonging to the family of Zimlan Luria of Padua,[w] may God his Rock protect him and grant him long life, [C 67] which was next to the dwellings belonging to the Calimani family, may God their Rock protect them and grant them long life. My son died exactly one year later, on the night of

---

[3] B.T. Hullin 56b.   [4] Adaptation of Psalm 55:15.
[5] Actually, the 9th of Heshvan 5377 fell on a Thursday (October 20, 1616).

the arrival of Tuesday the 9th of Heshvan 5378 [November 7, 1617], in the very same room and in a bed located on the very same spot. [That is] because I had moved to that apartment immediately after the death of that scholar. May both their souls rest in the Garden of Eden.

During Sukkot [October 4–12, 1618], at the request of the physician Hayyim Alatini[x] of blessed memory, I went to Ferrara with my son Zebulun, may God his Rock protect him and grant him long life, to attend the wedding of that doctor's widowed sister to Leon Costantin of Crete.[y] On my return, on Simhat Torah 5379 [October 12, 1618], I became sick right away with a dangerous illness that turned into a case of tertian fever,[6z] which lasted forty-four days before God relented and cured me.

Since the time of my son's death I had longed to find a mate for my daughter Esther, may she be blessed above all women of the house, who is called Sterella. I said that if God would but enable me to establish her comfortably in her husband's house,[7] I would change my way of life and my behavior and would retire to a life of solitude in some place, because for me, all joy has become darkened,[8] and I will not be comforted until the Comforter [i.e., Messiah] comes.

I looked around for her throughout the city, but could not find anyone. It did not work out until Tevet 5379 [December 1618–January 1619], when it was arranged by heaven. [MS 18a/ כט] A match for her was concluded with a young man, then eighteen years of age, named Jacob, may God his Rock protect him and grant him long life, son of Jekutiel, known as Fiz, may God his Rock protect him and grant him long life, who lived in a small village called La Motta,[a] for "the daughter of so-and-so is designated for so-and-so,"[9] and even from across the sea.

Then I began to consider how I would assemble the amount of dowry that I had pledged on her behalf—five hundred ducats in cash and three hundred in goods—in addition to the money to pay for the arrangement of the match and for the wedding, which in the end really amounted to almost a thousand ducats. My friends seduced me and prevailed over me,[10] [C 68] so that I came to an

---

[6] Hebrew *kadahat shelishit*. See historical note z.   [7] Ruth 1:9.   [8] Isaiah 24:11.
[9] B.T. Sotah 2a and elsewhere.   [10] Adaptation of Obadiah, verse 7.

agreement with the members of the Ashkenazic Torah Study Society, may God their Rock protect them and grant them long life. And, at the beginning of the month of Shevat[11] 5380 [began January 6, 1620], I entered the school they had established to teach students, with the *haver* Jacob Jozvil Levi,[b] may God his Rock protect him and grant him long life, as my assistant teacher,[12] and to give public sermons as I had already been doing. I committed myself for a period of sixteen months ending at the beginning of the month of Iyyar 5381 [began April 23, 1621], at a salary of 250 ducats a year. But the job was very burdensome to me.[c]

There, too, I had no rest from my son Zebulun, may God his Rock protect him and grant him long life. And, in Second Adar 5380 [March 6–April 3, 1620] he went to sea in an armada[13] to travel around as he wished. He was away for about three months, after which he returned home. In Sivan 5380 [June–July 1620] I went away myself for about a month, to Verona, Mantua, and Ferrara, and then returned to the school.[d]

On the 6th of Elul 5380 [September 4, 1620], through God's kindness, the wedding of my daughter Esther, may she be blessed above all women of the house, to her aforementioned mate took place when I gave her all that I had pledged for her, more and not less.[e] Instead of joy, however, there was trembling over my son Zebulun, may God his Rock protect him and grant him long life. A feud had broken out between him and certain cruel, violent, and powerful Christians,[f] and it dragged on for three months before I was able to appease them and make peace with them. Nonetheless, during Sukkot [5]381 [October 12–20, 1620], my wife, my aforementioned son, and I went to bring my daughter Esther to settle comfortably into her husband's house.[14] We stayed there joyously during the holiday and returned home safely immediately thereafter.

At the end of Elul 5380 [ended September 27, 1620] my son Isaac, may God his Rock protect him and grant him long life, had

---

[11] Another, undecipherable word was corrected by Modena to read Shevat.

[12] Literally, "second teacher."

[13] In the manuscript the second-to-last letter of this word might be either *r* or *d*, consonants that Modena formed almost identically, and "armada" seems a plausible reading. See also fol. 34b.

[14] Ruth 1:9.

arrived naked and bare from Egypt, after more than twelve years during which he had been all over the Levant. I spent [C 69] about fifty ducats to ransom him from the ship and clothe him, and brought him home. I said, "Perhaps he will revive my spirit and help to support me." But just as he had done before he left, he once again began going around with reckless and worthless men, playing games of chance and associating with drunkards. Finally, at the beginning of the month of Iyyar 5381 [began April 22, 1621], I directed him to return to the Levant and also spent about twenty ducats to send him off on his own. May God instill in his heart the right path, so that he will no longer disgrace my name wherever he goes.

During the autumn of 5381 [1620] I also engaged in evil, losing everything by playing games of chance. As [MS 18b/ ב] a result, I was obliged to extend my term of burdensome employment shut up in that school until the beginning of the upcoming month of Shevat [5]382 [began January 12, 1622]. Now, in Iyyar [5]381 [April–May 1621], I am troubled and distressed with many debts, in the very week that the Torah portion containing the verse "and if you shall say 'what shall I eat' "[15] is being read. May God take pity [on me].

On the night of the arrival of Friday the 16th of Iyyar 5381, at the fifth hour of the night [11:00 P.M.] on May 7[16] [1621], my daughter Diana gave birth to a son under an auspicious star. His father named him Isaac, may God his Rock protect him and grant him long life, after my saintly, revered father of blessed memory and after the father of my wife, may she be blessed above all women of the house. May God raise him [the child] to fear him and perform his commandments. Amen.

In Tammuz [5]381 [June–July 1621] I went with my wife to Padua to attend the wedding of the daughter of our relative Moses Simhah,[g] may God his Rock protect him and grant him long life. Then in the month of Elul [August–September] I accompanied her

---

[15] Leviticus 25:20. The Torah portion was Behar-Behukkotai, and it was read during the week ending on Saturday, the 24th of Iyyar (May 15, 1621).

[16] The phrase "at the fifth hour of the night on May 7" was added above the line by Modena and marked with a caret. At the fifth hour, that is, 11:00 P.M., it was technically still May 6. This journal entry and the following four are separated from one another by lines.

to La Motta, where she remained with our daughter Esther, may she be blessed above all women of the house, until Yom Kippur [September 25], at which time she returned home.

In Kislev [5]382 [November–December 1621], Zebulun was put in jail for twelve days, punished by the five magistrates.[h] [C 70] I paid thirty-two ducats on his behalf, impoverishing ourselves to secure his release.

At the end of Tevet 5382 [ended January 11, 1622], a celebration was held in the Great Synagogue at the conclusion of the study of the talmudic tractate Ketubbot. Eighteen sermons were delivered, and on the last night, which was the second day of Shevat [January 13, 1622], I gave the sermon before a huge standing crowd, packed in as never before, with many Christians and noblemen among the listeners. Poems and melodies were composed [for the occasion], and Zebulun sang a song that I had written.[i] The listeners could not stop praising his sweet voice. I was extremely happy because my term of duty in the school had ended, and I had emerged into the freedom for which my soul had longed all that time. Even though I was empty-handed and had many debts, I praised the living God. I decided after Passover to lead myself along the proper path with his help, may he be praised.

Passover 5382 [March 26–April 3, 1622] was transformed for me from a time of happiness to one of sorrow, and from a holiday to a time of mourning, gloom, trouble, and darkness. Alas, O Righteous One of the universe! Alas, O Judge of the universe! How my sins have multiplied and my transgressions have increased! It is now a full fifty-one years since my birth, with things getting worse and worse. There is never a day whose curse is not greater than the one before. I have had neither rest nor peace, with anxiety[17j] following anxiety and calamity following calamity, in money matters, in heart, and in body. I hardly have strength to hold the pen in my hand and to write down what happened to me as a result of God's disfavor. How can the paper fail to become wet[18] from the tears that fall upon it? O, my heart, which moans like a piped instrument,[19]

---

[17] Job 3:26. See historical note j.

[18] The word *yemuyyam*, derived from the noun *mayim*, "water," is not found in Hebrew dictionaries. Perhaps it constitutes a neologism created by Modena.

[19] Adaptation of Jeremiah 48:36.

break so that my life can end! Death seems to me so good.[20] No other rest would be good for me, because for hundreds of years until now, there has been no evil like the one that God visited upon me on account of my many wicked deeds.

[MS 19a/ אל] Four years beforehand my oppressed, bitter, and impetuous[21] son Zebulun, may God avenge his blood, had been forced to serve at a trial as a witness against certain accursed scoundrels and treacherous murderers. Since the days of the violent men who lived at the time of the destruction of the Temple there had not been the likes of them, the accursed brothers—may their names be blotted out from this world and their bones be ground to dust [C 71] in hell in the world to come—Shabbetai and Moses Benincasa, known as da Hindelina. May their names be blotted out, those brothers! May their portion be cursed in the earth.[22] May their sons speedily become orphans and travel about in search of bread like the descendants of Canaan.[k]

Because of this, they bore a permanent grudge against him. They did not show it in their faces or words, but rather always spoke peaceably with him and me, while harboring treachery in their hearts.[23] Finally, in the month of Av [5]381 [July–August 1621], while my son, may God avenge his blood, was speaking with the violent Shabbetai, may his name be blotted out, the latter began to quarrel with him. He struck him on the cheek and pursued him with a slaughterhouse knife to Cannaregio.[l] There, my son, may God avenge his blood, spotted a sword on a villager's shoulder, grabbed it, and became the pursuer himself. He struck him [Shabbetai] lightly on one arm, but the latter threw himself into the water and thus escaped from my son.

When I heard about this, and before the conflict went farther, I entreated the nobleman, my lord Signore Alvise Giustinian,[m] and he made peace between them. Thus the brothers, may their names be blotted out, once again passed themselves off as friends, while the fire of hatred burned ever more fiercely in their hearts.

On the night of the burning of leaven [the night before the first evening of Passover], the night of the arrival of Friday, March 25,

---

[20] Cf. Bereshit Rabbah 9:5.   [21] Habbakuk 1:6.   [22] Job 24:18.
[23] Adaptation of Jeremiah 9:7.

5. Interior of the Great Ashkenazi Synagogue, La Scola Grande Tedesca, in the Ghetto Nuovo, where Modena often preached sermons.

[5]382 [1622], the two brothers, may their names be blotted out, formed a conspiracy with the bastard Isaac of the Spagnoletta family[n] and the bastard Abram Ciompo della Bel, who were called "mules" because they were bastards, and with four Sephardim— David Mocatto, may his name be blotted out; Moses Emmanuel, may his name be blotted out; and the brothers Isaac and Jacob Montalti, the sons of the midwife[24]—eight men hated by God. They feared Zebulun because they knew of his courage, namely, that he had the heart of a lion and would not retreat in the face of battle.

The bastard Isaac stalked him on the way to the house of the Levantine. Just as I arrived, for I had been informed about it and had gone looking for him to bring him home, they came out of hiding, pretending that they wanted to beat up someone else. The bastard called to him and said, "Come down, for your friends are in a fight; come [C 72] to their aid!" On the run, the impetuous one came down, passing me by without my recognizing him. As soon as he emerged they surrounded him and struck him on the head, bruising him without drawing blood. Then they stabbed him in the throat with a sword or a spear, so that he fled, shouting, "Father, Father, I am dying!"

Blood spurted out like a spring, and as he could not make it home, he went to the house of my brother-in-law Johanan, may God his Rock protect him and grant him long life. There he threw himself into bed, rolling in blood. Before the doctor could arrive, he had lost his lifeblood. By the time [the physician] bandaged his wounds there was no longer enough of it left to keep him alive, and his entire right side lost all feeling. Immediately after reciting the confessional prayer and the prayers for mercy, he lost consciousness from the blow to his head and never again uttered an intelligible word. He lay near death for four nights and three days until Monday, the first of the intermediate days of the holiday [of Passover, Monday, March 28, 1622] [MS 19b/לב], when his soul departed and he passed on to eternal life.

He was buried that day next to his brother, my son Mordecai of blessed memory. Upon his coffin while it was being carried was placed his blood-soiled clothing. This sight, and the sound of my

---

[24] Italian word *comare*, written in Hebrew letters.

cries and those of my woebegone wife, caused every heart and eye to shed tears. Even Christians and Turks grieved. At the cemetery there was an eighteen-year-old Christian citizen from the Dolfin family° who had known him, and he grieved so much that immediately after returning home he took to his bed and died within four days. There was no one who had ever spoken with him [my son]— including many Christian commoners who were acquaintances of his—who did not weep over his death. Such a cruel death!

He was thirteen days short of twenty-one years, good-looking and handsome. There was nobody like him in this community. He sang with a voice as sweet as that of God's angel. He was wise, understanding, and cheerful, and a writer of both prose and poetry. He was brave in battle, and none had a heart as courageous as his. Alas, I had always told him, "Your big heart will kill you!" His courage and weapons he only used in zeal for his God and to hallow his name, for he could not endure the debasement of any Jew.[25] And he never touched one of his own people.[1p]

Four months before his death, the citizen Signore Lorenzo Sanudo had told his horoscope, saying [C 73] that he would be killed between the ages of twenty-one and twenty-two. Alas, my eyes witnessed such a cruel death visited upon him! His bloody state will never disappear from before my eyes for the rest of my life. My tears have been my bread, day and night.[2] My soul refuses to be comforted,[3] for there can be no consolation. I simply pray to God: "Please unleash your hand and cut me off. Take my soul from me. Then I shall cease to have anxiety from sinning before you, and shall have rest and quiet."

After his death I did not turn away[4] from seeking revenge against those who had spilled his blood. For five months I spent money and worked hard until they were all brought to "the staircase"[5q] by the magistrates of the Bestemmia, acting on order of the heads of the [Council of] Ten.[r] Among those summoned was Elia Muchia-

---

[25] Hebrew: "hillul shem yehudi," literally, the profanation of the name of a Jew, an adaptation of the standard expression, "hillul ha-shem," meaning the profanation of God's name.

[1] The entire phrase beginning with "His courage" was added by Modena above the line and marked with a caret.

[2] Psalm 42:4.   [3] Psalm 77:3.   [4] Isaiah 50:5.

[5] Hebrew *ha-sulam*. See historical note q.

chion, for I suspected that he was the one who had given the order to kill him[6] over a forsaken whore[7s] named Simhah, the daughter of Nissim Shoshan, whom he also had desired. They were all put into banishment[8] and expelled permanently from all territories belonging to the republic, may its honor be exalted. No one was permitted to speak about them for ten years. A fine of one thousand lire would be turned over to anyone who might capture them within the borders, and they would have their heads cut off.[t] Only the "mule" Ciompo della Bel remained [in Venice], while the eight departed in disgrace. I also saw revenge taken on others—those who had been in collusion over, or had incited, or had rejoiced in his murder. I still pray to the living God evening, morning, and afternoon by reciting Psalm 109. May God take revenge on those who shed innocent blood for no reason and grant rest to him, and may his death be his atonement. But I am living against my will and am losing heart,[9] for to me it has seemed as if my two sons died at the same time, and my soul refuses to be comforted.[10]

I[11] give thanks to God the living God for having allowed me to hear while still alive about the dog's deaths of the murderers Shabbetai and Moses da Hindelina, may their bones be ground to dust in hell.[12] They died in Livorno, the second of the two in [C 74] 5395 [1634/1635]. Of the others, some died as a result of calamities, some became apostates, and of some not a trace remains. Blessed is he who has granted me revenge.

[MS 20a/ לב] Here[13] I shall list in memorandum form some of my writings, especially those which have already been printed, both Hebrew and Italian works, and, in addition, books in which my name is mentioned because of poems of mine that I wrote therein, or because of prefaces or proofreading. It is a source of great com-

---

[6] Manuscript is vocalized "meshalleah u-metzavveh," presumably to avoid ambiguity. As vocalized in the Kahana edition, page 41 (as a passive), the phrase has the very opposite meaning.

[7] Cf. Isaiah 23:16.

[8] Italian word *banditi*, in Hebrew letters, with Hebrew *d* in place of the *t*.

[9] Cf. Job 37:1.   [10] Psalm 77:3.

[11] This passage, squeezed in at the bottom of the page immediately following the words "my soul refuses to be comforted," constitutes an addition made after 1635.

[12] The acronym used here, y-ʿ-b, is spelled out before, fol. 19a: "yishtahaku ʿatzmoteihem be-geihinnom."

[13] The section is set off by a parenthesis.

6. Page of the manuscript of *Hayyei yehudah*
containing Modena's "bibliography."

fort to me[u] that, despite death and these evil times, my name will never be blotted out among the Jews or in the world at large, as long as the earth remains.[14]

(1) *Sur mera*[v]—*Turn from Evil*—a dialogue in praise and condemnation of games of chance. I composed it in my youth, at the age of thirteen, and it was printed in [5]356 [1595/1596]. I did not want to have my name mentioned in it, so as not to begin with such an inconsequential work.

(2) *Sod yesharim*[w]—*Secret of the Upright*—in which are collected several arcane remedies. It was printed soon after the previously mentioned work, and on the title page my name is alluded to in an acrostic only: "Yatza ha-kol u-va derekh ha-melekh, etc."[15]—"All went out and came on the King's highway."

(3) *Tzemah tzaddik*[x]—*Flower of the Virtuous*—which is the book *Fior di virtù*, translated by me from Italian into Hebrew. It discusses the improvement of ethical qualities. I substituted a saying of the rabbis [of the Talmud] of blessed memory for every reference from their [i.e., the Christians'] Scriptures or saints. It was printed in [5]360 [1599/1600], and there, too, my name is mentioned in an acrostic only: "Yosher ha-ahavah veha-hibbah da'at ha-hakhamim, etc."[16]—"The sincerity of love and devotion is in the knowledge of the sages."

(4) *Midbar yehudah*[y]—*The Wilderness of Judah*—twenty-one of my sermons, printed in 5362 [1601/1602]. It has achieved renown in Italy because of its pleasant words and clear language.

(5) *Galut yehudah*[z]—*The Exile of Judah*—translations of words from throughout the Bible into Italian, accompanied by some grammatical rules. It sells now for ten lire a copy, while originally it had been valued at three lire, because not even one copy of it is left.

(6) *Lev ha-aryeh*[a]—*Heart of the Lion*—on "place" memorization. No one to this day has written a book on that subject. It was printed in that same year.

(7) *Beit lehem yehudah*—*Bethlehem in Judah*[17]—an index to the sayings in the book *'E[in] y[israel]*[b] [5]385 [1625].

---

[14] Genesis 8:22.

[15] The acrostic occurs in the initial consonants, *y-h-v-d-h* = Yehudah (Judah).

[16] As at the previous note, the acrostic occurs in the initial consonants.

[17] Updating the list of his writings begun in the wake of Zebulun's murder in 1622,

(8) An[18] abridgment of Abravanel on the Haggadah, entitled *Tzeli esh—Roasted in Fire*—5389 [1628/1629].[c]

[C 75] (9) *Tefillot le-khol yemei ha-shavua' ve-'al kol tzarah she-lo tavo—Prayers for Every Day of the Week and for Every Trouble, May it not Come*—very beautiful. Printed in a very small volume and therefore not sold.[d]

(10) *Tzori la-nefesh[e]—Balm for the Soul*—a confessional for a person on his deathbed.[19]

(11) *Beit yehudah[f]—House of Judah*—additional sayings from the Gemara not included in '*E[in] y[israel]*.

(12) *Sefer riti[g]*—The *Riti*—printed in Paris.

(13) *Pi aryeh[h]—The Mouth of the Lion*—a supplement to *G[alut] y[ehudah]*.[20]

(14) Poems and Prefaces:[21i]

    a. in the book *Torat ha-adam;*[j]

    b. in *Sefer ha-hinnukh;*[k]

    c. entreaties for the dead, printed in *Tzidduk ha-din* and in the book *Yihus ha-tzaddikim;*[l]

    d. in *Shomerim la-boker* for the day preceding the new moon;[m]

    e. in *Kohelet ya'akov*[n] by the sage Barukh;

    f. in *Divrei shalom;*[o]

Modena added the title of this book, printed in 1625, above the line and marked it by using a caret.

[18] This title and the next five [items 9–13] were added by Modena in the margin as he updated his list of writings after 1622.

[19] The writing in the margin of the manuscript is tiny and has been crossed out (see fig. 6). The first word after the title is *viddui*, "confessional." The next is *l-sh-m*, the abbreviation for *li-shekhiv mera'*, literally, "for someone dangerously ill." The book, which was published in 1619 (see historical note e), also appears in the original "bibliography" among works containing poems or prefaces by Modena (see item 14j). Its repetition in the margin, just a few lines below its occurrence in the body of the text (see fig. 6), poses something of a mystery. Possibly Modena, on rereading and updating this page in the autobiography, realized that he had omitted *Tzori la-nefesh* from his original list of authored works and decided to restore it to its rightful place by adding it in the margin as close as he could to the section listing books completed by 1622. Later, then, someone who could not explain the duplication to himself crossed out the reference in the margin.

[20] The abbreviation *g-y* in the manuscript stands for *Galut yehudah*. The title of the book is written out in full below the letters *g-y* in another hand.

[21] The word "prefaces" (*hakdamot*) was added by Modena above the line and marked by a caret, presumably when he came to the first item (*Kaf nahat*) containing a preface by him rather than a poem.

g. in *Keter shem* [C 76] *tov*[p], in the name of Disus;

h. in the Large Ashkenazic Mahzor;[q]

i. in the small edition of the Mishnah with commentary called *Kaf nahat*;[r]

j. in *Tzori la-nefesh*,[s] a confessional written for the G[emilut] H[asadim] Society (Society for Good Deeds);

k. in *Imrei shefer*,[t] the sermons of the sage Naftali;

l. in *Ma'amadot*[u] with commentary;

m. in the Passover Haggadah with illustrations and complete translation;[v]

n. in the new edition of the *Mikra gedolah*[w]—Large Bible;

o. in *Sefer ha-levushim*;[x]

p. in *Yefeh 'einayim*;[22][y]

q. in *'Etz shatul*,[z] a commentary on *Sefer ha-'ikkarim*;

r. in the *Songs of Solomon* Rossi[a] of Mantua;

s. *Belil hamitz*,[b] for the *haver* Joseph Hamitz the physician, my student, may God his Rock protect him and grant him long life;

t. in *Sefer yeri'ot 'izzim*; [C 77] and many, many more that I cannot remember.[c]

(15) Among the vernacular ones:

a. in the book *Tevat noah*[d] by Don Marco Marini, one very beautiful poem of mine, composed when I was fifteen years old, was printed;

b. in the collection of rhymes praising Doge Grimani;[e]

c. in the book *Ester* by H. Rieti;[f]

d. in *Barekhi nafshi* by the same author;[g]

e. in a book of rhymes in honor of the Fabbri wedding in Bologna;[h]

f. in the *Pastorale trionfi*[i] by Y. Alatini of blessed memory;

g. The tragedy of *Ester*,[j] in its entirety; and in many other works like these.[k]

Some works that are in my possession have not been printed; of these some are complete and others have not been completed, such as:

[22] Updating the list, Modena squeezed in this item (printed in 1631) at the end of a line in the left margin. The color of its ink is black and contrasts with the poorer ink used in the body of the text at this point, which has turned reddish brown.

(16)[1]

    a. *Ha-avot liyhudah*[m]—*The Fathers According to Judah*—a commentary on Tractate *Avot*;

    b. a commentary of the five Megillot;

    c. a commentary on Proverbs;[n]

    d. a commentary on the Haggadah;[o]

    e. a commentary on Psalms;

    f. a commentary on Samuel;[p]

    g. *Beit yehudah*[q]—additional sayings from the Gemara omitted by the author of *'Ein yisrael*.[23]

(17) Books completed:[r]

[MS 20b/ רב]

    a. a book that teaches how to write [C 78] letters[s] in the Holy Tongue [Hebrew];

    b. a commentary on the Haftarot and on their connections with the weekly Torah portion;

    c. The Book of the Wisdom [of Solomon], Ecclesiasticus, Hasmoneans, and others,[t] translated into the Holy Tongue;

    d. *Shirei yehudah*[u]—*The Poems of Judah*—a collection of my poems;

    e. a collection of my legal rulings; I entitled it *Ziknei yehudah*[24v]—*The Elders of Judah*;

    f. There is no end to my sermons and commentaries on the entire Torah, scattered here and there;

    g. *Sha'agat aryeh*[w]—*The Roar of the Lion*—an answer to a certain book against the Oral Law;

and many others, besides:

    h. *Meshal ha-kadmoni*[x] in Italian, newly cast;

    i. *The Pastoral of Rachel and Jacob;*[y]

and many rhymes of mine, to which, if God decrees life for me, I shall add others, even though my hands have be-

---

[23] After *Beit yehudah* appeared in print in 1635, Modena added the title above in the margin, next to the list of books already published when he began to compile his "bibliography" in 1622. See also item 11.

[24] The second phrase, giving the title, was added above the line by Modena later on and marked by a caret. Its color is black and contrasts with the reddish brown color of the ink used for the text. The interpolation was possibly made in 1630, when, at the age of sixty, Modena collected his responsa together. See historical note v.

come weak following my son's death, because for whom do I toil?[25]

In[1] Tammuz 5382 [June–July 1622], because my wife and I were still extremely sad and upset over the murder [of our son], may God avenge his blood, I brought my daughter Diana, may she be blessed above all women of the house, and my son-in-law, the *haver* Jacob Levi, and their young son Isaac, may God his Rock protect him and grant him long life, to live with me in part of my house in the Ghetto Nuovo. [The house] belonged to Rabbi M. Merari,[2] may God his Rock protect him and grant him long life, and I had moved there in Kislev [5]379 [November–December 1618]. Their company relieved me a little of my anxieties.

In Iyyar 5383 [May 1623] I went to Mantua[a] to escort Diana Copio, who married one [C 79] of the Massarano sons.[b] Being fearful of bandits,[c] we were escorted by thirty-six harquebus bearers. We encountered fifty Corsican mercenaries, who took us to be bandits, as we did them. Without speaking both sides began to load and draw their harquebuses. We were at the time between Sanguinetto and Castel d'Ario,[2d] and the women and some of the men, I among them, fled into hiding, until finally they recognized one another and greeted one another in peace. We then proceeded together to Castel d'Ario, where we dined with rejoicing and with happy hearts. From there we proceeded to Mantua, where I wrote the story of this incident in very beautiful Italian terza rima.[3e]

I preached there downstairs in the Great Synagogue[4f] before a large audience, to the glory of the King of the king of kings.[5] Many Christian friars were also there, and my words were pleasing to those who heard them.

In 5384 and 5385 [autumn 1623–autumn 1625] nothing of note

---

[25] Ecclesiastes 4:8.

[1] A switch at this point in the text to a better ink, which has retained its original black color; an enlarged letter *t* in the first word, "Tammuz"; and a space all seem to indicate the passage of time since the writing of the previous section.

[2] Modena's Hebrew transliteration reflects alternate names for these towns (Sanguine and Castellara), which I have found on seventeenth- and eighteenth-century maps of the Duchy of Mantua.

[3] Hebrew "melitzah shelishiyyah notzrit."

[4] Manuscript reads *mi-tahat le-b-h-k-g* (= "le-veit ha-keneset ha-gadol"), though the *m* of *mi-tahat* is not clearly written. Modena preached downstairs in a small study room. The main sanctuary was on the top floor.

[5] Adaptation of and play on Proverbs 14:28.

befell me, for the world went on as usual. God, may he be blessed daily, did not desert me, and I was able to survive with just two Jewish students[g] and a few Christian ones.[h]

At the beginning of 5386 during Sukkot [October 14–21, 1625], the sage Rabbi I[saac] Gershon,[i] may God his Rock protect him and grant him long life, decided [C 80] to go to the Holy Land. The task of preaching on alternate Sabbaths in the Great Synagogue, may God its Rock protect it and grant it long life, was therefore handed over to me and to my son-in-law, the *haver* J[acob] L[evi], may God his Rock protect him and grant him long life. From that time on, I have always preached twice each Sabbath, either in that synagogue or in that of the Sephardim,[j] as well as every morning, in addition to teaching the Haftarah in the Italian synagogue[k] and the weekly lesson on a steady basis. Blessed is he who gives strength to the weary and who increases the power of those without strength.

In Kislev [5]386 [November–December 1625], a son of my daughter Diana, may she be blessed above all women of the house, died of smallpox.[6] His name was David. He was fourteen months old and had been my daily delight. My sorrow was so great that I left the lodgings I was in and went to live nearby in a place belonging to Meir Cigala, may God his Rock protect him and grant him long life. That dwelling was more spacious for me.[l]

[MS 21a/לה] On Monday morning,[m] the 18th of Kislev 5386 [December 17, 1625], while I was hurrying from the Rialto to San[7] Cassian, I came to a certain path that led to Campo San Cassian.[n] I wanted to enter it, but thought I would shorten the distance by taking a different path. Just as I had backed up about three steps, a strong gust of wind blew down a chimney—that is, a *camin*[8]—on the very path I had originally intended to take, at exactly the spot from which I had taken those three steps backward. Had I entered that path it would have fallen on my head and wounded me mortally. Blessed is he who redeems and saves.

During that winter I lost so much money playing games of

---

[6] See fol. 7a, note 24.   [7] See fol. 15a, note 8.

[8] Italian in Hebrew letters, so spelled (rather than *camino* as generally in Italian), reflecting the dropping of the final vowel in the Venetian dialect. Similarly, immediately above, Cassian instead of Cassiano.

chance that I was compelled at Passover time to take a loan of 152 ducats from the members of the Ashkenazic Torah Study Society,[9] may God their Rock protect them and grant them long life, to be deducted six ducats a month from my salary, in order to pay my debts. I vowed not to play games of chance until the money was fully deducted, which would take twenty-five months.[o] Today a year has gone by without income and without [C 81] students and earnings.[p] I do not know how I shall find flock to graze or how I shall find some teaching,[10] or whence will come my help, if not from God in heaven.[11]

On the eve of Passover [5]387[12] [March 31, 1627], my brother-in-law and cousin,[13] Johanan Simhah of blessed memory, my wife's brother, passed away. My heart was truly grieved, for he had been like a brother to me, and now I was left alone without relatives or sons. For even my son Isaac, may God his Rock protect him and grant him long life, wanted never to return home, notwithstanding my many pleas to him after the death of Zebulun, may God avenge his blood, to come and comfort me, a thing he refused to do. Instead, he wanders in exile from city to city, and the reports I hear of him are not good.[14] O God, how long will you continue to oppress and afflict me?

Between Rosh Hashanah and Yom Kippur [September 13–19, 1627] I received the good news that my son Isaac, may God his Rock protect him and grant him long life, had arrived at the Lazzaretto[q] from Izmir,[r] and after Sukkot [ended October 3, 1627] he came home. My heart and that of my wife, may she be blessed above all women of the house, rejoiced, for I thought that he would bring me comfort in my troubles. He stayed here until after Shavuot 5388 [ended June 8, 1628], but then a different spirit began to move him[15] to return to the Levant. Although I strongly implored

---

[9] Manuscript has the abbreviation *t-t-'-y*. The first three letters stand for "talmud torah ashkenazi"; the *y* is an abbreviation for the blessing "may God . . . long life."

[10] Cf. Ezekiel 34:15, where the prophet quotes God as saying: "ani er'eh tzoni va-'ani arbitzem" (I shall graze my flock and I shall let them lie down). Modena adopted this imagery for his own teaching of young students (see, for example, Yacob Boksenboim, ed., *Iggerot rabbi yehudah aryeh mi-modena* [Tel Aviv, 1984], no. 21), cleverly playing on the word *arbitz*, "I shall lie down," which in the rabbinic idiom *le-harbitz torah* means "to teach Torah."

[11] Psalm 121:1–2.   [12] So in the manuscript; cf. Carpi edition, p. 81 line 3.

[13] The term used for cousin is *ah sheni*, "second brother."

[14] 1 Samuel 2:24.   [15] Adaptation of Judges 13:25.

and entreated him not to leave me, he would not listen. In the week that the Torah portion beginning "Send thou [men]"[16] was read [June 17–24, 1628], he went to Izmir, where he still remains. It is punishment for my sins and transgressions that of my three sons one died, one was murdered, and one lives in exile.

In Kislev 5389 [November–December 1628] I married off the daughter of my brother-in-law Samson Levi of Ancona—her mother is my wife's sister Simhah and her name is Esther—to Ephraim Ostiglia, may God his Rock protect him and grant him long life. My wife and I assumed the burden of raising about 450 ducats for her. I arranged that she should have ninety ducats from the estate of my brother-in-law Johanan of blessed memory and assembled the rest from friends, benefactors,[s] and my own pocket. May God remember this for my benefit.

[MS 21b/ יב] When the Torah portions Tazria and Metzora were read in 5389 [April 28, 1629][17] I preached in the synagogue of the Sephardim, may God their Rock protect them and grant them long life. In attendance were the brother of the king of France,[t] who was accompanied by some French noblemen and by five [C 82] of the most important Christian preachers who gave sermons that Pentecost.[18] God put such learned words[19] into my mouth that all were very pleased, including many other Christians who were present. All the congregations gave great praise and thanks. There had never been anything like it during my thirty-seven continuous years in this work of God. People wrote to distant places all over Italy about how unique it was. Both before and afterward, noblemen and other great men came to hear my sermons, notably Duke Candale and Duke Rohan,[u] among others. May God be praised by all for imparting the grace to his servant to hallow his name in public before gentiles.[20] May it not become [a source of] pride and haughtiness for me.

---

[16] Numbers 13:2, at the beginning of the Torah portion Shelah [Numbers 13:1–15:41], which was read in 5388 during the week ending on Saturday the 23rd of Sivan (June 24, 1628).

[17] Leviticus 12:1–13:59 combined with 14:1–15:33. Read in 5389 on the Sabbath, the 5th of Iyyar (April 28, 1629).

[18] Hebrew: 'atzeret, in the Talmud a name for the Jewish holiday of Shavuot, which is celebrated fifty days (seven weeks) after the beginning of Passover. Here it designates the Christian festival of Pentecost, which occurs on the seventh Sunday after Easter.

[19] Isaiah 50:4.   [20] Adaptation of Ezekiel 39:27.

Oh that my head were waters and my eyes a fountain of tears, that I might weep,[21] lament, and curse the day I was born to see toil and anger.[22] Each day is ever more accursed [than the one before]. Job said,[v] "I had neither peace nor quiet nor rest, but disquiet came";[23] to which I can add, "Disquiet came and difficulty and additional distress. My days may end, but my difficulties will not."

A son-in-law of perfect virtues[24] to me was Rabbi Jacob, son of Kalonymos Halevi, may their memory be blessed. Like a pomegranate he was full of wisdom in Torah, in Kabbalah,[w] and in secular subjects. He was a God-fearing preacher and pious, more modest than all others, beloved in heaven and pleasing to those on earth. He loved my daughter, his wife, like himself and honored her more than himself.[25] He was happy with his lot in life and saw good in all his toil. His profession was dancing, and his knowledge of Torah and his deeds were without blemish. His penmanship was excellent, and he used clear language when he wrote. I cannot sufficiently praise him. He used to comfort me in my sorrow over my losses, namely, the sons who left me and who are no longer here. He restored my soul.

The day after Shavuot [May 30, 1629], he took to his bed, and on the night of the arrival of Thursday, the beginning of the month of Tammuz [5]389 [June 21, 1629], he passed away. There was no one here, humble or great, who did not weep over him, for without a doubt he left behind no one like him in these congregations. The departure from this place of such a saintly person made an impression, for during that summer about sixty people died[x] in our holy community, may God their Rock protect it and grant it long life, and of these more than twenty were noted for their learning, honesty, and wealth. They were all heads of their families and, for the most part, more excellent than those who survived. But this was of no significance to me, as they say, "For sorrow shared with others is no comfort to me,"[1] but rather adds to my hurt and pain.

---

[21] Jeremiah 8:23.   [22] Psalm 10:14.   [23] Job 3:26.

[24] The phrase "hatan tamim le-ma'alot" is meant to echo the phrase "hatan damim la-mulot" (a bridegroom of blood because of the circumcision), which Moses' wife Zipporah uttered after circumcising their son (Exodus 4:26). Regarding the error in the Kahana edition see the preface.

[25] An undecipherable word has been crossed out in the manuscript, for which *mi-gufo*, "than himself," was substituted.

[1] Here Modena reversed the rabbinic folk-saying, "tzarat rabbim hatzi nehamah" (sorrow shared is sorrow halved [literally, half comfort]).

He was survived by the boy Isaac, may God his Rock protect him and grant him long life, then eight years of age, and by my daughter, his wife, then seven months pregnant. They came to live in my house and within my walls,[2] and the eyes of all of us overflowed with tears all day.

On the night of the arrival of Friday the . . .[3] of Elul of that year [5389: August–September, 1629], my daughter gave birth to a girl, and we turned her over [C 83] to a wet nurse at great expense.[4] She named her Richina, may she be blessed above all women in the house. May God, the Father of orphans and the Judge of widows, have compassion upon her and her brother and mother. She died afterward at the age of ten[5] months.[y]

All through that summer I was ill with pains in my stomach.[z] The boy Isaac, may God his Rock protect him and grant him long life, took ill, too, and was on the point of death. But I cried out to God, who heard my cry and miraculously cured him. May it be his will to give me the ability to raise him to know the Torah and to fear God, as a father would wish to do for his own son.

[MS 22a/ לב]In the month of Av 5389 [July–August 1629], Esther, the daughter of my brother-in-law Samson Levi of blessed memory, passed away. She is the one I had worked hard to marry off to Ephraim Ostiglia, may God his Rock protect him and grant him long life. Two days later, her mother, my wife's sister Simhah, died, may she be blessed above all women. Amen. Blessed are you, O Lord, the true Judge, who decided to visit my sins upon me and my sons and my relatives, as well as upon all my admirers, so that I should never rejoice in anything I do. You are righteous, O Lord, and your decrees are just.

In Adar 5390[6] [February 1630], I quarreled with the members of the Small Committee,[a] the [Jewish] heads and leaders of the city,

---

[2] Isaiah 56:5.

[3] Modena did not remember the exact day of the month, so he left a lacuna of two dots in the manuscript. Elul 5389 began on Monday, August 20, 1629.

[4] A passage of perhaps ten words has been thoroughly crossed out at this point, making it undecipherable.

[5] When updating his journal, Modena added this sentence later in the space remaining on the same line in which he asked God to "have compassion upon her, etc." The letter representing the number of months looks like a v (= 6). But because Richina's death is reported on the next page of the manuscript as Tammuz [June–July] 1630, the letter is probably an elongated y (= 10).

[6] Modena first erroneously wrote sh-p-t ([5]389), then rubbed it out (leaving visible traces) and substituted the correct date h-sh-tz (5390).

LEON MODENA

over a decision they had made two years earlier to forbid, under penalty of ban and excommunication, certain types of games of chance.[b] Not in order to praise games of chance, but rather to show that they lacked the authority to ban such a thing and thereby cause many to stumble into transgression, I composed a nice and forceful legal decision,[c] had it printed with lead type,[7] and sent it throughout the dispersed communities of Israel.

Back in Kislev 5390 [November-December 1629], my son Isaac, may God his Rock protect him and grant him long life, had arrived in Livorno, where he had stayed about seven months without even wanting to come to see me here in Venice. May God forgive him.

In Sivan [May–June 1630] I went to Modena[d] with my student, the young Barukh Luzzatto,[e] may God his Rock protect him and grant him long life, [C 84] to arrange his marriage to the daughter of Simhah Sanguini,[f] may God his Rock protect him and grant him long life. We went there and back with great difficulty in three weeks' time, because the passes were being closed one after another on account of the plague that was then beginning to spread throughout Italy. When we reached the Grand Canal there was a storm in which we almost perished.[8]

In Tammuz [June–July 1630], the little girl Richina,[g] the daughter of my daughter Diana, passed away.

[5]391 [1630/1631].[9] From that time on the pestilence began to spread all over. The hand of God weighed heavily on the Jews throughout Italy, bringing war, famine, and plague. The sorrows that befell the holy community of Mantua[h] had not been felt since the time of the destruction of the Temple, and the holy community of Modena was almost destroyed by the pestilence. Then it reached Venice, and after it began in the Ghetto Vecchio with Moses Tzarfati of blessed memory, during the Days of Repentance [September 7–16, 1630]; and during Sukkot [September 21–29, 1630] with Jacob Cohen, known as Scocco,[i] it spread further, until by today, the beginning of the month of Second Adar 5391 [March 5, 1631],

[7] Cf. Job 19:24.
[8] This sentence is squeezed into the margin.
[9] The year [5]391 (began September 7, 1630), during which the devastating plague of 1630–1631 raged, is written in the margin. The beginning of a new section is indicated by a line separating it from the notices for the year 5390. Modena recorded his description of the plague contemporaneously.

134

about 170 people[j] have died. There has been great panic in the various congregations, and many, especially the Sephardim, have left the city for the Levant or for Verona.[k]

Seven hundred and fifty bales worth much money were sent to the Lazzaretto, and almost all of them were destroyed or lost. For approximately a year Jews have been forbidden to buy and sell or engage in business negotiations; hence there has been no earning. The government also took more than 120,000 ducats[l] from the Jews. An unprecedented rise in prices has been the worst blow of all, causing many Jews in these communities to become impoverished,[10] the rich becoming middling and the middling poor, and no one taking pity any longer on the poor, for there is no money.[m] [C 85]

And I, in my poverty, not only have I had my widowed daughter Diana and her son, may God his Rock protect him and grant him long life, in my house for the past two years, but my daughter Sterella, may she be blessed above all women of the house, whose husband has not been able to return home for a full year,[n] has also become my financial responsibility. Indeed, all of them are my responsibility in these strange times. But despite all this, God in his mercy and truth[11] has not ceased to deal wondrously with me,[12] and this year I have spent more [MS 22b/ נ״ב] than five hundred ducats between household necessities and repayment of debts without having to resort to donations from anybody. I earned these [ducats] by using my pen, my tongue, and my wits, and God in his great kindness had mercy.

Indeed, he has continuously protected me, for his hand has struck all the surrounding dwellings, and even the [apartments on the] staircase where I live. Above and below me and on all sides, left and right, people have taken ill and died from the plague. But to this day God has not allowed the agent of destruction to enter my apartment to cause affliction. May he not abandon or desert me or the members of my household. Amen.

Between the beginning of the month of Second Adar [began March 5, 1631] and the 11th of Sivan [June 12, 1631], even though the pestilence had increased in severity in every quarter of the city, God made a wondrous division between their camp and the camp

---

[10] Judges 6:6.   [11] Cf. Genesis 24:27.   [12] Cf. Joel 2:26.

of Israel, and nobody became ill or died in the two ghettos. The gentiles were astonished at this wondrous thing.[o] Only we Jews did not appreciate the miracle wrought for us, and people in our communities continued to do evil in the sight of God by quarreling, slandering, stealing, cursing, lying, and swearing falsely. Thus God's anger was kindled[p] against his people, and [they] began to be afflicted [by the plague] on the 11th of Sivan. He did not relent and heal them, however, and once again, many people began to die[q] in both ghettos. Nonetheless, the death toll among the Jews never reached the rate of mortality in the rest of the city. It was not so in the communities of Verona and Padua,[r] for God's hand struck them, and less than one-third survived. No one escaped, for there was not a house without its dead. May the Merciful One have pity on his creatures.

Throughout this time my son Isaac, may God his Rock protect him and grant him long life, was in Livorno. When he did decide to come to visit me, he was unable to do so, for all passes leading from the cities were closed because of the pestilence. Finally, he set out again by sea, in order later to return. Even if he tarries I will wait for him.[13] May God return him in safety.

Regarding the stars and constellations that God placed in the heavens to rule over those below and guide them, acting as secondary causes, I always thought that no one could escape their power and that nothing was hidden from their wrath.[14] Even though they are not totally determinative, they have a strong tendency to compel action. Thus, they forced me all my life to persist in the folly of playing games of chance, even though inside I knew well its faults and evil. [C 86] When I was just a twelve-year-old child, I exposed its evil in public in the essay *Sur mera*[s]—*Turn from Evil*—which was printed in [5]356 [1595/1596] here in Venice and was reprinted in Prague in [5]375[15] [1614/1615] because of its sweet language. Had it [playing games of chance] not stunned me and thrown me to the ground so many times I would have been content all my life with my lot, happy that God has granted me the knowledge and

[13] A pious wish used in connection with the Messiah. [14] Adaptation of Psalm 19:7.

[15] Manuscript reads *sh-ʿ-h* (= [5]375), which is indeed the year the Prague edition was published. Cf. Carpi edition, p. 86 line 2.

wisdom to please not only the far-flung exile of Judah[16] but also noblemen and benefactors who are not of our people, even now, near the end [of my life], at sixty years of age and at the height of the plague and other troubles mentioned before.

On the 17th of Tammuz [5]391 [July 17, 1631], the date that commemorates five things[t] that befell the Jews because they were evil and sinful, the spirit of foolishness seized me and I resumed playing games of chance. From then until Kislev 5392 [November–December 1631] I lost more than five hundred ducats, most of them owed to people who had lent them to me. My expenses because of high prices added weight to my lament.

[MS 23a/כב] As mentioned before, the plague continued in the city and among the Jews through Heshvan 5392 [November 1631]. Then God in his great mercy took pity, and the bitterness of death turned away.[17u] There was great celebration in the city, and everyone gave thanks to his God.[18v] In addition, a fast was decreed in all the holy congregations for the eve [Tuesday evening, November 25, 1631] of the new moon of Kislev, with a prayer service for the new moon during the day [Wednesday, November 26], including [the prayer] "Nishmat Kol Hai"[w] and with the pleasant sound of joyfulness. A collection was taken up in every synagogue, which will be used to make a silver object to commemorate the deliverance.[x] Blessed is he who redeems and saves, blessed is he and blessed is his name.

In the month of Kislev 5392 [November–December 1631], I arranged for the marriage of my daughter Diana, may she be blessed above all women, amen, the widow of Rabbi Jacob the son of Kalonymos Halevi, may their memory be blessed, to the *haver* Moses Fano, commonly known as Saltaro, may God his Rock protect him and grant him long life, the son of the erudite Rabbi Judah of blessed memory and of my cousin Fulvia, the daughter of my uncle Rabbi Abtalion Modena of blessed memory. He [Moses] lived in Padua. In the aforementioned plague, his mother, his two daughters, his wife, and his brother had died. During Purim of [5]392

---

[16] I.e., the Jewish people. Note the author's choice of an expression that contains his own name.
[17] I Samuel 15:32.   [18] Adaptation of Jonah 1:5.

7. Gravestone marking the mass grave of Jewish ("Hebrei") victims
of the plague of 1630–1631.

[March 8, 1632], along with my wife, my daughter Esther, and her husband, may God his Rock protect him and grant him long life, I was there in Padua, where the wedding took place joyously. May it be your will that they have a long life together and see sons, and may God's work succeed in their hands. And may my wife and I see this, too. Amen.

Young Isaac, the son of my aforementioned daughter, stayed to live with me. May God grant me the ability to raise him to worship God and to teach him books and wisdom, in which he has already shown promise, until he achieves marriage and success in our lifetime.

Following the wedding of my aforementioned daughter, nothing worth noting happened to me, because until the beginning of the month of Iyyar 5393 [began April 11, 1633] [C 87] all I did was play games of chance, for better or worse.

In Adar 5393 [February–March 1633] my daughter Diana gave birth to a girl. She named her Angelitta after her brother,[y] my son Mordecai of blessed memory, for she had loved him deeply.

Throughout the plague my son Isaac, may God his Rock protect him and grant him long life, was living in Livorno, until finally he agreed to return home at my request and arrived here in the month of Tevet 5394 [December 1633], physically, though not financially, sound. He was like a spoiled child, living with his father.

From the beginning of the month of Iyyar 5393 [began April 11, 1633] until Passover 5394 [began April 12, 1634], I had peace and rest,[z] because I refrained from playing games of chance. God was with me and caused me to make a good living. I also completed and put in order many of my writings. I would have found some satisfaction in this had not old age suddenly overcome me and my wife,[a] may she be blessed above all women of the house. She and I are both in steadily declining health and there is no health in our bones.[19] Each day and night bring indications that our end is near.[20] My sorrow is doubled, for she is truly my other half. If, God forbid, she should die before me, I shall die twice. On the other hand, if I should die before her I shall die only once.[21] Our lives and the length of our days are in the hands of our Creator, who will do what is good in his eyes.

[19] Cf. Psalm 38:4.   [20] Adaptation of Psalm 19:3.   [21] Adaptation of Genesis 46:30.

In Adar 5394 [February 1634] I began to print my book *Beit ye-hudah*,[22] a supplement to *'E[in] y[israel]*[23] All my wishes were centered on it. May it be God's will that I be granted to see it through to completion, for it is my entire salvation and desire.

[MS 23b/ מ] In Tammuz 5394 [June–July 1634] my son Isaac, may God his Rock protect him and grant him long life, married Sarah, may she be blessed above all women of the house, the daughter of Joseph Finzi of blessed memory. She had been divorced from her previous husband, not, God forbid, on account of any reproachable act, but because the marriage was not working out on account of her husband, not on account of her. He [Isaac] moved into his own lodgings because my dwelling was too small to hold all of us. May he have children, enjoy long life, and may God's work succeed in his hands.

From the month of Av [5]394 [July–August 1634] until the beginning of the month of Adar [5]395 [began February 19, 1635], God blessed the work of my hands, and I accumulated a bit more money than I had ever had since being on my feet.[24] But the constellations caused me to act foolishly, and in the months of Av and Elul 5394 [July–September 1634] I lost about two hundred ducats playing at games of chance, and later on, during the months of Heshvan, Kislev, Tevet, and Shevat [5]395 [October 23, 1634–February 18, 1635], about another four hundred, so that I ended up shorn of everything. From the beginning of the month of Adar 5395 [began February 19, 1635] to the present I have desisted from that vice. Through God's kindness that does not cease[25] to provide me with what I need, [C 88] I would have lacked nothing were it not for the fact that old age is overcoming me and my wife, and we are not healthy but, rather,[1] weak and sad.

Previously I mentioned the start of the printing of my book *Beit yehudah*, a supplement to the sayings contained in the book *'E[in]*

---

[22] Modena's introduction to the book is, in fact, dated Adar 5394.

[23] See Modena's own list of writings, fol. 20a, items 11 and 16g, with notes.

[24] The expression *'al 'omdi*, "on my feet," apparently carries an allusion to Daniel 8:18, in which Daniel is placed back on his feet by the angel Gabriel after having fallen to the ground on his face. Elsewhere, Modena uses the imagery of being thrown to the ground to describe his addiction to games of chance (see fol. 22b). "Being back on my feet" seems to mean refraining from games of chance and engaging in constructive forms of employment.

[25] Adaptation of Lamentations 3:22.   [1] Play on Psalm 73:4.

y[israel]. Never in my entire life had I so desired anything as to see it printed and distributed and disseminated among the dispersion of Israel, for I was certain that from it I would earn merit and honor and an everlasting reputation, which would never be lost. I began to have it printed in Adar 5394 [February 1634], as mentioned before. Many impediments intertwined[2] concerning it, however, and the matter dragged on until Heshvan 5395[3] [October–November 1634]. Before that, in Elul [5]394 [August–September 1634], some scoundrels from among our own people had informed the Cattaver about the printing,[b] and it closed down the print shop. It remained tightly sealed off[4] for about six months. Then it was reopened, and they [the printers] returned to their work and to printing my aforementioned book, which was almost entirely done by my grandson Isaac min Haleviim, may God his Rock protect him and grant him long life. I had introduced him to that craft about two years earlier so that he would learn to derive benefit from working with his hands in a clean and easy craft[5] and, at the same time, not desist from his studies.

On Wednesday the 28th of Iyyar 5395 [May 16, 1635], police suddenly entered the print shop and arrested my grandson Isaac along with two of his young friends; they put them in prison, in darkness,[6] and sealed off the print shop once again. I was very distressed when, despite great efforts at intercession, I was unable to conclude the matter and set him free. With difficulty, after fifteen days, they allowed him to leave the darkness [C 89] for light,[c] though still in prison, and he remained there for a total of sixty-six days.[d] I went back and forth every day, with labor and effort and great expense, until God in his great kindness had mercy, and by decree of the Quarantia Criminal,[7c] he was released without fine on Friday the 28th of Tammuz 5395 [July 13, 1635].[8]

During the month of Av 5395 [July–August 1635] I became ill

---

[2] Lamentations 1:14.

[3] The date of Heshvan 5395 is problematic because the printing took until Rosh Hashanah of 5396 (September 13, 1635) to complete (see below); presumably this date constitutes a slip of the pen on the part of the author.

[4] Job 41:7.   [5] Mishnah Kiddushin 4:14.   [6] Isaiah 42:7.

[7] Written in Hebrew letters and reflecting the dropping of the final vowel in the Venetian dialect.

[8] The 28th of Tammuz fell on the Sabbath, beginning Friday night, July 13. Possibly Isaac was released on Friday night.

with shortness of breath and stomach pains and was confined to my sickbed for about twenty days. My son-in-law and daughter, may God their Rock protect them and grant them long life, came from Padua to visit me. Afterward God relented and cured me, though I still continued to experience shortness of breath.

[MS 24a/ מא]   In Adar 5396 [February–March 1636], my daughter Diana, may she be blessed above all women of the house, gave birth to a son under an auspicious star. My wife, may she be blessed among women—amen—and I went to Padua to bring him into and establish him in the Covenant, and he was circumcised by the learned physician, Rabbi David Hayyim Luria,ᶠ may God his Rock protect him and grant him long life. His father named him Abtalion Hai,⁹ may God his Rock protect him and grant him long life, after his grandfather and my uncle, the gaon Rabbi Abtalion of blessed memory. May it be God's will that he become like him in Torah, wisdom, and longevity. Amen.

By that Rosh Hashanah [September 13, 1635]¹⁰ I had completed the printing of the book *Beit yehudah.* I paid for all the expensesᵍ of printing, which were approximately 250 ducats, totally on my own and without a loan from anyone, from the income that God had granted me from proofreading other printed books and from what I earned from the sale of those books in Venice, Ferrara, and some other territories in Italy. I also sent some of them to the Levant, Germany, and Flanders, where some are being sold daily.

After my son Isaac got married, he showed himself capable of turning away from evil, if not of doing good, for about a year. Then, in the month of Av [5]396 [August–September 1636], I became ill with the same stomach and breathing symptoms I had had in [5]395 [1635]. They had let up a little during the cold weather, but when it became hot again they bothered me greatly. At that time my aforementioned son Isaac was discovered to be playing games of chance and treading [C 90] a bad path. Up to the present it has been about eighteen months. He does not visit me or talk to

⁹ The word "Hai" (living) was added above the line in ink of a higher quality, which has retained its original black color and contrasts with the poorer ink—now turned reddish brown—used by Modena when first writing this section.
¹⁰ The first edition of *Beit yehudah* bears the date 5395, reflecting the fact that the type was set before the start of the Jewish New Year (5396).

me, nor I to him, for I have borne reproach[11] because of him. May God, who has shown me no joy, but only sorrow and grief, from the three sons I have had, be praised. From the three of them I have had nothing but sorrow and grief. But as the students whom I have nurtured and raised up to be Torah scholars and teachers in Israel are called sons, they give me comfort.

During the winter months of 5396 [1635/1636] I also taught Italian and other things to an honored nobleman, lord M. Lodovico [Louis] Iselin, a Frenchman close to the king. He admired me greatly, and I earned about one hundred ducats from him. He left me his likeness and image, namely, his portrait[12] as a token of his affection and wanted to have a likeness of me made by the skilled and well-known painter Cavalier Tiberio Tinelli.[h] But Tinelli died when the portrait was just about completed, and it was lost. Everyone said that it was worth its weight in gold.[13]

That winter I devoted my energies to teaching and to matters of the yeshiva,[i] and also wrote an essay refuting the doctrine of transmigration of souls. I called it *Ben david* [j]—*The Son of David*—because I composed it at the request of David Finzi, who lived in Egypt,[k] so that he would be comforted by it after the death of his dearly beloved nine-year-old son.[l] I sent it to him, along with some small books and a small, square portrait of me as a remembrance. Subsequently I sent him twenty copies of my book *Beit yehudah*, but in three years I have received neither a letter nor anything else from him in return.

[MS 24b/ מב] On Purim of 5396 [March 21, 1636], the entire community turned from joy to mourning when trouble began[m] for the community as a whole, for some individuals in particular, and for myself. Indeed, I have always had my share of troubles, whether they be those of individuals or of the community, in addition to my personal ones.[14]

It was because the crime of Grassin[15] Scaramella and Sabbadin Catelano[n] was discovered. They had received [C 91] goods and

---

[11] Cf. Psalm 69:8.   [12] Italian word *ritratto*, written in Hebrew letters.

[13] Modena squeezed this sentence in later on, below the final line of this passage.

[14] The translation of this paragraph represents an attempt to convey the meaning of a rather difficult Hebrew passage without doing excessive violence to the original.

[15] Known in Hebrew as Gershon. See historical note.

cash—silk, silk clothing, and gold—worth seventy thousand ducats, stolen by some Christians in the Merceria[16] from the merchant
Bergonzi, and had put them in a room in one of the houses in the
ghetto.[o] A worthless scoundrel named Isaac the son of Jacob Se-
nigo, may his name be blotted out, had informed against them and
disclosed the affair.[p] The government agents came and arrested
Sabbadin, who showed them where the money was, but Grassin
escaped. Menahem d'Angelo and Isaac Scaramella[q] were involved
with them through the accusation, even though they were innocent. On Purim the ghetto compound was closed off in order to
conduct a house-to-house search for them in great haste. The outcry against and contempt for all Jews on the part of everyone in the
city—nobles, citizens, and commoners[r]—increased as usual. For
when one individual committed a crime, they would grow angry
at the entire community,[17s] calling us a band of thieves and [saying]
that every kind of crime is concealed in the ghetto. Ever since then,
they [the Jews] have been the object of scorn and hatred, instead of,
as formerly, being loved by all.

Then calamity was added to calamity. On the first day of Passover 5396 [April 20, 1636], the Zorzetti brothers, Mordecai—who
died later as an apostate while in prison—and Jacob[t]—who is now
serving a sentence on a galley—were arrested for giving a bribe to
the Quarantia[u] in a case involving two Christians, because the
aforementioned Grassin Scaramella informed[v] against them in order to take his revenge. May God refuse to forgive him, for he destroyed and harmed six families of upright men.[18w]

Then my personal heartbreak and grief began. After having been
saddened over Grassin and Sabbadin, who were admirers of mine,
the situation became drastic and affected me personally. My son-
in-law Jacob Motta,[x] also a friend of the Zorzetti, had become involved with them in the aforementioned affair. Afraid and anxious,
he fled for his life to Ferrara[y] with several other unfortunate and
honest Jews who were fearful for that same reason. The affair lasted
about a full year, with constant fear and trembling, which became

---

[16] Italian written in Hebrew letters. See historical note.

[17] Adaptation of Numbers 16:22.

[18] The passage "because the aforementioned Grassin Scaramella . . . upright men"
was added by Modena above the line and marked by a caret. Later on, as events unfolded,
for the sake of completeness Modena updated his narrative with these significant details.

worse each day. My daughter Esther, may she be blessed above all women of the house, mourned for her husband because he was far away from her.[z]

All the while, I also feared greatly for myself, and horror took hold of my flesh,[19] because Isaac Vigevano[a] of Rovigo had been arrested and had stated that I had spoken with him as if [C 92] I knew about the affair of those Jews who had bribed the nobles. I had no peace,[b] day or night. Then, at the beginning of the month of Adar [5]397[20] [began February 25, 1637], my anxiety and fear increased considerably. One of the nobles who had been denounced for accepting a bribe was a dear friend of mine,[c] and I worried that they would say I had been involved with him in that affair. Even though I was innocent of any transgression, it was nonetheless a time of anger and wrath, with punishments and arrests being made for every slight suspicion. So I left for Padua[d] and stayed there for ten days like someone in hiding. I wanted to flee to Ferrara, but God mercifully dissuaded me from becoming a banished person[21] for no fault. I agreed, therefore, to return home a little before Purim, and immediately following my arrival I delivered a sermon that night in the "garden" marking the end of the winter term.

[MS 25a/גל] Afterward, on the 7th of Adar [5]397 [March 3, 1637],[22] sentence was handed down on all those terrified Jews, and they were ordered to be banished[23] forever, under severe restrictions of banishment.[24c] Additionally—and this had never been heard of since the time of our ancestors—they banished from the entire state[25f] fathers, sons, and brothers of every one of those Jews. As a result, not only had my son-in-law Jacob to seek a new home, but also his two brothers who lived in La Motta had to go awan-

[19] Job 21:6.
[20] The color of the ink in the text at this point is black. The date is written above the line, marked by a caret, and written in ink of poorer quality, which has turned reddish brown on the page.
[21] Italian word *bandito*, written in Hebrew letters, with Hebrew *d* in place of the *t*.
[22] There is a problem with the chronological sequence here, because Purim, mentioned in the previous sentence, falls on the 14th of Adar. Perhaps Modena meant to write "17th of Adar," which fell on March 13. The records of the Venetian Council of Ten preserved in ASV indicate that the convicted Jews were notified of the sentence on March 12 (see historical note e), and the 17th of Adar actually began at sundown, March 12.
[23] Italian word *banditi*, written in Hebrew letters, with Hebrew *d* in place of the *t*.
[24] Italian word *bando*, written in Hebrew letters.
[25] Hebrew: *maʿamad*. See historical note f.

dering.[1] My son-in-law settled permanently in Ferrara.[g] Because it is proper for a wife to go to live in her husband's house, my daughter Esther, long life to her, went with all her household articles to Ferrara at the beginning of the month of Nisan [5]397 [began March 26, 1637]. Thank God, she now lives there as befits wives of honorable Jewish men. My son-in-law is engaged there in trade, transacts business honestly, and is admired by the people, both for his own sake and for mine, because the people of that holy community, may God their Rock protect them and grant them long life, always liked me from years gone by. He has been there now for about two years. May God keep them healthy and calm.

My wife and I have to grieve that we have been left alone, old and in poor health. Our dear, beloved daughter, who was a great help to us and who tended to us in times of sickness or need, now lives far away from us. Today we sit wretched and lonely, having neither support nor help, except from God, who sends his assistance.

[C 93] While my heart was still full of sorrow because of the separation from my son-in-law and daughter, there came an enormous anxiety, fear, and heartache the likes of which I had never before experienced among the very great multitude of troubles and sorrows that had mounted upon me every day since I was born. About two years earlier[h] I had given a certain Frenchman who knew the Holy Tongue [Hebrew], M. Giacomo [Jacques] Gaffarel,[i] a certain book to read. I had written it more than twenty years earlier at the request of an English nobleman, who intended to give it to the king of England.[j] In it I relate all the laws, doctrines, and customs of the Jews at the present time in their dispersion. When I wrote it I was not careful about not writing things contrary to the Inquisition, because it was only in manuscript and was meant to be read by people who were not of the pope's sect.[k]

After reading it, that Frenchman asked me to leave it with him and he would print it in France. I agreed, but did not think of editing out the things that the Inquisition in Italy might find unacceptable in a printed book.

Two years later,[l] after I had given up hope that the Frenchman

[1] Jeremiah 9:9.

might print it, on the second day of Passover 5397 [April 10, 1637], someone brought me a letter from him, in which he told me that he had printed the book in Paris.[m] He did not divulge to whom he had made the dedication or whether he had changed anything in the book, or the like.

My heart immediately began pounding, and I went to look at a copy of it[n] that I still had from the time I had written it. I saw four or five things of importance of which it is forbidden to speak,[o] much less to write, [MS 25b/ מו] and needless to say to print, against the will of the Inquisition. Heartbroken, I shouted and tore at my beard until I almost lost my breath. I said to myself, "When this book is seen in Rome, it will become a stumbling block for all the Jews and for me, in particular. They will say, 'How insolent are they to print in the vernacular, informing the Christians not only of their laws, but also of some matters contrary to our religion and beliefs.' " As for me, where could I go? I could not escape to Ferrara or to any other place in Italy.

But, I was imagining the danger so much greater than it actually was—for in the end the items turned out not to be so forbidden— that my sighs were many and my heart faint,[2] and I almost went out of my mind, [C 94] and none of my friends could comfort me. Then God, the kind and merciful, put into my mind the idea to seek the advice of the inquisitor, may he be blessed and praised, for he had always acted like one of the righteous gentiles in his dealings with me.[p] So I made a voluntary declaration to the Inquisition,[q] which protected me on every count and on which I relied. Thus, after about a month of indescribable pain and sorrow, I relaxed.

Not long afterward the aforementioned Frenchman arrived in Rome, and from there he sent me a copy of the book that had been printed in Paris. I saw that he had been clever and considerate enough to delete the four or five items over which I had worried.[r] He had also addressed a letter to me in the introduction, enthusiastically praising and glorifying me and my work.[s] He dedicated the book to a nobleman, the ambassador of the king of France, who had just come here[t] to take up residence near the government of Venice, may its glory be exalted. This ambassador wrote me a letter

---

[2] Cf. Lamentations 1:22.

HISTORIA
DE RITI HEBRAICI
Vita &osseruanze degl'
Hebrei di questi tempi
DI
LEON MODENA RABI H.º
Da Venetia
Gia stampata in Parigi,
& hora da lui corretta e
riformata
Con licenza de Supriori
IN VENETIA 1638.
Appresso Gio Calleoni

8. Title page of the 1638 Venice edition
of Modena's *Historia de' riti hebraici*.

in his own hand praising me on his own behalf and on behalf of the king. Thus, I was greatly relieved of my fear and apprehension.

Despite this, because many errors in correct spelling had occurred during that printing, and there still remained a few things that I feared might not seem proper to the Catholics," I decided to print it a second time here in Venice, deleting and adding^v items as I wished for that purpose. It is sold today by their booksellers, and so far, about six months having passed, nothing but praise for it has been heard. I dedicated the second edition, like the first, to that ambassador,^{w} and he gave me a gift of thirty-four ducats, which defrayed the costs of printing.^{x}

In Sivan 5397 [May–June 1637], I went to Ferrara with my wife. We stayed there for a while with my daughter Esther, may she be blessed above all women of the house. Then we returned home safely. One month afterward, however, my wife became ill. [C 95] One Friday night while getting out of bed she fell down and struck her shoulder against the corner of the wall. For about a year she could not extend that arm. On top of that, during the winter she developed a kind of gout in the other arm, so that she could not use either one. Finally, God had mercy on her and on me, and after Passover [5]398 [April 1638], without the care of a physician, except for the True Healer, she was able gradually to stretch and move her arms sufficiently to perform necessary tasks.

In Heshvan 5398 [October–November 1637], I went to Padua to see my daughter Diana and found myself objecting to the way her husband ran his household. This went on until Passover [March 30–April 6, 1638]. After Passover, my daughter, along with her young son and daughter, may God their Rock protect them and grant them long life, came and stayed here with us for a month and a half, daughter living with parents. [MS 26a/ מה] At that time, about the 10th of Sivan [May 23, 1638], while my daughter Diana, may she be blessed above all women of the house, was still here, I went to Ferrara via Padua and Rovigo to see my daughter Esther, long life to her. I arrived there safely on Wednesday and was healthy and happy with her until the Sabbath. Then, on the Sabbath day, after midday, I was seized by stomach pains, shortness of breath, and persistent thirst. I lay on my sickbed for twelve days, taking medicines and cathartics.

When I saw that my illness was dragging on, I chose to return home, even though I was still sick and weak. My daughter Esther, long life to her, came along to help me and to provide for my needs on the way. I traveled first to Rovigo, then by coach to Padua, and from there by boat to Venice, at very great expense. When I arrived home, I began to regain my strength, and the pains and shortness of breath subsided. My thirst, however, continued through the summer. From morning to evening I drank well water, pharmacists'[3] water, and medicinal water concoctions, sparing no expense. My daughter Esther stayed here for about fifteen days, and then my daughters both returned safely to their husbands' homes.

Beginning in the month of Shevat[y] 5398 [January–February 1638], my son Isaac, may God his Rock protect him and grant him long life, began to transgress greatly. Instead of earning money to provide food for his family, as a man should, from morning to evening he played games of chance, mad though they be.[4] In the end he chose to go away, and I assisted him so that he could wander afar. He forsook his family, left his wife lonely and sad, and went to Livorno and from there [C 96] to Amsterdam. He said he wanted to get to Brazil[z] in the Indies, may God forgive him. He could have lived peacefully and quietly in his home, making me happy and supporting and sustaining me in my old age. But he vanished and has not been here[5] from the beginning of the month of Sivan [began May 14, 1638] until now,[6] as he wanders about the earth.[7] It is only my sins and transgressions that have caused me to be able to say that of my three sons, one died, one was murdered, and one lives in exile.

The only comfort I have left in my misery is from my grandson Isaac min Haleviim, may God his Rock protect him and grant him long life, the son of my daughter Diana, long life to her. For about ten years, since the death of his father of blessed memory, I have

---

[3] The Hebrew letters are *b-s-m-y-m*, and under the first two, marks for the vowel sign *a* seem to have been written. Apparently the word is *bassamim*, literally "perfumers," and means pharmacists, because they dealt with herbs.

[4] The phrase contains a clever pun on the Italian word *giocare*, "to play" (games of chance), and on a biblical verse, Job 4:20, as well as an adaptation of Ecclesiastes 2:2.

[5] Adaptation of Psalm 37:36.   [6] This section was written in 1639; see below.

[7] Genesis 4:12, 14 (referring to Cain).

reared him in my house, and he has been like a son to me. Now, at
about eighteen years of age,[8] he obeys me, understands Scripture
and Aggadah, and preaches in public, pleasing his listeners.[a] He has
a clean and easy craft in printing, which is, after all, also the work
of Torah. I love him all the more because in his face and character
traits he resembles in all respects my son Mordecai, may he rest in
peace. May God grant him a good life and one that will be much
longer than his [Mordecai's].[9] Perhaps God will grant me the privilege of experiencing some joy and happiness from him before I die.
After my death, may he grant me and my wife, may she be blessed
above all women of the house, our reward in the world to come for
having raised an orphan[b] in our home, with all the trouble and pain
involved in child rearing.

Since then, all through 5398 [1637/1638] and up to the present,
on my account many friars have spoken well of the Jews while
preaching in their churches, praising me greatly in their sermons
before large audiences of gentiles in terms that would not be believed were they related, so that my fame has grown even greater
among the gentiles than it was before.

On the eve of Rosh Hashanah[10] 5399 [September 8, 1638], I was
informed by the members of the household of the honored Abraham Aboab,[c] may God his Rock protect him and grant him long
life, that they would no longer pay my salary of six ducats a month
at the yeshiva.[d] Leo di Cervi[e] went along with them by canceling
preaching in his home during the winter. As a result, I was left with
half of what I needed to meet my expenses and with no outside
earnings, at a time that my wife and I were growing old.[f] Blessed[11]
is the Lord, who has been with me for the past four years, helping
me to refrain completely from evil games of chance, and may he
take pity for the remainder [of my life].

[8] Manuscript reads "ve-'ad ha-yom ke-ven y-h [= 18] shanah," with two words, *harei hu,* "he is," in smaller letters, inserted above the line after the word *ha-yom,* "now," and marked with a caret. Isaac was born in May 1621; his father died in June 1629. Therefore this section of the autobiography was written in 1639.

[9] The passage, "I love him . . . than his [Mordecai's]," was added above the line and marked with a caret. The black ink contrasts in color with the ink of the body of the text at this point, which has turned reddish brown, evidence of a later revision by the author.

[10] The abbreviation *r-h* for Rosh Hashanah, "New Year," was added above the line.

[11] Modena celebrated his (temporary) victory over gambling by writing an enlarged *b* in the word *barukh,* "blessed."

[MS 26b/ מו ; C 97] At the beginning of the month of First Adar 5399 [began February 5, 1639], I arranged a match for my grandson Isaac, may God his Rock protect him and grant him long life, with Esther, long life to her, the only daughter of Judah Monte Scudolo,^g may God his Rock protect him and grant him long life. He is learned in Torah and comes from a family of good lineage. I thought, now that I and my wife are old, I would find him a refuge that would be good for him after our death. This would be his third set of parents to take care of him. May it be [God's] will that it be under an auspicious star and that I live to see his wedding and the sons who be born to him.

During that Purim [March 20, 1639] my wife developed podagra, or gout in her legs, and from then until now,[12] she has been walking with a slight limp in the house. Her arms also began to swell from this, and increasingly old age overcomes us, with accompanying poor health.

In Iyyar [5]399 [May–June 1639] the members attending our communal yeshiva rose up to close a breach[h] caused by certain transgressions, especially some lecherous and criminal acts that were going on openly in our community. Isaac di Alva, a complete sinner, was placed under the ban, and although we did everything with permission of the magistrates of the Cattaver, complete with the signatures of three of them, someone informed on us, and we eight rabbis were summoned to court. After much investigation, they let us return to our homes on bail of sixteen thousand ducats, two thousand per person.[i] In fear and apprehension and with expense and pleading, we worked hard until,[13] through God's mercy, we were acquitted by two members [of the Cattaver] around the 20th of Sivan [June 22, 1639].

In Elul 5399 [September 1639] the world began to enter a period of chaos.[14j] [C 98]

In Heshvan 5400 [November 1639] about thirty men from the Sephardic congregation, may God their Rock protect them and grant them long life, got together to restore the yeshiva to its former glory.

---

[12] This section was written in 1639, a few months after Modena's wife's illness began.

[13] The words 'ad ki, "until," were added by Modena above the line.

[14] This comment and the next notice, for Heshvan 5400, were added by Modena in the blank space preceeding the item for the 15th of Kislev.

On the 15th of Kislev 5400 [December 11, 1639], I took ill with stomach pains for about twelve days, and, though I recovered then, I continued to experience those pains constantly, especially during the summer of that year.

On the 9th of Adar [March 4, 1640] the wedding of my grandson Isaac,[k] may God his Rock protect him and grant him long life, to his aforementioned mate took place. My daughters Diana and Esther, long life to them, were here for about a month and a half, after which each returned to her husband's house. Isaac was honored with the title *haver* by all the ranking authorities in the yeshiva, may God their Rock protect them and grant them long life. At that time he left my house and moved into the house of his father-in-law, the aforementioned Judah M[onte] S[cudolo],[15] in accordance with the stipulations [of the betrothal agreement] that he could reside with him and have the latter pay his expenses for three and a half years while he continued to busy himself with study, preaching, and the craft of printing to the best of the ability granted him by God.[16] My son-in-law M[oses] S[altaro] so embittered me at the wedding that it turned into agony for me.[17]

At the beginning of the month of Sivan [began May 22, 1640] I was in Padua. At that time the second printing of my book *Galut yehudah* was completed,[l] with a new supplement I had made for it, consisting of [definitions of] terms used by the talmudic rabbis of blessed memory and by the commentators. I called it *Pi aryeh*[m]— *The Mouth of the Lion*—because all my life I had labored to benefit the public. About six months earlier I had completed a treatise against the Kabbalah. I entitled it *Ari nohem*[18n]—*The Roaring Lion*— because of my great anger[19] at one of those [kabbalists] who had spoken wrongly in his books against the great luminaries[o] of Israel, especially "the eagle" Maimonides of blessed memory. But it was never printed.[p]

---

[15] The two letters, *m-s*, are an abbreviation of Judah's family name.   [16] Cf. Ezra 7:9.

[17] The statement about the behavior of the son-in-law is a later addition by the author. He inserted it in the blank space he had left when originally recording the notice and used ink of a poorer quality, which has turned reddish brown on the page.

[18] By a slip of the pen, Modena wrote *Ari no'em* (The Lion Speaks)! "Ari No'em" formed part of Modena's signature motto: see the introduction to *Magen ve-herev*, Ambrosiana MS Q 139 sup., fol. 2a (copied and introduced by Modena's grandson, Isaac min Haleviim).

[19] 1 Samuel 1:16.

During Tammuz, Av, and Elul, until the end of [5]400 [late June through mid-September 1640], I was ill with aches and pains and could not muster the strength to study and write as in other summers and as I had intended to do [that summer].

From Rosh Hashanah [5]401 [September 17, 1640] through Shavuot [May 15, 1641], the two-millennium-long era of chaos[q] became more firmly established.

On the 5th of Tevet 5401 [December 18, 1640], at midnight, a daughter was born to my grandson Isaac, may God his Rock protect him and grant him long life. He named her [C 99] Sarah, may she be blessed above all women of the house, after his father's mother.[20] May God cause her to be worthy of marriage and good deeds.[r] Amen.

[MS 27a/ מז] In [5]401, close to Hanukkah [began December 9, 1640], my wife took seriously ill for about a month, and from then on, throughout the winter, she was sad and distressed for no reason. The following Passover [began March 26, 1641] she became sick again, and her illness lasted a long time, until Sivan [May–June 1641], when my daughter Diana came from Padua and stayed here for about a month and a half and then left. About two months later [she came again][21] and stayed here until Rosh Hashanah [5]402 [September 5, 1641], because all that summer either both of us or my wife alone were sick and depressed.

That Sivan [began May 10, 1641] my wife assumed a strange mood, and she began to quarrel with me and make me angry. This has been and will be the destruction, ruin, and desolation of my money, body, honor, and soul until this day. If I were to live another hundred years I would not recover from any of those four things. God is the one who knows whether she fought with me for no reason, when I had committed no wrong and there had been no evil deeds or transgressions on my part. I cannot write about how foolish she was, or of how from day to day I was led astray by her wheedling from failure to failure and from evil to evil. I can only give an outline.

[20] The word *em*, "mother," was added by Modena above the line and marked with a caret.

[21] Kahana (p. 60) suggested that a word was missing in this passage and supplied the word *hazrah*, "she returned." A simpler solution lies in assuming an ellipsis of the verb "came" (*ba'ah*), found in the previous sentence.

We quarreled all day long from the month of Sivan [May–June 1641] until after Sukkot [ended September 27, 1641]. I would grow angry and shout and act foolishly. My blood would boil, my heart would flutter, and my insides would churn up. From time to time she would vow to keep still and to cease being boisterous, but a few days later she would resume her foolish behavior. We carried on this way during the entire summer of 5401 [1641] and during the whole month of Tishre 5402 [September–October 1641]. On the 4th of Heshvan 5402 [October 8, 1641] I took her with me to Padua on condition that there be peace between us. We stayed there with my daughter Diana, may she be blessed above all women of the house, for five days. Immediately upon our return, however, my wife resumed her old provoking, so that I could no longer bear it.

Meanwhile, I developed an abcess, pus, and a pulmonary infection.[5] And about the middle of the month of Kislev [November 1641], I became bedridden with fever, pains, and [other] severe symptoms, in particular the shortness of breath called asthma. Finally, at the beginning of the month of Tevet [began December 4, 1641], the doctors diagnosed me as dying. I recited the deathbed confessional prayer, while in the synagogues prayers were offered up for me as I was dying. But God did not wish to kill me.[22] Nonetheless, my illness kept dragging on, and the shortness of breath and pains grew worse and worse, until I got sick and tired of staying in bed and began to get up in the month of Shevat [January 1642]. But I still suffered from insomnia every time I got back into bed, and it lasted for about seven months. It was so difficult for me to speak, pray, or preach that I despaired, saying, "I will no longer be able to serve the public as I have for the past forty-nine years, or even to associate with other living beings."

[C 100] Because I had spent about 130 ducats in cash on my illness by the beginning of the month of Shevat [began January 2, 1642], and because my wife did not stop causing me grief day and night, I became angry at myself, lost control, and returned to the "sin of Judah" [of which I have] written[23] several times, namely playing games of chance, which utterly consumed me and schemed

---

[22] Play on Judges 13:23.
[23] Adaptation of Jeremiah 17:1. Dots over the name "Judah" signal the play on the author's name.

against me.[24] I did so much more evil than on previous occasions that I lost six hundred ducats in the course of a full year. I am still burdened with debts from this amounting to more than three hundred, and I have nothing left to buy food for my household.

At the beginning of the month of Nisan [5]402 [began April 1, 1642], I was forced to move out of the house belonging to Meir Cigala of blessed memory, where for seventeen years I had lived comfortably. On account of my illness my knees had grown weak and, being short of breath, I could no longer climb the stairs. I moved to a house belonging to Moses Luzzatto,[1] which was located next to his store.[25] It was a dark and gloomy place, which I called "The Cave of Makhpelah,"[1] with high rent and expenses. And though [good or bad fortune immediately following a move to a new place] does not constitute divination, it does act as an omen,[2] for I was sick there, too, and the days were difficult and [marked by] loss [of money]. All this resulted from a single cause, for anger and wrath took away my health and made me ill, illness prevented me from climbing stairs, and that forced me into this dark and poorly lit dwelling, because it is low.

[MS 27b/ מח] In Iyyar 5402 [May 1642] I received a letter from my son Isaac, may God his Rock protect him and grant him long life, from Brazil in the Indies, telling me that he was a rich and leading merchant there, and that he possessed more than four thousand reals, as well as black slaves. He said that he would yet return to his home and his wife and that he would send gifts to her and to me. But about eight months have passed since then, and I still have not even seen another letter. Whatever happens, may he live and be successful, for he is my son. Then, at the end of [5]403 [summer 1643], I heard disturbing rumors [C 101] that he had played games of chance and lost everything. To this day, in Nisan [5]404 [April–May 1644], he has been destitute and has not written more.[3]

---

[24] Adaptation of 2 Samuel 21:5.   [25] Italian word *bottega*, written in Hebrew letters.

[1] The name of the cave that Abraham purchased from the sons of Heth as a tomb for his deceased wife, Sarah, and where he, too, was later buried; see Genesis 23. The name "Makhpelah" derives from the Hebrew root meaning "double" and was doubtless meant by Modena to allude to the "high rent" he paid.

[2] B. T. Hullin 95b.

[3] The passage regarding the rumors of Isaac's gambling, "Then, at the end, . . . not written more," was added later on, in Nisan 1644. Modena inserted it in the blank space following the words "for he is my son," which were written at the beginning of 1643.

In Sivan [5]402 [June 1642] I went to Ferrara with my daughter Diana, may she be blessed above all women of the house, and her husband and son, may God their Rock protect them and grant them long life, to attend the wedding of Moses, the brother of my son-in-law Jacob Motta. We stayed there for eight days with my daughter Esther, may she be blessed above all women of the house, and then returned home safely. My expenses were great, and, there, too, my son-in-law M[oses] S[altaro] irked me.[4]

After I returned home I began to eat, drink, and act in every way contrary to doctors' orders concerning my illness. This way I rid myself of some of my illness, particularly the shortness of breath and the insomnia that had weighed heavily upon me for the previous eight months. Due to God's kindness it seemed to me that I was cured when an abscess in my lung burst and healed and I expelled blood from my mouth and became well,[5] even though old age is a natural illness that grows ever more severe upon me, with rupture, pain, and weakness. May God be praised, therefore, for everything.

In[6] 5403, from Rosh Hashanah [September 25, 1642] until the 16th of Heshvan [November 9, 1642] I played evil games of chance constantly, [going] from failure to failure, until, because of my heavy debts and depleted resources, I vowed to stop until the upcoming Passover [April 1643]. Now three verses from the Torah, Prophets, and Hagiographa distress me. From the Torah: "And if you will say, what shall we eat"[7]; from the Prophets: "The creditor has come to take"[8]; and from the Hagiographa: "For my loins are filled with burning, and there is no soundness in my flesh."[9] God have mercy.

Beginning the previous Elul 5402 [August–September 1642], I had begun to reprint the prayers I had published twenty years earlier, entitling them *Tefillot yesharim—Prayers of the Upright*—with a nice supplement.[11] I presented it as a gift to the holy community

---

[4] The statement about the son-in-law appears to have been added later by Modena. It was inserted in the blank space following the sentence "My expenses were great." See fol. 26b, note 17.

[5] The phrase, "when an abscess . . . and became well," was added by Modena above the line and marked by a caret.

[6] An enlarged letter *h* (the 5 in 5403) introduces this section.   [7] Leviticus 25:20.

[8] 2 Kings 4:1.   [9] Psalm 38:8.

of Rome,ᵛ may God its Rock protect it and grant it long life, and I received twenty-five ducats in return. Because I mentioned the names of the officeholders individually, however, there was some resentment over the order of the names.ʷ So I printed the dedication a third time, but I remained alienated from them.

Starting that Elul [5]402 [August–September 1642], my son-in-law Moses Saltar greatly sinned against my daughter, his wife. Because I complained about this, he has ceased writing to me for about the past four months.

Since the previous Sivan [5]402 [June 1642], I had sold or pawned several of my books and writings for a sum of more than 100 ducats.ˣ I also presented some of them as gifts to students and admirersʸ and others, and through the end of [C 102] [5]403 [1642/1643], the value [of the books I gave away] was more than 150 ducats.

From Heshvan 5403 [October–November 1642] through Adar 5403 [February–March 1643], I worked in the way that God desires, with his help and that of my admirers. Then, at the end of Adar [ended March 20, 1643], I left the house of Moses Luzzattoᶻ and moved into a small, cramped dwelling that belonged to Isaac the son of S[amuel]¹⁰ Obadiahᵃ next to the butcher Isaac, known as Rosso.¹¹ᵇ But I had no rest there.¹² Although [good or bad fortune immediately following a move to a new] place, [the birth of a] child, [or the taking of a] wife does not constitute divination, it does act as an omen.¹³ My wife took sick two or three times, and I became involved in defending Simhah the son of Meshullam the butcher,ᶜ on whose account for various reasons I had worn myself thin for about three months.¹⁴ My wife squabbled with me continuously whenever I recalled the evil she had done to me, and so on.

For the six months that I lived there I did not earn even six ducats, and all my endeavors went awry and lacked success. Because of the commotion made by the women neighbors [MS 28a] and other

---

¹⁰ The abbreviation b-sh follows the name Isaac. Presumably this means ben Shemuel.

¹¹ Hebrew adom, "red," the word used among Italian Jews as the Hebrew equivalent of the family name de Rossi. Azariah de Rossi, mentioned earlier in the autobiography, was known in Hebrew as Azariah min Haadummim.

¹² Lamentations 5:5.   ¹³ B.T. Hullin 95b.

¹⁴ Passage not clear; it seems to read ke-mishalosh. This entire section and much of these last pages of the autobiography are written in an unfirm hand by a tired, ailing, and weak Modena.

annoyances, I was forced to leave that place, too. On Rosh Ha-shanah [5]404 [September 14, 1643], I took up temporary residence in a house belonging to Naftali Cohen Scocco, where lived the haver A[braham] Stella,[d] may God his Rock protect him and grant him long life. He let me have it for eight months only, after which I would have to find another place to live. Thus exile was decreed for me even within the city itself.

Between Rosh Hashanah [5]404 and Hanukkah [began December 6, 1643], [a time of] bitterness and impetuousness for me all my life, I engaged in efforts to bring my son-in-law Jacob Motta, may God his Rock protect him and grant him long life, back to Venice from his banishment,[15] for because of the war with the pope,[e] it had been decreed that with the approval of the Council of Ten anyone in banishment[16] could return on payment of money toward the wages[17] of mercenary soldiers. On the day preceding Hanukkah they denied him permission,[f] [C 103] and I was saddened by this. I compounded my sorrow when, on the first night of Hanukkah, I resumed playing accursed games of chance. I persisted in this until the beginning of the month of Adar [began February 8, 1644] at great monetary loss, as well as much loss of honor, the likes of which I had never experienced before, and quarreling at home, too.

In the month of June [5]403 [1643], my daughter Esther, may she be blessed above all women of the house, had come here on account of the war and remained for eleven months. She was here during all the bad happenings I have just mentioned. Afterward, at the beginning of the month of Nisan [began April 7, 1644], she returned home,[g] and my daughter Diana arrived. She remained until the holiday of Shavuot [June 10–11, 1644], also at a time of sadness and pain and quarrels with my wife, with whom God has punished me.

In the month of Adar [5]404 [February–March 1644] I left off playing games of chance and sought to work and to struggle on account of those three biblical verses that are written on the facing page.[18] But I did not even find young students, for God closed off to me every source of income, whether large or small, on all sides.

---

[15] Italian word *bando*, writtten in Hebrew letters.
[16] Italian word, *banditi*, written in Hebrew letters.   [17] Play on Judges 5:2.
[18] See above, fol. 27b. The "three biblical verses" are written on the facing page in the manuscript (p. 48 of the Hebrew pagination), exactly opposite this statement.

That Sivan, after Shavuot [ended June 11, 1644], I left the house of the aforementioned Naftali and moved into the house of Moses Luzzatto, where I had lived once before until Adar [5]403 [February–March 1643], as [written] on the facing page,[19] lacking in everything and without income or success. I do not know why God continues to treat me so roughly.[20]

Beginning that Nisan [April–May 1644], I had two or three students, who came for a part of each day to study and to write. I passed that entire summer until Rosh Hashanah [5]405 [September 1, 1644] as best I could.

Because of the complaints of my wife, who has not stopped vexing me for the past five years and who did not want to live in that house, I moved out, and, after much effort, moved in Tishre 5405 [September 1644] into a house belonging to Mordecai Baldoz. I remained there all winter and had an income of about 250 ducats.[h] With this I paid some debts and supported my household to the best of the ability granted me by God.

At the beginning of the month of Nisan 5405 [began March 28, 1645], my wife became ill with gout and was bedridden for two and a half months. [C 104] I brought my daughter Diana from Padua to tend to her, along with other servant girls, all at great expense. After she recovered, her feet and hands remained immobilised, but not her tongue, and her words were as cutting as a sword.[21] All day long she would not be silent.

[MS 28b] I wish to write here as a record the many endeavors[i] I have tried in order to earn my living, trying without success.[22]

Jewish pupils	Poems for weddings and gravestones
Gentile pupils	Italian sonnets
Teaching writing	Writing comedies

---

[19] The passage describing Modena's departure from the house of Moses Luzzatto at the end of 5403 (fol. 27b) is, indeed, written "on the facing page" in the manuscript, some lines below the "three biblical verses." Cf. Carpi edition, p. 103 n. 20 and p. 22 of his introduction, for a different interpretation.

[20] Genesis 42:7.   [21] Adaptation of Proverbs 12:18.

[22] In the manuscript, the list that follows is divided into two parallel columns, with wide spaces between entries, in contrast to the closely written lines of the rest of the text. In order to highlight the list further, Modena devoted a separate page to it (see fig. 9).

9. Page of the manuscript of *Hayyei yehudah* containing Modena's
list of twenty-six professional endeavors.

Preaching	Directing them
Sermons for others	Drawing up contracts
Cantorial work	Translating[24]
Secretary for societies	Printing my writings
Rabbinate	Proofreading for print
Decisions [of Jewish Law]	Teaching arcane remedies and amulets [C 105]
Judging	Selling books of arcane remedies
Yeshiva	Commercial brokerage
[Conferring] diplomas of "rabbi" and "*haver*"	Matchmaking
Letters for abroad	
Music[23]	

[MS 29a] Who will give me learned words of lamentations, moaning, and woe[25] so that I may speak and write of how much worse my luck has been than that of any other person? I shall suffer and bear what began to make me desolate on the day I was born and has continued without respite for seventy-six whole years.[j] Indeed, from then until now, when there has not been a day that has not been more accursed than the one before, there has been no one like me in the entire kingdom of heaven and among all created beings.

On the 16th of Tammuz 5405 [July 10, 1645], my beloved son-in-law, Jacob of La Motta of blessed memory, passed away in Ferrara. He was forty-five years old, at the height of his good fortune, at a time that every day he acquired more wealth and honor. He remained my last hope of settling down and finding respite in a city and community that I liked and that liked me. My heart has been stricken like grass and has withered,[26] and I am left without breath.

That same week I went to Ferrara to oversee the matter of my

---

[23] Three items were added later on—Secretary for societies; Decisions [of Jewish law]; and Music—in a poorer ink, which turned reddish brown and which contrasts by its browning with the black color of the ink used in the original list of twenty-three jobs. The insertions did away with the original, uniform spacing between items (see fig. 9). Updating the curriculum vitae!

[24] Italian word *tradurre*, spelled *tradur* in Hebrew transcription, reflecting the dropping of the final vowel in the Venetian dialect.

[25] Ezekiel 2:10.   [26] Adaptation of Psalm 102:5.

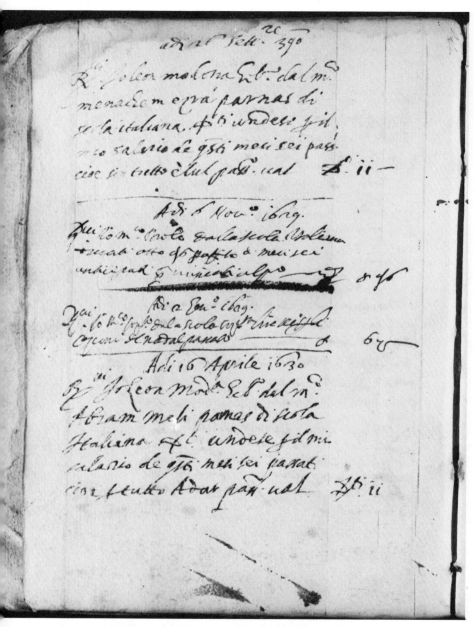

10. Page from the expense ledger of the Italian Synagogue
in Venice containing Modena's handwritten receipts (first and last
entries) for salary payments for services performed,
dated September 20, 390 (= 1629) and April 16, 1630.

daughter's dowry,[k] and quarreled about it with the brothers of my son-in-law of blessed memory. I granted them a full year in the matter of the dowry, at the end of which they repaid it with great stinginess, as God would wish. In Heshvan [5]406 [October–November 1645] they released her by properly performing the ceremony of Halitzah[l] there in Ferrara. She immediately returned to my house, a sorrowful widow, and still lives with us, ministering to her father and mother. May God reward her for her deeds.

In Nisan 5406 [March–April 1646] my wife became ill with gout, and my daughter Diana came and stayed here until Shavuot [May 20]. Actually it was in Nisan [5]407, and during the intermediate days of Passover [April 22–25, 1647] that my daughter Diana came to stay, as just mentioned.

From the time my son-in-law died until now—Sivan 5407 [June–July 1647]—I have continuously worked hard and labored[m] and have not lacked any necessities. Yet day in and day out I have been bickering. I am saddened and pained on account of the matter alluded to, am spending money on my wife's illness, and am depressed because of her. But now,[1] at this time, the day after Shavuot 5407 [June 11, 1647], I am bereft of possessions and have no hope of being able to subsist. My debts increase, and I am also afflicted[n] on behalf of others with the ruin of my honor, money, body, and soul.[2] I do not know what will happen, whether [C 106] heaven's mercy will not almost miraculously extend itself to be a shield for me, or my spirit and soul will be gathered to him, for everything must end.

Despite all this, all summer long and during the month of Tishre [5]408 [October 1647], because of the holidays, I endured with many expenses. Nothing was lacking, for the Lord of Hosts sent his aid. From writing letters, from rendering decisions on matters of Jewish law, and from other things, which I myself do not remember, I spent, but had something left over. But my wife was continuously sick in bed, and the expenses for the gout and catarrh[o] were great. For about a year now she has been in pain and dire straits with bad sickness, which, in the nature of things, will not

---

[1] Manuscript reads ʿattah; cf. Carpi edition, p. 105 line 24.

[2] The abbreviation b-kh-m-g-n apparently stands for "be-khilyon kevodi mammoni gufi ve-nafshi." Cf. fol. 27a.

allow her to live much longer. I also cried out bitterly every night with chest illness and shortness of breath, until by the end of Heshvan [5]408 [November 1647] the illness so overcame me that all day and all night I could not keep silent, as I shall describe next.

[MS 29b] All summer and winter, up to the present time, I have had so much sorrow and trouble over an obligation I had assumed toward the aforementioned butcher and have become worn so thin that on the 26th of Heshvan [5]408, on the Sabbath when the Torah portion Hayyei Sarah was read,[3] I threw myself into bed and summoned doctors for my chest illness and shortness of breath. All their medicines made me feel worse, and I developed such a fever that they feared for my life and hinted to me that I ought to recite the confessional prayer and make out my will. I did this on the 28th of Heshvan [November 26], in the presence of ten men, three of whom were rabbis.[p] But I have endured for three months,[q] even though for the last month[r] I have been getting out of bed every day, and every night my illness is worse than the night before. In addition, I have contracted a rupture down below [which causes me to] roar like a lion[s] all the time. These past three months I have had my daughter Diana, may she be blessed above all women of the house, here, but she and Esther and my neighbor cannot adequately minister to my wife and me. She, like me, is steadily waning and has no rest, day or night. What can I say about my expenses these past three months and the predicament I am in while writing, today?[4t]

[MS 30a–34a blank]

[MS 34b, C 107] Miseries of my heart in brief.[5u]

Apart from the banishments, the death of my sons, and the other matters recorded here. Beginning about four years after my settlement here in Venice, that is, beginning in 5371 [1610/1611].[6]

[3] Genesis 23:1–25:18. It was read on the 25th of Heshvan (Saturday, November 23, 1647). The 26th of Heshvan began on Saturday night.

[4] The bottom two-thirds of the page in the manuscript are blank, as are the next nine pages.

[5] This section begins following nine intervening blank pages in the notebook. The brief "memorandum" notes that Modena jotted down here are largely cryptic, and the translation of some of the passages should be considered tentative. In some cases the allusions are clarified by the more discursive recitation of the same events in the body of the autobiography. See excursus 2 and Natalie Davis's introductory essay, note 38.

[6] Date added above the line. This is the year of the first event recorded below. Modena dated his permanent settlement in Venice from Adar 5367 (February–March 1607; see fol. 14b), even though he had been born there in 1571, had lived there from 1592 until

11. Pages of the manuscript of *Hayyei yehudah* containing
the section entitled "Miseries of my heart in brief."

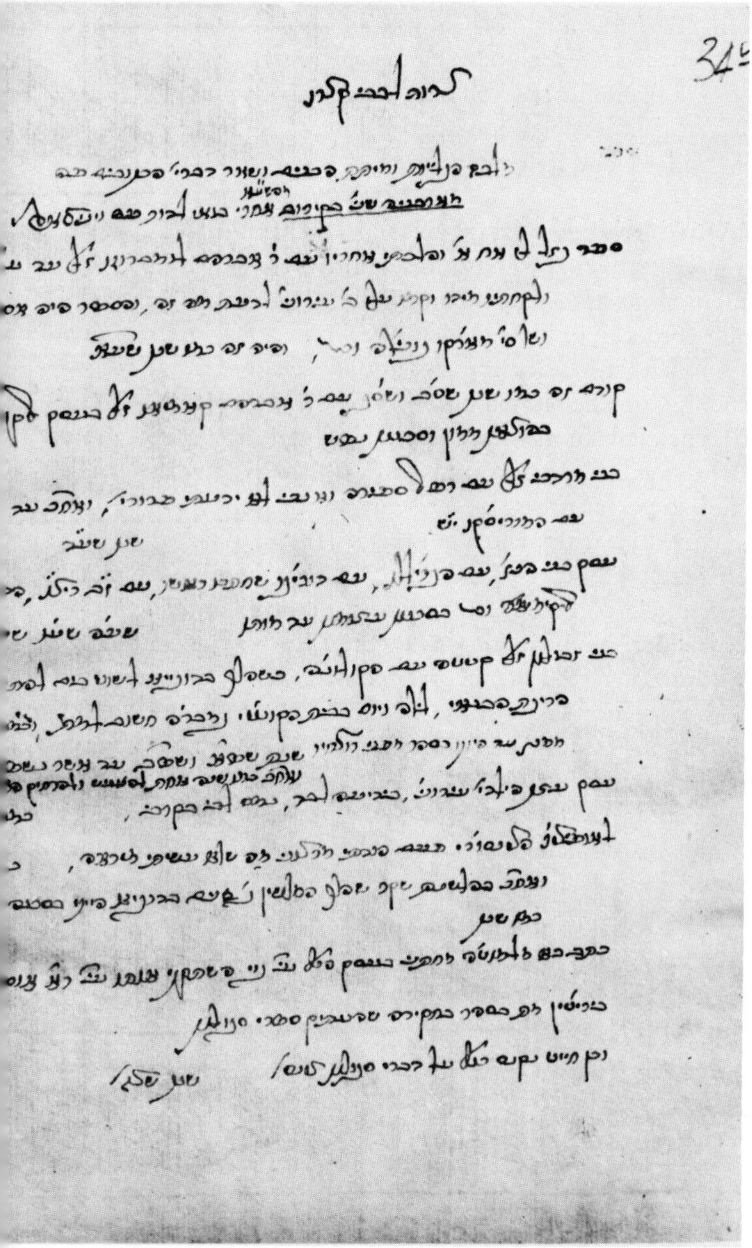

34

A certain friar stole a book from me, and, along with Abraham Lombroso[v] of blessed memory, I pursued him to San[7] Marino. When I took it from him, two citizens set upon me to find out what it was. It was a proscribed book and belonged to Signore Marco Gonnella, and so on. It happened about the year [5]371 [1610/1611].

Prior to that, about the year [5]362 [1601/1602] and [5]363 [1602/1603], engaged in alchemy and so on with Abraham Cammeo[w] of blessed memory at monetary expense and in mortal danger.

My son Mordecai[x] of blessed memory with Raphael Spira,[y] and I did not know a bit,[8] and afterward, until his death, with the Morisco, may his name be blotted out. [5]374 [1613/1614].

[C 108] The affair of my aforementioned son with Grillo,[z] with Dorigo who was decapitated, and with Z. B. Rizzo, all over alchemy, and so on, at great danger, until his death. [5]375 [1614/1615], [5]376 [1615/1616], and all of [5]377 [1616/1617].

My son Zebulun of blessed memory. Quarrel with the Colonna when he went to travel around for pleasure in the galley. The murder of the builder. Night and day in the house of Conte Gambara, taken for dead. Then some danger from him until he was taken into custody [as protection] against those who wished to murder him. [During] the years [5]381 [1620/1621] and [5]382 [1621/1622], until finally his blood was shed like water. Afterward about one year to punish and banish the murderers.[9a]

The matter of the council of young citizens,[b] of which I only have knowledge. My heart melted within me. About the year. . . .[10]

Once, out of fear, I made a voluntary declaration to the Uffizio Censori[c] about something I had not even done; about the year [5]384 [1623/1624]. Subsequently, as a result of a false denunciation

---

1604 (see fols. 11b–14a), and spent the year between May 1609 and April 1610 living in Florence (see fol. 15a).

[7] See fol. 15a, note 8.

[8] The last word in this phrase poses a mystery. The translation "a bit" for the assumed *perurim* is very tentative.

[9] This sentence was added later on by Modena using ink of a higher quality, which still retains its original black color and contrasts with the poorer ink used in the rest of the passage, which has turned reddish brown.

[10] The year is left blank in the manuscript.

for which the informer served three years on a galley, I was in great danger about the year. . . .[11]

A letter about the aforementioned matter from my son-in-law in La Motta arrived via a gentile. Through A[braham] Osimo I calmed him down.[d]

Beretin died in jail during inquisitorial proceedings for copying books of arcane remedies.

Also a tailor was fined, as mentioned before, in connection with proscribed arcane remedies. [C 109] In the year [5]397 [1636/1637].

[MS 35a] 5390 [1629/1630]. The quarrel with Panarotti.[12e]

5387[13] [1626/1627]. Isaac Padovan.[f]

5395 [1634/1635]. Tobias Saphira, may his name be blotted out, from the Italian synagogue.

5399 [1638/39]. Joseph Hamitz.[g]

My grandson Isaac,[h] may God his Rock protect him and grant him long life, was in prison for sixty-six days on account of the print shop. In the year 5395 [1635].

Some little books[i] of arcane remedies were given to a Frenchman to send to Paris, and another Frenchman was caught. 5397 [1636/1637].

The matters affecting my son-in-law Motta began on Passover [5]396 [April 1636]. From that time the matter concerning Isaac Vigevano, Lippamano, and "the boat"[j] intensified, and for others as well, until the day that judgment concerning them was handed down—a full year. It is impossible to contemplate how much pain, anger, fear, and dejection I have experienced.

I gave a golden tray to the ambassador of Spain and he held onto it for fifteen days. I thought it lost.

[The matter of] the book Riti[k] published in France, as I have written here, surpassed all the rest.

Books of arcane remedies were given to the Genoese noblemen, and from them they have spread, and so on [5]399 [1638/1639], and from the writer.

---

[11] The year is left blank in the manuscript.

[12] The four short items, for 5390, 5387, 5395, and 5399, in that order, were added at the top of a page in ink of a higher quality, which still retains its original black color and contrasts with the poorer ink on the rest of the page, which has turned reddish brown.

[13] Manuscript reads h-sh-p-z (5387). Cf. Carpi edition, p. 109 line 1.

From [5]392 at Purim time [March 8, 1632], when I married off my daughter Diana, may she be blessed above all women of the house, to Moses Saltar, who has embittered her life with troubles[14] . . . until this day.

Last affliction[15] as severe as Sheol. Since the beginning of the month of Sivan [5]401 [began May 10, 1641] and to this day, it is the cause of all the evil that has befallen me and will yet befall me until the day of my death, which has been hastening to overcome me for more than ten years, and so on—evil, ruination of honor, money, body, and soul.[m]

Some false accusations, defending Simonetto the butcher[n] against imprisonment on account of debts and the Criminal,[160] five years.

[5]404 [1643/1644]. How hard I toiled to return my son-in-law Jacob Motta from his banishment[17] without success.[p]

[C 110] I will not say "last affliction" as before because there is no end to my miseries. Nonetheless, a heavy blow came with the death of my son-in-law[q] in Tammuz 5405 [July 1645]. If not for that, I would by now have decided to dwell in Ferrara to rest there. Thus I remain forlorn, my days coming to an end because of calamities, in fear and dire straits.

[MS 35b–36a] So that it be known (although without merit) what fame I have had, in July 1634 there came to me a book printed in London in England in the year 1631, the title of which is, as will be written below here or on the facing page:[18r]

[on the facing page, 36a][19]

---

[14] The word in the manuscript following *tzarot*, "troubles," appears to be composed of the letters *m-sh-m-r-t*. Its meaning is not clear.

[15] Cf. Isaiah 8:23.

[16] Written in Hebrew letters and reflecting the dropping of the final vowel in the Venetian dialect.

[17] Italian word *bando*, written in Hebrew letters.

[18] This sentence, in Italian, is written on two lines from left to right across the top of facing folio pages 36a and 35b and ends on 35b (see fig. 12). Apparently Modena was not sure when he wrote these lines whether he would transcribe the title page of Selden's book directly below or "on the facing page," namely fol. 36a. He decided on the latter. Anthony Grafton of Princeton University and Aaron Katchen of Brandeis University provided valuable assistance in understanding the vernacular passages on fols. 35b–36a.

[19] For the sake of realism, Modena laid out the text in the format of a title page (see fig. 12). The spacing and lining, however, do not coincide exactly with the layout of the

John Selden[s] Lawyer (J.C. = Juris Consultus)
On
the Succession[t] to the Possession of the Deceased or
On the Right of Inheritance According to the Laws of the
Jews that were in Use at the Time that
their Republic was at its Height, One Book
drawn from the Bible, from Both Talmuds, and from Selected
Rabbinic Writings, that is, from the Sources,
the Digest,[u] and the Most Learned
Teachers of the Hebrew Law

"and even in its [the soul's] close bondage [it] rejects
the body's filth"[20]

London
printed by William Stanesby and for sale at
Edmund Weaver and John Smithick
1631

[MS 35b] o[n] p. 60 it states thus:[21]
We learn this from the Italian compendium on the rites, life, and
customs of the Jews[v] by Leon of Modena the Jew, who is even today, so I hear, archisynagogus in Venice. The most learned Mr.
William Boswell[w] kindly shared with me an autograph copy that
he had received from him: and[22] in the latest edition in 16°, which I
have, it is on p. 105.[23]

---

title page of the 1631 edition. The Latin text, with Modena's spelling retained, is as
follows: "Joannis Seldeni J.C. De successionibus in Bona defuncti, seu iure hereditario.
Ad leges Hebreorum quae florente olim eorum Republica in usu, Liber singularis ex
sacris literis, utroque Talmude et selectioribus Rabinis, id est ex Juris Ebraici fontibus,
Pandectis, atque consult[iss]imis magistris desumtus.—et sordes, arcta inter vincla, recusat. Londini. Typis Guillielmi Stanesbeii, et prostant apud Edmundum Weaver et
Joannem Smithick. M DCXXXI."

[20] The Latin quotation is from the poem *Psychomachia* by the early Christian writer
Prudentius (Loeb edition, vol. 1, p. 342, line 907). I am grateful to Abraham Wasserstein
of the Hebrew University of Jerusalem for tracking down the reference for me when he
was a visitor at the Institute for Advanced Study, Princeton, in 1986 and 1987.

[21] Latin (Modena's spelling retained): "Discimus haec, ex Leonis Mutinensis Judaei,
qui Venetiis hodieque, ut audio, Archisinagogus est, compendio Italice conscripto de
Ritibus, vita et moribus Ebreorum. Exemplar mecum pro summa sua humanitate communicavit V[ir] Cl[arissimus] erudi[ti]ssimusque Guilielmus Boswellus, qui ab eo autographum accepit."

[22] A note in Modena's own words in Italian: "E nell'ult[im]a editione in 16° che io ho
è a c. 105."

[23] So in the edition of Leiden, 1638, revised by the author. Following Boswell's name,

Per cui ni sappia (ben ch'senza merito) qual sia sta

In Inghilterra l'anno 1631 il titolo del q.

Joannis Seldeni J.C.

De

successionibus in Bona defuncti, seu iure Seredi

Ad leges Hebreorum que florente olim eor

Republica in uso, Liber singularis

ex sacris literis utroque Talmude et selec

Rabinis id est ex Juris Ebraici fontis

Pandectis atque consultimis magistris

desumtus.

— et sordes, areta inter uincla, recusat

Londini

Typis Guilielmi Stanesbeij, et prostant ap.

Edmundum Weauer et Joannem

Smithick

M·DCXXXJ.

12. Pages of the manuscript of *Hayyei yehudah* containing testimonials about Modena by illustrious Christian and Jewish authors.

...ma Luglio 1634 mi capitò un libro stampato in Londra
come qui sotto sarà scritto, o qui d'incontra:

A. C. bo. con dice

Discimus Eae, ex Leonis Mutinensis Judaei, qui
Venetiis hodieque, ut audio, Architinagogus est,
compendio Italicè conscripto de Ritibus
vita et moribus Ebreorum. exemplar mecum
pro summa sua humanitate communicavit
V. Cl. eruditissimusque Guilielmus Boswellus,
qui ab eo autographum accepit:

e nell' ult.^a editione in 16 delo 60 è a c̄. 105

לו קפיטר די לונדרא ...
...
...
...

Io Abraham Israel vidi librum
cui titulus: Valgeus de Confessione
auriculari. uoi in Addenda. dicebat
Leo Mutilensis int. hebraes venetos doctiss.

In[24] addition, the bishop of Lodève, in the large book—which I have not been privileged to see—that he compiled on all the printed Hebrew books, lists all my writings and praises and extols me highly.[x]

The all-encompassing and learned sage Rabbi Manasseh ben Israel,[y] in the book of his written in Spanish,[25] . . . mentions me among the class of commentators and preachers, saying that one should read the books of "the most learned Rabbi Judah da Modena."[26]

[in another hand][27] I, Abraham Israel, have seen a book entitled *Dallaeus on the Oral Confession,*[z] where, in the addenda, he said: Leo of Modena, the most learned among the Venetian rabbis.

[MS 37a, C 111] Will[1]

Several years ago it occurred to me that I should make out my will for the day of my death, and I already wrote some of it. But times having changed in every respect, I wished to rewrite it in accordance with my current wishes at the end of Tammuz 5407 [beginning of August 1647].

I have no wealth or riches in my home to dispose of, for it is empty and lacking in everything, praised be God. My everlasting gift is my written works: compositions, sermons, commentaries,

---

Selden expanded the passage as follows: "Eques Auratus atque apud Ordines Belgiae foederatos serenissimi Regis Magnae Britanniae Orator, qui a Leone autographum accepit."

[24] The following section, mentioning the commendations of the bishop of Lodève and Manasseh ben Israel, is in Hebrew.

[25] Modena left a lacuna of four dots; he either did not know or had forgotten the title of Manasseh ben Israel's book. It was, perhaps, one of the unpublished works listed at the end of Cecil Roth's *A Life of Menasseh ben Israel* (Philadelphia, 1945), pp. 304–305 (a suggestion I owe to Miriam Bodian). Modena may never actually have seen the book.

[26] Italian phrase "Il doctissimo Rabi Juda da Modena," written in Hebrew letters. *Doctissimo* is a Latinate form of the Italian word *dottissimo*.

[27] This sentence, written in Latin, was copied on this page by someone who at one time saw, and perhaps read, the manuscript of *Hayyei yehudah*. Latin: "Ego Abraham Israel Vidi librum cui titulus dallaeus de Confessione auriculari ubi in Addenda dicebat Leo mutinensis int. Rabinis venetiis doctissimus."

[1] In the manuscript, this, the later of Modena's two Hebrew wills, comes first, and the one written in 1634 follows, on the final page (fol. 38a). The will of 1634 was copied in a strong hand (as is most of the autobiography) and still retains the original black color of the ink. The later will (1647/1648) betrays the less firm hand of the aged, ailing Modena, and the ink has turned reddish brown on the page, indicating that its source was a batch of ink of poorer quality than that employed to copy the earlier will.

and novellas of different kinds, all in great number. They are written in a small hand[2] and in outline form, which, if written out and explained, would constitute a burden fit for a camel.[a] Some of them are mentioned above on page 33,[3] especially the printed ones. In a different generation their renown would be great and they would be more pleasing than many others.[b]

I[4] wrote this much at the end of Tammuz 5407 [beginning of August 1647], as an introduction to my will, which I would have liked to have completed on my own, but could not. Then, around the end of Heshvan 5408 [November 1647], I became ill with shortness of breath, from which I am now, at the end of Shevat [late February 1648], suffering worse. On the 28th of Heshvan [November 26, 1647] I recited the confessional prayer in the presence of ten men, including three rabbis, namely, Rabbi Simhah Luzzatto,[c] Rabbi Nehemiah Saraval,[d] and Rabbi Shemaiah di Medina.[e] [C 112] After the confession I asked everyone else to leave, and, in their presence, I gave one manner of disposition concerning my writings, compositions, and books. About fifteen days later I changed my mind about that manner and summoned Abraham H[aver] T[ov],[f] may God his Rock protect him and grant him long life, Isaiah Nizza,[g] and[sh] . . . and arranged it in a different manner. And now, on this day, having changed my mind also about the second, I hereby arrange it in accordance with my latest wish, which I want to be executed when I pass away unless I write differently below.

First,[6] at the end of the first month following my death, I direct my grandson Isaac min Haleviim, may God his Rock protect him and grant him long life, to assemble all my writings and compositions and those by others than myself, and separate the Hebrew ones from those in Italian, under my curse lest he overlook anything, even one page. Then he should summon some wise and trustworthy Torah scholar who, in the presence of the *haver* Moses

---

[2] Hebrew *etzba' ketanah*; it seems to mean "in tiny letters."
[3] Modena's list of writings begins, indeed, at the top of the page numbered *lamed gimel* (= 33) by him (fol. 20a).
[4] The continuation of this will is written in an even shakier hand than the section above.
[5] Modena left a blank in the manuscript. Evidently he had forgotten the name of the other person he had summoned. See historical note h.
[6] An enlarged letter *r* begins the word *rishonah*, "first."

son of Judah Luzzattin[i] of blessed memory and Solomon son of
Mordecai Ashkenazi,[j] may God his Rock protect him and grant
him long life, should first take everything written in Italian and
divide [MS 37b] these works into four portions, as equal as possible.
Then, as decided by lot, two portions should be sent to Abtalion
son of the *haver* Moses Fano, may God his Rock protect him and
grant him long life, my daughter's son, who lives in Padua; another
portion to that Solomon Ashkenazi; and the fourth portion to my
grandson, the *haver* Isaac min Haleviim. Then, as much as I have
written at that time of my treatise against the Christians, *Magen ve-
herev*,[k] and of my quarto-sized journal,[l] in which I wrote memorandum notes for some things to be written in that treatise [C 113],
should be given to the *haver* Moses son of J[udah], mentioned before.[m] In addition, in the presence of the Torah scholar who is to
divide up [my writings], he should be given twelve of my sermons,
namely, for Hanukkah, for Shabbat Shirah,[n] for Shabbat Zakhor,[o]
for Shabbat Hagadol,[p] for Passover, for Shavuot, for the Sabbath
before the 9th of Av,[q] for [Shabbat] Nahamu,[r] for the new year, for
[the Sabbath of] repentance,[s] for Sukkot, and for the eighth Day of
assembly.

All the rest of my writings, treatises, begging letters,[t] journals,[u]
and memorandum notes,[v] as well as every treatise and writing by
others than myself, no matter what it be, in manuscript, should go
to my grandson Isaac min Haleviim in entirety. From the printed
books, in addition to the Kuzari[w] and Kohen-Job[x] and another
book that he already has but which I cannot remember, he should
take my copy of *Keli yakar*,[y] treating it as precious on account of
the notes that I jotted down therein,[z] and, in addition, the books
Divrei shelomo,[a] *'Akedah*,[b] and Abravanel on the Torah,[c] which are
incomplete, and my books *Midbar yehudah, Galut yehudah*, and *Lev
aryeh*. All the rest of the printed Hebrew and Italian books should
go to whomever will be judged my legal heir.[d] It will amount to
very little.

Such is my final wish, unless I write something below. Today,
Monday the first day of the month of Adar 5408 [February 24,
1648], sick and faint of body and soul and in every other respect.
Only let my supplication ascend to God to have mercy on my soul.

[MS 38a, C 114] With God's Help
Will^e

For many years I have had in mind making a will and arranging
things for the time of my punishment [i.e., death] regarding what
should be done with my body, writings, books, and compositions,
because I have no wealth or riches for disposal. And now, on this
Tuesday[7] the 3rd of Sivan 5394 [May 30, 1634], my head and limbs
being heavy, and feeling weak, I took my pen in hand lest time and
chance befall me this very minute.[8] This is my word and my wish.
First of all regarding burial, eulogy, and gravestone:

Many years ago I had a dream[9] that I was asked about the manner
in which my burial should be conducted, and I responded, "In such
a manner." I now decree and order that so it should really be done.

The[10] coffin should be rectangular, instead of with a sloped top.^f
Upon it let them place only books I have written,^g both printed
ones and ones in manuscript. But let them take care with those in
manuscript lest someone lay hands on them. Therefore, let them
lay out only the large and well-bound ones.

The cantors shall not chant behind my coffin Tokhahot^h for
others but rather either the Maʿalot Psalm [that begins] "I will lift
my eyes unto the mountains";[11] or [the text that begins] "For unto
thee, O Lord, do I lift up my soul"[12] and ends "His soul shall abide
in prosperity and his seed shall inherit the land";[13] or [the text] composed by my grandson I[saac] m[in] H[aleviim], may God his Rock
protect him and grant him long life, [that begins] "O thou that
dwellest in the covert of the Most High."[14]

Regarding the eulogy, both at the cemetery and afterward during

---

[7] There is a hole in the manuscript where the words *yom g* (= "the third day" of the
week, namely, Tuesday) were written. The tail end of the letter *g* is preserved.

[8] Ecclesiastes 9:11. Only the first and last letters of the word *ka-regaʿ*, "this very minute," are preserved, owing to the hole in the manuscript (see previous note).

[9] On this page in the manuscript there is a tear along the right-hand margin. The page
has been glued to another sheet of paper, and at the beginning of line 6, someone added
two letters *n-ʾ* to the truncated word *-lamti*. The completion *neʾelamti* that was printed
in the Kahana edition, p. 69, makes little sense here. Most likely the word is *halamti*, "I
had a dream."

[10] At the beginning of the line in the manuscript, part of the letter *h* is visible at the
tear along the margin.

[11] Psalm 121.   [12] Psalm 86:4.   [13] Psalm 25:13.

[14] Psalm 91:1. The comment about his grandson was added by Modena later on.

the first month, I had already decided to demand that there be no eulogy at all when I began to compose a eulogy of my own to be recited by my son-in-law Rabbi Jacob min Haleviim of blessed memory. (Written in the margin:[15] [and after] his death, my grandson the son of Rabbi J[acob] mentioned above.) But God took him away before taking me. Without me I do not want people to listen to my voice, but rather to do as they wish. I would only adjure them in the name of God, and if I could I would so decree, that they not dwell at length on my praise but only say that I was not a hypocrite; that my beliefs were consistent with my actions;[16] that I was a God-fearing man; that I turned from evil[17] more in private than in public; that I showed no more favoritism to admirers or relatives or myself for my benefit than seemed to me to be proper; that I was well liked by people, both great and humble; and let them make the effort to quote in my name original verses or sayings.

Let them bury me[i] near the entrance to the cemetery that leads out to the field, next to my mother, sons, grandfather, and uncle.[j] Let them march around my grave according to the custom of the Levantines.[k]

[MS 38b] Let my son Isaac, may God his Rock protect him and grant him long life, come to the Italian synagogue all the [first] year to recite Kaddish.[l]

Before three months have passed let them erect a durable gravestone that will last as long as possible, inscribed exactly as the following words are.[18]

The words of the deceased:

From above they have transferred to the possession
of Judah Aryeh

[15] In the margin the manuscript contains part of a note (the beginning is torn away) by the author: "[ve-aharei] moto nekhdi ben m-h-r-r-y ha-n-l (= moreni ha-rav rabbenu ya'akov ha-nizkar le-'eil]." Apparently Modena subsequently decided to allow his grandson to substitute for his deceased son-in-law in reciting the eulogy he had composed for himself and added this codicil in the margin.

[16] Hebrew *tokhi ke-vori*, "my inside [was] like my outside."

[17] A play on the title of his book on games of chance, *Sur mera'*, "Turn from Evil."

[18] Modena does not mean that the text must be reproduced exactly, because further on he states that changes may be made. Rather, he means that the inscription should be laid out in a particular form, which he proceeds to show by copying the inscription in large, square letters and by dividing each line into hemistichs of poetry. See Carpi edition, p. 115.

13. Leon Modena's gravestone, showing the exposed
first lines of his epitaph.

Modena,[19] now acquainted with him
   and at peace,[20]
Four cubits of ground in this compound
By making the acquisition binding[21m]
   and eternal.
   Died, on the day . . .

If, however, one of my poetically minded students sees fit, they
may put the second stich before the first and substitute for "now
acquainted with him and at peace" the line "Herewith hidden and

[19] Modena separated the word *mi-modena*, "(from, of) Modena," into two smaller
words, *mi-mo dina*, "from whom [namely, God], judgment," creating a clever pun.
[20] Cf. Job 22:21.
[21] Hebrew: *kinyan sudar*, literally "acquisition by shaking a handkerchief [*sudar*]," here
apparently meant as a pun on the verb *sudar*, "arranged," hence the translation, "binding." See historical note m.

concealed"—as appears best to them. And this latter way seems right to me.[n]

At[22] the beginning of the month of Nisan [5]402 [began April 1, 1642], I left the Cigala place and went to live in the h[ouse] of M[oses] L[uzzato], in "the Cave of Makhpelah."[o] One year.

In Adar [5]403 [February–March 1643] I left the Luzzatto place to live in the little dwelling of I[saac] O[badiah].[p] Seven months.

On Rosh Hashanah [5]404 [September 14, 1643] I entered the house of Cervo.[q] Nine months.

In Sivan [5]404 [June–July 1644] I returned to the h[ouse] of M[oses] L[uzzatto].[r] Four months.

In Tishre [5]405 [September 1644] I entered the house of Baldoz,[s] until the upcoming Tishre of [5]408 [began September 30, 1647], which will make three years.

Kislev [5]402 [November–December 1641] to the house of Pomis. Seventeen months.

[5]403, end of Sivan [June 1643] to Monsel[ice]. Fourteen months.

Rosh Hashanah[23] [5]404 to Cannaregio.[t] Fourteen months.

Heshvan [5]405 [began October 31, 1644] to Scoz. Six[24] months.

About Sivan [5]405[25] [May–June 1645] to Pomis.

[22] The following brief notes by the author about his peregrinations from residence to residence during the years 5402–5408 are found at the bottom of the last page of the manuscript. With one minor exception regarding a name, all of the information accords with what Modena wrote above in the autobiography. The part that begins "Kislev [5]402 to the house of Pomis. Seventeen months," separated from the previous section by a line and appearing as five short jottings on two lines, does not have its counterpart above, and its proper interpretation is unclear. It is written in an even shakier hand than the previous part.

[23] Before the words "Rosh Hashanah" the name of the month of Elul (the last month before the beginning of the new year) is rubbed out. Elul 5403, the final month of the year, began on August 16, 1643, and Rosh Hashanah 5404 fell on September 14.

[24] Or "Seven months"; the letter is either *v* (= 6) or *z* (= 7).

[25] Manuscript reads *t-h* [5]405. Cf. Carpi edition, p. 116 n. 7 (end).

Historical Notes

HOWARD E. ADELMAN AND

BENJAMIN C. I. RAVID

A PART FROM Modena's autobiography, *Hayyei yehudah*, the most important primary source for reconstructing his life is his letters, primarily written in Hebrew but with some in Italian, and they are extensively cited in these historical notes. In almost all cases, they have been consulted in manuscript, even when previously published. A selection of Modena's Hebrew letters (taken from two British Library manuscripts, Or. 5395 and 5396) was published by Ludwig (Judah Leib) Blau as *Kitvei ha-rav yehudah aryeh mi-modena* (Budapest, 1905), republished by him with the first modern critical biography of Modena under the title *Leo Modenas Briefe und Schriftstücke* (Budapest, 1906), and again under the same title with an expanded introduction (Strasbourg, 1907). Blau also contributed some notes to the first Hebrew edition of *Hayyei yehudah* by A. Kahana (1911). But like Kahana, who had not seen the original manuscript of *Hayyei yehudah*, Blau also had not seen the manuscripts of the texts he published, which had been carelessly copied for him. Subsequently a new collection of Hebrew letters by Leon Modena, *Iggerot rabbi yehudah aryeh mi-modena*, meticulously edited by Yacob Boksenboim, has appeared (Tel Aviv, 1984). It partially overlaps with, and improves, the edition done by Blau, and also includes additional letters from a manuscript that had been unknown to him (Moscow–Guenzburg 356). Other important sources for these historical notes include Modena's works of various genres, published and unpublished, such as rabbinic responsa, sermons, polemics, poetry, prefaces, dedications, registers of Venetian Jewish communal organizations, material preserved in ASV, and references to him in the writings of his contemporaries.

There are numerous recent and accessible general histories of Venice, written from varying perspectives. Special mention should be made of F. C. Lane, *Venice: A Maritime Republic* (Baltimore, 1973), with extensive bibliography. More specialized works dealing with the period of Modena's life include W. Bouwsma, *Venice and the Defense of Republican Liberty: Renaissance Values in the Age of the Counter Reformation* (Berkeley, 1968); B. Pullan, *Crisis and Change in the Venetian Economy in the Sixteenth and Seventeenth Centuries* (London, 1968); P. F. Grendler, *The Roman Inquisition and the Venetian Press, 1540–1605* (Princeton, 1977); and G. Arnaldi and M. P. Stocchi, eds., *Storia della cultura veneta* 4.2 (Vicenza, 1984).

On the Jews of Venice, C. Roth's *The Jewish Community of Venice* (Philadelphia, 1930) is dated and must be used with great caution. R. Calimani's *Storia del ghetto di Venezia* (Milan, 1985), now being translated into English, constitutes a useful synthesis of the increasingly large number of specialized studies on the Jews of Venice. Recent book-length treatments of key aspects of the history of the Jews of Venice include: B. Pullan, *Rich and Poor in Renaissance Venice: The Social Institutions of a Catholic State to 1620* (Cambridge, 1971); B. Ravid, *Economics and Toleration in Seventeenth Century Venice: The Background and Context of the Discorso of Simone Luzzatto* (Jerusalem, 1978); B. Pullan, *The Jews of Europe and the Inquisition of Venice, 1550–1670* (Totowa, N.J., 1983); and the texts in P. C. Ioly Zorattini, *Processi del S. Ufficio di Venezia contro ebrei e giudaizzanti*, 5 vols. to date (Florence, 1980–). Mention must also be made of the Hebrew book on the rabbinate in Renaissance Italy by R. Bonfil, *Ha-rabbanut be-italiah bi-tekufat ha-renasans* (Jerusalem, 1979), now being translated into English, and proceedings of a conference on the Jews of Venice, *Gli Ebrei e Venezia*, ed. G. Cozzi (Milan, 1987), with an extensive bibliography, pp. 867–910.

For a general introduction to the Jews in Renaissance and Counter-Reformation Italy, see M. A. Shulvass, *The Jews in the World of the Renaissance*, trans. E. Koss (Leiden, 1973, from the Hebrew of 1955); C. Roth, *The Jews in the Renaissance* (Philadelphia, 1959); S. W. Baron, *A Social and Religious History of the Jews* (Philadelphia, 1952–), vol. 13, pp. 159–205, and vol. 14, pp. 3–146; and *Italia judaica*, vols. 1 (Rome, 1983) and 2 (Rome, 1986). For a comprehensive treatment of the life and writings of Modena, see the doctoral dissertation of H. E. Adelman, "Success and Failure in Seventeenth Century Venice: The Life and Thought of Leon Modena, 1571–1648" (Brandeis University, 1985).

FOLIO 4a

a. *Judah Aryeh*: The name Judah, popular among Jews, was first given to the fourth son of Jacob and Leah in the Bible. On the basis of a verse in the blessing of Jacob, Genesis 49:9, "Judah is a lion's whelp," Judah came to be associated with the lion, "Aryeh," in Hebrew and "Leone" in Italian; see V. Colorni, "La Corrispondenza fra nomi ebraici e nomi locali nella prassi dell'ebraismo italiano," *Judaica minori* (Milan, 1983), pp. 741–743. Leone became Leon in the Venetian dialect, which tended to drop final vowels, a phenomenon noticeable throughout the autobiography in the Hebrew transcription of Italian words.

b. *Isaac*: Numerous further references to Isaac will be encountered in the autobiography.

c. *Mordecai*: On Mordecai see *The Life of Judah*, fol. 5a.

d. *Moses*: Moses, the great-great grandfather of Leon Modena, is the earliest ancestor mentioned in the autobiography and was, it appears, the only one who actually lived in Modena. He is mentioned in the introduction of Solomon bar Shem Tov Atiah, *Perush tehillim* (Venice, 1549); I. Reggio, *Behinat ha-kabbalah* (Gorizia, 1851), p. vi; and N. Libowitz, *R. yehudah aryeh modena* (New York, 1901), p. 3. On a David son of Moise da Modena who ran a loan bank in Pavia in 1512, see S. Simonsohn, *The Jews in the Duchy of Milan*, 4 vols. (Jerusalem, 1982–1986), no. 1328.

e. *known as Angelo*: In Italy Jews named Mordecai were often called Angelo because of a rabbinic tradition that the biblical Esther's uncle Mordecai was the prophet Malachi, whose name means "my angel," hence Angelo in Italian. Roth, *Venice*, p. 168; Colorni, "La Corrispondenza fra nomi ebraici," pp. 763–765; Simonsohn, *Milan*, no. 1724. Modena sometimes called Mordecai "Malachi": Boksenboim, *Iggerot*, no. 145. Later a niece named after Mordecai was called Angelitta; see *The Life of Judah*, fol. 23a.

FOLIO 4b

f. *I had neither tranquility . . . and then disquietude came upon me*: This verse from Job 3:26 was often used by Modena either wholly or in part at critical periods of his life, in the tradition of the medieval Hebrew poets who adopted biblical verses as their motto.

g. *my son Mordecai*: The events leading up to Mordecai's death in November 1617 due to his alchemical experiments are described in *The Life of Judah*, fols. 15b–16a, 17a.

h. *what new happens to me*: Modena did not carry out this promise, but rather periodically added sections and also made interpolations in previously written entries. By paying attention to such phrases as "now," "up to now," "at this time," one can usually determine approximately when a section was written.

i. *After that will come my will*: At the end of Modena's autobiography two wills appear, one from 1634 and the other from 1647–1648; see excursus 2.

j. *came from France*: Presumably his ancestors left France as a result of one of the numerous fourteenth century expulsions of the Jews, which occurred in 1306, 1311, 1322, 1349, and 1394; see S. Schwarzfuchs, "The Expulsion of the Jews from France (1306)," in *The Seventy-Fifth Anniversary Volume of the Jewish Quarterly Review*, ed. A. Neuman and S. Zeitlin, (Philadelphia, 1967), pp. 482–489; R. Chazan, *Medieval Jewry in Northern France* (Baltimore, 1973), pp. 191–205.

k. *family tree*: On the interest in family trees among the Jews of Italy, see Isaac min Haleviim, *Medabber tahpukhot*, ed. D. Carpi (Tel Aviv, 1985), p. 103.

l. *Rabbi Solomon*: Modena will describe Solomon in more detail further on; see *The Life of Judah*, fol. 5b.

m. *Rabbi Aaron*: Aaron Berechiah of Modena (d. 1639), a leading mystic and poet of his generation; see I. Tishby, "Ha-'imut bein kabbalat ha-'ari le-kabbalat ha-ramak," *Zion* 39 (1974): 8–85; an English summary is found in the back of the journal, pp. 10–15.

n. *in Modena*: Modena was an independent duchy north of Rome, ruled by the dukes of Este. The problem of Jewish family names in Italy (see the preface to this volume) is illustrated here by the appearance of two men who apparently have the same last name in Hebrew, *mi-modena*, which means "of Modena" and can be rendered in Italian as "da Modena." Solomon Modena was from Bologna so, as with his nephew Leon, Modena was simply his last name. Moses *of* Modena, however, actually lived in Modena. Although he may also have been a distant blood relative, he was immediately related to Leon by virtue of his marriage to Solomon Modena's daughter Imperia, Leon's cousin (*The Life of Judah*, fol. 5b). For a discussion of the traditions of family names among Italian Jews, see Shulvass, *Renaissance*, pp. 32–37.

o. *Viterbo*: A town slightly northwest of Rome under papal rule where there had been an active Jewish community since the early fourteenth century; see C. Roth, "Il Primo Soggiorno degli ebrei a Viterbo," *RMI* 20 (1954): 367–371; A. Milano, "Sugli Ebrei a Viterbo," in *Scritti in memoria di Guido Bedarida* (Florence, 1966), pp. 137–149.

p. *the first to establish a pawnshop there*: This claim has not been substantiated to date by research on the history of the Jews of Modena; see A. Balleti, *Gli Ebrei e gli estensi* (Reggio-Emilia, 1930), pp. 16–17. For a general discussion of Jewish moneylending, see S. Stein, "Interest Taken by Jews from Gentiles: An Evaluation of Source Material (Fourteenth to Seventeenth Centuries)," *Journal of Semitic Studies* 1 (1956): 141–164; J. Rosenthal, "Ribbit min ha-nokhri," in his *Mehkarim*, 1 (Jerusalem, 1967): 253–323; Baron, *Social and Religious History of the Jews*, vol. 12, pp. 132–197; the documents published in R. Chazan, *Church, State, and Jew in the Middle Ages* (New York, 1980), pp. 197–220; and *EJ*, s.v. "moneylending" and "usury." For a specific discussion of events in Venice, see R. Mueller, "Les Prêteurs juifs de Venise au Moyen Âge," *Annales* 30 (1975): 1277–1302; Pullan, *Rich and Poor*, pp. 476–578; L. Poliakov, *Jewish Bankers and the Holy See from the Thirteenth to the Seventeenth Century* (London, 1977, from the French of 1967), pp. 199–210; B. Ravid, "The Socioeconomic Background of the Expulsion and Readmission of the Venetian Jews, 1571–73," in *Essays in Modern Jewish History: A Tribute to Ben Halpern*, ed. F. Malino and P. Albert (Rutherford, N.J., 1982), pp. 27–55; B. Ravid, "Moneylending in Seventeenth Century Vernacular Jewish Apologetica," in *Jewish Thought in the Seventeenth Century*, ed. I. Twersky and B. Septimus (Cambridge, 1987), pp. 257–284; B. Pullan, "Jewish Moneylending in Venice: From Private Enterprise to Public Service," in *Gli Ebrei e Venezia*, pp. 671–686.

q. *our crest*: On Jewish family crests in Italy, see C. Roth, "Stemmi di famiglie ebraiche italiane," in *Scritti in memoria di Leone Carpi*, ed. D. Carpi and A. Milano (Jerusalem, 1967), pp. 165–184 (with a sketch of the Modena crest on p. 167).

r. *all those who ruled Modena—popes, emperors, dukes, and the like*: At the beginning of the sixteenth century, numerous parties made claims on Modena, and the city changed hands several times. On the Jews of Modena, see I. Sonne, "Le-toledot kehillat boloniah bi-tehillat ha-me'ah ha-16," *HUCA* 16 (1941): 35–40.

FOLIO 5a

s. *Bologna*: South of Modena, Bologna had one of the most thriving Jewish communities in Italy during the sixteenth century, and records indicate that on Friday, February 24, 1505 the house of Isaac and Joseph Modena, rich Jewish bankers, burned. It was situated on the corner of Israda Maggiore (no. 213) and Pazzuola di S. Michele dei Perosetti. V. Rava, "Gli Ebrei in Bologna," *EI* 20 (1877): 295. On the expulsion of the Jews from Bologna in 1569, see D. Carpi, "Gerush ha-yehudim mi-medinat ha-kenesiah biymei ha-apifior pius ha-hamishi u-mishpetei ha-hakirah neged yehudei boloniah, 1566–1569," in *Scritti in memoria di Enzo Sereni*, ed. D. Carpi, A. Milano, and U. Nahon (Jerusalem, 1970), pp. 145–165.

t. *only during the past ten years and but two or three times*: From the available sources it appears that Leon Modena had visited the city of Modena once, about 1608. His next reported visit was to be in 1630; see *Ari nohem*, ed. N. Libowitz (Jerusalem, 1929), p. 49, and *The Life of Judah*, fol. 22a.

u. *Leon Modena da Venezia*: Modena consistently referred to himself in three ways: in Italian as Leon Modena; in Hebrew as Yehudah Aryeh Mimodena; and in Latin as Leo Mutinensis.

v. *Mordecai*: 1480–1530. He was called, perhaps with some exaggeration, "the wonder of his generation," *mofet ha-dor*, based on B.T. Hullin 103b: Bonfil, *Ha-rabbanut*, p. 220. Much of the information about Mordecai in the autobiography is confirmed by Aaron Berechiah of Modena in his *Ma'avar yabbok* (Mantua, 1626; Zhitomir, 1851), fols. 7a–8a.

w. *Beit Yosef of the gaon Caro*: Joseph Caro (1488–1575), the well-known author of the Shulhan Arukh, which became the basic guide for everyday conduct for traditional Jews, was born to a Sephardic family. After the exile of 1492, his family moved to Portugal, Egypt, and Turkey, and he finally settled in Safed. Caro finished his Beit Yosef, a commentary on Jacob ben Asher's Arba'ah Turim, in 1542, but it was not published until 1550–1558. Thus his and Mordecai Modena's efforts were simultaneous but independent. On Caro see H. Adelman, "From Zion Shall Go Forth the Law: On the 500th Anniversary of the Birth of Joseph Caro," *JBA* 45 (1987–1988): 143–157.

x. *rabbinic explanations, legal rulings, and other treatises*: Some of Mordecai Modena's opinions are still extant; see M. Montefiore, "Un Recueil de consultations rabbiniques," *REJ* 10 (1885): 186; A. Marx, "R. yosef ish arli be-tor moreh ve-rosh yeshivah be-sienah," in *Sefer ha-yovel li-khevod levi ginzburg li-mele'at lo shiv'im shanah* (New York, 1946), p. 280; M. Ghirondi, *Toledot gedolei yisrael* (Trieste, 1853), no. 49, pp. 244, 246; JTSA, ENA, 890, now edited by Y. Boksenboim, *She'elot u-teshuvot mattanot ba-adam* (Tel Aviv, 1983), no. 57. Aaron Berechiah of Modena showed his great-grandfather's collection of rabbinic decisions to Leon Modena sometime between 1618 and 1630, and Modena made summaries of them that are still extant; see Ancona, Comunità Israelitica, MS 7, fol. 13a–b; *Ziknei yehudah*, ed. S. Simonsohn (Jerusalem, 1956), p. 16; and *Devar shemuel*, ed. Samuel Aboab (Venice, 1702), no. 19.

y. *Charles V*: 1500–1558, king of Spain and Lombardy, 1516–1556, Holy Roman emperor, 1519–1556. He was associated with many other significant Jewish personalities of the period including David Reuveni, Solomon Molcho, Gracia Mendes, and Josel of Rosheim.

z. *medical diploma while he was there*: According to Roth, who did not cite any sources, in 1528 Angelo (Mordecai) Modena was the first Jew ready to graduate from the medical school at Bologna, and in order for him to receive his degree in 1529, it was necessary for the papal governor to intervene: Roth, *Renaissance*, pp. 38–39; idem, "The Medieval University and the Jew," *Menorah Journal* 19 (1930–1931): 135; the texts, concerning Angelo di Isac in the year 1528, have been published by V. Colorni, "Sull'Ammisibilità degli ebrei alla laurea anteriormente al secolo xix," *RMI* 16 (1950): 210. Charles V was crowned king of Lombardy by Pope Clement VII in Bologna in 1530, the year Mordecai Modena died.

a. *Shalshelet ha-kabbalah: The Chain of Tradition,* by Gedaliah ibn Yahya, was first published in Venice in 1587. In the Jerusalem edition (1961/1962) Mordecai is mentioned on p. 146.

b. *your verse from the Bible*: On Jewish bibliomancy, the practice of using the Bible for purposes of divination, see J. Tractenberg, *Jewish Magic and Superstition* (New York, 1939), p. 216. This activity was widespread among Italian Jewry, as can be seen from the numerous examples of it cited in the autobiography. The verse requested from the boy was probably the last one he had studied.

FOLIO 5b

c. *Isaac Gallico*: Another Gallico served as tutor to Leon Modena, Mordecai Modena's grandson; see *This Life of Judah*, fol. 7b.

d. *four male children*: Mordecai also had at least two daughters, the name of only one of whom, Sarah, is known. It is surprising that Leon Modena never mentioned these aunts or any of their offspring. Information about them is available only from other authors; Marx, "R. yosef ish arli be-tor moreh ve-rosh yeshivah be-sienah," pp. 279–284.

e. *at the time*: Based on the information available in the autobiography and in Marx's essay cited in note d, above, at the time of Mordecai's death, Isaac was nine years old, Solomon, between six and eight years, Shemaiah, between three and six years, and Abtalion, eighteen months old.

f. *Rabbi Solomon*: Solomon Jacob Raphael Modena was a great rabbinic scholar who lived from about 1522 or 1524 until 1580. In 1542 he made plans to stay in Siena, a town in Tuscany in central Italy. He intended to study and to live with Ishmael Rieti, his sister's wealthy father-in-law, who ran a small school in his house there. In Siena Solomon studied letter writing, music, and Latin with Joseph Arli, a rabbi, scholar, kabbalist, writer, and teacher. The correspondence from Rieti and Arli to Solomon Modena is still extant. JTSA 3759, 3833; Marx, "R. yosef ish arli be-tor moreh ve-rosh yeshivah be-sienah," pp. 279–285. Isaac ben Immanuel Lattes ordained Solomon in 1546, and his ordination diploma, which is also still extant, contains expressions of great praise: Bonfil, *Ha-rabbanut*, p. 220. Solomon Modena wrote a Hebrew apologetic treatise defending rabbinic Judaism against the accusations of the apostate Alessandro Franceschi and showing that Jews did not harbor anti-Christian views; see D. Ruderman, "A Jewish Apologetic Treatise in Sixteenth Century Bologna," *HUCA* 50 (1979): 253–275. Solomon was also involved in commerce in Bologna, where he had amassed great wealth. Some of his business letters are still extant: D. Kaufmann, "Letters of Salomon di Modena to Abraham del Bene," *JQR* o.s. 8 (1896): 523–524. After he left for Ferrara in 1566, the Jewish community of Bologna accused him of tax delinquency: Ruderman, "Bologna," p. 261. In his *Me'or 'einayim* (Mantua, 1573), fol. 9b, Azariah de Rossi (ca. 1511–1578), the leading critical Jewish historian in Italy during the sixteenth century (see historical notes to fol. 6a), listed Solomon Modena as a philanthropist in Ferrara at the time of the great earthquake of 1570. In the margin of his own copy of *Me'or 'einayim*, preserved in the Biblioteca Palatina, Parma, MS 983, Leon Modena noted this reference to his uncle.

g. *Fioretta*: According to her grandson, Aaron Berechiah of Modena, whom she reared, Fioretta (Batsheva) was an expert in the Torah, Mishnah, Talmud, Midrash, Jewish law, especially Maimonides, and kabbalistic literature, such as the Zohar: *Ma'avar yabbok*, fol. 7a; S. Assaf, *Mekorot le-toledot ha-hinnukh be-yisrael* (Jerusalem, 1930–1943), vol. 4, p. 54; C. Roth, *The House of Nasi: Doña Gracia* (Philadelphia, 1947), pp. 68–69; A. Pesaro, "Le Donne celebri israelite," *VI* 29 (1881): 33–34; and on Jewish women in the Renaissance, see Roth, *Renaissance*, pp. 44–58; Shulvass, *Renaissance*, pp. 159–168.

h. *passed through Venice*: Because of its geographic location, Venice had served for centuries as a point of departure for pilgrims to the Holy Land, both Jewish and Christian, from northern and central Europe. For an interesting, almost contemporary, account of a journey from Venice to Cyprus on a Venetian ship, see the Hebrew letter of Elie di Pesaro, published by B. Goldberg in *Hayyei ʿolam* 5 (1879–1880): 6–25, reprinted in *Masaʿot eretz yisrael*, ed. A. Yaari (Ramat Gan, 1976), pp. 165–196, and translated into French by M. Schwarz as "Voyage ethnographique de Venise à Chypre," *Revue de geographie* 5 (1879): 206–228. See also the general summary with quotations by H. Barnaby, "A Voyage to Cyprus in 1563," *Mariner's Mirror* 56 (1970): 309–314 and the article of J. Shatzmiller to appear in the proceedings of the congress on "The Mediterranean and the Jews: Banking, Finance, and International Trade: 16th–18th Centuries" held at Bar-Ilan University, June 1984.

i. *alchemy*: On alchemy, see historical notes to fol. 14a.

j. *Vignola*: South of Modena and west of Bologna.

FOLIO 6a

k. *Abtalion*: 1529–1611. Abtalion went to Padua to attend medical school and also studied Talmud there with Meir ben Isaac Katzenellenbogen, the famous Maharam of Padua (1473–1565): *Mikveh yisrael*, ed. Judah Saltaro Fano (Venice, 1607), fol. 36b. Meir's son, Samuel Judah Katzenellenbogen (1521–1597), a leading Venetian rabbi of the period, reported that Abtalion Modena was an outstanding scholar in Gemara, rabbinic decisions, and all "lofty knowledge," *hokhmah rammah*; see *Mikveh yisrael*, fol. 35a.

l. *Azariah de Rossi . . . praises him many times in his book "Meʾor ʿeinayim"*: He mentioned Abtalion only twice in *Meʾor ʿeinayim*, citing him as a scholar of the academy of the Sephardim in Ferrara who, in addition to possessing a large collection of books and manuscripts, was noted for his wisdom and critical ability to identify additions to printed editions of traditional Jewish texts. See Azariah de Rossi, *Meʾor ʿeinayim* (Mantua, 1573), fols. 86b and 123a and ed. D. Cassel (Vilna, 1866), pp. 233, 323. Copies of the book were rare because access to it had been severely curtailed by the rabbis of Italy, who were afraid that de Rossi's methodology and presentation, especially in the third section, would pose a threat to the religious faith of young Jews. Modena nevertheless obtained a copy of the first edition of 1573. He used the margins to record important events in his own life as well as his reactions to some of de Rossi's ideas. Indeed, many of Modena's most significant writings, such as those on Kabbalah, can only be fully understood in the light of his reading of Azariah de Rossi. Modena's copy of *Meʾor ʿeinayim*, with his handwritten comments in the margins, is preserved in the Biblioteca Palatina in Parma. On the life and work of de Rossi, see S. Baron, *History and Jewish Historians*, ed. A. Hertzberg and L. Feldman (Philadelphia, 1964), pp. 167–239; J. Weinberg, "Azariah dei Rossi: Towards an Appraisal of the Last Years of His Life," *Annali della Scuola normale superiore di Pisa* 8 (1978): 495–511; Y. Yerushalmi, *Zakhor: Jewish History and Jewish Memory* (Seattle and London, 1982), s.v. index; R. Bonfil, "Some Reflections on the Place of Azariah de Rossi's *Meor enayim* in the Cultural Milieu of Italian Renaissance Jewry," in *Jewish Thought in the Sixteenth Century*, ed. B. Cooperman (Cambridge, 1983), pp. 23–48; A. Melamed, "The Perception of Jewish History in Italian Jewish Thought of the Sixteenth and Seventeenth Centuries," in *Italia judaica*, vol. 2, pp. 137–170.

m. *Gregory XIII*: Gregory XIII (1572–1585) had ordered the Jews to surrender all talmudic and rabbinic works, even if they had already been censored. Abtalion also defended the right of Jewish doctors to treat Christian patients; see W. Popper, *The Censorship of Hebrew Books* (New York, 1899), p. 66; Baron, *Social and Religious History of the Jews*, vol. 9, p. 205.

n. *Judah Fano, commonly known as Saltaro*: Fano is on the Adriatic coast of Italy south of Pesaro; Saltara is slightly west of Fano. Judah's son Moses later married Leon Modena's daughter Diana in 1632. These two men are each known variously as Saltaro, Fano, or Saltaro Fano. The names were interchangeable probably because of the close proximity of the two towns. Indeed, reflecting the fact that Italian Jewish family names from this period do not usually correlate with the names of the cities in which the persons actually lived, Judah is also called "Judah the son of Moses Saltaro Fano of the inhabitants of Venice"; see *Mikveh yisrael*, title page; *Ziknei*, nos. 6, 9, 56, 61; Boksenboim, *Iggerot*, nos. 64, 73, 90, 93, 117; *The Life of Judah*, fol. 23a.

o. *At the age of seventeen*: Also at the age of seventeen Isaac Modena was one of the *tuvei ha-'ir*, the leaders of the Jewish community of Bologna, who had endorsed a communal ordinance on November 1, 1536 limiting the taking of evidence to a court composed of three scholars at least twenty-five years old who had to work in the presence of a judge: Sonne, "Bologna," p. 40. At the same age, Alessandro Bivago told Isaac what would happen to him year by year for the rest of his life; see *The Life of Judah*, fol. 16b.

p. *emerged from guardianship*: The first of his brothers to reach adulthood, Isaac Modena took personal charge of his father's estate at this time, relieving the guardians of their obligations; see *The Life of Judah*, fol. 5b.

q. *the quarrel between the brothers continued*: Further details on this controversy can be gleaned from a series of letters written to Isaac Modena by Joseph Arli. He suggested that Isaac was holding onto his brothers' property and advised him that, as the eldest, it was his responsibility to make peace among them: JTSA 3833.69, fol. 35a–b; 3759.32–33, fols. 20a–22a. Although Arli's account does not essentially contradict Leon Modena's, it seems to indicate that Isaac was at least partially responsible for some of the controversy. Modena actually possessed Arli's letters in 1618 when he wrote about this controversy in his autobiography; see Boksenboim, *Ig-*

gerot, no. 76. Clearly, then, when he wrote his autobiography Modena intentionally colored his description of the events so that his own father would not appear in a bad light to future generations of the family, for whom the autobiography was intended.

r. *one hundred thousand*: This figure could represent either lire or ducats. For a contemporary description of Venetian coins, see the account by Thomas Coryat, an Englishman who traveled through Venice in 1608: *Coryat's Crudities* (London, 1611), pp. 285–286; (Glasgow, 1905), pp. 422–423. The autobiography contains many references to Venetian and other Italian currencies.

s. *He could answer*: Isaac Modena made a deep and lasting impression on Leon, and in both the autobiography and his letters Modena mentions him many times.

FOLIO 6b

t. *Samuel Hezekiah*: See *The Life of Judah*, fol. 7a.

u. *532-*: Between 1566 (5326) and 1569 (5329), during the aforementioned persecutions brought about by Pope Pius V, which culminated in the expulsion of the Jews from Bologna on January 26, 1569, Isaac left for Ferrara with his wife Peninah, their children, his brothers Solomon and Abtalion, and his mother Gentile, leaving behind their possessions: Carpi, "Gerush ha-yehudim," pp. 145–156; Ruderman, "Bologna," p. 260. Among their activities in Ferrara was the establishment of a small synagogue for Jews from Modena; see Boksenboim, *Iggerot*, no. 58.

v. *Johanan Halevi*: Rachel had another brother, Lazzaro Levi (d. 1581), who in 1558 assisted Solomon Usque in producing a Purim play called *Ester*, the earliest Jewish dramatic production in the vernacular that is still extant; see historical notes to fol. 20a.

w. *Apulia*: (Puglia) A province in southeastern Italy on the Adriatic coast.

x. *Meir Parenzo, who is mentioned by name in several printed books*: Meir Parenzo (d. 1575) and his brother Asher were important publishers in Venice. At first associated with the great Christian publisher of Hebrew books Daniel Bomberg (1483–1553), in whose shop he worked with Cornelio Adelkind and Guillaume de Be, Meir began to publish books under his own name with his own printer's mark in 1547, issuing at least ten titles between 1547 and 1549; see B. Ravid, "The Prohibition Against Jewish Printing and Publishing in Venice and the Difficulties of Leone Modena," in *Studies in Medieval Jewish History and Literature*, ed. I. Twersky (Cambridge, 1979), p. 148, note 19.

y. *Abraham*: Modena became very close to him; see *The Life of Judah*, fol. 9a–b.

z. *Abraham Rovigo*: On Abraham Rovigo (b. 1504), his life, the controversies in which he was involved, and his writings, see E. Kupfer, "R. avraham ben menahem me-rovigo ve-ha'avarato min ha-rabbanut," *Sinai* 61 (1967): 142–162.

a. *a huge and severe earthquake struck Ferrara*: The earthquake occurred on Friday, November 17, 1570. Many books incorrectly convert the Hebrew year 5331 to 1571; because the date, the 19th of Kislev, occurred during the autumn after the beginning of the Jewish New Year but before the beginning of the secular new year, it should be 1570.

b. *"Me'or 'einayim" by the aforementioned sage de Rossi*: De Rossi's description of the earthquake is contained in the first section of *Me'or 'einayim*.

c. *Venice*: Modena's family lived at this time in the house of Isaac Luzzatto in the Ghetto Vecchio, a fact that Modena recorded in the margin of *Me'or 'einayim*, Parma 983, fol. 4a, but not in his autobiography. On the origins of the word "ghetto" and the history of the institution, see excursus 1.

d. *I was born in the breech position*: If Modena was accurate when he stated that he had been conceived in the Hebrew year 5331, which began on August 31, 1570, then he was at least five weeks premature at birth. The frank breech position, doubled over with the rump facing backward, is sometimes associated with premature birth.

e. *Menahem Azariah Fano*: The fact that Fano (ca. 1548–1620), a prominent rabbi and kabbalist in Italy, circumcised Modena is also reported in *Ari nohem*, p. 9. Fano's register of circumcisions, recently discovered, also records this event as occurring on an unspecified Monday in May, 1571, but according to its editor this date must be corrected to April 30: R. Bonfil, "Yedi'ot hadashot le-toledot hayyav shel r. menahem azariah mi-fano u-tekufato," *Perakim be-toledot ha-hevrah ha-yehudit biymei ha-beinayim uve-'et ha-hadashah mukdashim la-profesor ya'akov katz*, ed. I. Etkes and Y. Salmon (Jerusalem, 1980), pp. 98–134. Modena's relationship with Fano continued for many years; see Boksenboim, *Iggerot*, nos. 28–31, 86; *Ziknei*, p. 198; *Ari nohem*, p. 49. Modena may also have studied with Fano, taught his children, and delivered a eulogy for him. Boksenboim, *Iggerot*, no. 44; Kaufmann 312. Fano's involvement in Jewish communal affairs is documented in Simonsohn, *Milan*, s.v. index. For recent studies on Fano see R. Bonfil, "Halakhah, Kabbalah, and Society: Some Insights into Rabbi Menahem Azariah da Fano's Inner World," in *Jewish Thought in the Seventeenth Century*, pp. 39–61; and A. Altmann, "He'arot 'al hitpathut torato ha-kabbalit shel r. m. a. mi-fano," *Mehkarim be-kabbalah mugashim le-yishayahu tishby be-mele'at lo shiv'im ve-hamesh shanim, Mehkerei yerushalayim be-mahashevet yisrael* 3 (1983–1984): 241–267, English summary, pp. xii–xiii.

f. *godparents*: Modena consistently used the term *baʿalei berit*, based on Genesis 14:13, for the woman who brought the infant in and for the man who held him during the circumcision; see *Riti*, 4.8.4.

FOLIO 7a

g. *remained in Venice for about eight months and then set out to return to Ferrara*: The departure of the Modena family from Venice in mid-December 1571 may have been prompted by external events. In December 1571 a motion was passed in the Venetian Senate providing that as a gesture of gratitude to God for the victory over the Turks at Lepanto, the infidel Jews, who allegedly had exploited the poor and were disloyal to the state, should not have their charter renewed but should rather be expelled from Venice at the end of the two-year grace period provided for in case of nonrenewal; consequently the Jews were required to wind up their affairs and leave. Eventually in 1573 the charter was renewed and subsequently continually renewed until the end of the Republic; see Pullan, *Rich and Poor*, pp. 537–542; Ravid, "Socioeconomic Background of the Expulsion," pp. 27–55; idem, "Love, Money and Power Politics in Sixteenth Century Venice: The Perpetual Banishment and Subsequent Pardon of Joseph Nasi," in *Italia judaica*, vol. 1, pp. 159–181; B. Arbel, "Venezia, gli ebrei e l'attività di Salomone Ashkenasi nella guerra di Cipro," in *Gli Ebrei e Venezia*, pp. 163–190.

h. *manager*: Hebrew *manhig*. Samson Meshullam was also a Hebrew scholar; see Boksenboim, *Iggerot*, no. 1.

i. *La Giara*: Ferrara was then under the control of the dukes of Este. A street named La Giara still exists today.

j. *Panetto*: This nickname could be either derisive or affectionate.

k. *bad ways*: This may be a reference to his gambling; see *The Life of Judah*, fols. 8b and 13b.

l. *Hazanetto*: Like Panetto, this nickname could be either derisive or affectionate. For another name possibly formed this way, see *The Life of Judah*, fol. 13a.

m. *Rabbi Azriel Basola, the son of the gaon Rabbi Moses*: Like Menahem Azariah Fano, both Basolas were kabbalists. On Moses Basola (1480–1560), who left Venice for the land of Israel in 1521–1522, see Sonne, "Bologna," pp. 44–45; *Ari nohem*, p. 84; and I. Tishby, "Ha-pulmus ʿal sefer ha-zohar ba-meʾah ha-shesh-ʿesreh be-italiah," in *Perakim: Yearbook of the Schocken Institute for Jewish Research at the Jewish Theological Seminary of America* (Jerusalem, 1967–1968), vol. 1, pp. 131–182, especially, p. 172, reprinted in *Hikrei kabbalah u-shelukhotehah* (Jerusalem, 1982), pp. 79–132, especially, p. 120.

n. *Haftarah*: The portion from the Prophets that follows the Torah reading on Sabbaths and holidays.

o. *at the age of three I recognized my Creator*: The legends in rabbinic literature, for example, in Bereshit Rabbah 64:4 (ed. J. Theodor and H. Albeck [Berlin, 1912–1927], vol. 2, p. 703), give two opinions as to the age at which Abraham discovered monotheism: forty-eight (some manuscripts read forty, which is the age given by Maimonides in his Mishneh Torah, Hilekhot Akum 1:3) and three. Modena had, of course, to select the version giving the age of three, which conformed to his self-image as a precocious child. Modena's accomplishments, and even the phrases he uses to describe them, were not unique in Italy; see Assaf, *Mekorot le-toledot ha-hinnukh be-yisrael*, vol. 2, p. 114, cf. p. 123.

p. *Cologna*: Cologna da Veneto is located southeast of Verona and northwest of Este. Between 1574 and 1588, the Venetian Senate approved the requests of several villages and small towns, including Cologna, to contract with Jewish moneylenders to help alleviate serious financial problems; see Pullan, *Rich and Poor*, pp. 542–545.

q. *ritually fit for use*: Possibly the prominence given by Modena in his adult recollections to this childhood episode reflects the major controversy over the ritual bath at Rovigo; see Howard Adelman's introductory essay.

r. *Gershon Cohen*: Some of his Judeo-Italian sermons are still extant in manuscript; see C. Roth, "Catalogue of Manuscripts in the Roth Collection," in *Alexander Marx Jubilee Volume* (New York, 1950), no. 718, p. 531.

FOLIO 7b

s. *servant girl*: The Modena family was apparently prosperous in Cologna, for it engaged servants and a semiprivate teacher and possessed property large enough to require a long search.

t. *Malachi Gallico*: An Isaac Gallico had lived with Mordecai Modena and presumably had tutored Modena's father; see *The Life of Judah*, fol. 5b. This family was involved in the kabbalistic circles of Safed. A namesake of Malachi Gallico was a rabbi in Cori, a village near Rome, the Jewish community of which planned to move en masse to Tiberias with Joseph Nasi in 1566; see D. Kaufmann, "Don Joseph Nassi, Founder of Colonies in the Holy Land, and the Community of Cori in the Campagna," *JQR* o.s. 2 (1889–1890): 291–297.

u. *"The young pumpkin is known by its young shoot"*: Elsewhere Modena recorded the strong desires for prominence, accomplishment, and adulation he had developed by the age of five: "Since I was five years old and ready for the study of Bible I asked: When will I accomplish something? Woe is me if I shall die at this time and go out as an empty wind and all my work will be in vain if I leave this place without making a lasting impression"; *Midbar yehudah* (Venice, 1602), fol. 3a.

v. *Montagnana*: A medieval walled town surrounded by a moat. A community of Jews had lived in Montagnana since the late fourteenth century:

C. Roth, *A History of the Jews of Italy* (Philadelphia, 1946), and Pullan, *Rich and Poor*, s. v. index. Later in life Modena communicated with several good friends who were from that town; see Boksenboim, *Iggerot*, nos. 34, 35, 36; *Ziknei*, nos. 4, 5.

w. *Zerah Halevi*: Modena wrote poems and responsa for him; see S. Bernstein, ed., *The Divan of Leo de Modena* (Philadelphia, 1932), nos. 82, 173, 239; Blau, *Kitvei*, no. 49; Boksenboim, *Iggerot*, no. 36; *Ziknei*, nos. 5, 34.

x. *prison*: For a description from a slightly later period of the capriciousness of Montagnana's rulers, who condemned a Jew to a cruel and humiliating death for having struck a Christian, and for the way in which the Jews tried to buy justice on his behalf, see Boksenboim, *Iggerot*, nos. 187–188.

y. *fifteen hundred scudi*: A popular silver coin roughly equivalent to a ducat; see Boksenboim, *Iggerot*, no. 29, and Grendler, *Roman Inquisition*, p. xv.

z. *Alvise Mocenigo*: He was a namesake of the recent doge Alvise Mocenigo IV (1570–1577).

FOLIO 8a

a. *Eliakim Macerata*: His full name was Eliakim son of Isaiah Moses Macerata: H. Neppi, *Zekher tzaddikim li-verakhah* (Trieste, 1853), p. 17, no. 33. Macerata was mentioned in the introduction of *Tikkunei ha-zohar* (Mantua, 1558) as having possessed one of the original manuscripts of this work: Tishby, "Ha-pulmus ʿal sefer ha-zohar," p. 143, n. 47. On the Jewish community of Macerata, south of Ancona, see R. Bacchi, "Ricordi ebraici in Macerata," *RMI* 8 (1933): 299–303.

b. *nephew*: The Hebrew *nekhed*, like *nipote* in Italian, can mean either nephew or grandson, depending on the context.

c. *Mordecai Modena*: The son of Leon Modena's late uncle Shemaiah Modena.

d. *Jehiel Tardiolo*: He later served in Revere and Mantua; see S. Simonsohn, *History of the Jews in the Duchy of Mantua* (Jerusalem, 1977), p. 735.

e. *Hezekiah Finzi*: The son of Benjamin Finzi, he was considered one of the greatest talmudists of his generation, according to Modena; see *Divan*, no. 203.

f. *Alfasi*: A compendium of the legal material in the Talmud compiled by Isaac of Fez (al-Fasi, 1013–1103). Advanced students studied this code because the Talmud itself had been banned in Italy since 1553; on the censorship and availability of talmudic tractates in Venice, see *Zeraʿ anashim*, ed. D. Frankel (Husyatin, 1902), no. 23; Popper, *Censorship of Hebrew*

Books, pp. 34–35; D. Kaufmann, "Die Verbrennung der talmudischen Litteratur in der Republik venedig," *JQR* o.s. 12 (1901): 533–538; Grendler, *Roman Inquisition*, pp. 89, 91–92, 117, 140; M. Benayahu, *Ha-yehasim shebein yehudei yavan liyhudei italiah mi-gerush sefarad 'ad tom ha-ripublikah ha-venetzianit* (Tel Aviv, 1980), pp. 207–209. Nonetheless, from Modena's writings, it appears that some copies of talmudic tractates could be found; see *Riti*, 2.2.7; Boksenboim, *Iggerot*, nos. 36, 309; BL 5395, fols. 1b, 13b.

g. *preaching*: Modena's sermon here represents the classical paradigm of a Jewish sermon. Each sermon had to include two subjects: a verse from the weekly portion and some lines from rabbinic literature. The preacher's task was to explore the relations between them. On teaching young Jewish boys to preach in Italy, see D. Ruderman, "An Exemplary Sermon for the Classroom of a Jewish Teacher in Renaissance Italy," *Italia* 1 (1978): 7–38, and on Jewish preaching in Italy in general, see I. Bettan, *Studies in Jewish Preaching* (Cincinnati, 1939), pp. 192–272. On the sermons of Leon Modena, see E. Rivkin, "The Sermons of Leon da Modena," *HUCA* 23.2 (1950–1951): 295–317; Howard Adelman's introductory essay; and historical notes to fols. 13b and 20a. On Modena's preaching in Ferrara, see *The Life of Judah*, fol. 14a.

h. *instruction . . . Latin*: From the letters Modena wrote for his students in Venice between 1596 and 1603, it is possible to reconstruct what they studied. On Sunday, Monday, and Tuesday mornings they studied the laws of the Sabbath according to Rabbi Moses (either Sefer Mitzvot Gadol, Semag, by Moses ben Jacob Coucy of the thirteenth century or Moses Maimonides' Mishneh Torah, because Semag had been burned in Venice in 1553 with the Talmud). On Wednesday and Thursday mornings they studied Rashi and the portion of the week with commentaries, and on Saturday, Psalms. On weekday afternoons they studied the Prophets in order, letter writing, and Italian. Older students studied the laws of women and the dietary laws orally from Nedarim, Shevuot, and Hullin; see Boksenboim, *Iggerot*, nos. 36, 288, 289, 307, 312.

On the Jewish curriculum in Italy see Roth, *Renaissance*, pp. 271–304; Shulvass, *Renaissance*, pp. 168–172; Ruderman, "Exemplary Sermon," pp. 7–38; Assaf, *Mekorot le-toledot ha-hinnukh*, vol. 1, p. 157; vol. 2, pp. 93–237; vol. 4, pp. 27–37, 51–56; and the forthcoming article by H. Adelman, "The Educational Program of Leon Modena and Jewish Attitudes to the Study of Hebrew in Seventeenth-Century Venice."

i. *Samuel Archivolti*: 1515–1611, a leading rabbi and scholar in Italy. He and Isaac Modena had been in Bologna together prior to 1568. Like Modena's uncle Abtalion, Archivolti had been a student of Meir Katzenellenbogen, the Maharam of Padua (1473–1565). Archivolti was Modena's most famous teacher, and his influence on Modena shaped the latter's activities for the rest of his life. Archivolti's main interests and activities fore-shadow some of the major features of Modena's later accomplishments: composing Hebrew poems (S. Bernstein, "Shirim hadashim le-r. shemuel archivolti," *Tarbiz* 8 [1936–1937]: 55–68, 237), preparing Hebrew letters (*Maʿayan ganim* [Venice, 1553]), teaching Hebrew grammar (*ʿArugat ha-bosem* [Venice, 1602]), developing works on Jewish ethics (*Degel ahavah* [Venice, 1551]), pursuing rabbinic scholarship (*Heʿarot le-sefer he-ʿarukh* of Nathan b. Jehiel of Rome [Venice, 1553]), writing about synagogue music (I. Adler, *Hebrew Writing Concerning Music* [Munich, 1975], pp. 96–102), teaching Jewish girls as well as Christian students (G. Jarè, "Samuele Archivolti rabbino di Padova," *CI* 3 [1864]: 14–16, 48–50), proofreading for Hebrew publishers in Venice, acting as secretary of the Jewish community (see citations in historical notes to fol. 17b), and serving as head of a ye-shiva and of a rabbinic court. See D. Kaufman, "Samuel Archivolti on Paintings and Sculpture in the Synagogue," *JQR* o.s. 9 (1897): 263–269. Modena continued to correspond with Archivolti; see *Ziknei*, no. 1; Bok-senboim, *Iggerot*, nos. 5, 14, 17, 37, 40, 44, 92, 145, 218–223; and he wrote an elegy when Archivolti died; *Divan*, no. 205.

FOLIO 8b

j. *Moses, the son of Benjamin della Rocca*: Modena's teacher, Moses ben Benjamin della Rocca Basola, was the nephew of Azriel Basola, who had previously taught Modena.

k. *About this time*: 1583; see *The Life of Judah*, fol. 13b.

l. *an evil path of wastefulness and loss*: Perhaps another reference to Sam-uel's gambling; see *The Life of Judah*, fols. 7a and 13b.

m. *four thousand ducats*: *The Life of Judah*, fol. 13b states that his share was between three thousand and four thousand ducats.

n. *"Kinah shemor"*: In Italian, "Chi nasce, muor." An octet is an eight-line poem with a rhyming pattern of a b a b a b c c, then popular in Italy. Modena created a work, the first in Hebrew, that sounded the same and had approximately the same meaning in two completely unrelated lan-guages. On this poem, see D. Pagis, *ʿAl sod hatum* (Jerusalem, 1986), pp. ix, 167; idem, "Baroque Trends in Italian Hebrew Poetry as Reflected in One Unknown Genre," in *Italia judaica*, 2, pp. 263–277.

o. *it is printed in my book "Midbar yehudah"*: Midbar yehudah was published in Venice in 1602; see *The Life of Judah*, fol. 20a. "Kinah Shemor" is on fol. 80b. The text of "Kinah Shemor," in both Hebrew and Italian, is repro-duced in Roth, *Renaissance*, p. 307.

p. *without a teacher or master*: Thus, at about the time he reached the age of Bar Mitzvah, an event he never mentioned anywhere despite its signif-icance in Jewish society, Modena's formal education came to an end.

FOLIO 9a

q. *to play games of chance*: On gambling, see Howard Adelman's introductory essay and *The Life of Judah*, passim.

r. *When I reached Venice*: In order to take a boat to Ancona.

FOLIO 9b

s. *I composed elegies for him*: This elegy for Abraham, which is still extant, included idyllic visions of family life, a panegyric on his half-brother's good qualities, and a section of echo poetry, a form of poem in which the sounds of the final syllable or two at the end of each line were repeated twice. Each repetition was necessary for the meaning of the poem, and because of Modena's use of homonyms, each time the sounds were repeated they had different meanings; see Blau, *Kitvei*, no. 26; D. Kaufmann, "Echogedichte," *ZHB* 1 (1896): 22–25, 61– 64, 114–117, 144–147.

t. *I continued in this profession until 5372 [1611/1612]*: This hiatus in the teaching of children in 1611/1612, which began when Modena was ordained a rabbi and elected cantor, did not last long.

u. *because it did not seem fitting to me*: At first Modena had found teaching to be satisfying, but after a year of it, he realized that it could become drudgery. Nonetheless, he continued to view it as an opportunity for favor and honor; see Boksenboim, *Iggerot*, no. 26. Moreover, teaching advanced students turned out to be a great source of comfort to him.

v. *After this*: The antecedent is not clear. Was this after the death of his half-brother, in the spring of 1588, or after he began teaching in the spring of 1589? The uncertainty affects the sequence of the next few passages.

w. *dream divination*: On this activity, see Trachtenberg, *Jewish Magic and Superstition*, pp. 241–243. For Modena's own prayer for such occasions, see his *Tefillot yesharim* (Venice, 1661), fols. 41a–45a.

FOLIO 10a

x. *lingered in Venice*: Modena's travels brought him into closer contact with many friends with whom he had been corresponding and who now studied in Venice in a study group, a *havurah*. Modena wrote a poem describing how distraught he had felt before coming to Venice and being reunited with his friends, and expressing great sadness over the prospect of his upcoming departure for home; see *Divan*, no. 90.

y. *symbolic acquisition*: In Hebrew, *kinyan*. Modena refers here to the custom of the prenuptial agreement (*shiddukhin*) in which the conditions (*tena'im*) are agreed upon concerning the future marriage, including matters such as the date and place of the wedding and the financial obligations of each family. This ceremony usually took place at least a year before the wedding. The relationship of the couple after this ceremony was similar to the modern institution of engagement. The agreement was usually marked by a written document, a handshake, the exchange of presents, the breaking of a plate, and by both parties holding a kerchief in symbolic affirmation of the agreement (*kinyan sudar*); see *Riti*, 2.6.1; *The Life of Judah*, fol. 38b and textual notes; *Riti*, 4.3.1; E. Horowitz, "Havurat 'hassi' betulot' be-venetziah: bein masoret le-hiddush u-vein ide'al li-metzi'ut," *Tarbiz* 56 (1987): 357–358, n. 59.

z. *that I had described more than a year previously*: Because Modena's mother had only raised the idea of marriage recently, his dream had to have preceded her machinations.

a. *in Bologna*: By 1590 Isaac Modena had recovered from his incapacitation. In the spring of that year he spent two months in Bologna, where the Jews had been allowed to return in 1586; but they were expelled again in 1593. Because of his father's absence, many business and travel obligations became Leon's responsibility; see Boksenboim, *Iggerot*, no. 12.

b. *I also invited my friends and relatives*: Some of these invitations are still extant, including those for Abtalion Modena, his wife, his son-in-law Judah Saltaro Fano, and Samuel Archivolti; see Boksenboim, *Iggerot*, no. 13 (May 27), 14.

c. *we did not touch each other even with our little fingers*: Modena wrote about premarital modesty in relations between bride and groom in his *Riti*, 4.3.1.

FOLIO 10b

d. *I wrote to my revered father*: It is puzzling that Modena had to write his father, which implies either that Isaac had not made the trip to Venice for his son's wedding or that the father had some pressing reason for leaving his son's side at this time of great distress.

e. *Friday the 5th of Tammuz 5350 [July 6, 1590]*: The 5th of Tammuz 5350 actually fell on the next day, Saturday, July 7, the Sabbath on which Modena was granted the title of *haver* (see historical note m). Modena associated the two milestones, hence, probably, the conflation: Friday the 5th of Tammuz.

f. *Solomon Sforno*: Solomon Shemaiah Sforno, a rabbi and a salaried employee of the Italian synagogue, whose job included teaching and preaching; see *The Life of Judah*, fols. 13a and 16a.

g. *Italian synagogue*: The ghettos of Venice contained at least five synagogues: in the Ghetto Nuovo, La Scola Grande Tedesca (Ashkenazic, 1528), La Scola Canton (Ashkenazic, 1531–1532), and La Scola Italiana (Italian-Ashkenazic, 1575), and in the Ghetto Vecchio, La Scola Levantina (Sephardic, the usual date of 1538 is difficult to accept because Jews had not been allowed to reside in the Ghetto Vecchio until it was assigned to them in 1541) and La Scola Spagnola (Sephardic, 1583). These synagogues occupied the upper stories of the buildings. On the lower stories were smaller rooms called *scuola* (plural *scuole*), *midrash*, or *talmud torah* (as opposed to *scola* meaning synagogue) used for study as well as for worship and preaching. On the synagogues of the ghetto of Venice see E. Morpurgo, "Inchiesta sui monumenti e documenti del Veneto interessanti la storia religiosa, civile e letteria degli ebrei," *CI* 49 (1911): 62, 145; A. Ottolenghi, *Per il IV Centenario della scuola canton* (Venice, 1932); Y. Pinkerfeld, *Batei ha-keneset be-italiah* (Jerusalem, 1964); U. Fortis, *Jews and Synagogues* (Venice, 1973); D. Cassuto, *Richerche sulle cinque sinagoge di Venezia* (Jerusalem, 1978); and C. Krinsky, *Synagogues of Europe: Architecture, History, Meaning* (Cambridge, 1985), pp. 378–386.

h. *gaons*: These were the leading rabbinic authorities of the city.

i. *Katzenellenbogen*: Samuel Judah, 1521–1597, the son of the famous Meir ben Isaac of Padua, was one of the most influential rabbis of his generation in Jewish and Christian circles and one of the few Venetian rabbis ever identified as *av beit din*, implying membership on a rabbinical court or perhaps even its head; see *Midbar yehudah*, fol. 67b; *Ziknei*, p. 60; Blau, *Schriftstücke*, pp. 108–109; A. Ziv, "Ha-rav shemuel yehudah katzenellenbogen," *Ha-darom* 34 (1972): 177–201.

j. *Jacob Cohen*: d. 1596, another prominent Venetian rabbi who joined the rabbis of Venice in most of their major decisions; see Blau, *Schriftstücke*, pp. 108–109; *Ziknei*, p. 43.

k. *Avigdor Cividal*: d. 1601, a student of Katzenellenbogen and his successor in the position of leadership among the gaons. These three gaons had much influence with the lay leaders who sat on the communal board, the *va'ad katan*.

l. *Levantine Jews, who at that time abounded in important persons*: Jewish merchants had been coming to Venice from the Levant since at least the later fourteenth century. In 1541, in response to their complaint that they did not have sufficient room in the Ghetto Nuovo, the Venetian government assigned them space in the Ghetto Vecchio across the canal. In 1589, the Venetian Senate issued a ten-year charter granting both Levantine and Ponentine (Iberian) Jewish merchants the right to reside in Venice as Venetian subjects with very favorable commercial privileges. This charter led to an increased immigration of Jews from both the Levant and Iberia, and indeed many of those coming from the Levant were probably originally of Iberian provenance; see excursus 1, "The Venetian Ghetto in Historical Perspective"; B. Ravid, "The First Charter of the Jewish Merchants of Venice," *AJSR* 1 (1976): 187–222; idem, *Economics and Toleration*, pp. 25–49; B. Cooperman, "Venetian Policy Towards Levantine Jews and Its Broader Italian Context," in *Gli Ebrei e Venezia*, pp. 65–84.

m. *haver*: An honorific bestowed in Italy upon students who had not yet attained the levels of learning and age that merited rabbinical ordination; see Bonfil, *Ha-rabbanut*, pp. 27–28, 63 note 263 (mentioning Modena), and elsewhere (see index).

n. *Cardinal d'Este*: See *The Life of Judah*, fol. 7b.

o. *Katz*: Written *k-tz*, an abbreviation of *kohen tzedek*, "righteous priest"; see Boksenboim, *Iggerot*, nos. 6, 7, 10.

FOLIO 11a

p. *"I have nothing to bequeath to you"*: This is a simple ethical will, common among medieval Jews who had more advice than money to leave their children; see I. Abrahams, *Hebrew Ethical Wills* (Philadelphia, 1926), and Natalie Davis's introductory essay.

q. *especially fifteen of them*: The implication is that the worst period in Modena's father's life began in 1576, when Modena was only five. In the introduction to *Midbar yehudah* Modena wrote that until he was thirteen (hence, in 1584), life had been relatively easy for the family.

r. *the day of his death was short*: Because of the approaching Sabbath eve, which came early during the winter.

s. *if it really exists*: Here Modena expresses skepticism about the kabbalistic belief called *hibbut ha-kever*. The beating of the dead by demons and the way to avoid it by being buried on Friday afternoon are described by Modena's cousin, Aaron Berechiah of Modena: *Siftei renanot*, chap. 42, in his *Ma'avar yabbok*; see fol. 19a of that work for a summary of the chapter. On *hibbut ha-kever*, see "Masekhet hibbut ha-kever," *Beit ha-midrash* 1, ed. A. Jellinek, (Leipzig, 1853), pp. 150–153; Trachtenberg, *Jewish Magic and Superstition*, p. 74; and M. Cohen, "Leone da Modena's *Riti*: A Seventeenth-Century Plea For Social Toleration of Jews," *JSS* 34 (1972): 299–300.

t. *I buried him there in Montagnana*: This cemetery was located "contra della Spina" near the wall; see Morpurgo, "Inchiesta," p. 203.

u. *a year later I placed a tombstone*: Modena requested a tombstone inscription for his father from Samuel Archivolti because he felt the praise for his father would be more credible if he did not write it himself. But eventually Modena had to do so; see A. Berliner, *Luhot avanim* (Frankfurt am Main, 1881), no. 184; Boksenboim, *Iggerot*, no. 17.

FOLIO 11b

v. *laying out money*: In a letter Modena related that he had lost 150 ducats in four to five months because of this abortive partnership; see Boksenboim, *Iggerot*, no. 17.

w. *and came to Venice*: When Modena arrived in Venice, about 1,043 Jews lived in the ghetto, out of a total population of about 140,000. For a full discussion of the population figures of the Jewish community of Venice, see B. Ravid, *Economics and Toleration*, pp. 75–77; Pullan, *The Jews of Europe*, pp. 157–158.

x. *the 15th of Kislev*: Based on a letter Modena wrote at this time, Boksenboim suggests that Modena arrived between the 24th and the 29th of Kislev, November 29–December 5; see *Iggerot*, no. 17.

y. *underneath that of my father-in-law*: This apartment was probably in the Ghetto Vecchio, based on information in Boksenboim, *Iggerot*, no. 81; *Me'or ʿeinayim*, Parma 983, fol. 4a.

z. *Abraham the son of Meir Luzzatto*: The student was five years old at this time, as he was thirteen years old in 1597; see Boksenboim, *Iggerot*, no. 299.

a. *the first time that I preached a sermon in the Great Synagogue before a large audience*: This reference is to the Ashkenazic congregation. According to a letter, it was because of his excellent ability to speak Italian that Modena had first been asked to become a teacher and a preacher for an unspecified Venetian congregation in May 1593, after having lived in the city for six months. He agreed he would preach on Shavuot (Sunday, May 6) and began preparing his sermon well in advance: Boksenboim, *Iggerot*, no. 26. That sermon was probably given in the Italian synagogue, his own congregation and the one in which he was ordained. It was affiliated with the Ashkenazic congregation, and for certain major Sabbaths during the year its preachers would be invited to address the larger congregation of the Great Ashkenazic Synagogue; see Haleviim, *Medabber*, pp. 75–76.

b. *Midbar yehudah*: Fols. 8a–14a. According to the introduction to *Midbar yehudah* (fol. 4a), Modena continued to preach at the Ashkenazic congregation during the next year until he was offered a position by Kalonymos Belgrado. On *Midbar yehudah*, see *The Life of Judah*, fols. 13b and 20a.

c. *Kalonymos Belgrado*: Caliman Belgrado (1532–1612) was a wealthy Venetian Jew; see L. Luzzatto, "Mosè Belgrado e il S. Uffizio," *VI* 51 (1903): 388–391; P. C. Ioly Zorattini, *Leandro Tisanio: Un Giudaizzante sanvitese del Seicento* (Florence, 1984), pp. 17–29; and for his will, idem, "Il Testamento di Caliman Belgrado," *Mi-mizrah u-mimaʿarav* 5 (1986): vii–xxiv.

d. *in the "garden"*: Belgrado had built and rented out seven houses in what had once been a garden or orchard in the Ghetto Vecchio; see Pullan, *The Jews of Europe*, p. 158. Though called "the garden," Modena wrote elsewhere that the sessions at Belgrado's school met "in his house and between his walls" (*Midbar yehudah*, fols. 4a, 59a–63a). At Belgrado's "garden" academy Modena came into contact with many important people in the Venetian Jewish community. In the morning the rabbis of Venice met there under the leadership of the chief authority among them, who, after

1602, was Benzion Zarfati, called gaon and head of the yeshiva (*Midbar yehudah*, fols. 3a-4b, 79b). Another important rabbi who taught there was Naftali Ashkenazi (1540–1602), a scholar and mystic from the land of Israel who spoke Hebrew. The Hevrat Tzedakah (the Charity Society), which helped sponsor the school, also met there. Modena viewed this as his yeshiva and midrash, and many of his preaching and teaching duties, which included instructing female students, centered around it; see *Midbar yehudah*, fols. 3a–4b, 55b.

e. *I was the first preacher there*: He used a similar expression in *Midbar yehudah*, fol. 55b, "for me to be the first to preach on the day of the Sabbath."

f. *For the past twenty-five years*: From 1593 to 1618 he preached regularly not only while he was in Venice but also during the time he spent in Ferrara and Florence.

g. *Even many esteemed friars, priests, and noblemen come to listen*: Soon after his arrival in Venice, Modena, together with some other Jews, often attended a society of learned men. There they listened to sermons and in turn were asked questions about Judaism. Modena wrote with great relish about this experience to his old friend Gershon Cohen. He told Cohen that he would love to tell him what had been discussed, but could not, because he was not permitted to write about these matters, which should be discussed only orally (Boksenboim, *Iggerot*, no. 24, quoted in English translation in Y. Yerushalmi, *From Spanish Court to Italian Ghetto* [New York and London, 1971], pp. 353–354). On Modena's preaching to Christians, see Haleviim, *Medabber*, pp. 80–81. Although Haleviim mentioned that Modena had preached before kings, there is no other evidence of his having done so.

FOLIO 12a

h. *Jacob, the son of Meir*: He died in 1612; see *Luhot avanim*, no. 58.

i. *petechiae*: This term refers to a skin rash, which can be a sign of various diseases.

j. *to travel around*: Beginning in 1594 and for many years thereafter, the pattern of looking for work and settling for a position at which he was not happy repeated itself almost every autumn.

k. *Eliakim Cohen Panarotti*: A relative of Modena's; see *The Life of Judah*, fol. 13a and historical notes; and Haleviim, *Medabber*, p. 29.

l. *Satan fooled me into playing games of chance*: Modena's first report in his autobiography of his experiences with gambling. On a later occasion, he identified his tempter as a Christian friar; see *The Life of Judah*, fol. 13a. Modena may have turned to gambling to make ends meet following a year of financial setbacks and little income. He may also have turned to gambling as a form of holiday entertainment common on Hanukkah among Jews. But quite probably, the general prevalence of gambling in Venetian society was enough to induce him to engage in that activity. On gambling in Venice, see G. Dolcetti, *Le Bische e il giuoco d'azzardo a Venezia, 1172–1807* (Venice, 1903), with some observations about the Jews on pp. 141–144.

FOLIO 12b

m. *in the Ghetto Nuovo*: This move took place at the end of the school year, in late Sivan or early Tammuz. It appears to constitute the first time that Modena lived in the Ghetto Nuovo. On the ghetto, see excursus 1.

n. *and died*: Two weeks after the birth of this infant daughter, Modena wrote of his uncertainty whether she would live; see Boksenboim, *Iggerot*, no. 35 and pp. 28–29.

o. *She was buried here in Venice*: Because she died shortly before the beginning of the Sabbath, she could not be transported to Montagnana to be buried next to her husband.

p. *the following epitaph*: The text of this epitaph is also in *Luhot avanim*, no. 99, with some variations.

q. *Cento*: This town is centrally located between Ferrara, Bologna, and Modena. There, under the dukes of Este of Ferrara, the Jews enjoyed many privileges; see L. Modona, "Illustri Ebrei centesi," *VI* 46 (1898): 4–10; G. Volli, "La Comunità di Cento e un suo documento inedito del 1776," *RMI* 7 (1951): 205–209.

r. *Paciotto Revere*: The name Paciotto comes from the root *pace*, "peace." His Hebrew name, Shalom, has the same meaning and was the name Modena used in a poem he wrote on the occasion of the wedding of Paciotto's son; see *Divan*, no. 65.

s. *I changed my mind about the move*: Again Modena attempted to leave Venice in the autumn. An outpouring of concern by friends, relatives, and Jewish leaders persuaded him not to leave; see Boksenboim, *Iggerot*, no. 37.

t. *The duke of Ferrara*: Alfonso II of Este (d. 1598).

u. *danger of war*: Papal forces were trying to take control of the area. They were ultimately successful. In 1598 Cento was incorporated into the papal states, and in 1636 a ghetto was established for the 100–150 Jews who lived there.

v. *I supported the members of my household with honor through my writings and compositions*: Missing from collections of Modena's writings from 1597 to 1599 are the usual dated occasional pieces, letters for students, letters for the rabbis, and tombstone inscriptions. Rather, in these years the greatest number of his dedicatory poems for books appeared in works published by di Gara, Zanetti, and Bragadini. Modena was proud of this aspect of his career. He recorded almost every one of these poetic dedications in his collection of poems and itemized them in the list of his writings that appears in his autobiography; see *The Life of Judah*, fol. 20a.

FOLIO 13a

w. *the night of the 13th of Second Adar*: The next day was Purim, and for it Modena wrote a poem about vacuums that reveals knowledge of new scientific ideas; see *Divan*, no. 58.

x. *Gutzeln*: Earlier he was referred to by his Hebrew name, Eliakim Cohen Panarotti; see also Boksenboim, *Iggerot*, p. 318, note 1.

y. *to teach his children and board at his table*: Here is yet another change of jobs before the beginning of the school year. Modena could not make a living by writing and publishing alone, so he had to make new, and probably frustrating, residential and career plans, moving into the house of Panarotti to serve as a tutor. By this time Modena felt as if he had become a prisoner of his work, though he was also able to preach almost every evening during the winter at the midrash of Belgrado; see Boksenboim, *Iggerot*, nos. 36, 28, 29, 38.

z. *Spagnoletto*: A family name that will appear later in the autobiography; see *The Life of Judah*, fol. 19a.

a. *three hundred ducats*: For the second time Modena records gambling losses. The difficulties that had initially led to his gambling had only become more acute since his last bout. His correspondence provides several expressions of his concern about his expenses and his frustration over unfulfilled needs; see Boksenboim, *Iggerot*, nos. 36, 35; *Ziknei*, no. 4.

b. *and paid all my debts*: This hiatus in his gambling corresponds to an increase in the number of extant letters he wrote for the Venetian rabbis from the summer of 1599 through 1600.

c. *I began to preach in the house of study of the Ashkenazic Torah Study Society*: This occasion was the first time he preached for them during the week. He had already begun to preach for them on the Sabbath as early as April 22, 1600; see *Midbar yehudah*, fol. 98b.

d. *Proverbs of Solomon*: See *The Life of Judah*, fol. 20a and historical notes. As elsewhere in the autobiography and in his letters, here Modena boasts about his skill as a preacher, one of the few professional accomplishments about which Modena wrote with unabashed immodesty.

e. *I brought him into the covenant of the holy sign*: The circumcision, on the 6th of Iyyar (May 8, 1601), is reported by Modena in a letter; see Boksenboim, *Iggerot*, no. 39.

f. *Doge Marin Grimani*: Marino Grimani (1596–1606) was praised often by Modena; see Blau, *Kitvei*, nos. 105, 64; *Divan*, no. 53; and *The Life of Judah*, fol. 20a, item 15b.

g. *called him Marin*: A masculine name from *mare*, "sea." Presumably this name was chosen because of the nautical associations of the name Zebulun in the blessing of Jacob: "Zebulun shall dwell at the shore of the sea" (Genesis 49:13). According to Colorni, "Corrispondenza fra nomi ebraici," p. 791, it is the only case of correspondence between these two names.

FOLIO 13b

h. *Rabbi Joseph Pardo*: Pardo (d. 1619) was a prominent Levantine rabbi and merchant in Venice. He had emigrated from Salonika to the land of Israel, traveled to Venice in 1589 when the Jewish merchants received their first charter, returned to the Levant between 1591 and 1596, and subsequently came back to Venice intermittently after 1596: G. Cohen, "Le-toledot ha-pulmus ʿal setam yeinam," *Sinai* 39 (1975): 63, 71, 73; Benayahu, *Ha-yehasim*, pp. 177–181. Record of Pardo's merchandise being transported from Constantinople to Venice in 1595 has been preserved in a notarial record of insurance transactions because the boat became immobilized off Ragusa (Dubrovnik): A. Tenenti, *Naufrages, corsaires et assurances maritimes à Venise, 1592–1609* (Paris, 1959), p. 167. Pardo had been deeply committed to raising money for the Jews of the land of Israel, and Modena's relationship with him began when Modena was writing fundraising letters for the Venetian rabbis in 1600. In the course of a year Modena's work for Pardo expanded to include writing letters for such activities as the redemption of Jewish captives, Jewish education, and Hebrew publishing, as well as traditional ritual issues. At the end of October 1600, as ships were about to depart for the eastern Mediterranean, Pardo raised 853 ducats in three days; see D. Carpi, *Peʿulat kehillah kedoshah italiani shebe-venetziah le-maʿan ʿaniyei eretz yisrael be-shanim [5]336–[5]493* (Tel Aviv, 1979), pp. 17–21; Boksenboim, *Iggerot*, nos. 183, 189, 204; Benayahu, *Ha-yehasim*, pp. 113–116, 207–209, 318; idem, "Defusei turkiah she-einam ella defusei italiah," *Sinai* 72 (1973): 76, 184; Blau, *Kitvei*, nos. 81, 152, 153; L. della Torre, "Cenno storico sulla famiglia Pardo," *VI* 8 (1860): 45–48. On Pardo's tombstone, see D. Henriques de Castro, *Keur van grafsteenen op de nederl. -portug. -israel. Begraafplaats te Ouderkerk aan den Amstel* (Leiden, 1883), pp. 60–62.

i. *became inspired to employ me*: Modena's industry and ability in executing projects for Pardo must have made an impression on the latter. Yet before he hired Modena for the project mentioned here, Pardo consulted with Rabbi Moses Alpalas (born ca. 1540), a preacher at the Levantine synagogue and an author, who recommended Modena for the job because of his impressive sermons; see Benayahu, *Ha-yehasim*, p. 130; *Parashat ha-kesef*, introduction, Oxford, Canon Misc. 204 (Neubauer, *Catalogue*, no. 2549.1), cited in A. Neubauer, "Quelques Notes sur la vie de Juda Leon de Modène," *REJ* 22 (1891): 82–84.

j. *twenty-seven authors*: Modena and Pardo came to an agreement that each week Modena would review each verse of the biblical portion and all the printed commentaries on it. Modena thought that a week would be enough time for each portion because, as he says below, he now had his own apartment and did not have a full-time teaching job to distract him from the project; see *Parashat ha-kesef*, introduction.

k. *the plain meaning of the text*: This is one of the four traditional methods of Jewish Bible commentary summarized by an acronym, PARDES, which stands for *peshat* (plain meaning), *remez* (allegorical), *derash* (sermonic), and *sod* (mystical). In his introduction to the commentary, Modena related that Pardo explicitly requested that he not use the allegorical, sermonic, or mystical interpretations, but only the plain meaning of the text.

l. *impressive and beautiful work*: Modena left his commentary in rough-draft form with almost incomprehensible editings and scribblings. In the introduction he wrote that he found some satisfaction in this commentary and occasionally a solution to a difficulty in the Torah. He called it *Parashat ha-kesef* because he wrote it for the money (*kesef*). In 1632 his grandson, Isaac min Haleviim, who was ten years old at the time, copied it over, and his version is still extant as Oxford MS Canon Misc. 204; see excursus 2, "Who Wrote the Ambrosiana Manuscript of *Hayyei yehudah*?"

m. *Bereshit, Pinhas, Mattot, and Mas'ei*: Modena began his work on Tuesday, July 10, 1601, the week of portion Balak (Numbers 22:2–25:9). He omitted mention of this portion in the autobiography, but it is contained in the manuscript version of the commentary. Pinhas (Numbers 25:10–30:1) is dated July 25 (25th of Tammuz); Mattot (Numbers 30:2–32:42) is dated August 27 (29th of Av); Mas'ei (Numbers 33:1–36:13) that year combined with Mattot. Therefore, at the end of two months he had finished only four portions. In the autumn, Modena agreed to begin a new scheme by starting with Bereshit, (Genesis 1:1–6:8), which fell on October 20, but this portion took him five months to complete.

n. *for I did not refrain from playing games of chance. When Rabbi Pardo saw that I was not devoting myself to the task, he took it way from me and did not wish to see it finished*: In the introduction to the commentary, Modena claimed that he found the work more difficult than he had initially expected. Resumption of the winter teaching and preaching at Belgrado's may have taken much of his time. At this time his work on the commentary for Pardo began to founder, and a losing streak at gambling began, lasting until the spring of 1602, when for a while he began to win again. In his introduction to the commentary Modena did not mention that his gambling had influenced Pardo's decision to cancel the project but rather that Pardo had suffered business reverses. If that were true, it may have limited his ability to finance Modena's project as early as 1602, so that when Modena fell behind in his writing schedule, Pardo simply found a convenient pretext for terminating it.

o. *Having left the Panarotti house in the month of Tammuz [5]361 . . . in my own house with a few students*: This move, which represented another change of jobs at the beginning of the school year, coincided with the inception of the commentary for Pardo. Modena remained on good terms with Panarotti, and in 1617 he composed the invitations for the wedding of one of his daughters; see Boksenboim, *Iggerot*, p. 362.

p. *alone and idle*: By the spring of 1602, Modena's work publishing Hebrew books, writing letters for the rabbis, and aiding Pardo tapered off drastically. In the introduction to his first volume of sermons, *Midbar yehudah*, Modena summarized his feelings about life at the age of thirty-one: "So the days have increased and I, a thirty-one-year-old, am like a seventy-year-old with gray hair because of the many tempests of my head and heart . . . as long as the strength waned the desire waxed . . . but goodness and kindness have pursued me all the days of my life until today . . . today I am in the wilderness away from all good" (fol. 4b).

q. *Midbar yehudah*: From late June until mid-August 1602, Modena labored frantically on the publication of his first volume of sermons at Zanetti's, for whom he had done much work in the past. Although he and most other Jewish preachers delivered their sermons in Italian, his notes, some of which are still extant, consisted of topics and verses from biblical and rabbinic literature in Hebrew or a complete text written in Italian using Hebrew characters; see BL Or. 5396, fols. 30a–32a; Ancona 7, fols. 33a–37b. As was customary among Jews, Modena later wrote his sermons for publication entirely in Hebrew. He wrote each day and sent the pages to the publisher to be set and printed. In a note at the end of the published volume, the proofreader complained about the condition of the manuscript because words were missing, redundant, scratched, blurred, and splotched. Modena agreed to refine his manuscript, but was not able to do so for lack of time. On Modena's sermons, see Boksenboim, *Iggerot*, no. 40; Rivkin, "Sermons of Leon da Modena," pp. 295–317; I. Rosenzweig, *Hogeh yehudi mi-ketz ha-renasans* (Tel Aviv, 1972); Howard Adelman's introductory essay; and historical notes to fol. 20a.

r. *widely distributed among the Jews*: These words, of course, were written later, sometime after 1618. A year after its publication in 1602, however, only four or five copies of *Midbar yehudah* had been sold outside Venice; see Boksenboim, *Iggerot*, no. 41.

s. *in my possession more than four hundred sermons, in addition to commentaries on the Torah and many anthologies*: A manuscript that may have been written by Modena, conforming to this description, is still extant; see Kaufmann 312.

t. *they go about their business honestly*: Modena stayed in touch with Solomon and Mordecai for many years; see *The Life of Judah*, fol. 15a.

u. *Ancona*: As was often the case when he needed work for the upcoming year, about the time of the Jewish New Year Modena left Venice. On the Jewish community of Ancona, see L. A., "Gl'Israeliti in Ancona," *EI* 18 (1870): 221–222, 316–318; 19 (1871): 18–19, 108–109; C. Ciavarini, *Memorie storiche degli israeliti in Ancona* (Ancona, 1898).

FOLIO 14a

v. *I was without students*: Not only did he lack students, but during the school year 1602–1603 he had few opportunities to write letters, tombstones, or wedding poems.

w. *the vanity of the craft of alchemy*: In other writings, such as a sermon delivered sometime before 1602, Modena appears to have regarded more seriously the validity of alchemy; see *Midbar yehudah*, fol. 81b. Modena's knowledge of alchemy, however, eventually led him to consider it a chicanery founded on obscure expressions; see *Ari nohem*, p. 30; Trachtenberg, *Jewish Magic and Superstition*, pp. 303–304 n. 1; E. J. Holmyard, *Alchemy* (Edinburgh, 1957), p. 13.

x. *Abraham di Cammeo*: At this time he was only a *haver*. Later he became a rabbi and served in Rome; see Boksenboim, *Iggerot*, nos. 54, 72.

y. *Calimani*: For references to members of the Calimani family see Pullan, *Rich and Poor*, p. 549; and idem, *The Jews of Europe*, p. 150.

z. *at the age of six*: That many of Modena's letters for young boys were written as part of dictation exercises for children like the four- or five-year-old Simhah Calimani is demonstrated by a letter in his collection written between July 15 and July 27, 1604 over the name of this boy; see Boksenboim, *Iggerot*, no. 309.

a. *after I had left Venice for Ferrara*: A few lines below in *The Life of Judah* Modena indicates that he left for Ferrara at the end of Elul 1604. That must have been between September 19 and 24, after Mordecai, his eldest son, celebrated his Bar Mitzvah in Venice on Saturday, September 18 (Parashat Nitzavim); his birthday was actually on the 20th of Elul (Wednesday, September 15). A copy of the Italian sermon (written in Hebrew characters) that the young Modena preached on that occasion is extant in manuscript: Ancona 7, fols. 33a–35b.

b. *poverty and distress*: About this time Modena had to pawn some of his writings to raise money. He borrowed two zecchini from Simone Luzzatto on the pledge of six of his manuscripts, one of them an Italian pastoral no longer extant, called either *Rachele* or *Rachele e Giacobbe*, on the condition that Luzzatto would not allow any copies to be made. Later Modena became furious when he discovered that Luzzatto had allowed one of the pawned manuscripts to be copied; see Boksenboim, *Iggerot*, nos. 143, 144.

(On Luzzatto, see historical notes to fol. 37a.) Modena's distress was compounded by a painful abcess in his gums during the summer of 1604 that kept him from working, eating, and sleeping. His activities consisted of negotiating the sale of some books and writing letters for others; see Boksenboim, *Iggerot*, no. 43.

c. *Ferrara*: At the beginning of the seventeenth century, about 1,530 Jews lived in Ferrara, a decrease of about 500 since papal forces took the city in 1598. At that time pawnshops and synagogues were closed, including the synagogue that had been established by the Modena family after their arrival in 1566 (see Boksenboim, *Iggerot*, no. 58), and other limitations were placed on Jewish life. Soon, however, because of popular opposition, rules against Jewish moneylending activities and residence restrictions were relaxed. On the Jews of Ferrara, see Roth, *Italy*, p. 314; Blau, *Kitvei*, no. 188; *Ziknei*, nos. 38, 88; Kaufmann 155.90; A. Pesaro, *Memorie storiche sulla comunità israelitica ferrarese* (Ferrara, 1878), p. 34.

d. *Joseph Zalman*: A wealthy merchant, philanthropist, and educated Jewish leader who aided the poor and oppressed. When not in Reggio or Carpi on business, he presided over a large extended family. In addition to teaching the young children Hebrew and Bible, among other subjects, Modena helped care for Joseph Zalman's family in his absence, reporting news to him and assisting with the betrothals of his children; Boksenboim, *Iggerot*, nos. 48, 77, 82, 83, 84, 276; *Divan*, nos. 212, 213; *Lev ha-aryeh* (Venice, 1612), fol. 4a; (Vilna, 1886), fol. 2a. After Modena's death, among those to whom his grandson Isaac min Haleviim turned for support during a time of distress were members of the Zalman family; Haleviim, *Medabber*, p. 31.

e. *After a month I brought my wife and children*: In a letter written on December 6, 1604, Modena indicated that for two months his wife and children had been living with him in Ferrara. Not only is it difficult to reconcile exactly the dates given in the autobiography with those in the letter, but in the letter he implies that all his children (his three sons and two daughters) were living with him in Ferrara. From the autobiography, however, it is clear that Zebulun had remained in Venice. See Boksenboim, *Iggerot*, no. 46. Mordecai was thirteen years old at the time, Isaac eleven, Diana six, Zebulun three, and Esther one year old.

f. *Great Synagogue*: In Ferrara Modena also preached at congregations Adat Abirim and Naveh Kodesh; *Lev ha-aryeh*, fol. 2a.

g. *I was overcome by depression*: In addition to missing Venice, Modena felt that his role in life had changed for the worse. In Venice he had considered himself a communal religious worker, while in Ferrara he felt he was merely a teacher for a distinguished private family, and he missed the camaraderie and the public aspects of his work in Venice; see Boksenboim, *Iggerot*, nos. 45, 46, 48; *Divan*, no. 28.

FOLIO 14b

h. *Because the air in Ferrara bothered my son Mordecai*: Benvenuto Cellini (1500–1571), the famous Renaissance artist and autobiographer, and Azariah de Rossi both mentioned the vapors and the fog in Ferrara: B. Cellini, *Autobiography*, trans. G. Bull (Harmondsworth, 1956), p. 246; and H. Friedenwald, *Jews and Medicine* (Baltimore, 1944), vol. 2, p. 398. After Mordecai recovered from diarrhea he developed a severe cold and then contracted a disease that affected his legs and limited his freedom of movement. He was particularly upset because his uncle Moses had to replace him in an upcoming comedy, probably the yearly Purim play in Venice. After moving to Venice in the spring of 1605 Mordecai worked in a store where he kept the records in Hebrew and prospered; see Boksenboim, *Iggerot*, nos. 42, 82.

i. *Joseph Zalman . . . passed away*: He died on August 22, 1606 (19th of Av) after a brief illness lasting two days: *Divan*, nos. 123, 233. Four days later, on August 26, Simon Copio, another major supporter of Modena in Venice, died. Six months later another unnamed patron in Venice, in whom Modena had placed much hope, became perilously ill. This event caused him further anguish: "What can I do, if all the people inclined to love me and help me are taken from the world?"; see Boksenboim, *Iggerot*, no. 85.

j. *Therefore, I intended to move back to Venice*: In November 1605 Modena had made a trip to Venice to look into the possibilities of moving back there. Thus, despite the authority he now enjoyed as a rabbi in Ferrara, he soon tired of this role and missed the intellectual life of Venice. About Purim 1606 he had arranged to rent an apartment at a high price from a member of the Copio family. When he tried to leave for Venice, the congregation in Ferrara crowded around him and would not let him board the carriage. Instead they committed him against his will to another year or two of work there; see Blau, *Kitvei*, no. 109; Boksenboim, *Iggerot*, nos. 72, 74.

k. *the "garden"*: On the academy of Kalonymos Belgrado see *The Life of Judah*, fol. 11b.

l. *the house of study of the Torah Study Society*: The school sponsored by the Ashkenazic Torah Study Society, where Modena had been preaching since 1600; see *The Life of Judah*, fol. 13a.

m. *my wife's relative Moses Copio*: Modena had planned to move in with this family in the spring of 1606. He had dedicated *Midbar yehudah* to Moses Copio and his late brother Simon, the father of Sarra Copia Sullam, the distinguished author, poet, and *salonière* (see historical notes to fol. 20a). Moses appears regularly as an insurer of merchant cargo and as a merchant himself in notarial records from 1592 to 1609. Simon appears in the same documents during the same years but only as an insurer; Tenenti, *Naufrages*, s.v. index.

n. *may his name be blotted out*: Modena's hostility to Moses Copio was probably due to Copio's conversion to Christianity; see L. Schiavi, "Gli Ebrei in Venezia et nelle sue colonie," *Nuova Anthologia di scienze lettere ed arti* 3d ser. 47 (1893): 502–503. Nevertheless, Modena was in contact with Abraham Copio, Moses' son, in 1640; see BL Or. 5395, fol. 19b; Haleviim, *Medabber*, p. 85.

o. *the house belonging to the Treves family*: This family was probably that of Isaac ben Mordecai Gershon Treves, usually called Isaac Gershon, who had come to Venice from Safed sometime before 1576, joined the Venetian rabbinate between 1602 and 1608, and supported himself by working as a proofreader of Hebrew books, particularly those by kabbalists from Safed. He was also the leading preacher at the Great Synagogue; see Neppi, *Zekher tzaddikim li-verakhah*, p. 145, no. 27; *Ziknei*, nos. 21–22; D. Tamar, *Mehkarim be-toledot ha-yehudim be-eretz yisrael uve-italiah* (Jerusalem, 1970), pp. 108–109, 113–114; Haleviim, *Medabber*, p. 76.

p. *Patras in Morea*: A port city in the northern Morea (Peloponnese) across from Lepanto, under Turkish control. On Jewish life there, see Benayahu, *Ha-yehasim*, pp. 60–79. Shortly after Isaac's departure Modena wrote to a friend that the reason he had sent his son to the Levant was "to afflict him and to straighten him, because his head had swelled," *gavar ʿalav moho*, and that Isaac now could not wait to return, "may his return be better than his departure"; see Boksenboim, *Iggerot*, no. 95.

q. *Zante*: Now called Zakinthos, an island in the Adriatic, between Corfu and Crete, just south of Cephalonia. It was a Venetian possession from the late fifteenth century until the end of the Venetian Republic in 1797. On Jewish life there, see Benayahu, *Ha-yehasim*, p. 79.

FOLIO 15a

r. *220 ducatoni*: This sum was equivalent to about 250 ducats a year. According to Modena a ducatone equaled seven Venetian lire. According to Coryat it equaled eight lire; see Boksenboim, *Iggerot*, no. 276 and Coryat, *Crudities* (1611), p. 285, (1905), p. 422.

s. *smitten by priests and afflicted*: After his arrival in Florence, in a letter written to his old friend Abraham Cammeo, Modena alluded to this incident using the same phrase employed here but describing the incident only as "an unpleasant experience"; Boksenboim, *Iggerot*, no. 95.

t. *boil at the base of my throat*: See Boksenboim, *Iggerot*, no. 98.

u. *I quarreled with the aforementioned Abraham and some other members of the community*: Reasons for his quarrel included the following aspects of his life in Florence described in his letters: his income was not adequate; his teaching load was oppressive and grew worse every day; he spoke about matters of faith before Christian nobles; he harshly criticized Florence in his letters to Venice; as early as August 1609 he had tried to obtain another teaching job in Padua. Reluctantly Modena agreed to remain at the position in Florence until the spring. Modena was most frustrated because many people in Venice could not understand why he was so unhappy in Florence; see Boksenboim, *Iggerot*, nos. 95, 99, 100, 101, 104.

v. *we constantly longed for and yearned to return to Venice*: In Florence during the autumn of 1609, shortly after the Jewish New Year, Modena saw the realization of a long-awaited dream. At last, at the age of thirty-nine years, he received his rabbinic ordination from the gaon Leib Saraval, the leading rabbi in Venice; see Boksenboim, *Iggerot*, p. 17, nos. 90, 101, 102, 103, 145.

w. *teaching*: One of Modena's most distinguished students from this period of his teaching career was Saul Levi Morteira (1596–1660), who had been born in Venice and subsequently left in 1613 to accompany Dr. Elijah Montalto, physician to the queen mother, Maria de Medici, to Paris. In 1616, after the death of Montalto, Morteira settled in Amsterdam. There he served as a teacher, rabbi, and senior rabbi. He ordained Manasseh ben Israel, drew Modena into controversies, and taught and later excommunicated Spinoza; see historical notes to fol. 24a.

x. *San Vito*: San Vito al Tagliamento, a city north of Venice between Conegliano and Udine. The Romanin family was prominent in Jewish affairs there; see Boksenboim, *Iggerot*, nos. 241, 206; Zorattini, *Leandro Tisanio*, pp. 6–15.

FOLIO 15b

y. *the "haver" Jacob Levi*: The son of Kalonymos and Sarah Levi, he was Modena's favorite son-in-law; see *The Life of Judah*, fols. 15b, 21b.

z. *relying on heaven's mercy*: On a yearly salary of about two hundred ducats, this dowry was beyond Modena's means; see Howard Adelman's introductory essay.

a. *eulogy for him*: Abtalion died in Ferrara, but Modena eulogized him in Venice. Two other important Jewish leaders with whom Modena had close relations died between 1611 and 1612, Samuel Archivolti in March 1611 and Kalonymos Belgrado in February 1612; but as usual, Modena did not record these events in his autobiography.

b. *all my doings were worthless*: The self-deprecation in the autobiography contrasts markedly with a description in a letter by Modena of the fullness of a day in his life at about this time:

When the morning light shines I cannot avoid getting up with the dawn to go to the synagogue. Immediately afterward it is time to go to the midrash. There

214

I come to teach the laws from the Shulhan Arukh to the congregation. Next I get up and go immediately to the yeshiva for *pilpul* with the members. From there I go to the elementary school to serve my sentence, as the wicked do in hell. The students number approximately thirty-three or thirty-four. [Modena wrote the words "mourning," *evel*, and "poverty," *dal*, the numerical values of whose letters are thirty-three and thirty-four, respectively.] I remain there until lunch, having consumed nothing yet but my weeping mixed with my drink [Psalms 102:9]. Then I must go to teach writing to the two children of the prominent members of the community for an hour. Then they call me and I reply by returning to serve my sentence, dictating to my students and teaching. Then, afterward, when the congregation gathers again, I preach for half an hour every day. Then I return to serving my sentence rebuking the students. Until 5:00 P.M. they do not allow me to catch my breath. I must also study in preparation for teaching the laws and the Midrash as well as for the Sabbath sermons. And if a document or a letter arrives that requires a response for which I will be paid, I must steal the time, which is just not available. I swear, I am consumed by heat during the day and by exhaustion at night. If today were not Friday, if my son were not preaching tomorrow, and if this time that I usually use to prepare my sermon had not been available to write you, you still would not have seen this letter. . . . Although I am tired and weary, as mentioned, I find relaxation even if I have but half an hour each week to delight in the love of dear friends and to have pleasing conversations. In Florence my sermons were known to the little fish in the Arno and in Venice they are novelties to the big fish in the sea. (Boksenboim, *Iggerot*, no. 105)

Modena's account of his daily schedule is reminiscent of that which Maimonides gave of his own schedule in his oft-cited letter to Samuel ibn Tibbon, the translator of his *Guide of the Perplexed*; see F. Kobler, *Letters of Jews Through the Ages* (New York, 1952), vol. 1, pp. 211–212; and I. Twersky, *A Maimonides Reader* (New York, 1972), pp. 7–8.

c. *I completed the printing*: Modena had returned to work for the Christian Hebrew publishers of Venice as an expediter and proofreader of books. The books he worked on included *I trionfi* by Angelo Alatrini and the Mishnah with the commentary *Kaf nahat* (see *The Life of Judah*, fol. 20a). The phrasing here implies that he was also doing some of the printing, which was illegal for Jews. Similar phrasing is also found in a letter Modena wrote about the same book, "I am still occupied with the printing of a book"; see Boksenboim, *Iggerot*, no. 93, 11 Adar, 1609; Ravid, "Prohibition Against Jewish Printing," pp. 135–153.

d. *Galut yehudah*: Sensitive to pedagogic needs, Modena organized *Galut yehudah* as a complete program to bring students to the level at which they could read and understand the Bible. In this book the essential Hebrew words of every book of the Bible and portions of the liturgy are listed in the order of their appearance and translated into Italian. It also contains a brief summary of the rules of Hebrew grammar in Italian and lists of basic Hebrew nouns, particles, and verbs; see historical notes to fol. 20a.

e. *Lev ha-aryeh*: In *Lev ha-aryeh*, Modena again demonstrated his keen interest in creating innovative pedagogical devices to attract young students to Hebrew studies. He developed a course in memory improvement with particular emphasis on the Hebrew language, culminating in a list of the 613 commandments of rabbinic Judaism according to Maimonides. He was especially pleased that he was the first to use gentile ideas about memory training in the service of Hebrew. Modena's interest in this topic is indicated by the fact that he owned a book on localized memory techniques printed in Venice in 1603; see Ancona, "Inventario," pp. 260–267. On the classical art of memory improvement through concentration on "places" (*loci*) and "images" (*immagine*), and its popularity during the Italian Renaissance, see F. Yates, *The Art of Memory* (Chicago, 1965). For studies of *Lev ha-aryeh*, see D. Margoliot, " 'Al ha-zikkaron," *Korot* 5 (1972): 759–772; and G. Sermoneta, "Aspetti del pensiero moderno nell'ebraismo italiano tra rinascimento e eta barocca," in *Italia judaica*, vol. 2, pp. 17–35.

One tantalizing example of Modena's methods is the following: "If you want to remember what the study of that which is beyond nature is called in Greek, namely metaphysics, remember a bed [*mittah* in Hebrew] with a man and a woman lying on it or, if you remember that it is *metafisica* in Italian, imagine a half of a woman doctor, that is *metà* [half] *fisica* [a term for a woman doctor]" (*Lev ha-aryeh*, 3.10).

f. *patriarch of Aquileia, Ermolao Barbaro*: The Venetian patrician families of Barbaro and Querini, along with the Grimanis, controlled the Patriarchate of Aquileia. It was one of the most affluent ecclesiastical offices in the country, yielding between five thousand and ten thousand ducats a year in revenue; see D. Chambers, *The Imperial Age of Venice, 1380–1580* (London, 1970), pp. 112–113; O. Logan, *Culture and Society in Venice* (New York, 1972), pp. 30–31.

g. *dance and music teacher*: Jews regularly held this position in Renaissance Italy; see Roth, *Renaissance*, pp. 271–304; Shulvass, *Renaissance*, pp. 241–246; O. Kinkeldey, "A Jewish Dancing Master of the Renaissance," in *Studies in Jewish Bibliography and Related Studies in Memory of Abraham Solomon Freidus* (New York, 1927), pp. 329–372; Simonsohn, *Milan*, nos. 3663, 4196.

h. *at ten months of age*: In this passage, written about April 1621 (see historical notes to fol. 16b), Modena refers to two children who were born and died in infancy during Jacob and Diana's early years of marriage and before the birth of Modena's grandson, Isaac, in May 1621 (see *The Life of Judah*, fol. 18b). Diana lost two others infants in later years, David in 1625 (fol. 20b) and Richina in 1630, two months after her husband, Jacob, passed away (fols. 21b, 22a).

i. *On the 10th of Tishre*: The unspecified antagonism must have been great, because Mordecai fled Venice on a Yom Kippur (always the 10th of Tishre), which coincided that year with the Sabbath.

FOLIO 16a

j. *six and a half lire per ounce*: This was approximately the value of a ducat in Venice at the time.

k. *coppella*: A vessel used to distinguish gold and silver from other metals.

l. *I knew that it was real*: A procedure using copper and arsenic to produce copper arsenide, a white, solid metal that resembled silver, was performed by alchemists, who accepted the results as silver because for them color was the most important characteristic; see Holmyard, *Alchemy*, p. 26.

m. *Great Synagogue*: The Ashkenazic synagogue.

n. *the Church of San Geremia*: Directly outside the ghetto, which was located in that church's parish.

o. *Abraham Haver Tov*: Abraham Haver Tov (Buoncompagno) and his father Solomon published most of Modena's early books at the Christian Hebrew presses of Venice: *Sur mera'* and *Sod yesharim* at di Gara's and *Tzemah tzaddik* at Zanetti's. Haver Tov was a proofreader of Hebrew books in Venice. About 1639 Modena recorded a magical formula he had learned from Haver Tov, who had gone to Mantua to work as a proofreader; see BL Or. 5395, fol. 5a.

p. *Bible with commentaries* ("*Mikra gedolah*"): The publisher Modena found in 1616 for this version of the rabbinic Bible was Bragadini. Modena assured potential buyers that this edition would be totally free from any iniquities in the eyes of the censor, so that no accusations could be leveled against it; see Boksenboim, *Iggerot*, no. 112.

q. *four hundred subscribers*: Bragadini had wanted 400 advance subscriptions, but only 160 people signed up in Venice. Therefore, Modena wrote to other communities, such as that of Rome, to find agents to take orders for the book, and sent Mordecai to Verona, Mantua, Ferrara, and other communities to enroll subscribers. Though still bleeding from his alchemical experiments, Mordecai was able to enroll the necessary number of subscribers. Here Modena incorrectly gives his son credit for having solicited all 400 subscribers. The book appeared in print within the year (1616/1617); see Boksenboim, *Iggerot*, no. 112.

FOLIO 16b

r. *written [i.e., copied] from his hand in [a copy of] his book that is in my possession*: In 1834 S. D. Luzzatto wrote to Solomon Rapoport that he had seen an old manuscript notebook that contained Azariah de Rossi's poem about his dream, which he mentioned had also appeared on his tombstone

(*Iggerot*, no. 96, p. 291 [July 4, 1834]; S. Rapoport, "Mikhtav 14," *Kerem hemed* 5 [1842]: 161; *Me'or 'einayim*, ed. L. Zunz [Vilna, 1863], fol. 12b). In the introduction to the 1866 edition of *Me'or 'einayim*, David Cassel, the editor, claimed that he had seen this poem at the end of Modena's annotated copy of *Me'or 'einayim*. Cassel's citation indicates, however, that his source for the poem had been a copy made by somebody else from another manuscript. The text of the autobiography is ambiguous. It does not indicate clearly whether Modena actually had a text of the poem *in* de Rossi's hand or *copied* "from his hand," nor does it make clear whether the poem was in a copy of *Me'or 'einayim* or in some other work by de Rossi that is now lost. In Modena's copy of *Me'or 'einayim* in Parma no such poem is found. The problem of the original source of this poem is further complicated by Roth, who reports that Azariah de Rossi's tombstone inscription was a translation of Latin hexameters from a 1542 tombstone prepared by Cardinal Gasparo Contarini for his own grave; Roth, *Renaissance*, p. 325. According to Cassel, the full text of de Rossi's poem is:

On my bed lingering Kislev [5]335 [1574]
Appeared to me one saying "you have
Three more years"
Therefore in the year [5]338 [1577/1578] my soul will pass through
Please good master forgive, whiten the darkness of crimson.

s. *Alessandro Bivago*: Bivago was the name of a Jewish family from Spain; see Ruderman, "Bologna," p. 258.

t. *I am fifty now*: Modena turned fifty on the 29th of Nisan (April 19, 1621).

FOLIO 17a

u. *outside the ghetto*: As Jews had not been allowed to live outside the ghetto in Venice since 1516, perhaps this remark was meant as a reference to his impending death.

v. *9th of Heshvan 5378*: The date of Mordecai's death is confirmed by a contemporary chronicle by David Matzah of Corfu, *Ma'aseh ha-shem* (Venice, 1618), cited in Benayahu, *Ha-yehasim*, pp. 327–328, 148; and by *Luhot avanim*, no. 51.

FOLIO 17b

w. *Zimlan Luria of Padua*: (d. 1624), he was an important lay leader in Padua who quarreled with Rabbi Samuel Archivolti. Modena wrote extensively on behalf of the Venetian rabbis about this disagreement; see JTSA 8950.6 and D. Carpi, ed., *Pinkas va'ad kehillah kedoshah paduah* (Jerusalem, 1973–1979), vol. 1, s.v. index. Modena also prepared his epitaph; see *Divan*, no. 263.

x. *the physician Hayyim Alatini*: He was a rabbi and physician in Ferrara; see *Ziknei*, p. 190.

y. *Leon Costantin of Crete*: Modena ordained him; see *Ziknei*, pp. 59, 60, 198.

z. *tertian fever*: In tertian fever the fever recurs every third day.

FOLIO 18a

a. *La Motta*: A small village north of Vicenza on the Venetian terra firma.

b. *Jacob Jozvil Levi*: He was also a poet; see *Luhot avanim* 2, ed. S. Bernstein, *HUCA* 10 (1935): 483–552, no. 40.1; Haleviim, *Medabber*, pp. 110–111.

c. *very burdensome to me*: Because of the heavy duties connected with this position Modena had to resign from some of his other secretarial positions. On Saturday evening, December 28 (22d of Tevet), 1619 he asked for permission from the board of the Fraterna di Maritar Donzelle della Natione degli Hebrei Tedesca di Venezia, the Society for the Dowering of Brides, to hand his duties over to his son-in-law Jacob Levi. This move was approved by a vote of twelve to three; see Regolazione della Fraterna di Maritar Donzelle della Natione degli Hebrei Tedesca di Venezia, ASV, Scuole Piccole e Suffragi, b. 733, fol. 62b (242a). References to this record book, long considered lost, have been supplied by Harvey Sukenic, who located it and is using it in his dissertation on confraternities (*hevrot*) in the ghetto of Venice in the early modern period, which he is writing at Brandeis University. On this episode see Horowitz, "Havurat 'hassi' betulot,' " pp. 362–371. This job may have prevented Modena from working at the Italian synagogue from 1619 through 1626. In JTSA 8593 there are no records of his having been paid there during that period. He did record in the autobiography (fol. 20b) that he was working at the Italian synagogue in 1625.

d. *returned to the school*: Here is another example of a trip taken by Modena at the end of the school year. The word for school here, as in the Regolazione mentioned in the previous note, wherein it clearly refers to the school of the Ashkenazim ("Hebrei tedeschi"), is *beit midrash*. Hence this term is used interchangeably with the word, *hesger*, used above for the same school. For other references to the term *hesger*, see Y. Boksenboim, *Iggerot melammdim* (Tel Aviv, 1986), p. 5.

e. *more and not less*: After requesting help on Thursday evening, July 9 (9th of Tammuz), 1620, by Thursday evening, September 4 (6th of Elul), 1620—the night before Esther's wedding—when Modena still had not raised the necessary dowry, the Fraterna di Maritar Donzelle granted him fifty ducats for Esther and another twenty for his work in settling a controversy between that group and the Society for Gemilut Hasadim. This action was contrary to the rules of the Society for the Dowering of Brides because the sum of fifty ducats was double what other brides received and because Esther was under the usual age of eighteen. These details are found in the aforementioned record book of the society, Regolazione, fols. 62a (244b), 63a–b (241b–a), 64a (240b); see M. Soave, "Vita di Giuda Arie Modena," *CI* 2 (1863): 287–288; and Horowitz, "Havurat 'hassi' betulot,' " pp. 362–365.

f. *Christians*: This feud involved the murder of a builder; see *The Life of Judah*, fol. 34b.

FOLIO 18b

g. *our relative Moses Simhah*: He is not to be confused with Modena's late brother-in-law of the same name; on this Moses Simhah, see *Luhot avanim*, no. 126; *Divan*, no. 256.

h. *five magistrates*: Modena did not specify which five magistrates had arrested his son. The reference is either to the Cinque Savii alla Mercanzia, who had jurisdiction over the Ghetto Vecchio and to a considerable extent also over the Levantine and Ponentine Jews living there, or to I Cinque alle Pace, who were responsible for supervising the public peace.

i. *Zebulun sang a song that I had written*: It was published and distributed. Modena recorded it in his *Divan*, no. 141. On such events, see Haleviim, *Medabber*, pp. 48–49.

j. *I have had neither rest nor peace, with anxiety*: This verse is Modena's "motto" from Job; see *The Life of Judah*, fol. 4b.

FOLIO 19a

k. *like the descendants of Canaan*: Elsewhere Modena indicated that those who killed his son had been Jews; see Salamone de Rossi, *Ha-shirim asher li-shelomoh* (Venice, 1623), fol. 3a, reprinted Frankfurt am Main, 1925; see also Adler, *Hebrew Writings Concerning Music*, pp. 212–214.

l. *Cannaregio*: Cannaregio is the name of one of the major canals of Venice, which passes by the gate of the Ghetto Vecchio, and also the name of the district in which the ghetto is located.

m. *Alvise Giustinian*: The Giustiniani were one of the leading noble families of Venice.

n. *Isaac of the Spagnoletta family*: Modena had lived with this family in 1598; see *The Life of Judah*, fol. 13a. For an Isaac Spagnoletto in the 1620s, see Pullan, *The Jews of Europe*, pp. 56, 266.

FOLIO 19b

o. *Dolfin family*: It was a member of the Dolfin family named Zacaria who proposed about Eastertime 1516 to the Venetian government that the Jews who were then spread out all over the city be sent to live in the Ghetto Nuovo; see excursus 1, "The Venetian Ghetto in Historical Perspective."

p. *never touched one of his own people*: Zebulun's murder is described in his own tombstone inscription: *Luhot avanim*, no. 52. Jews murdering other Jews in Italy was not an entirely unknown phenomenon; see *Ziknei*, no. 121; *Luhot avanim* 2, nos. 19, 24, 35, 70, 83; D. Kaufmann, "A Contribution to the History of the Venetian Jews," *JQR* o.s. 2 (1890): 302; and for the general background, G. Ruggiero, *Violence in Early Renaissance Venice* (New Brunswick, N.J., 1980).

q. *to "the staircase"*: In the ducal palace there are several spectacular staircases, *scala* in Italian, many of which are associated with justice. For example, the Scala dei Giganti, "The Giants' Staircase," built in 1505, was anachronistically considered to have been the scene of the beheading of Doge Marino Faliero in 1354. The Scala dei Censori, "The Staircase of the Censors," led to an opening in a wall decorated with a marble lion's head, where secret denunciations were made to the captain of the police and the guards of the Council of Ten, under whose control were also the Esecutori contro la Bestemmia, described in the next note. See T. Okey, *Venice and Its Story* (London and New York, 1903), pp. 241–251. Another massive staircase in Venice associated with justice was that inside the Campanile, the "Tower of St. Mark." At its base was the Logetta, where patricians sat in judgment; Coryat, *Crudities* (1905), pp. 325–327. Modena uses the Hebrew equivalent of *scala*, *sulam*, apparently intending justice in general, without stating to which specific staircase he is referring.

r. *the magistrates of the Bestemmia, acting on order of the heads of the [Council of] Ten*: The Council of Ten, created in 1310, assumed jurisdiction over matters of police, public safety and security, and internal stability and discipline. The only reference located to date in the Venetian archives to this incident is a unanimous ruling of the Council of Ten of June 28, 1622. It provided that the proceedings initiated by the suit of Leon Modena, identified as "Jewish rabbi," against the brothers Sabbadin and Moyse Benincasa, called D'Endelina, who were accused of the murder of Modena's son Marino and other crimes committed also with others, be turned over to the magistracy of the Esecutori contro la Bestemmia, so that it could administer justice in accordance with its procedures. The text in ASV, Council of Ten, criminale, filza 49, reads:

Che'l processo formato a querela di Leon Modena Rabbi hebreo contra Sabbadai et Moyse fratelli Benincase detti d'Endelina imputati della morte data a

Marino suo figliuolo, et di altri delitti commessi anco in compagnia d'altri sia con tutto il caso rimesso alli Essecutori nostri contra la Biastema affine che secondo'l rito del loro magistrato amministrino giustitia.

The Esecutori contro la Bestemmia was founded in 1537 to combat blasphemy and evil living, and thus by extension came to have jurisdiction over a wide range of activities, including gambling, taverns, excommunication, printing and censorship, immigration, and aspects of sexual relations between Christians and Jews. According to a letter from the inquisitor of Ferrara, Isaac Spagnoletto allegedly lived during the 1620s in both the Venetian townhouse and also the country villa of a certain Christian lady; see Pullan, *The Jews of Europe*, p. 266.

s. *a forsaken whore*: On Jewish whores in Venice, see Pullan, *The Jews of Europe*, pp. 157, 162, 277; and Horowitz, "Havurat 'hassi' betulot,' " pp. 355–356. Additionally, in 1650 a Jewish prostitute named Sicile Polacca, who lived in the Ghetto Vecchio, was expelled from the Venetian state by the Esecutori contro la Bestemmia; see *Leggi e memorie venete sulla prostitutione fino alla caduta della repubblica* (Venice, 1870–1872), p. 348, no. 140.

t. *they would have their heads cut off*: Beheading was one of the standard punishments for individuals who were banished from the Venetian state but subsequently returned and were apprehended; see Coryat, *Crudities* (1611), p. 189; (1905), p. 330.

FOLIO 20a

u. *It is a source of great comfort to me*: Privately Modena measured his success by his writings that appeared in print and not by his accomplishments in the classroom, in the pulpit, or as a member of the rabbinate. As is noted in excursus 2, "Who Wrote the Ambrosiana Manuscript of *Hayyei yehudah*?" Modena updated this bibliographical list several times by adding titles in the margin and between lines (see fig. 6, Modena's page numbered with Hebrew letters, *lamed-gimel*, "33"). Only a few of his works were written and printed at the time he began the list in the autobiography (1622).

v. *Sur mera*ʿ: The title, *Turn from Evil*, is based on Psalms 34:15 and 37:27. Although in *The Life of Judah*, fol. 22b, Modena wrote that he had composed it at the age of twelve, in *Ziknei*, no. 78, he related, as here, that he had written it at the age of thirteen. Modena carefully pointed out that the dialogue both praised and condemned gambling, a fact overlooked by many modern writers. In each of its six parts Modena used a different method of argumentation, for each of which he marshaled the pros and cons, supported with proof texts from Hebrew literature. It was published by Abraham Haver Tov at the press of di Gara in 5396 [1595/1596] and republished in Prague (and perhaps Venice) in 1615, Leiden, about 1656, and Vilna in 1899 (reprinted in 1903 and photoreproduced in Jerusalem in

1971). *Sur mera'* has been translated into Latin, Judeo-German, German, French, and English: H. Gollancz, "On Games of Chance," in *The Targum to the Song of Songs; The Book of the Apple; The Ten Jewish Martyrs; A Dialogue on Games of Chance* (London, 1908), pp. 162–205; sometimes it appeared under the name of *Tzahkan melummad* or *Talmid tzahkan.* Thirty-five years after the original printing, Modena acknowledged his authorship publicly; see *Ziknei,* no. 78 and Plantavit, *Bibliotheca rabbinica,* no. 478, p. 610.

w. *Sod yesharim*: Based on Psalms 111:1. This work contains a hundred of what Modena calls *segullot,* which he describes in Hebrew on the title page as "a treasure-trove of secrets, marvelous cures, and amazing things" (*matmonei mistarim refu'ot pela'ot ve-divrei nora'ot*). Plantavit's Latin description of the book uses the phrase *naturae arcana,* "natural mysteries," in *Bibliotheca rabbinica,* p. 610, no. 476. This genre of literature was well known under the rubric of "books of secrets." These books, often call "receipt books," contained a mixture of medical remedies and magical formulas ("recipes") for achieving various purposes. It is highly likely that Modena named his books *Secret of the Upright* because he was fully aware of this genre. On this literature, see L. Thorndike, *A History of Magic and Experimental Science* (New York, 1941), vol. 6, pp. 215–220. In *Sod yesharim* Modena included formulas such as how to grow one's signet on a peach pit (no. 1), how to grow a peach without a pit (no. 2), how to guess a number (no. 40), how to guess a coin (no. 47), how to stop bed wetting (no. 68), how to handle a snake (no. 69), how to remove a spot (nos. 82, 83), how to treat diarrhea and vomiting (no. 92), how to remember one's daily lessons (no. 3), and how to use a secret manual alphabet with most of the letters being indicated by Hebrew mnemonics, such as signaling the letter '*ayin* with the eye ('*ayin*; no. 29). One typical formula—for pregnancy, taken from Galen—included drinking a burned rabbit's stomach with wine at the beginning and end of the menstrual period (no. 55). Modena's interest in these formulas continued after the publication of *Sod yesharim*; see *The Life of Judah,* fols. 34b–35a; *Ari nohem,* p. 76; Isaac min Haleviim, introduction to *Magen ve-herev,* in *Ma'amar magen ve-tzinnah,* ed. A. Geiger (Breslau, 1856), fol. 11b; and BL Or. 5395, fol. 5a. *Sod yesharim* also contains fifty riddles with answers and a curriculum for Jewish education. Manuscript versions of Modena's riddles were circulated among the Jews of Yemen. One researcher of Yemenite Jewish folklore reported many of Modena's riddles exactly as they appear in *Sod yesharim* as oral traditions "from the mouth of the people" created by Jews from the East whose Hebrew was influenced by Arabic; see Y. Ratzhaby, "Ahuda na," *Yeda'-'am* 2 (1954): 36–42; cf. Pagis, *'Al sod hatum,* pp. v, 17, 18, 19, 49, 50, 60, 72. For a discussion of these riddles and their role in Modena's Jewish educational program, see H. Adelman's paper, "The Educational

Program of Leon Modena and Jewish Attitudes to the Study of Hebrew in Seventeenth-Century Venice." *Sod yesharim* was first published by Abraham Haver Tov at di Gara's. The first edition bears the date 5355 [1594/ 1595], with the letters arranged to spell the Hebrew word *be-simhah*, "with joy" [= 355]. It was republished in 1598/1599 at Zanetti's; see L. Nemoy, "A Hitherto Undescribed Edition of Leon Modena's *Sod yesharim*," *JQR* n.s. (1933–1934): 48–50. Subsequent editions include Verona, 1647; Amsterdam, 1649; Frankfurt am Main, 1682; and an abridged version (Jerusalem, ca. 1880).

x. *Tzemah tzaddik: Flower of the Virtuous*, based on Jeremiah 23:5. This work was published by Solomon and Abraham Haver Tov at Zanetti's in 1600. *Fior di virtù*, one of the most popular books of the Renaissance, had already been translated into almost every European language. An excellent English translation with introduction is available in L. Rosenwald and N. Fersin, *The Florentine Fior* (Washington, D.C., 1953). Modena preserved the highlights of the original anonymous *Fior di virtù* in his *Tzemah tzaddik*. Most of the time Modena closely followed the text of *Fior di virtù*, and his statement, "I substituted a saying of the rabbis of blessed memory for *every* reference from their Scriptures or saints," is not completely accurate. Sometimes he substituted for some of the Christian quotations by Matthew, Augustine, Gregory, Bernard of Clairvaux, or Pope Innocent verses from the Torah and Jewish sources such as the Talmud, Midrash, or Solomon ibn Gabirol. At other times, however, he retained the citation, merely removing the Christian attribution. By contrast, he retained attribution to pagan authors. Modena did eliminate a few sections with unalterable christological significance as well as some examples from the Hebrew Bible that might have offended contemporary ethical standards: *Fior di virtù*, chaps. 9, 8, 17, 12; *Tzemah tzaddik*, chap. 16. The most revealing changes Modena made were in the chapters in which the subject of women was treated: for example, *Tzemah tzaddik*, chap. 6; *Fior di virtù*, chap. 7. The one chapter he omitted was that on amorous love, in which much attention was paid to the physical pleasures of love between a man and a woman (*Fior di virtù*, chap. 5). In translating and editing *Tzemah tzaddik* Modena's purpose, as an innovative teacher, appears to have been to attract students to the study of Hebrew texts and Jewish teachings. *Tzemah tzaddik* was republished at Vilna in 1865 (without illustrations); New York, 1899; and Tel Aviv, 1949. On *Tzemah tzaddik*, see M. Steinschneider, "Jehudah (Leon) Modena und *Fior di virtù*," *MGWJ* 41 (1896–1897): 324–326.

y. *Midbar yehudah*: Based on Judges 1:16 or Psalms 63:1, the title, literally *The Wilderness of Judah*, was evidently meant to be a play on words. The consonants can also be vocalized *mi-devar yehudah*, "from the word of Judah." It was published only once, by Zanetti in 1602. Modena presented the first book he published in his name with a mixture of trepidation and confidence. In his introduction he apologized, saying that the sermons were the unripe fruit of his youth; that the husk might be larger than the kernel; that they might constitute a spiritual desert, as the name implied; and that he had hastily completed the book in only six weeks. He was, nevertheless, proud of his accomplishments as a preacher and presented in his introduction much biographical information, assuming the readers would be interested in his personal life. In his dedication to Simon and Moses Copio, he compared his patrons to the godparents at a circumcision and, in a letter, he called this book his "firstborn"; see Boksenboim, *Iggerot*, no. 40; Rivkin, "Sermons of Leon da Modena," pp. 295–317; Rosenzweig, *Hogeh yehudi mi-ketz ha-renasans*; see historical notes to fol. 13b.

z. *Galut yehudah*: The title of the book, *The Exile of Judah*—taken from Jeremiah 24:5—has a twofold meaning. It refers to Modena's own exile from Venice in Ferrara and Florence, during which he began to prepare the book, and it also alludes to the exile that caused the Jews to forget the Hebrew language, a state of affairs that Modena decries in his preface. The book also has an Italian title, *Novo dittionario hebraico et italiano*. It was first published in Venice in 5372 (1612) by the Jew Giacomo Sorzino. A second edition was published in Padua in 5400 (1640), with a supplement entitled *Pi aryeh*; see item 13, historical note h. Modena had wanted to publish a complete Italian translation of the Bible both for students in the schools and also for teachers, who often were at a loss for the proper expression in Italian for a biblical word. For reasons that he did not state, however, he bemoaned the fact that he could not do so. The main impediment to such an undertaking was no doubt the Catholic authorities' fear that any dissemination of the Bible in the vernacular would stimulate dissent. This fear led them to prefer that only the doctrinally safe Latin version be available to the masses, who could not understand it. On other contemporary attempts to translate the Bible into Italian, see M. Berenblut, "A Comparative Study of Judeo-Italian Translations of Isaiah" (Ph.D. diss., Columbia University, 1949). For more discussion of the work *Galut yehudah*, see historical notes to fol. 15b.

To raise money sometime before 1621, Modena took all sixty remaining copies of the first edition of *Galut yehudah* and sold them cheaply to Jacob Cohen of Tripoli, who then resold them for four lire each. Subsequently, Modena advised someone who requested a copy from him that even if he himself wanted a copy he had to buy it from Cohen like everybody else (Boksenboim, *Iggerot*, no. 119, July 29, 1621). Evidently by the time Modena made this entry in his autobiography a year or so later, no more copies were available, so the price had climbed to ten lire.

a. *Lev ha-aryeh*: Published in Venice in 5372 [1611/1612] by Sorzino. The title, *Heart of the Lion*—based on 2 Samuel 17:10—includes one of Modena's names, as did *Midbar yehudah* and *Galut yehudah*. *Lev ha-aryeh* was republished at Vilna in 1886. This book is discussed in the historical notes to fol. 15b.

b. *Beit lehem yehudah* . . . *'E[in] y[israel]*: Published in Venice on July 18, 1625 by Bragadini at Calleoni's press. This entry was written by Modena above the line and marked by a caret (see textual note). The title, *Bethlehem in Judah*—based on Judges 19:2, 18—could also be translated *A Source of Bread for Judah*, meaning that he hoped to earn money from the publication of this book. On the first edition, see B. Ravid, "*Contra Judaeos* in Seventeenth-Century Italy: Two Responses to the *Discorso* of Simone Luzzatto by Melchiore Palontrotti and Giulio Morosini," *AJSR* 7–8 (1982–1983): 329, note 59. Because the Talmud had been banned in Italy since 1553, rabbinic materials had to be garnered from other sources, which, though censored, had not been proscribed. Non-legal material was often taken from the major collection of Aggadah from the major collection of Aggadah from the Babylonian and Palestinian Talmuds, *'Ein ya'akov*, compiled by Jacob ibn Habib (1445–1515), which because of the Inquisition was called *'Ein yisrael*. See N. Porges, "Der hebraeische Index expurgatorius: *Sefer Ha-zikkuk*," in *Festschrift zum siebsigsten Geburtstage A. Berliner's* (Frankfurt am Main, 1903), pp. 292–293. Modena's manuscript of *Hayyei yehudah* gives only the initials "E. Y.," which could stand for either title. The importance of *Beit lehem yehudah* was that it provided preachers and students with an index to a major rabbinic source available in Italy. It was republished in Prague in 1705.

c. "*Tzeli esh*" . . . *[1628/1629]*: As mentioned in the textual note, this title and the next five (items 9–13) appear in the margin rather than in the body of the text (see fig. 6). *Tzeli esh* was not yet written in 1622 when Modena compiled his original list of writings. After Modena's illustrated Haggadah translation of 1609 (see item 14m) had sold out in 1629, Gershon ben Moses Parenzo, the son of the first edition's benefactor and a relative of Modena's mother's first husband, commissioned him to reissue it with a commentary so that in addition to appealing to "children and people of low understanding" it would also be attractive to the "mature and knowledgeable." Asked to use his judgment in selecting a commentary for this new edition, Modena decided not to use his own commentary on the Haggadah. Instead, he prepared an abridgment of Isaac Abravanel's *Zevah ha-pesah* (1506) without adding anything of his own. He called this commentary *Tzeli esh*, (*Roasted in Fire*), based on Exodus 12:8–9, because "like the sacrifice, when roasted it shriveled, diminished, and shrank, but still tasted good." Modena wrote that he used only about one-fiftieth of Abravanel's commentary but felt that it was enough for the commentary to be understood. The printing of this Haggadah was supervised by Israel Zifroni and carried out by Pietro, Alvise, and Lorenzo Bragadini in the shop of Giovanni Calleoni. *Tzeli esh* appeared in the Judeo-Italian, Yiddish, and Ladino versions of the Haggadah, which were published simultaneously. *Tzeli esh* was republished at Venice in 1664 and 1695 and at Sulzbach in 1774 and 1834, and a photoreproduction of the 1629 edition has appeared (Benai Berak, 1975). See Y. Yerushalmi, *Haggadah and History* (Philadelphia, 1974), plates 49 and 50.

d. *"Tefillot le-khol yemei ha-shavua' ve-'al kol tzarah she-lo tavo"* . . . *not sold*: In the introduction to his *Tefillot yesharim* of 1642, he noted that it had first appeared twenty years earlier. Confirmation of the relation between the book listed here in the autobiography and *Tefillot yesharim* is the similarity of the subtitle of the 1642 edition, *le-khol yom me-shiv'at yemei ha-shavua' devar yom be-yomo*, and the fact that the 1661 edition of *Tefillot yesharim* is called a "third edition." Still, the title of the first edition was not included in Modena's original list of the year 1622, but, rather, was added in the margin. The book simply may not have been completed by the time Modena began compiling the original list, or, because the book was not distributed, as Modena states, he omitted it. Because there are, in fact, no known versions of the earlier edition, the contents of the 1642 edition, which included prayers for every day of the week with planetary images, a psalm for the day, and prayers against every trouble, may give an indication of what it contained. *Tefillot yesharim* was subsequently issued at Venice in 1717, 1754, 1775, 1787, 1793; Mantua, 1734, 1756; Pisa, 1779, sometimes with many additional prayers or sometimes in the very small 32mo format. On Modena's efforts to publish the 1642 edition, see *The Life of Judah*, fol. 27b.

e. *Tzori la-nefesh: Balm for the Soul*. The full title, *Tzori la-nefesh u-marpeh la-'atzem*, is a variation on Proverbs 16:24. In December 1617, about two months after the death of his son Mordecai, Modena prepared this ritual manual. The Ashkenazic Gemilut Hasadim Society (the Society for Good Deeds), a burial society, sponsored the publication, which was designed for every member of the society to take with him to the house of a person who had been sick for five days. The cantors and sextons of every synagogue were required to notify the leaders of the society, who were in turn required, within one hour, to gather a rabbi who would be acceptable to the sick person and ten members of the society, or at least of the Ashkenazic congregation, to pray for him or her and to hear his or her confession. The manual also included Hebrew formulas written with feminine verb forms for women to confess in that language. If a member of the society refused to come, he would be fined a ducat. The society authorized the publication of the book on January 3, 1618 (6th of Tevet), and it was published in Venice in 1619 by Pietro and Lorenzo Bragadini in the shop of Giovanni Calleoni. Modena received twenty-five ducats for his labors. See also the textual note and item 14j.

f. *Beit yehudah: House of Judah*. First published at Venice in 5395 [1635] and subsequently in many editions of *'Ein ya'akov/ 'Ein yisrael*. Modena had begun this work between 1622 and 1624 and by 1625 had sent the manuscript to the printers (see item 16g). But he could not attempt to publish it again until early 1634, and then a number of problems hampered its production (see *The Life of Judah*, fols. 23a–24a). During 1634 he extensively revised it, rereading the Talmud in search of further innovations (Ancona 7, fol. 11a; *Ziknei*, p. 193; *Beit yehudah*, Niddah, 48a). It finally appeared shortly before the Jewish New Year in 1635, and this entry was subsequently made in the margin of the autobiography. The publisher was listed on the title page as Giovanni Vendramin, and in the colophon Isaac min Haleviim stated that he printed the book at the age of fourteen, a fact confirmed in *The Life of Judah*, fols. 23a–24a; on *Beit yehudah*, see B. Safran, "Leone da Modena's Historical Thinking," in *Jewish Thought in the Seventeenth Century*, pp. 381–398.

g. *Sefer riti*: Between 1614 and 1615, Modena wrote a description of the Jewish religion in Italian at the request of "an English Lord," probably Sir Henry Wotton, to give to King James I (1603–1625). The entry in the margin of the autobiography was made sometime after the manuscript was printed for the first time in 1637 at Paris by Modena's Christian acquaintance, Jacques Gaffarel (1601–1681). The full titles are given in Howard Adelman's introductory essay and a facsimile of the title page and further details appear later in *The Life of Judah* (see fig. 8). The *Riti* was the first work written by a Jew in the vernacular to present the rites and beliefs of the Jewish religion to Christians. Modena's purpose was to describe Jewish practices in a favorable light and to counter the erroneous notions about them often held by Christians. The major impetus for writing the *Riti* was the publication of a description of the Jewish religion by the Protestant Hebraist and rabbinic scholar, Johann Buxtorf (1564–1629). His *Synagoga judaica*, which appeared in the original German in 1603 and in Latin in 1614, presented much information on Judaism, but in a very negative light, making it appear superstitious. The *Riti* was republished many times in Italian as well as in English, French, Dutch, Latin, and Hebrew. On the *Riti*, see Cohen, "Leone da Modena's *Riti*," pp. 287–321; historical notes to fol. 25a; and the remarks in the three introductory essays.

h. *Pi aryeh*: See fol. 20a, historical note z. The title is based on Psalm 22:22 and alludes, of course, to Modena's middle name in Hebrew. In May, 1640 Iseppo Foa of Padua sponsored a republication of *Galut yehudah*. Modena prepared a supplement for this edition, which, because it required vowels, was printed in Venice at the shop of Giovanni Calleoni. *Pi aryeh (The Mouth of the Lion)*, was a twenty-four-page alphabetical listing of Hebrew and Aramaic rabbinic terms translated into Italian, with about fifty on each page. To facilitate usage, the terms were given in the forms in which they appeared in the literature instead of according to their roots. Modena had considered dedicating this edition to Cardinal Barberini (1597–1679), a relative of Pope Urban VIII (1623–1644) and founder of the Barberini library. But instead, for an unspecified reason, he dedicated it to Giovanni Vislingio (1598–1649), a German who was chief professor at Padua, where he taught anatomy and botany, and whose accomplishments included pioneering work in the dissection of humans and a trip to the land of Israel to study its flora. *Pi aryeh* also appeared separately in Venice in 1647/1648; see Boksenboim, *Iggerot*, no. 133; Roth, "Leone da Modena and the Christian Hebraists," pp. 397, 401; I. Benjacob, *Otzar ha-sefarim* (Vilna, 1880), p. 457, no. 58; and historical notes to fol. 26b.

i. *Poems and Prefaces*: Many of these works are found in Modena's *Divan* and in his collections of letters.

j. *Torat ha-adam*: A work by Nahmanides on the rituals involved in sickness, death, mourning, and dying, as well as on reward and punishment, published in 1594/1595 by di Gara; see *Divan*, no. 21.

k. *Sefer ha-hinnukh*: A thirteenth-century work on the commandments usually attributed to Aaron Levi of Barcelona, published by di Gara, 1600/1601; see *Divan*, no. 26.

l. *Yihus ha-tzaddikim*: Modena wrote two prayers to be recited at the graves of Jews buried in the land of Israel, which were included in 1598/1599 by Gershon bar Asher Scaramella in this book, published by Zanetti. This Scaramella died in 1633/1634. Subsequently Modena describes in his autobiography a scandal in 1636 involving a different Grassin (= Gershon) Scaramella; see *The Life of Judah*, fols. 24b ff.; Boksenboim, *Iggerot*, p. 284, note 8; *Divan*, nos. 195, 196.

m. *"Shomerim la-boker" for the day preceding the new moon*: Modena had many contacts with the Shomerim La-boker Society, a group with strong ties to the land of Israel and the Kabbalah, the members of which rose in the morning to do penitence, often accompanied by whippings, especially on the day preceding the new moon, known as Yom Kippur Katan, the Minor Day of Atonement. The poem mentioned here, called *Yom zeh yehi mishkal*, has appeared in many prayerbooks and is available in Hebrew with an English translation in T. Carmi, *The Penguin Book of Hebrew Verse* (Harmondsworth, 1981), pp. 491–492; see also *Divan*, no. 197; I. Davidson, *Thesaurus of Medieval Hebrew Poetry* (New York, 1929), vol. 2, no. 1724; and L. Zunz, *Literaturgeschichte der synagogalen Poesie* (Berlin, 1865), pp. 427–428, who dated it 1614.

n. *Kohelet ya'akov*: A commentary on Ecclesiastes by Barukh b. Barukh published in 1598/1599 by Zanetti; see Benayahu, *Haskamah*, pp. 39, 42, 53, 249–251, and idem, *Ha-yehasim*, pp. 189–192. On the role of Baruch Bembaruch as a merchant, see Tenenti, *Naufrages*, s.v. index.

o. *Divrei Shalom*: Published in 1595/1596, the poem Modena wrote for this collection of sermons by the kabbalist Isaac b. Samuel Adrabi appeared in the name of Samuel Disus; see *Divan*, no. 25.

p. *Keter shem tov*: A commentary on the Torah by Shem Tov Melammed published in Venice in 1600/1601 at the request of Samuel Disus, in whose name the poem appeared; see *Divan*, no. 24; cf. Benayahu, *Ha-yehasim*, pp. 139–140.

q. *the Large Ashkenazic Mahzor*: In Hebrew, "Mahzor ashkenazi ha-gadol." Published by Bragadini in 1599, the poem by Modena included his name in an acrostic. His title was then *haver*. This poem was republished in S. Bernstein, "Sheloshah piyyutim hadashim le-r. y. a. mi-modenah," *'Alim* 4 (1935): 107–108. The Small Ashkenazi Mahzor, "Mahzor ashkenazi ha-katan," was also published.

r. *Kaf nahat*: A two-volume edition published by Pietro Bragadini and printed by Giovanni Calleoni in 1614. The commentary was based on Rashi and edited by Isaac ben Solomon Gabbai, a typesetter for Bragadini. In addition to serving as the proofreader, Modena wrote a preface and contributed the commentary on Pirkei Avot, basing his work on that of Rashi. Modena's commentary, which was not in the first edition, published by di Gara in 1609, must not be confused with an original, no longer extant commentary to Pirkei Avot, which Modena once started to write; see item 16a on fol. 20a.

s. *Tzori la-nefesh*: The reference here is to Modena's contribution of an introduction to this book, which he also compiled; see historical note e to item 10 on fol. 20a and also the textual note.

t. *Imrei shefer*: In 1601 Modena wrote a dedicatory poem in praise of this collection of sermons by Naftali ben Joseph Ashkenazi (1540–1602), a kabbalist of Safed and Egypt. The book was published by Zanetti. Modena also wrote a letter asking wealthy Jews to buy Ashkenazi's book so that he could support his family; see *Divan*, no. 27; Boksenboim, *Iggerot*, no. 247.

u. *Ma'amadot*: Sometime between March 20 and April 10, 1606, while living in Ferrara, Modena visited Venice and wrote a poem for the proofreader of *Seder ma'amadot* by Moses ben Joseph Aryeh of the land of Israel, which was published by di Gara; see *Divan*, no. 23; Benayahu, *Haskamah*, pp. 256–258.

v. *Passover Haggadah with illustrations and complete translation*: The Venetian Haggadah of 1609, planned by Israel Zifroni and published by di Gara, represented a bold innovation in the development of Haggadah illustration and translation. It continued to influence the publication of the Haggadah and was reprinted at least five times during the next three centuries; see Yerushalmi, *Haggadah and History*, pp. 40–41. One of the major innovations of the project consisted in issuing three almost identical editions with complete translations of the entire Hebrew Haggadah in the three other languages of the Venetian Jewish community, Judeo-Italian, Ladino, and Yiddish. Modena made the Judeo-Italian translation and helped prepare a special edition on vellum for Gershon Parenzo. On the next-to-last page Modena included a sentence in Hebrew, which contained an acrostic of his own name, stating that he was the translator. For a facsimile edition with an introduction in Hebrew and English, see B. Narkiss, *The Venice Hagada of 1609* (Jerusalem, 1974); see also A. Yaari, "Tofes meyuhad shel haggadah shel pesah, venetziah 369 [i.e., 1609] 'al klaf," *KS* 30 (1955): 113–117.

w. *Mikra gedolah*: The title of this collection, which usually appears in the plural as *Mikra'ot gedolot*, literally meaning "Large Bible," refers to the scriptural text accompanied by the classic commentaries of the major medieval rabbis. This edition of the rabbinic Bible was edited by Modena's former student Jacob Lombroso in 1638/1639. The text of Modena's preface is available in S. Bernstein, *Divan*, pp. viii–ix (erroneously dated 1624), and in P. Naveh, *Leket ketavim* (Jerusalem, 1968), pp. 287–288.

x. *Sefer ha-levushim*: Mordecai ben Abraham Jaffe (ca. 1535–1612), a prominent rabbi and scholar from Prague, prepared ten books with the word *Levush* in the title. Their purpose was to establish a middle ground in terms of length and regional variations between the Beit Yosef of Joseph Caro and his Shulkhan Arukh as glossed by Moses Isserles' Mappah; Jaffe often made reference to new kabbalistic doctrines in his explanations of the law. See I. Twersky, "The Shulhan Aruk: The Enduring Code of Jewish Law," *Judaism* 16 (1967): 154–155; reprinted in idem, *Studies in Jewish Law and Philosophy* (New York, 1982), pp. 130–147; and *The Jewish Expression*, ed. J. Goldin (New York, 1970), pp. 322–343. This Venetian edition of *Sefer ha-levushim* was authorized on December 4, 1620 by the local rabbis; see Benayahu, *Haskamah*, p. 268.

y. *Yefeh 'einayim*: Modena both proofread and wrote a dedicatory poem for this collection of homiletical commentaries on the weekly portions from the Torah by Samuel ben Isaac Yafeh Ashkenazi. The edition was published in 1631; see *Divan*, no. 39, and textual note.

z. *'Etz shatul*: The publication of this commentary by Gedaliah ben Solomon of Poland on Joseph Albo's book on the articles of faith, *Sefer ha-'ikkarim*, was edited by Modena's friend Abraham Haver Tov and completed on Tuesday, September 8 (21st of Elul), 1618 by Pietro and Lorenzo Bragadini in the shop of Giovanni Calleoni. Modena's poem appeared on the last page, fol. 144b; see also *Divan*, no. 36.

a. *"Songs of Solomon" Rossi*: Modena was in charge of preparing for press this first book of Hebrew music ever published, *Ha-shirim asher li-shelomo*, the title of which was based on the first verse of the Song of Songs, the biblical book attributed to King Solomon. Modena had persuaded his friend and regular guest in Venice, Salamone (Solomon) de Rossi (ca. 1570–1639), a musician and composer in the ducal court of Mantua who had also been writing and performing choral music for the synagogue, to publish his work. De Rossi gave Modena thirty-three compositions for religious festivals and special Sabbaths. Modena had no model for a Hebrew music book and had to solve the problem of how to print together Hebrew and music, which are read in opposite directions. He decided to print both from left to right, in the order of the musical notes rather than that of the Hebrew words, because most singers knew the Psalms and liturgical pieces by heart and did not need to read the words carefully when they sang. His responsibilities in connection with the publication of this work included editing, arranging, and proofreading. The murder of Zebulun interrupted Modena's work on it. But, even though he had personally eschewed music since his son's death, he felt that delaying the publication of de Rossi's book would deprive the Jewish people, and especially the children whom he wanted to be inspired to learn music, of an important work. Modena was, nevertheless, sad because he anticipated opposition to the music by the self-proclaimed pious types, who, he felt, fled from everything new. It was printed by Pietro and Lorenzo Bragadini in 1623. Eight separate versions, known as part books, were issued: Canto, Alto, Tenore, Basso, Quinto, Sesto, Settimo, and Ottavo. Apparently, some impressions of each version contained introductory material consisting of a dedication to Moses Sullam by Salamone de Rossi; anonymous dedicatory poems; a foreword by Modena; Modena's responsum of 1605 on the permissibility of music (*Ziknei*, no. 6; translated in Kobler, *Jewish Letters Through the Ages*, vol. 2, pp. 416–419; S. Freehof, *A Treasury of Responsa* [Philadelphia, 1963], pp. 160–166; and C. Leviant, *Masterpieces of Hebrew Literature* [New York, 1969], pp. 540–543); five rabbinic approbations by rabbis Benzion Zarfati, Leib Saraval, Barukh ben Samuel, Ezra Fano of Mantua, and Judah ben Moses Fano of Venice; and a copyright signed by four rabbis, Isaac Gershon, Moses Cohen Porto, Leon Modena, and Simone Luzzatto. A complete set is to be found in the Bibliothèque Nationale, Paris (photocopy available in the music libary of the Jewish National and University Library, Jerusalem). See I. Adler, *Les Incunables hébraiques de la Bibliothèque Nationale* (Paris and Jerusalem, 1962), pp. 47–48. The basso edition's title page is in F. Rikko, *Salamone de Rossi, Shir ha-shirim asher le-shelomo*, 3 vols. (New York, 1967–1973), with an English translation of the introductory material, a modern resetting of the music, and a selective bibliography. The Hebrew text is available in a critical edition, with extensive bibliographical references, in Adler, *Hebrew Writings Concerning Music*, pp. 212–221, 285–288. A recording of this music was made by the New York Pro Musica, Noah Greenberg, director: *The Music of Salamone Rossi, Hebreo, de Mantua*, Columbia Records, Y 35226. On Leon Modena and Jewish music in Venice, see I. Adler, "The Rise of Art Music in the Italian Ghetto," in *Jewish Medieval and Renaissance Studies*, ed. A. Altmann (Cambridge, 1967), pp. 321–364; idem, "La pénétration de la musique savante dans les synagogues italiennes au xviiᵉ siècle: Le Case particulier de Venise," in *Gli Ebrei e Venezia*, pp. 527–535.

b. *Belil hamitz*: In honor of Joseph Hamitz's graduation from medical school in Padua on Tuesday, December 19, 1623, Modena edited a collection of twenty-eight pages of congratulatory poems and letters for his former student, written by rabbis from Venice and other northern Italian cities. This book was published by Bragadini at the press of Calleoni. Modena wrote an introduction and a poem for Hamitz. There are only three extant copies of this book, and each is slightly different. They are to be found in the libraries of the Hebrew Union College in Cincinnati, the Collegio Rabbinico Italiano in Rome, and the Jewish Theological Seminary of America in New York, the latter missing a leaf. In 1937 N. Libowitz republished the JTSA version as *Seridim mi-kitvei ha-filosof ha-rofe veha-mekubbal r. yosef hamitz* (Jerusalem) and in 1938 reissued it with the additional leaf, copied from the copy in Rome; see also *Divan*, no. 77; S. Bernstein, "Mi hibber et ha-sefer *Belil hamitz*," *Ha-tzofeh le-hokhmat yisrael* 15 (1931): 231–243 and Libowitz, *Seridim*, pp. 327–328; Haleviim, *Medabber*, p. 87.

c. "*Sefer yeriʿot ʿizzim*" *and many, many more that I cannot remember*: *Yeriʿot ʿizzim*, a rhymed book on the commandments by Simon b. Samuel Yerushalmi, was published by di Gara in 1597; see *Divan*, no. 31. It is interesting that Modena, whose views were turning against Kabbalah at the time he wrote his autobiography, "forgot" about most of the poems, introductions, prefaces, and authorizations he had written earlier for many books that included kabbalistic themes. The works he could not remember include: (1) *Seder ha-nikkur*, a work on ritual slaughter by Giacomo Sorzina published in 1595; see *Divan*, no. 22. (2) *Ner mitzvah*, Samuel ben Joseph Cohen-Tzedek's collection of sermons published by di Gara in 1598; see *Divan*, no. 30. (3) *Zemirot yisrael*, published in 1599, a collection of poems by Israel Najara (1555–1625), a kabbalist from Safed; see *Divan*, no. 29. (4) *Arzei levanon*, a collection of kabbalistic works published by di Gara in 1601; see Bernstein, "Sheloshah piyyutim hadashim," pp. 106–107. (5) *Beit moʿed*, a collection of fifty kabbalistic sermons by Menahem ben Moses Rava of Padua, published in 1605. Modena's poem here expresses his admiration for the kabbalist and his work and insists that the material in it is true. Modena also proofread this book; see *Divan*, no. 28. (6) *Apiryon shelomo*, by Abraham Sason, the first presentation of Lurianic ideas in print, published with Modena's help in 1608; see *Beit 'eked sefarim*, ed. B. Friedberg (Antwerp, 1928), *kaf*, no. 549; M. Steinschneider, *Catalogus librorum hebraeorum in Bibliotheca Bodleiana* (Oxford, 1852–1860; repr. Berlin, 1931), col. 709; Tishby, "Ha-pulmus 'al sefer ha-zohar," pp. 159–161. (7) *Torat ha-bayit ha-arokh*, a compendium of laws, their talmudic sources, and differences of opinions about them held by the rabbis of early medieval Iraq (the gaons) and Europe, by Solomon ibn Adret (Rashba, ca. 1235–1310), the spiritual leader of Spanish Jewry. In addition to his work on the actual production of the book in 1607, Modena was involved in raising funds for its publication; see Blau, *Kitvei*, no. 143; Boksenboim, *Iggerot*, nos. 92, 248. (8) *Hibbur havat ya'ir*, by Abraham ben Yehiel Cohen Porto (Venice, 1628/1629); see Benayahu, *Haskamah*, p. 279. (9) *Minhagim le-r. isaac tirna 'im orhot hayyim leha-rosh* (Venice, 1616); see *Divan*, no. 44. (10) *Kenaf renanim*, by Joseph Yedidiah ben Benjamin Yekutiel Carmi (Venice, 1627); see Benayahu, *Haskamah*, p. 278. (11) *Tesoro de preceptos*, by Isaac Atias (Venice, 1627). (12) *Sefer elim*, by Joseph Solomon Delmedigo (Amsterdam, 1629; Odessa, 1864). (13) *Hurvot yerushalayim* (Venice, 1631; Tel Aviv, ed. M. Rozen, 1981). (14) *Planta vitis*, by Jean Plantavit de la Pause (Lodève, 1645); see Blau, *Kitvei*, no. 179. (15) *Seder keri'ah ve-tikkun le-leil hag ha-shavu'ot ve-hosha'na rabbah* (Venice, 1647/1648); see Benayahu, *Haskamah*, p. 279. (16) Mention should also be made of Modena's authorization of *Sefer ha-yashar*, a controversial pseudepigraphical work published at Venice in 1625; see Benayahu, *Haskamah*, pp. 270–275; Y. Dan, "R. yehudah aryeh mi-modena ve-*sefer ha-yashar*," *Sinai* 88 (1976): 197–198; idem, "'Od 'al *sefer ha-yashar*, venetziah 1625," *Sinai* 88 (1976): 94–95. On Modena's attitude toward Kabbalah, see historical notes to fols. 24a and 26b.

d. *Tevat noah*: This book, published in 1593, was also called *Arca Noae*, the Latin equivalent of the Hebrew. It was written by Marco Marini (1541–1594), a distinguished Christian Hebraist, censor of Hebrew books, and proofreader for di Gara; Blau, *Kitvei*, no. 179; *Divan*, no. 47; Popper, *Censorship*, p. 56. Marini had studied with Archivolti and published a Hebrew grammar in 1580, so his request for a poem from Modena in 1586 indicated that already at the age of fifteen Modena was considered a serious poet.

e. *collection of rhymes praising Doge Grimani*: Marino Grimani, doge of Venice from 1595 to 1606. Still extant is a poem Modena wrote in Hebrew for one of the priests at the Seminary of San Antonio to sing for the doge on his visit there: *Divan*, no. 53. The poem was accompanied by an oration in Hebrew that repeated the same praises for the doge: Blau, *Kitvei*, nos. 64, 105. For a discussion of a manuscript of a Hebrew prayer written in his honor, see *VI* 49 (1901): 327, 348–349; 55 (1907): 623–625.

f. *"Ester" by H. Rieti*: This person could be either Hananiah Eliakim

Rieti (1561–ca. 1623), the Mantuan poet, or Hezekiah Rieti, noted for his Italian translations of biblical books such as Proverbs (Venice, 1617); see Simonsohn, *Mantua*, p. 731 and s.v., index.

g. *"Barekhi nafshi" by the same author*: While this work appears to refer to the aforementioned H. Rieti, no work with this title by such a person is known. It probably refers to a poem from the ethical treatise *Hovot ha-levavot* by the eleventh-century Spaniard Bahya ben Joseph ibn Paquda. Bahya's poem was translated into Italian by Yohanan Mordecai (Angelo) Yehudah ben Solomon Alatrini and published as *L'Angelica tromba* at Venice in 1628. In his *Divan* Modena wrote, as he did here, that a poem of his had been published in Alatrini's translation; see *Divan*, no. 41 and the demur of Bernstein.

h. *in honor of the Fabbri wedding in Bologna*: Modena's *Divan* (no. 54) contains a poem written for the wedding of unnamed Christians from Bologna. The poem had been printed with an Italian translation and distributed among the wedding guests.

i. *Pastorale trionfi*: In 1611 Modena supervised the publication of an Italian Jewish pastoral drama, *I Trionfi*, written in 1575 by the late Angelo (Elhanan Yehudah) Alatini when he was rabbi in Castelnuovo, and not to be confused with the classic work by Francesco Petrarca (1304–1374) with the same title. In his introduction to his own play *L'Ester* (Venice, 1619) Modena contended that he had contributed nothing of his own to Alatini's work; M. Soave, "Sara Coppio Sullam," *CI* 16 (1877): 31; A. Piattelli, "*Ester*: L'Unico Dramma di Leon da Modena giunto fino a noi," *RMI* 34 (1968): 163–172; Roth, *Renaissance*, p. 269.

j. *The tragedy of "Ester"*: About 1613, a group of Jews in Venice wanted to reissue for the third time Solomon Usque's Purim drama about Esther, one of the earliest Jewish plays. It had been written about 1558, first presented to a group of Venetian nobles in 1559, and revived in 1592. In addition to his general interest in drama, Modena was particularly interested in this project because his uncle Lazzaro Levi had been associated with the original production and because a drama, *La Reina Esther*, on the same subject by Ansaldo Cebà (1565–1623), an aging diplomat who had entered monastic retirement in Genoa, was published in 1613 and 1615 in Genoa. Modena considered Usque's verses insipid and his style primitive, and, advising this group of Jews to wait before reissuing the play, volunteered to adapt it according to the newest dramatic standards. His version, *L'Ester*, was not published until 1619, and he claimed then that two-thirds of it was now his own original material.

The preface to which Modena refers here was a dedication to Sarra Copia Sullam, wife of Jacob Sullam and a leading Jewish cultural and philanthropic figure in her own right in Venice. Early in 1618 Sarra had a miscarriage, and during her recovery she read Cebà's play. She wrote Cebà of her admiration and spiritual love for him, reporting that she carried his book with her and slept with it under her pillow. Cebà wrote back that he wanted to continue to correspond with her and hoped to convert her to Christianity. This correspondence continued, becoming both more polemical and more titillating. Sarra had intellectual relationships with several other Christian men of letters for whom she provided financial backing as well as charming conversation. One member of her circle was Modena. He was impressed by her, and to compete with her Christian sycophants, he dedicated his play *L'Ester* to her on Purim, February 28, 1619. (The book actually bears the date "1618," but as the Venetian new year began only on March 1, it was actually published in 1619 and the date given corresponds to Purim 1619.) Very little has been published on Sarra Copia Sullam in English: G. Karpeles, "Women in Jewish Tradition," in *Jewish Literature and Other Essays* (Philadelphia, 1895), pp. 124–128; E. Sarot, "Ansaldo Cebà and Sarra Copia Sullam," *Italica* 31 (1954): 138–150; Kobler, *Letters of Jews Through the Ages*, vol. 2, pp. 434–448. For the most extensive treatment of her to date, see the series of articles by C. Boccato, the most recent of which is "Nove Testimonianze su Sarra Copio Sullam," *RMI* 46 (1980): 272–287. An analysis of her life and writings is being prepared by Howard Adelman.

k. *and in many other works like these*: Modena wrote a dedicatory poem in Italian for the pastoral *L'Amor possente* by his student Baruch Luzzatto in 1630; C. Boccato, *"L'Amor possente, favola pastorale di Benedetto Luzzatto hebreo da Venetia*, composta durante la peste nel 1630," *RMI* 43 (1977): 36–47; on Baruch Luzzatto, see historical note e to fol. 22a. In his *Divan*, no. 50, are also Hebrew and Italian poems for Alberto de Pompei's life of Frederico Gonzaga II; but the only extant work by this author is his *Vita di Francesco II Gonzaga IIII marchese di Mantova* (Mantua, 1625), which has no such poem by Modena. In 1601 Modena wrote poems in Hebrew and Italian honoring the birth of the dauphin of France. They were published in quarto on a broadside by Zanetti. During the 1640s Modena sent the poems with a Latin translation to Claude Mallier, the former French ambassador to Venice, for presentation to Louis XIII. Modena also sent a copy of the poems to Plantavit, who published them in 1645; see Howard Adelman's introductory essay and historical notes to fol. 28a.

l. Most of the works listed in this section in the original bibliography are no longer extant.

m. *Ha-avot liyhudah* means *The Fathers According to Judah* and recalls the title of the extracanonical minor tractate of the Talmud, *Avot de-rabbi natan* (*The Fathers According to Rabbi Nathan*).

n. *commentary on Proverbs*: This commentary may have developed from the series of public lectures Modena gave on Proverbs beginning in 1601; see *The Life of Judah*, fol. 13a.

o. *commentary on the Haggadah*: Modena must have written this work between the time he finished this list and 1629, for in 1629, in his introduction to *Tzeli esh*, he described it as a completed book. He called it *Ge'on yehudah* (*The Pride of Judah*), based on Jeremiah 13:9. He apologized for the immodest title (implying that he, Judah, was a gaon, an honorific reserved for the most learned rabbis) by saying that the Exodus was the exaltation of all Israel.

p. *commentary on Samuel*: This work is still extant at Oxford, Bodleian Library, MS Canon Misc. 204 (Neubauer, *Catalogue*, no. 2549.2); see Neubauer, "Quelques Notes sur la vie," p. 84.

q. *Beit yehudah*: Begun between 1622 (as indicated by its appearance in Modena's list begun in that year) and 1624, the manuscript had been sent to the printers by 1625 (*Beit lehem yehudah* [Venice, 1625], introduction), but it did not appear then because "the angels of God injured me many times"; see *Beit yehudah* (Venice, 1635), introduction; and item 11.

r. *Books completed*: While this heading could refer to the preceding list of books, it is more likely that it refers to the ones that follow, most of which were complete though not yet published by 1623, the year of the latest publications listed here in Modena's original bibliography (items 14r, s). While some were revised at a later date prior to their publication, most were not published during Modena's lifetime at all, and some were subsequently lost entirely.

FOLIO 20b

s. *to write letters*: In 1606 Modena turned in earnest to a project that he had long felt to be of benefit to students because it had not been done before: the preparation of a *Guide for the Perplexed in Writing Hebrew*. He had begun to collect letters and poems to serve as models of good Hebrew style. Modena had been saving his own letters as well as gathering samples from the leading Hebrew writers in Italy. He also hoped to include other examples of writing, such as contracts, minutes, memorandums, commentaries, responsa, endorsements, exegesis (with and without errors), treatises, prayers, ethics, proverbs, and jokes, as well as simple, serious, bombastic, and freestyle writing; see Boksenboim, *Iggerot*, pp. 343–345; on Hebrew letter writing, see Boksenboim, *Iggerot melammedim*. While in Venice on a short trip Modena learned that Samuel Archivolti, who had already dealt with aspects of Hebrew writing in *'Arugat ha-bosem* (Venice, 1602), was preparing another work similar to his own nearly completed book on letter writing. Modena became very concerned because he feared that Archivolti's work would supersede his own. He communicated this fear to Archivolti, hoping that what he had heard was not true and that he could publish his own modest work shortly. Modena pointedly accused

Archivolti of having once already usurped an idea of his, which he had shared with him ten years earlier. Modena also advised Archivolti that he had a copy of an earlier letter he had sent Archivolti explaining this project (Boksenboim, *Iggerot*, no. 81). There is no evidence of a reply from Archivolti, and in 1607 Modena was still soliciting sample letters. Reference in two letters indicate that Modena did finish the book, giving support to the notion that the word "complete" used above refers to the books that follow it (Boksenboim, *Iggerot*, nos. 88, 161). Like Archivolti's book, Modena's was never published, and the manuscript is no longer extant; see Boksenboim, *Iggerot*, nos. 75, 76, 79–81, 87–89; Ruderman, "Exemplary Sermon," pp. 9–13.

t. *The Book of the Wisdom [of Solomon] . . . and others*: These books are part of the Apocrypha, holy books of the Jews dating from the later second temple period, which were not, however, included by the Jews in their Bible, usually because of their obvious late or pseudepigraphical nature. Rather they were preserved by the Catholic church, first in Greek and then later in the Latin Vulgate. Accordingly, they were inaccessible to the average Jew in the days of Modena. His translation was not published and is no longer extant.

u. *Shirei yehudah*: After Modena had written a draft of each poem in a notebook, he would copy it or have it copied into his permanent collection of his poetry; Blau, *Kitvei*, no. 179. About 370 of the 400 poems it once contained are still extant in a manuscript at Oxford, Bodleian Library, MS Mich. 528, olim 759 which was published with an English introduction by S. Bernstein under the title *The Divan of Leo de Modena*.

v. *Ziknei yehudah*: Modena arranged his responsa for publication on August 15, 1630, as the plague approached Venice. He called his book *Ziknei yehudah*, "The Elders of Judah"—based on 2 Samuel 19:12—because he relied heavily on the teachings of his ancestors and because he collected his opinions when he was an aged man of sixty. In his introduction Modena decried those who were sharp-witted in abstruse rabbinic reasoning (*pilpul*) and who tried to make "bean" from "elephant" and "elephant" from "bean," Hebrew puns on the word *pilpul*: *min pil, pul; u-min pul, pil*. His own method of deciding matters of Jewish law was based on the simple meaning (*peshat*) of every precept. His grandson Isaac later prepared this manuscript for publication between 1650 and 1655, but the book did not appear until 1956, when it was finally published by S. Simonsohn in Jerusalem.

w. *Sha'agat aryeh*: Sha'agat aryeh—*The Roar of the Lion* (alluding to one of Modena's given names)—was a gentle but comprehensive defense of rabbinic Judaism against the antirabbinic treatise called *Kol sakhal* (*The Voice of the Fool*), purportedly written sometime before 1500 by a Jew, Amitai Bar Yedaiah ibn Raz, of the Spanish city of Alcalá (de Henares?).

Much ink has been spilled discussing whether Modena was also the author of *Kol sakhal*; see, for instance, Reggio, *Behinat ha-kabbalah*; E. Rivkin, *Leone da Modena and the Kol Sakhal* (Cincinnati, 1952); J. Petuchowski, *The Theology of Haham David Nieto* (New York, 1954; rev. ed. 1970), pp. 39–46; and H. Adelman, "New Light on the Life and Writings of Leon Modena," in *Approaches to the Study of Judaism in Medieval Times*, ed. D. Blumenthal (Chico, Calif., 1985), vol. 2, pp. 109–122. The only extant copy of this manuscript is not complete, but it constitutes a work of careful calligraphy meant for private circulation and hence was presumably based on a completed work. A reference in Solomon Delmedigo's *Sefer elim*, p. 4, indicates that this work may have been completed.

x. *Meshal ha-kadmoni*: "The Fable of the Ancient," by Isaac ben Solomon ibn Sahula (b. 1244), a Hebrew writer, scholar, and kabbalist from Guadalajara, Spain. Written in rhymed prose and deriving its themes from rabbinic literature, it was first published at the end of the fifteenth century and again in Venice in 1546.

y. *The Pastoral of Rachel and Jacob*: The fact that Modena pawned a manuscript version of this book in 1604 provides one of the indications that the heading "Books completed" refers to the items that follow it. On this pastoral see Boksenboim, *Iggerot*, no. 144 and historical notes to fol. 14a.

z. *Rabbi M. Merari*: A Moses Merari was invested with the title rabbi by Modena himself (*Ziknei*, p. 179; Benayahu, *Haskamah*, pp. 268, 274), but in the writings of Isaac min Haleviim there are also references to a Menahem and a Manasseh Merari. Manasseh owned a store that was located under the portico opposite the Italian synagogue in the Ghetto Nuovo; see Haleviim, *Medabber*, p. 99.

a. *Mantua*: Out of its total population of roughly 50,000, about 2,325 Jews lived in the ghetto of Mantua when it was first established in 1612. Another 500 to 700 lived in the surrounding towns; see Simonsohn, *Mantua*, pp. 190–195.

b. *Massarano sons*: On the Massarano family see Simonsohn, *Mantua*, s.v. index.

c. *Being fearful of bandits*: The reason for these fears is found in a responsum Modena wrote in April 1623. The wedding was planned for the 1st of Sivan (Tuesday, May 30), in Mantua. As was the custom, the young man came to visit his fiancée during the intermediate days of Passover, April 17–21. While in Venice he learned that an ambush was being prepared to rob him between Venice and Mantua, on the way to the wedding, because word had spread that his was one of the richest Jewish families in Italy. Fearful for the safety of his family, the groom did not want to wait until the end of May to make the trip because by then the fields, crops, and trees would be in leaf and would provide many places for brigands to hide. Rather, he desired to leave for Mantua immediately so that the bandits would have neither the time to organize nor a place to hide. He also wished to advance the wedding by a month, from the 1st of Sivan to the 1st of Iyyar (May 6), 1623. This part of the plan, however, required rabbinic approval because the date fell during the period of Sefirah, a time of mourning between Passover and Shavuot when Jewish weddings were not performed. Hence, the question was submitted to Modena; see *Ziknei*, no. 47.

d. *between Sanguinetto and Castel d'Ario*: They either came by boat to Legnago or by road from Montagnana. These towns are located east of Mantua.

e. *terza rima*: There are no known copies of this poem.

f. *the Great Synagogue*: Founded in 1529 and enlarged in 1542, this Italian congregation was the main synagogue in the ghetto of Mantua. It was plundered in 1630 by the invading armies of Emperor Ferdinand II, subsequently relocated, and then demolished in the 1920s; see Simonsohn, *Mantua*, pp. 568–571.

g. *two Jewish students*: His two Jewish students were probably two cousins, Samuel and Raphael Nahmias, the sons of David and Joseph Nahmias, sons of the Marrano Isaac Nahmias, who reverted to Judaism. Modena ordained Raphael Nahmias sometime after 1625 (*Ziknei*, p. 197), and Samuel (1612–1683) studied with Modena prior to 1628. See E. Werner, "The Eduard Birnbaum Collection of Jewish Music," *HUCA* 18 (1943–1944): 18; Giulio Morosini, *Via della fede* (Rome, 1683), p. 793. In 1649, after Modena's death, Samuel converted to Christianity and took the name Giulio Morosini. His voluminous polemical work, *Via della fede*, contains many references to Modena as his teacher and to the customs of the Jews of Venice; see D. Simonsen, "Giulio Morosinis Mitteilungen uber seinen Lehrer Leon da Modena und seine jüdischen Zeitgenossen," in *Sefer ha-yovel le-avraham berliner*, pp. 337–344; Ravid, "*Contra judaeos*," pp. 328–351.

h. *and a few Christian ones*: One of them was Andreas Colvius (1594–1671), a native of Dort who from 1620 to 1627 accompanied Johan Berck, the Dutch ambassador to Venice. Colvius's collection of manuscripts included some by Modena that shed much light on the development of the latter's views on Kabbalah and Christianity; see F. Secret, "Notes sur les hébraisants Chrètiens," *REJ* 124 (1965): 158.

i. *I[saac] Gershon*: Mentioned previously in the historical notes to fol. 14b.

j. *of the Sephardim*: For the first time Modena mentions that he preached for the Sephardim, but it appears that he had been doing so for a while; see Atias, *Tesoro de preceptos*, p. 2.

k. *in the Italian synagogue*: He was cantor, teacher, and secretary of this congregation. He also established the manner in which people paid for their seats and the order of prayers. The time of this reference to Modena's employment in the Italian synagogue almost coincides with the renewal, in the autumn of 1626, of his receipts of pay for the preceding six months after a hiatus since 1619 in these entries in the congregation's expense ledger; see JTSA 8593, fol. 21b; 8594, pp. 13, 1, 14; on this manuscript see R. Pacifici, "I Regolamenti della scuola italiana a Venezia," *RMI* 5 (1930): 401; and Carpi, *Pe'ulat*, p. 15.

l. *more spacious for me*: This lodging was located several stories above ground level. From a comment in *The Life of Judah*, fol. 27a, it appears that he was to live here for seventeen years, his longest stay anywhere. According to testimony by Modena preserved in the archive of the Pia Casa di Catecumeni, "Pie Casa de Cattecumeni contro Università degli Hebrei" (July 30, 1637–March 24, 1638), in the Istituti di Ricovero e di Educazione, on February 3, 1638 he indicated that he was living in the Ghetto Nuovo; see Pullan, *The Jews of Europe*, pp. 89, 281. Hence this entire seventeen-year period was spent in that ghetto. Brian Pullan graciously made some of the information from these documents cited here and below available to us in a letter.

FOLIO 21a

m. *On Monday morning*: Actually it was a Wednesday.

n. *the Rialto . . . Campo San Cassian*: The Rialto, from either *riva alta*, high bank, or *rivo alto*, deep river, is the historical, political, social, and commercial center of Venice. Its most prominent landmark, the stone Rialto bridge with its covered shops, was completed in 1588, during Modena's lifetime. Campo San Cassian (Cassiano) is a square just north of the Grand Canal, slightly beyond the Rialto Bridge when approaching it from the ghetto.

o. *I vowed not to play games of chance . . . twenty-five months*: Typical of the prevalence of gambling at this time in Venice and the attempts by individuals to curtail their habit is a Hebrew document from Venice in the 1620s that contains a promise by a man that, beginning with the intermediate days of Passover, he would not gamble for two years. This vow, witnessed by two others, indicates that such an oath was a formal matter. This document, no. 163 in a collection of 363 Hebrew letters the location of which is no longer known, was published by M. Soave, "Vita di Giuda Arie Modena," *CI* 3 (1864): 78.

p. *earnings*: According to the figures given here, Modena was receiving at least seventy-two ducats a year from the Ashkenazic Torah Study Society. On Modena's income, see Howard Adelman's introductory essay.

q. *Lazzaretto*: An island in the Venetian lagoons, which in 1423 was set aside for the ill; in 1485, the Venetians introduced there the institution of quarantine, a forty-day detention of all ships suspected of being infested by plague; see Lane, *Venice*, p. 18. The name of the island could be derived from one of two possible New Testament associations: either Lazarus (Lazzaro), a man whom Jesus raised from the dead (John 11), later considered the protector of the infirm; or Nazareth (Nazaret), the place where Jesus grew up (Matthew 2:23; Luke 2:39, 51), transformed in the Venetian dialect and associated with a monastery originally on the island. Subsequently, the word came to be used for a charnel house or a pesthouse where people and also goods were quarantined on account of the plague; see C. M. Cipolla, *Faith, Reason, and the Plague in Seventeenth-Century Tuscany*, trans. M. Kittel (New York, 1979), p. 14.

r. *Izmir*: Formerly Smyrna, a port city in western Turkey on the Aegean Sea, then part of the Ottoman Empire.

s. *assembled the rest from friends, benefactors*: For an example of one of the letters Modena sent to raise this dowry, see Boksenboim, *Iggerot*, no. 122.

FOLIO 21b

t. *brother of the king of France*: The only full brother of Louis XIII (1601–1643) who was alive at this time was Gaston, duc d'Orléans (1608–1660). The duke and his mother, Maria de Medici (1573–1642), were involved in many plots against the king. Letters from the duke of Orléans to his brother King Louis XIII, along with several manifestos by the duke, mostly dating from 1632, are preserved in the Biblioteca Nazionale Marciana in Venice.

u. *Duke Candale and Duke Rohan*: Henri, duc de Rohan (ca. 1572–1638), was chief of the French Protestants until his defeat at La Rochelle in 1628. As a result of a compromise he made with Louis XIII, he had to live in Venice. There he served as commander in chief of the Venetian army and wrote his memoirs between 1629 and 1631. Henri de Hogoret d'Épernon, duc de Candale, was a close associate of the duke of Rohan. They lived in the same house in Venice, and, according to rumors current at the time that were designed to undermine the legitimacy of the duke of Rohan's heirs, it was the duke of Candale who was the father of Tancred, the son of Marguerite de Béthune, duchesse de Rohan; see J. Clarke, *Hugenot Warrior: The Life and Times of Henri de Rohan, 1579–1638* (The Hague, 1966), pp. 180–196.

v. *Job said*: Once again, Modena is citing his "motto verse."

w. *Kabbalah*: Jacob had studied Kabbalah with Ezra Fano, a teacher of Menahem Azariah Fano. Modena and Jacob had many heated arguments about Kabbalah and the Zohar. One of Modena's views that was particularly upsetting to his son-in-law was his assertion that Shimon bar Yohai did not write the Zohar and did not follow accepted rabbinic law. In his

Nahalat ya'akov, Jacob tried to respond to those who cast aspersions on the Kabbalah and its fundamentals and the authenticity of the Zohar. This manuscript, mentioned many times in *Ari nohem*, was recently rediscovered by Moshe Idel, in Oxford, Bodleian Library, MS 1955, fols. 1–91; see Idel, "Major Currents in Italian Kabbalah Between 1560 and 1660," in *Italia judaica*, vol. 2, pp. 252–253.

x. *sixty people died*: Although the etiology of this outbreak is unclear, the major plague of 1630–1631 was not a continuation of it; see C. M. Cipolla, *Fighting the Plague in Seventeenth-Century Italy* (Madison, Wisc., 1981), p. 84. By the time this outbreak had run its course in seven months, the total number of victims in the ghetto had reached 130, most of them sages, scholars, and heads of families; see *Ziknei*, no. 78, p. 114; and no. 79.

y. *at the age of ten months*: See *The Life of Judah*, fol. 22a.

z. *All through that summer I was ill with pains in my stomach*: This occurrence was the first of what was to become a chronic ailment for Modena, consisting of shortness of breath, stomach pains, nausea, and thirst, all of which made it difficult for him to function and caused him to be confined to bed. At first he was affected only during the warm months, but gradually the symptoms began to trouble him during the cold weather as well. From this point in the autobiography, Modena will increasingly refer to his failing health.

FOLIO 22a

a. *Small Committee*: In Hebrew, *va'ad katan*. It was composed of seven lay leaders representing the different Jewish communities in Venice. The "small committee" ratified the decisions made by the Kahal, which was composed of every Jew who paid more than twelve ducats in taxes a year (*Ziknei*, no. 78). Unfortunately, the minutes books of both the Small Committee and the Kahal are apparently no longer extant.

b. *two years earlier . . . certain types of games of chance*: In January 1628, supported by the Small Committee, the Kahal passed a ban against gambling. It described the ruin and destruction of families caused by games of chance and prohibited any Jew living in Venice, under pain of severe excommunication, from gambling inside or outside Venice, with a Jew or a Christian, on his own or through an agent. This ban was intended to last for six years and was to be proclaimed along with the other sumptuary regulations. Seventy-one members voted for it and thirty-two against it; see *Ziknei*, no. 78.

c. *a nice and forceful legal decision*: On Tuesday, February 11, 1630, Modena published a fifteen-page responsum challenging the validity of the ordinance against gambling. Modena dealt with two basic issues: first, was the prohibition against gambling sufficiently strong in Jewish tradition to jus-

tify enforcement with excommunication; and second, did those who enacted it have the authority to do so? In answer to the first question, Modena concluded that there was no clear prohibition against gambling. But
it was the second question that concerned him the most, as he indicated in
his autobiography. The major theme of all his arguments against the ban
was that the Kahal had acted improperly by failing to seek the authorization of the rabbis. The responsum was republished by Isaac Lampronti as
"Herem she-lo lishok" in *Pahad yitzhak* (Venice, 1808), fols. 53b–55b and
again in *Ziknei*, no. 78, preceded by a detailed introduction to it by Simonsohn. For a bibliography on Jewish gambling, see S. Baron, *The Jewish Community* (Philadelphia, 1942), vol. 3, p. 207 note 30; and for a
discussion of the subject, L. Landman, "Jewish Attitudes Toward Gambling," *JQR* n.s. 57–58 (1966–1968): 298–318, 34–61.

d. *I went to Modena*: This occasion may have been the first time Modena
was in Modena since 1608; see *The Life of Judah*, fol. 5a, and *Ari nohem*, p.
49.

e. *Barukh Luzzatto*: Also known as Benedetto Luzzatto, son of Moses
Luzzatto, a lay leader of the Italian synagogue and a favorite student of
Modena's, who invested him with the title of *haver*; see JTSA 8594, 2, fol.
159b; Blau, *Kitvei*, no. 182; *Ziknei*, p. 189; Ancona 7, fols. 55a–57a; Roth,
"Leone da Modena and the Christian Hebraists," pp. 398–401; Boccato,
"*L'Amor possente*," pp. 42–43; *Luhot avanim*, no. 186; and *Divan*, no. 88.

f. *the daughter of Simhah Sanguini*: On Sanguini see *Ziknei*, no. 81.

g. *Richina*: See *The Life of Judah*, fol. 21b.

h. *holy community of Mantua*: See Simonsohn, *Mantua*, pp. 52–53.

i. *Scocco*: See *The Life of Judah*, fol 28a.

j. *about 170 people*: According to the official records, by the end of September 1630, 13 Jews had died of the plague. The plague was at its worst
during October, when 101 Jews died, and November, when 102 Jews
died. From December to March the number of dead began to taper off:
33, 8, 69, 1. During the first seven months of the plague a total of 427 Jews
died. In the Jewish cemetery on the Lido a single mass grave was established for the victims. The marker reads "1631 HEBREI" (see fig. 7). On the
plague statistics, see C. Boccato, "Testimonianze ebraiche sulla peste de
1630 a Venezia," *RMI* 41 (1975): 463 and Ravid, *Economics and Toleration*,
p. 84 note 80. Their information does not concur with the figures in the
autobiography, but Modena himself, in an authorization he wrote for a
responsum, noted that by March 28, 1631, 300 had died; *Zera' anashim*,
no. 23, fol. 13a.

k. *Verona*: On the flight of Jews from Venice to Verona during the
plague, see I. Sonne, "Avnei binyan le-toledot ha-yehudim be-veronah,"
Zion 3 (1937–1938): 123–148.

l. *120,000 ducats*: In his *Discorso circa il stato de gl'hebrei et in particolar dimoranti nell'inclita città di Venetia* (Venice, 1638), fol. 29v, Simone Luzzatto wrote that in accordance with legislation of the Senate, the Jews advanced the government ten thousand ducats to be credited against their customs payments; see Ravid, *Economics and Toleration*, pp. 84–85.

m. *for there is no money*: The conditions described by Modena in this paragraph appear to be in line with the health ordinances for plagues during this period, which were particularly concerned with merchandise and travelers from abroad. Furs, carpets, and woolens were viewed as major sources of contagion, which probably accounts for the sequestration and destruction of bales of Jewish merchandise. The unemployment and impoverishment caused by measures against the plague often did more damage than the plague itself; see Pullan, *Rich and Poor*, pp. 215, 219, 316, 317; Cipolla, *Fighting the Plague*, pp. 5, 19, 73; idem, *Faith, Reason, and the Plague*, p. 24; and Abraham Catalano, *'Olam hafukh*, ed. C. Roth, in *Kovetz 'al yad* 16 (1946): 67–102.

n. *for a full year*: Esther and her husband were also having great marital strife at this time; see *Ziknei*, p. 1.

FOLIO 22b

o. *this wondrous thing*: The official records show the same trend but indicate that Modena was too enthusiastic in his statistics. In March 1 Jew died; in April, 10; and in May, 5. This pattern was typical of postepidemic mortality after the first major outbreak, as deaths became less frequent because the survivors were fewer and stronger than the victims had been.

p. *God's anger was kindled*: Christians also attributed the plague to God's hand, interpreting it as a sign of divine displeasure at Venetian defiance of the pope; see W. McNeil, *Venice: The Hinge of Europe* (Chicago, 1974), pp. 195–196.

q. *many people began to die*: This pattern is also typical of postepidemic mortality in which, after an initial high rate of deaths and a subsequent tapering off of casualties, gradually the number of deaths would increase, often particularly among infants; Cipolla, *Faith, Reason, and the Plague*, p. 102. In time the rate increased, but it never reached the initial high level. In June, 23 Jews died; in July, 22; in August, 19; in September, 31; and in October, 17; see Boccato, "Testimonianze," pp. 464–465.

r. *Padua*: Modena made a copy of excerpts from Abraham Catalano's description of the plague there, called *'Olam hafukh* (Ancona 7, fol. 6b); see historical notes to fol. 22a.

s. *Sur mera'*: See *The Life of Judah*, fol. 20a and historical notes.

t. *five things*: See Mishnah Taanit 4:6.

FOLIO 23a

u. *death turned away*: In sixteen months, by the time the plague had run its course in Venice, 46,000 people out of a total population of roughly 140,000, about one-third of all the inhabitants, had died. About 454 Jews died and many others fled. Soon, however, the Jewish population began to reach its previous levels. By 1642, there were 2,671 Jews in Venice; see Cipolla, *Fighting the Plague*, p. 100; Boccato, "Testimonianze," p. 463; Pullan, *The Jews of Europe*, p. 156; and Ravid, *Economics and Toleration*, p. 84 note 80.

v. *everyone gave thanks to his God*: The Christians of Venice attributed the end of the plague to the effective use of a treasured Byzantine icon, the Nicopeia, and the relics of Venice's first patriarch, Lorenzo Giustinian. November 21 was made a festival. See Lauritzan, *Venice*, p. 171; and W. Hazlitt, *The Venetian Republic, Its Rise, Its Growth, and Its Fall* (London, 1900), vol. 2, p. 212 (November 28). In keeping with medieval custom, even when responding to a shared natural disaster, Jews and Christians did not observe the same days of fasting and prayer; see J. Katz, *Exclusiveness and Tolerance* (New York, 1961), p. 96.

w. *"Nishmat Kol Hai"*: A prayer of gratitude to God for his mercies said on the Sabbath and festivals, at the Passover Seder, and by many today on Israeli Independence Day. It begins with the words, "The soul of every living being shall bless thy name, O Lord our God."

x. *to commemorate the deliverance*: Christian Venice also commemorated the deliverance. The doge sent a gold lamp to the shrine of the Madonna's house at Loreto, and the Senate ordered the construction of the Church of Santa Maria della Salute to thank the Virgin Mary for ending the plague; it was designed by Longhena and still stands today as a masterpiece of Baroque architecture.

y. *Angelitta after her brother*: See historical note to fol. 4a on the relation between the names Mordecai and Angelo.

z. *I had peace and rest*: Modena reformulates his "motto verse" from Job 3:26 positively to indicate relief from anxiety during this period of refraining from gambling. It is the only positive formulation in the autobiography.

a. *had not old age suddenly overcome me and my wife*: At this time Modena wrote his first Hebrew will, which he copied on the last leaf of the notebook in which he was writing his autobiography.

FOLIO 23b

b. *informed the Cattaver about the printing*: Because most of the printing was being done by Modena's grandson Isaac and his Jewish friends, it was illegal. Since 1548 Jews had not been allowed to work at publishing houses or to publish books, though this prohibition was not always enforced. In addition, talmudic materials were considered particularly odious by the authorities. Venice had accepted the view of the popes, and the Council of Ten had banned not only the Talmud or portions of it but also "compendiums, summaries, and other works dependent on it," which included ʿEin yisrael (Popper, Censorship, p. 35). In autumn 1634, in their petition seeking the renewal of their charter of 1629, the Jewish moneylenders of Venice, perhaps at Modena's request so that Beit yehudah could be completed, asked for permission to engage in printing and publishing Hebrew books. On December 29, the Senate approved a limited measure allowing for one or more of the deputies of the Jews to proofread those books necessary for their religious rites before they were printed. This law was a major setback for Modena, and his project was in great danger; see Ravid, "Prohibition Against Jewish Printing," pp. 142–145; idem, Economics and Toleration, pp. 125–126.

c. *in darkness . . . darkness for light*: The Venetian jails had both light and dark cells, depending on how much daylight penetrated, and prisoners would be placed in whichever seemed more appropriate.

d. *sixty-six days*: The amount of time Isaac spent in prison is unclear. From the 28th of Iyyar to the 28th of Tammuz, inclusive, only sixty days elapsed. In the brief notes at the end of the notebook containing the autobiography, fol. 35a, Modena gives the same problematic figure of sixty-six days. Elsewhere he mentions that Isaac was in jail for two and a half months (*Ziknei*, no. 108a). Isaac briefly mentions imprisonment in his own account of his life; see Haleviim, *Medabber*, p. 28.

e. *Quarantia Criminal*: The chief criminal court of Venice; see *The Life of Judah*, fol. 24b. The words "great expense" may indicate, in addition to the usual fees, the need to engage in some bribery.

FOLIO 24a

f. *David Hayyim Luria*: The son of Zimlan; see *The Life of Judah*, fol. 17b; *Belil hamitz*, fol. 10a; *Divan*, no. 79–80.

g. *I paid for all the expenses*: During the summer of 1635 another difficulty arose in connection with the publication of *Beit yehudah*. As Modena was finishing the book, he reported in a letter that there were no longer people who would sponsor the publication of books. Authors who wanted to publish their work now had to finance the costs out of pocket and then try to sell the books on their own. Modena learned that he would have to pay 250 ducats for *Beit yehudah* because paper and publishing costs had more than doubled since the plague; see *Ziknei*, no. 108a; cf. Boksenboim, *Iggerot*, no. 126.

h. *Tiberio Tinelli*: Tinelli (1586–1638) was a skilled Italian portrait painter. He studied under Giovanni Contarini and Leandro Bassano. Tinelli painted portraits of many members of the Venetian nobility and of Charles I of England, and he was particularly appreciated by Louis XIII of France, who knighted him. Tinelli died, probably by committing suicide, before completing Modena's portrait, which regrettably was lost, despite a claim in the nineteenth century that it had been located; see M. Landsberg, "Yigbor ha-shem hasdo," *Ha-melitz* 1 (July 27, 1861): 43–44.

i. *matters of the yeshiva*: Although Modena did not specify which "matters" faced the yeshiva, the fact that he states in the very next phrase that he "also wrote an essay refuting the doctrine of transmigration of souls" suggests that there may be a connection with a certain controversy in Amsterdam that came to the attention of the heads of the yeshiva of Venice during the winter of 1635/1636. The controversy had been precipitated by Modena's former student, Saul Levi Morteira, who now served as a rabbi in Amsterdam, when he preached a sermon in which he claimed that punishment for heretics, informers, and sectarians was eternal. Among the counterclaims made by his opponents was the argument that his view was contrary to belief in transmigration of souls (*gilgul*), an increasingly popular concept among Jewish mystics, according to which, through successive transmigrations of the soul, even a sinner damned to hell forever could find salvation. See A. Altmann, "Eternality of Punishment," *PAAJR* 40 (1972): 1–88. The hypothesis regarding the "matters of the yeshiva" advanced here is strengthened by the fact that Modena's "essay refuting the doctrine of transmigration of souls" ends with a discussion of the eternality of punishments; but see historical notes that follow.

j. *Ben david*: The treatise is a point-by-point refutation of the commentary of Isaac Abravanel (1437–1508) on Deuteronomy 25:5. While Modena devoted most of the treatise to proving the impossibility of the transmigration of the soul based on philosophical arguments, his central thesis was that the belief in transmigration of souls was not an old one for Jews but rather new. He attributed its origins to spurious kabbalists who unabashedly claimed that this belief was a major tenet of rabbinic Judaism. There are many manuscripts of *Ben david*; the only one that might be the original is in Warsaw; see F. Kupfer and S. Strelcyn, "Dwa lata pracy nad katalogiem rekopisow hebrajskich i aramejskich ze zbriorow polskichi," *Przeylad orientalistyczny* 2 (1953–1954): 153. One of the manuscripts from Oxford was published in *Ta'am zekenim*, ed. E. Aschkenazi (Frankfurt am Main, 1854), fols. 61a–64a. On Modena's views on the Kabbalah, see historical notes to fols. 20a, 26b.

k. *at the request of David Finzi . . . Egypt*: The fact that Modena wrote *Ben david* for Finzi in Egypt casts some doubt on the hypothesis, mentioned in note i, that he wrote it in response to the controversies in Amsterdam. None of the extant manuscript versions of this treatise mentions

Finzi, but are instead addressed to Modena's student, Joseph Hamitz, after 1639.

l. *nine-year-old son*: The attempt to provide comfort to a man who had just lost a son might lie in Modena's argument in *Ben david* that those who die young are not being punished for past sins and that God would not withhold his mercies from them.

FOLIO 24b

m. *trouble began*: This incident of 1636–1637 was a major one in the history of the Jews of Venice. Another account of the course of events, from the general perspective of the Jews of Venice, is contained in the eighth section of a seventeenth-century Hebrew chronicle entitled *Sippur ha-tzarot she-ʿavru be-italiah*, "A Story of the Misfortunes that Afflicted the Jews in Italy," apparently written sometime between 1637 and 1663 but first published only in 1949. That eighth section is called "The Threat of an Expulsion from Venice in 1636"; see M. Shulvass, "Sippur ha-tzarot she-ʿavru be-italiah," *HUCA* 22 (1949): 1–21 (Hebrew section); reprinted in idem, *Bi-tzevat ha-dorot* (Tel Aviv and Jerusalem, 1960), pp. 76–102; the eighth section is available in English translation in Ravid, *Economics and Toleration*, pp. 10–13. For the most part it is more general, and even vague because it is written in very flowery Hebrew; among the more significant points contained in it but not found in the autobiography of Modena is the assertion that the doge, Senate, and Council of Ten thought of expelling the Jews from the Venetian state (the charter of the Levantine and Ponentine Jewish merchants but not that of the Tedeschi Jewish moneylenders contained provisions allowing for its abrogation with certain notice—in other words, expulsion—before their expiration; but if a motion to expel the Jews was not formally introduced in a legislative body and voted upon, it may be impossible to find reference to it in the archives). Another significant point is that an Italian work by Simone Luzzatto played a role in averting this "expulsion." Presumably this claim is a reference to something closely related to his *Discorso*, published in 1638; see Ravid, *Economics and Toleration*, pp. 13–18. On Luzzatto, see historical notes to fol. 37a. Additional new information from the registers of the legislation of the Venetian Council of Ten preserved in ASV about this incident of 1636–1637, to be treated at length in a forthcoming study by B. Ravid tentatively entitled "Crime and Punishment in Seventeenth-Century Venice," has been incorporated into the historical notes that follow.

n. *Grassin Scaramella and Sabbadin Catelano*: Another Gershon Scaramella, probably not the same individual, was a leading member of the Society for Gemilut Hasadim in Venice. This society had sponsored many of Modena's literary works, including a poem that he had written a few weeks earlier for Scaramella in honor of the circumcision of his grandson Joseph (*Divan*, no. 75, the week of January 19, 1636). In any case, that Gershon Scaramella is not identical with the Gershon Scaramella who had published *Yihus ha-tzaddikim* with Modena's poems included in it in 1598; see *The Life of Judah*, fol. 20a, item 14c, and historical note l. Modena states below that both Scaramella and Catelano were friends of his.

    o. *had received goods and cash . . . Merceria . . . in one of the houses in the ghetto*: Legislation of the Council of Ten describes a series of events basically corroborating the account in the autobiography. On the night of March 1–2, four Christians—Nicoletto Zachera, a diamond cutter, and Camillo Scarpa or Scarpon, a potter, with Guglielmo Scala and Marco or Marchetto, two employees of the magistracy of the Cattaveri—had opened the door of the shop of Bartolomeo Bergonzi at the sign of the Madonna in the Merceria (the commercial district in Venice) with a key that they had forged and had carried away secretly gold cloth and silk worth about sixty thousand ducats. They took the goods by barge to the ghetto, where they were received by three Jews, Grassin Scaramella, with the cooperation of Menachem de Iseppo d'Angeli (Menahem d'Angelo of the autobiography) and Isaac Scaramella, the cousin of Grassin, who carried it around at night from place to place so that it would remain hidden. This "Bergonzi affair" was resolved on May 6, 1636, when the Council of Ten voted unanimously to banish the seven indicted individuals forever from the Venetian state. Also, all their property was to be confiscated and applied to reimbursing Bergonzi fully for the value of the unrecovered goods stolen from him, elsewhere estimated as worth about eight thousand ducats; cf. the account in the "Story," Ravid, *Economics and Toleration*, pp. 10–11.

    p. *disclosed the affair*: Modena may have been very angry at Senigo for informing directly to the Venetian authorities instead of going to the Jewish communal leadership, which had dealt with this type of scandal many times before by means of excommunication. The fact that Isaac Senigo and his alleged informing are not mentioned in the legislation of the Council of Ten should not be considered to cast doubt on the accuracy of Modena's account, because the legislation of the council was concerned primarily with meting out punishment, not with presenting a complete record of the course of events.

    q. *Menahem d'Angelo and Isaac Scaramella*: On these two individuals, see the preceding historical notes.

    r. *nobles, citizens, and commoners*: Modena here is alluding to the three lay legal estates into which Venetian society was divided: the *nobili*, *cittadini*, and *popoli*.

    s. *when one individual committed a crime, they would grow angry at the entire community*: In three places in his *Discorso*, without referring to any specific contemporary event, Luzzatto argued that it was not right to punish the whole group because of the misdeeds of some individuals; presumably, he is alluding to these events of 1636–1637 and assumes that the relevance of his point would be self-evident to his Christian Venetian readers. See Ravid, *Economics and Toleration*, pp. 18, 51–53; idem, "*Contra judaeos*," pp. 310–312, 340–342. Modena also apparently added a passage to the 1638 edition of the *Riti* in the light of these occurrences; Cohen, "Leone da Modena's *Riti*," p. 312. The change in the attitude of the Christian populace of Venice toward the Jews is also mentioned in the "Story": "and all this made us very odious indeed in the eyes of the people."

t. *Jacob*: See historical notes to fol. 25a.

u. *a bribe to the Quarantia*: In November 1633, the Council of Ten had begun investigating a case of corruption in the Quarantia Civile Vecchia, in which bribes had been given by a merchant named Marc Antonio Marta, through intermediaries, on behalf of Andrea and Marc Antonio dalle Nave to enable them to win their case against the Coroneri brothers under the clock of St. Mark's Square. Presumably Modena's reference in the "memorandums" at the end of the autobiography to "the boat" (*ha-oniyah*) in conjunction with his son-in-law Motta, Isaac Vigevano, and Lippamano, represents a translation of the Italian name "dalle Nave." When Modena actually came to write his autobiography, however, he chose not to mention the names of either dalle Nave or Lippamano in the text; see *The Life of Judah*, fol. 35a and historical note j.

v. *the aforementioned Grassin Scaramella informed*: The informing of Grassin Scaramella apparently began on March 20, when he was promised an immunity against prosecution for any involvement in the theft at Bergonzi's store in return for his information, for, although he was guilty, it did not appear that he was one of the principal offenders in the theft. But although the Council of Ten confirmed this immunity on March 27 by the vote of twelve to one, with two abstaining, the motion that he was indeed suited for the immunity, which required a three-fourths majority, failed to carry on three occasions, July 4 (6–4–5; 7–4–4), July 7 (10–4–2; 10–4–2) and July 9 (again 10–4–2). Accordingly on July 11 a divided council adopted on the third ballot a proposal to proceed against him (7–2–6; 7–2–6; 8–2–5). On September 22, he was sentenced to row at the oars in irons for ten years in one of the galleys of the condemned; in case he was unable to serve, his main hand was to be cut off and he was to spend the rest of his life in a dark cell. Alternate proposed punishments that were not adopted by the council were that he be sentenced to a dark cell for life, that he be sentenced to a dark cell for twenty years, and that he be hanged the following morning between the Columns of Justice in St. Mark's Square.

w. *six families of upright men*: See historical note e to fol. 25a.

x. *My son-in-law Jacob Motta*: See historical notes e and f to fol. 25a.

y. *Ferrara*: A part of the papal states since 1598, and thus beyond the jurisdiction of the Venetian authorities.

z. *he was far away from her*: Jacob stayed in touch through letters, which were often transmitted by Christians. He was also showing signs of strain, but Modena quieted him with the help of Abraham Osimo, a lay leader of the Italian synagogue; see *The Life of Judah*, fol. 34b, JTSA 8594, fol. 2; JTSA 8593, fol. 158b; JTSA 3920; Blau, *Kitvei*, no. 130; *Divan*, no. 93; Boksenboim, *Iggerot*, no. 157.

a. *Isaac Vigevano*: According to information contained in the registers of the Council of Ten, Isaac Vigevana (spelled thus) was arrested on May 16, 1636, by order of the Inquisitors of State; and a motion to release him, proposed in the Council of Ten on May 30, 1636, was defeated by the vote of 5–10–2. Then on February 18, 1637, noting that nothing new had emerged against him in the material on the cases read during the present month, the council approved by the vote of 16–0–1 the proposal that he be dealt with when and how the council saw fit, without a rereading of those cases. Subsequently, on March 24, 1637 a motion to proceed against him was defeated (0–9–7) and he was absolved. Presumably, this arrest was in connection with the affair related by Modena. On April 27, 1637, the Council of Ten again dealt with him; noting that he had previously been arrested by the Inquisitors of State in connection with another matter and then absolved by the Council of Ten, it approved by the vote of 12–2–1 the cryptic proposal that the matter concerning restoring to the Zerbina brothers the property stolen from them be referred to the appropriate magistracy, notwithstanding any immunity regarding the purchase of stolen property.

b. *I had no peace*: Again, Modena cites his "motto verse" from Job 3:26. In the brief "memorandums" at the end of the notebook containing the autobiography, Modena wrote that it was impossible to imagine the pain, anger, fear, and dejection that he was now experiencing; see *The Life of Judah*, fol. 35a.

c. *was a dear friend of mine*: Three judges, apparently all of the Quarantia, were implicated on the charge of accepting bribes and perverting justice: Lunardo Battagia, Gerolemo Lippamano, and Antonio Zorzi. Battagia and Lippamano were found guilty, deprived of their nobility, and banished perpetually from the Venetian state, with the stipulation that should they ever be caught returning, they were to be beheaded between the Columns of Justice in St. Mark's Square; Zorzi, against whom the Council of Ten had been much more reluctant to proceed, was ultimately acquitted. Because the name of Lippamano is found in the "memorandums" listed at the end of his autobiography, presumably that judge was his friend, and possibly the Hebrew word *sar* in this passage should be rendered "judge." The council also banished Paulina, the wife of Lunardo Battagia, for having participated in the crime of her husband (cf. the account in the "Story"). Coincidentally, according to Venetian tradition, the Lippamano family was of Jewish origin; see B. Ravid, "The Jewish Mercantile Settlement of Twelfth and Thirteenth Century Venice: Reality or Conjecture?" *AJSR* 2 (1977): 213–215.

d. *I left for Padua*: Before Modena left, he placed a gold tray in the custody of the Spanish ambassador, and on his return had trouble retrieving it; see the brief "memorandums" jotted down by Modena at the end of the notebook containing his autobiography, *The Life of Judah*, fol. 35a.

FOLIO 25a

e. *under severe restrictions of banishment*: On February 25, 1637 seven Jews—Grassin Scaramella (already, it was noted, banished for another very grave crime by the Council of Ten, namely, the theft at the store of Bergonzi), David Lonigo, Moise della Mendaressa, Giacob da Piran, Giacob della Motta, Salamon Allegri, and Marco Cigalla—were ordered arrested and, if not apprehended within three days, proceedings would be started against them in absentia. The charge against them was that with very great impudence and foolhardiness, they, together with others, were involved in various detestable ways in corrupting important judges. It was alleged that they had taken money from individuals involved in a civil case, who said that it was to be given to some specifically named people; but they deceitfully took some of the money for their own use and asserted that they had given it to some judges to whom they had not even dared to talk about it because of the integrity of those judges.

Subsequently, on March 6, the Council of Ten banished (by the vote of 15–0–2) those seven Jews from the Venetian state (Modena, imprecisely, gives the date that corresponds to March 3, but see textual note), with the provision that they were to be hanged between the Columns of Justice in St. Mark's Square should they be caught returning. Moreover, the unusual provision was added (by the vote of 15–2) that their fathers, brothers, and sons were also to leave the state within eight days. The records of the Council of Ten relate that six days later, on March 12, an official of the council went to the dwellings of the seven Jews and advised them of the sentence that they had to leave the Venetian state within eight days and never again return. Then, in accordance with the terms of the sentence, the names of the fathers, brothers, and sons of the banished were recorded: Grassin Scaramella had a one-year-old son; David Lonigo had two brothers, Cervo and Bebilion; while Jacob della Motta had two brothers, Joseph and Moses, who lived in La Motta.

Later, on April 6, action was taken against some more Jews. Anselmo and Zaccaria Cividal and Sabbadin Verdun were also perpetually banished from the Venetian state, and their fathers, brothers, and sons were ordered to leave within fifteen days; and Iseppo Bendana was banished. Interestingly, one Samuel Luzzatto was also implicated on the charge of having sought to corrupt justice for illicit gain. It was asserted that, driven by remorse and the fear of punishment, he had fled and now he was ordered to give himself up within three days in order to try to clear himself. A motion to accept an anonymous letter accusing him, together with Salamon Panarotto and Salamon de Consiglio, of engaging in corrupting justice was rejected by a vote of 5–9–2. Eventually, Samuel Luzzatto appeared before the Council of Ten and was acquitted by the vote of 12–2–2. Presumably he was a relative of Simone Luzzatto, and thus it is tempting to suggest that the involvement of a relative may have played a role in inducing Simone Luzzatto to intervene in the affair and to write his *Discorso*.

According to the account in the "Story," the doge, Francesco Erizzo, the Senate, and especially the Council of Ten "thought of expelling all the Jews from their land. However, God was with them . . . and assuaged the anger of the king [doge] and the nobles." The "Story" then relates how the actions of Rabbi Samuel Meldola, Rabbi Simone Luzzatto, and Rabbi Israel Conegliano were successful in preventing an expulsion of the Jews from Venice.

Modena characteristically was concerned in his autobiography with the incident primarily as it affected him and did not relate the final outcome. Although Sabbadin Catelano and Giacobo Zorzetto had been condemned to death by the Council of Ten, they both received many stays of execution and even promises of remission should their testimony lead to significant convictions in the matter of the corruption of justice. Finally, on May 14, the council ruled that their lives should be spared. It then decided that after Sabbadin Catelano had completed the sentence of ten years at the galleys passed on September 22 for his involvement in the theft at the store of Bergonzi, he was to spend the rest of his life in a dark cell. This punishment was approved by a 10–6 vote over a slightly more lenient measure that would have commuted the galley sentence and sent him directly to his life sentence in the dark cell. Three punishments were proposed for Giacobo Zorzetto. The one that was finally adopted provided that he serve in the galleys—but not the same one as Sabbadin—with chains on his feet for ten years; the others would either have directly jailed him for life without any galley service, or have provided that, like Sabbadin, he serve for ten years but on a different galley and then spend the rest of his life in jail.

The severity of the whole affair can be gauged from the next decision of the Council, which provided that all the material involved in "the matter of the Jews" be placed in the chest of the Inquisitors of State, from which it could not be removed for any reason unless proposed by all six ducal counselors and the three heads of the Council of Ten and passed unanimously by all members of the council. That material is still preserved in five notebooks; a detailed examination of them, which unfortunately could not now be undertaken because of faded ink which rendered many passages in the microfilm copy in our possession illegible, would reveal much information that would supplement that contained in the Council of Ten's legislation.

Finally, to prevent Jews from committing such abuses in the future, the Council of Ten ruled that without exception, no Jew was to go to the ducal palace, to any council, college, or magistracy, or to the courts of the Rialto, either as a petitioner or as a supporter or under any other pretext be involved in the cases of others, under pain of ten years in the galleys with chains on the feet, and in case he were not suited to such service, then he was to be hanged between the Columns of Justice in St. Mark's Square.

As a postscript, it should be related that sometime between 1638 and 1640 Modena wrote a letter requesting charity for an unnamed poor man who was in prison; in the margin of the copy Modena kept, he identified that person as Sabbadin Catelano; see Boksenboim, *Iggerot*, no. 194.

f. *the entire state*: The same Hebrew word, *ma'amad*, was used in the "Story" in the same sense. It is here translated as state (coming from the root *'md*, "to stand," like *stato* in Italian); cf. historical note f to fol. 28a, especially the phrase "per tutto lo stato nostro." Although usually it is used to designate the leadership of the different Jewish communities in Venice (for an example in Modena's own writings, see Boksenboim, *Iggerot*, nos. 207–208; also Haleviim, *Medabber*, pp. 48, 57, 96–99, 107), in the present context it must refer to the geopolitical entity of the Venetian Republic. Indeed, Modena twice used it in that sense in a letter urging charitable relief for the unfortunate Jews of Mantua, who had been expelled temporarily from the duchy following the German conquest in 1630 ("gershu otam mikol ha-ma'amad," Boksenboim, *Iggerot*, no. 200, where the editor takes the word to mean "territory" or "realm," rendering it in a note by the Hebrew word *mahoz*). Elsewhere in that same letter, Modena again used the term in connection with the governmental authorities who admitted the Mantuan Jewish refugees to their *ma'amad*.

g. *settled permanently in Ferrara*: Ferrara was outside of the Venetian Republic in papal territories.

h. *About two years earlier*: On this episode see Cohen, "Leone da Modena's *Riti*," pp. 289–292.

i. *Giacomo [Jacques] Gaffarel*: Gaffarel (1601–1681) was a French Catholic orientalist, Hebraist, mystic, and bibliophile with knowledge of the full range of Hebrew literature, including the Bible, rabbinics, and Kabbalah. He wrote *Abdita divinae cabbalae mysteria* in 1625 using kabbalistic methods, especially gematria, to justify Christian doctrine. It is available in French, *Profonds Mystères de la cabale divine*, trans. Samuel ben-Chesed

(Paris, 1912; reprinted Milan, 1975). Gaffarel was appointed librarian to Cardinal Richelieu (1585–1642), chief minister to King Louis XIII, who sent him to Italy in search of books and manuscripts. Gaffarel's interest in oriental mysteries, especially Persian talismans, almost led to his excommunication. On Gaffarel, see P. Gaffarel, "Jacques Gaffarel (1601–1681)," *Annales des Basses-Alpes: Bulletin de la Société scientifique et littéraire des Basses-Alpes* 11 (1903–1904): 374–406, 501–536; Modena is mentioned on pp. 508–510.

In the brief jottings made at the end of the notebook containing the autobiography, Modena related that several people had been fined and jailed by the Inquisition for copying proscribed books of arcane remedies; he also wrote that he had given some small books of arcane remedies to a Frenchman to send to Paris, and that another Frenchman was caught in 1637, perhaps a reference to Gaffarel; see *The Life of Judah*, fol. 35a.

j. *king of England*: James I (1566–1625), ruled 1603–1625.

k. *not of the pope's sect*: in other words, English Protestants.

l. *Two years later*: Modena wrote to his English friend Boswell at The Hague on September 8, 1634 that he had just revised the *Riti* and had given a copy of it to William Spencer, an Englishman from Wrexham and a fellow of Trinity College at Cambridge. To Boswell Modena also wrote that with the encouragement of friends and patrons, referring to Gaffarel, he was considering publishing the *Riti* at the end of the year in Paris to avoid Venetian censorship; see Roth, "Leone da Modena and His English Correspondents," pp. 40–41.

m. *he had printed the book in Paris*: The *Riti* was published in Paris on January 12, 1637. Gaffarel's letter was dated March 31, 1637. In his 1638 edition of the *Riti* Modena wrote that the first edition had been published in the first month of 1637, March, in accordance with the Venetian custom of beginning the year on March 1; for a discussion of the *Riti*, see historical note g to fol. 20a.

n. *I went to look at a copy of it*: According to Gaffarel's letter of March 31, which Modena reprinted in his edition of 1638 and which Chilmead published in his English translation of the *Riti* (London, 1650), Gaffarel had sent him a copy of the published book, but it did not arrive.

o. *four or five things of importance of which it is forbidden to speak*: Several themes in the *Riti* had been listed in the index of forbidden aspects of Hebrew books kept by the Catholic censors since the end of the sixteenth century. They included the discussions of the doctrine of transmigration of souls (*Riti* [1637], 5.10.2) and of the noneternality of punishment (*Riti* [1637] 5.10; see Popper, *Censorship*, p. 60), the exposition of the articles of faith with their assertion that the Messiah had not yet come, that God was one, indivisible, and incorporeal, and that there were no mediators (*Riti*

[1637], 5.11; Popper, *Censorship*, p. 83), and the discussion of conversion to Judaism, a crime in most Christian countries (*Riti* [1637], 5.2).

p. *the inquisitor, may he be blessed and praised, for he had always acted like one of the righteous gentiles in his dealings with me*: On Modena's camaraderie with an inquisitor, see Haleviim, *Medabber*, p. 72.

q. *I made a voluntary declaration to the Inquisition*: On Tuesday, April 28, 1637, Modena submitted a copy of his manuscript to the Inquisition, with an accompanying letter. On May 14 the Dominican friar Marco Ferro ruled that the most objectionable aspects of the *Riti* were the list of Maimonides' thirteen articles of faith and the description of the belief in transmigration of souls, and declared that the book merited destruction. Modena was instructed not to publish or circulate the manuscript or anything of its kind without permission and to denounce any other work like it. He was allowed to go in peace, but his manuscript remained with the Venetian Inquisition, where it is still preserved today under the title "Relatione de tutti riti, costumi et vita degl'hebrei" (ASV, Santo Uffizio, busta 94, Aprile–Maggio 1637; busta 157, under letter *L*; C. Roth, "Léon de Modène, ses *Riti ebraici* et le Saint Office à Venise," *REJ* 87 [1929]: 83–88).

r. *to delete the four or five items over which I had worried*: Many of the aforementioned theological issues that the Inquisition would especially resent were in fact retained in the 1637 edition. Thus it was not these discussions that Modena had been relieved to learn had been removed, and it remains unclear exactly which ideas Modena suspected might not seem proper to Catholics.

s. *praising and glorifying me and my work*: In the letter Gaffarel also raised some objections about material he felt Modena had overlooked, particularly certain practices with mystical and occult overtones. Additionally, he tried to convince Modena to convert to Catholicism. As in other instances in the autobiography, which he wrote for his family, Modena suppressed such unpleasantness, especially when it detracted from the image of fame among Christians that he wanted to project.

t. *ambassador of the king of France, who had just come here*: The Paris edition begins with a dedication dated January 12, 1637, to Claude Mallier, counselor to the king of France and ambassador to Venice, who, according to the text, had just been chosen as ambassador. Mallier, also identified in other works as M. de Houssay (see historical note w to this folio), served as ambassador from March 1638 till September 1640. See A. Baschet, *Histoire de la chancellerie secrète* (Paris, 1870), pp. 432–438. The dedication was signed "Leoni Mutinensi Rabbino Veneto."

u. *might not seem proper to the Catholics*: The reasons given in the preface to the 1638 edition included: first, to correct the many printer's errors of spelling and sometimes of wording that changed the meaning; second, to reformulate some passages; and third, to affirm the fact that he was the first person to write a work of this genre. (Modena may have been afraid lest his readers, especially in Venice, would have already seen the *Discorso* of Simone Luzzatto, also published in 1638, and would have assumed wrongly that he had been influenced by Luzzatto; see Ravid, *Economics and Toleration*, pp. 16–17, especially note 10.) In the privacy of his autobiography, Modena expressed the more ideological reason for the new edition, which was published by Giovanni Calleoni in July 1638.

v. *deleting and adding*: Cohen, "Leone da Modena's *Riti*," pp. 320–321 provides a chart comparing the differences between the two published versions of the *Riti* and discusses some of them in the body of the article. The title page of the 1638 *Riti* includes a small picture of Modena (see the frontispiece and fig. 8), the only one available, because the other two made of him (by Tinelli and the one he sent David Finzi in Egypt; see *The Life of Judah*, fol. 24a) are no longer extant. This picture shows no sign of a head covering, as would be required by Jewish practice and also Venetian law. For references to Modena's views on bareheadedness, see *Ziknei*, nos. 21–22.

w. *to that ambassador*: The dedication was to "il Signore Presidente D'Houssay," counselor of the Christian king and his ambassador to the serene Republic of Venice. After the "Praesidi de Houssay" left Venice he continued to patronize Modena; see historical notes to fol. 28a.

x. *which defrayed the costs of printing*: Thirty-four ducats seems low even for a book as small as the *Riti*, especially considering that *Beit yehudah* had cost 250 ducats to produce only three years earlier. The difference in the costs of publishing the two books may indicate how much more expensive it was to print Hebrew books than Italian ones.

FOLIO 26a

y. *Beginning in the month of Shevat*: Modena interrupted the chronology so that he could write about related events together.

z. *Brazil*: On Jewish life in South America at this time, see Martin Cohen, *The Jewish Experience in Latin America* (New York, 1971), vol. 2, and Baron, *Social and Religious History of the Jews*, vol. 15, pp. 322–350.

a. *preaches in public, pleasing his listeners*: In October 1637, for the festival of Sukkot, the sixteen-year-old boy delivered a sermon that had been delivered years earlier by Modena's son Mordecai, his uncle; see Ancona 7, fols. 35b-37b; Simonsohn, in *Ziknei*, p. 16.

b. *may he grant me and my wife . . . our reward in the world to come for having raised an orphan*: For details of Isaac's life, see his own account in *Medabber*.

c. *Abraham Aboab*: Abraham Aboab (d. 1642) had sponsored yeshivot in many other cities in which he had lived; see L. Lowenstein, "Die Familie Aboab," *MGWJ* 48 (1904): 674; Altmann, "Eternality of Punishment," p. 14; and Blau, *Kitvei*, no. 178.

d. *yeshiva*: On Sunday, June 20, 1638 the Jewish community of Verona authorized several families from Venice, including that of Aboab, to settle in Verona. Anticipating this move, which was to take place during the following year, Aboab may simply have canceled his contributions to the Venetian yeshiva as he made plans to leave the city; see Sonne, "Avnei binyan le-toledot ha-yehudim be-veronah," pp. 123, 145–148.

e. *Leo di Cervi*: He was a lay leader at the Canton synagogue; see Boksenboim, *Iggerot*, no. 244; *Luhot avanim*, no. 62.

f. *were growing old*: At sixty-seven, old age had caught up with Modena. Often in his works after 1638 he mentioned his age and complained about it; *Ziknei*, no. 114; Boksenboim, *Iggerot*, no. 126; *Mikra gedolah*, ed. A. Lombroso (Venice, 1639), introduction.

FOLIO 26b

g. *Judah Monte Scudolo*: Modena had lent him a book about this time (Boksenboim, *Iggerot*, p. 345). Writing to one of Isaac's prospective relatives, who was also a friend of his, Modena expressed delight over the match between his grandson and the daughter of Judah Monte Scudolo (Boksenboim, *Iggerot*, no. 128). The origins of the name Monte Scudolo are problematic. It is probably a diminutive form of Monte Scudo, a town southeast of Rimini; another town with a similar name, Montescudaio, is located southeast of Livorno.

h. *rose up to close a breach*: This passage reflects the mounting hostility between the rabbis and the lay leaders about this time. Writing in October 1638, Modena called his generation worthless because it despised the Torah (Boksenboim, *Iggerot*, no. 126). In March 1639 he called the people of Venice "thorns in my eyes" (Boksenboim, *Iggerot*, no. 129). Modena prepared two drafts of a document describing the long-standing mockery of the rabbis and gaons by the congregations of Venice. He called the lay leaders *hediotot*, common simple people, who were diminishing the glory of the Torah and denying the sages the power to order things correctly. The rabbis agreed to stand united against the lay leaders of any congregation that tried to deprive a rabbi of his power and authority to excommunicate. Further, if two rabbis agreed to a meeting, then all the others had to attend and to abide by any majority decision without hesitation; see Boksenboim, *Iggerot*, nos. 207, 208; cf. *Ziknei*, no. 99.

i. *two thousand per person*: For years the Cattaveri had been issuing edicts against the right of the Jews to excommunicate without their permission, even though that magistracy may not have had the full authority to do so (see Ravid, "Ripublikah nifredet," pp. 53–76). At the same time the Jewish lay leaders had opposed the power of the rabbis to excommunicate. Now, even though it appeared that the rabbis had followed the proper procedures, they had ended up in court, perhaps at the instigation of the Jewish lay leaders. Light may be shed on this event by looking at a similar occurrence, which involved the Capi dell'Università degli Ebrei. They were all imprisoned from September 1637 to March 1638 on charges of complicity in the escape of the wife and children of Leon Luzzatto, a convert to Christianity. In the trial that followed, it was suggested that the capi had not caused the rabbis to pronounce excommunication on the Jews involved as promptly or as strongly as possible. The public prosecutor, the Avogador Morosini, basing himself on the Libro Grande of the Jewish community, charged that the rabbis had at their disposal "la scomunica picola" and "la scomunica grande" and faulted them for not using the more serious of the two forms. Although one of the leaders of the Jewish community, Salamon Panaroto, argued that there was no difference between the two, it may be that also in this case it was the rabbis who were jailed for not doing all they could have to enforce the law. The source, found in the archive of the Pia Casa di Catechumeni, is cited in the historical notes to fol. 21a. It also remains unknown how Modena was able to raise his personal share of the bail money.

j. *period of chaos*: Perhaps an allusion to a famous messianic Midrash (see, e.g., B.T. Sanhedrin 97a–97b) that took on great significance for Christian kabbalists; see Secret, *Kabbalistes chrétiens*, pp. 11, 35, 49; Pullan, *The Jews of Europe*, p. 250; Ruderman, *Farisol*, pp. 54, 193, 195.

k. *the wedding of my grandson Isaac*: Modena's financial distress in 1640 was so severe that on January 8 he had to write to his grandson's fiancée's relatives, the Beer family, to ask for a hundred ducats (Roth, "Leone da Modena and the Christian Hebraists," p. 392). Isaac does not appear to have received the degree of *haver* at this time; Haleviim, *Medabber*, p. 38.

l. *the second printing of my book "Galut yehudah" was completed*: In the autumn of 1639, Modena learned that the republication of his *Galut yehudah* in Padua was almost complete except for two leaves. It was being printed in the shop of Giulio Crivellari under the sponsorship of Joseph Foa, who, according to Modena, was not particularly rich. Modena anticipated that it would take another month. Finally, for eight days, from May 18 to 25, Modena had to go to Padua to supervise personally the completion of the book; Boksenboim, *Iggerot*, no. 130, November 27, 1639. This work was one of the five Hebrew books published in Padua during the sixteenth and seventeenth centuries; see Amram, *Makers of Hebrew Books*, p. 38.

m. *Pi aryeh*: This supplement was published in Venice at Calleoni's shop because it required Hebrew vowel signs, which were not available in Padua. Foa did not want to sell individual copies for less than six lire each, in view of his substantial investment in the republication. He was willing, however, to sell them in lots of thirty or more for four lire thirteen soldi each, which he equated, apparently erroneously, with a half-ducat. Modena suggested selling them in even larger lots for four lire each; see Boksenboim, *Iggerot*, no. 133, May 30, 1640; and historical notes to fol. 20a.

n. *against the Kabbalah. . . . "Ari nohem"*: Modena's views on Kabbalah were based on extensive reading, and his reasons for opposing it were specific. They had developed gradually since he had first met Israel Sarug, the kabbalist missionary from Safed, in Venice during the 1590s. They had become firmly established by the middle of the following decade, and by 1626 most of his arguments had been written down and circulated. Although Modena had used many of the sources of *Ari nohem* in his earlier writings against Kabbalah and had mentioned in passing most of the ideas that were elaborated in it, this latest work on Kabbalah was a reaction to several new developments and contained a much stronger affirmation of his earlier standpoint.

o. *against the great luminaries*: Throughout the book Modena polemicized against the presentation of Maimonides' views by three kabbalists of earlier generations: Meir ibn Gabbai (1480–1540), author of *'Avodat ha-kodesh* (Mantua, 1545), Shem Tov ibn Shem Tov (1380–1441), author of *Sefer ha-'emunot* (Ferrara, 1556), and Eliezer Hayyim Gennazano (second half of the fifteenth century), author of *Iggeret hamudot*, a work that was then only in manuscript. Modena defended Maimonides in several ways, including reference to the favorable view of him by Nahmanides, himself a kabbalist (*Ari nohem*, chaps. 6 and 21). In context, however, this point was a minor aspect of this important book. Much of it was devoted to a polemic against Lurianic and Christian kabbalists, who, Modena felt, were a threat to rabbinic Judaism, like those Jewish kabbalists who had attacked Maimonides. For further discussion of Modena's views on Kabbalah, see M. Idel, "Differing Conceptions of Kabbalah in the Early 17th Century," in *Jewish Thought in the Seventeenth Century*, pp. 137–200; idem, "Major Currents in Italian Kabbalah Between 1560 and 1660," in *Italia judaica*, vol. 2, pp. 241–262; H. Adelman, "Rabbi Leon Modena and the Christian Kabbalists," in *Renaissance Rereadings: Intertext and Context*, ed. M. Horowitz, W. Furman, and A. Cruz (Urbana, Ill., 1988), pp. 271–286; historical notes to fols. 20a and 24a.

p. *it was never printed*: *Ari nohem* did, however, circulate widely in manuscript before it was finally published in 1840 by J. Fuerst in Leipzig. A subsequent edition was published at Jerusalem in 1929 by N. Libowitz. Of all the extant manuscripts of *Ari nohem*, the only one that might be the original is in Warsaw; see Kupfer and Strelcyn, "Dwa lata pracy," p. 153.

q. *two-millennium-long era of chaos*: See historical notes to fol. 26b.

r. *marriage and good deeds*: Here Modena followed the traditional Jewish blessing for a newborn girl, which includes only two of the three things asked on behalf of a Jewish boy at the time of his circumcision; it omits the hope that the daughter might also attain significant learning in Torah.

FOLIO 27a

s. *abcess, pus, and a pulmonary infection*: Modena used here rabbinic terms for internal adhesions in the lungs of a slaughtered animal.

t. *Moses Luzzatto*: See *The Life of Judah*, fols. 27b and 37a (with historical note i).

FOLIO 27b

u. *nice supplement*: Some of these prayers had appeared in *Kol sakhal* (see *Behinat ha-kabbalah*, p. 42) and *Kenaf renanim*, ed. Joseph Carmi (Venice, 1626), fol. 12a; see historical notes to fol. 20a.

v. *Rome*: In his dedication, he expresses his regrets that he had never been able to travel to Rome.

w. *resentment over the order of the names*: The names printed on the first page of the 1642 edition are Mordecai Tuscano, Raphael Yair, and Hayyim Natronai.

x. *more than 100 ducats*: This sale apparently accounted for about one-third of his library.

y. *to students and admirers*: In 1645 Plantavit wrote about Modena, "He is also the one by whose utmost care and diligence we have begun to build up our rabbinical library" (*Bibliotheca rabbinica*, p. 588, no. 323, also cited in Blau, "Plantavits Lehrer," p. 114).

z. *Moses Luzzatto*: See *The Life of Judah*, fols. 27a and 37a.

a. *Isaac the son of S[amuel] Obadiah*: Isaac was a lay leader in the Ashkenazic congregation; Haleviim, *Medabber*, p. 85.

b. *Isaac, known as Rosso*: See Haleviim, *Medabber*, p. 78.

c. *defending Simhah the son of Meshullam the butcher*: In the brief notes at the end of the notebook containing the autobiography (see *The Life of Judah*, fol. 35a) Modena mentions that this man, also called Simonetto, was defended by him "against imprisonment on account of debts and the Criminal," for which he would have had to spend five years in jail. Also, in the aforementioned trial of the Jewish lay leaders of Venice in January 1638, Modena appeared as a character witness for one of the accused (see historical notes to fols. 21a and 26b). On Modena's role defending Jews before the authorities, see Boksenboim, *Iggerot*, nos. 107, 108.

FOLIO 28a

d. *A[braham] Stella*: Called Kokhav in Hebrew—which, like *stella*, means "star"—he was a student of Modena's and a poet (Blau, *Kitvei*, no.

182; Boksenboim, *Iggerot*, no. 234; *Divan*, no. 68). The poet Immanuel Frances (1618–1710) chastised Stella for writing poetry in Italian and not in Hebrew; see *Metek sefatayim*, ed. H. Brody (Berlin, 1892), pp. 10–11.

e. *war with the pope*: The war with the pope was waged near Ferrara from December 1642 to May 1643.

f. *they denied him permission*: On November 20, 1643, a special committee of the Council of Ten appointed to supervise the matter of those banished or confined decided to authorize the release of Jacob della Motta, under certain conditions that can no longer be ascertained. The Council of Ten took up his case on December 4, 1643. Citing the report of that committee and the fact that a copy of the actual payment made had been presented to the Council, the three heads of the Council introduced a motion confirming and approving the release of Jacob and providing that he might "come, go, stay, and do business freely in this city and throughout our state as he could before he was banished, and his name is to be removed from every book, file, or protocol in which it had been written down." Passage of this motion required a three-fourths majority, and, despite the favorable recommendation of the committee and the attitude of the heads of the Council of Ten, the Council rejected the motion 5–10–2 on the second ballot (the first ballot vote of 5–8–4 was deemed inconclusive because there was no clear majority). Thus Jacob della Motta was never allowed to set foot in Venice again. The text in ASV, Council of Ten, comune, reg. 93, fol. 270r, December 4, 1643, reads as follows

Che la liberation di Giacob della Motta hebreo fatta a 20 del passato dalli deputati da questo consiglio sopra l'affare de banditi, relegati e confinati, con le conditioni che dalla copia hora letta si sono intese, sia confirmata et approbata, havendo portata copia auttentica dell'esborso effettivo fatto in cecca, et alla cassa del medesimo consiglio. Possa però esso Giacob venir, andar, star et pratticar liberamente per questa città, et per tutto lo stato nostro come poteva far prima che fosse bandito et il suo nome depennato da ogni libro, filza o raspe ove fosse notato . . .

Unfortunately, the files containing the complete records for that date, which may have included documents that would have shed more light on this matter, have been rendered unreadable by the ravages of nature.

g. *she returned home*: On March 31, 1644 the Treaty of Ferrara had been signed.

h. *250 ducats*: A large part of this sum was a contribution of 150 ducats sent to Modena by Claude Mallier, M. de Houssay, the former French ambassador to Venice (1638–1640), to whom Modena had dedicated both editions of the *Riti*. Modena sent him a copy of the Hebrew and Italian versions, with a Latin translation, of the poem he had written for the birth of King Louis XIII in 1601; see *Bibliotheca rabbinica*, p. 588, no. 323; and note 30 to Howard Adelman's introductory essay. Jochanan Wijnhoven and John Kirby of Smith College rendered assistance in understanding Plantavit's Latin.

FOLIO 28b

i. *many endeavors*: The items enumerated in this list can best be characterized as job descriptions that sometimes overlapped, rather than as separate careers, as has often been assumed; see Howard Adelman's introductory essay.

FOLIO 29a

j. *seventy-six whole years*: This passage would have been written in 1647.

k. *my daughter's dowry*: As it amounted to five hundred ducats in cash and three hundred in goods, recovering the dowry would be a great help for Modena and his family; see *The Life of Judah*, fol. 18a.

l. *Halitzah*: A ceremony, described in the Bible (Deuteronomy 25:9), whereby a widow who had not borne a son during her marriage is released by her brother-in-law from levirate marriage with him. The symbolic removal (*halitzah*) of the brother-in-law's shoe is the main feature of this ritual.

m. *I have continuously worked hard and labored*: The minutes of the societies for which he worked, such as the board of the Italian synagogue and ʿOzer Dallim (The Society for Helping the Poor), show that he regularly attended meetings in 1647 (JTSA 8594 and 8468). Until the end of 1647 he also served as the chief official translator of Hebrew documents for the Venetian government; see L. Luzzatto, "All'Illustre Dr. M. Steinschneider in Berlino," *VI* 31 (1883): 255.

n. *My debts increase, and I am also afflicted*: In the same vein, in the text of his lecture on Samuel, which he gave for the fourth time on June 17, 1647, at the study house of the Ashkenazic Torah Study Society, Modena wrote in the margin that he was losing his mind because of bad fortune in his old age. Each day, he complained, was worse than the previous one, and he was praying for his death; see Neubauer, "Quelques Notes sur la vie," p. 89.

o. *catarrh*: an inflammation of the mucous membranes.

FOLIO 29b

p. *three of whom were rabbis*: Their names are reported in his will of 1647–1648: Simhah Luzzatto, Nehemiah Saraval, and Shemaiah di Medina; see *The Life of Judah*, fol. 37a.

q. *three months*: That is, until about February 26, 1648.

r. *last month*: That is, since about January 26, 1648.

s. *roar like a lion*: Here Modena used a biblical allusion (cf. Job 4:10) to his name, Judah Aryeh (lion), to refer to the sounds made by his ruptured intestines.

t. *while writing, today*: Here the text of the autobiography ends. The final lines were recorded on or slightly before February 26, 1648, which coincides closely with the date on which Modena added the final touches to his revised last will and testament and copied it into the notebook containing the autobiography. That document was written in two stages, the first part in August 1647, and the second in November 1647, and it contains a final statement dated February 24, 1648 (*The Life of Judah*, fol. 37a–b). Modena's wife Rachel died shortly afterward on March 7 and Modena himself two weeks later; see Howard Adelman's introductory essay.

FOLIO 34b

u. *Miseries of my heart in brief*: For discussion of this section of the manuscript see excursus 2, "Who Wrote the Ambrosiana Manuscript of *Hayyei yehudah?*" and Natalie Davis's introductory essay, note 38.

v. *Abraham Lombroso*: He was a student of Modena's, who had officiated at his wedding in the Sephardic synagogue prior to 1602. Lombroso died in 1627. His brother, Jacob, was a noted grammarian. On Abraham, see *Divan*, no. 169; Blau, *Kitvei*, no. 182, 64; Boksenboim, *Iggerot*, no. 146; *Midbar yehudah*, fol. 81a; *Luhot avanim*, no. 31.

w. *Abraham Cammeo*: See *The Life of Judah*, fol. 14a, where he is called Abraham di Cammeo.

x. *My son Mordecai*: See *The Life of Judah*, fols. 15b–16a, 17a.

y. *Raphael Spira*: On his close friendship with Modena, see Boksenboim, *Iggerot*, no. 100.

z. *Grillo*: See *The Life of Judah*, fols. 15b, 17a.

a. *Zebulun . . . banish the murderers*: See *The Life of Judah*, fol. 18a.

b. *council of young citizens*: Possibly Modena is referring to developments in Venetian political life. During the 1580s new leaders arose in Venice called the Giovanni, "the Young Men," led by Leonardo Dona (1536–1612), who later served as doge (1606–1612). They had a large following loyal to the government, supporting its jurisdiction against the prerogatives of the clergy and claims of the pope, and advocating a French rather than a Spanish orientation. As the Giovanni and their followers took control of the different magistracies in Venice, they began to intervene more frequently in the affairs of the Inquisition, vying for jurisdiction over bigamists, Jews, prostitutes, blasphemers, magicians, infidels, and publishers; see Lane, *Venice*, pp. 393–394; F. Seneca, *Il Doge Leonardo Donà: La Sua Vita e la sua preparazione politica prima del dogado* (Padua, 1959); G. Cozzi, *Il Doge Nicolo Contarini: Richerche sul patriziato veneziano agli inizi del Seicento* (Venice, 1958); Grendler, *Roman Inquisition*, pp. 202–204, 206, 211, 218, 222–224, 252; Pullan, *The Jews of Europe*, p. 33.

c. *I made a voluntary declaration to the Uffizio Censori*: According to A. Da Mosto, *L'Archivio di stato di venezia* (Rome, 1937), vol. 1, p. 177, the magistracy of the two Censors was initially established in 1517 to deal with election intrigue. However, because of the rigor of the Censors, it was suppressed by the Great Council in 1521, but out of necessity reconstituted in 1524. Soon afterward its jurisdiction was extended to cover the wages of servants, wagering, and crimes committed by gondoliers. Presumably Modena's declaration in some way involved wagering.

d. *Through A[braham] Osimo I calmed him down*: See historical notes to fol. 24b.

FOLIO 35a

e. *Panarotti*: For an Eliakim Panarotti in the year 1594, see *The Life of Judah*, fol. 12a.

f. *Isaac Padovan*: He was a former pupil of Modena's who later served as a rabbi in Rome. He wrote two poems for Plantavit's *Planta vitis* in 1645 at Modena's 1639 recommendation and a poem for Modena's *Galut yehudah* in 1640. See *Divan*, no. 48; Blau, *Kitvei*, no. 182; Roth, "Leone da Modena and the Christian Hebraists," pp. 385, 398; Haleviim, *Medabber*, p. 79. On his rabbinic decisions, see *Ziknei*, p. 53 and nos. 110, 116, 158, 165.

g. *Joseph Hamitz*: See *The Life of Judah*, fol. 20b.

h. *My grandson Isaac*: See *The Life of Judah*, fol. 23b.

i. *Some little books*: See historical notes to fol. 25a.

j. *the matter concerning Isaac Vigevano . . . and "the boat"*: See *The Life of Judah*, fols. 24b–25a and historical notes.

k. *Riti*: See *The Life of Judah*, fol. 25a–b.

l. *Moses Saltar, who has embittered her life with troubles*: See *The Life of Judah*, fols. 25b–26a, 26b, 27b.

m. *ruination of honor, money, body, and soul*: See *The Life of Judah*, fol. 29a.

n. *the butcher*: See historical notes to fol. 27b.

o. *Criminal*: The Quarantia Criminal, the chief criminal court of Venice; see *The Life of Judah*, fols. 23b, 24b.

p. *How hard I toiled . . . without success*: See *The Life of Judah*, fol. 28a and historical notes.

q. *death of my son-in-law*: See *The Life of Judah*, fol. 29a.

FOLIOS 35b–36a

r. *here or on the facing page*: The passages on these facing pages have been discussed by Roth, "Leone da Modena and England," p. 211 and idem, "Leone da Modena and His English Correspondents," pp. 39–41.

s. *John Selden*: 1584–1654, a leading Christian Hebraist in England (*Dic-*

tionary of National Biography, vol. 17, pp. 1150–1162). On October 8, 1628, Modena signed a statement attesting to the authority of a Bible manuscript from 1304 that included a Masoretic text and Rashi's commentary. In 1659 Selden donated this book to the Bodleian Library in Oxford; see Roth, "Leone da Modena and His English Correspondents," p. 42.

t. *On the Succession: De successionibus* . . . (for the complete Latin title as transcribed by Modena see the textual note and fig. 12) is a book about inheritance according to Jewish law. Selden also cited Modena again in 1646 in his *Uxor ebraica* (M. Cowley, *A Descriptive Catalogue of the Manuscripts in the Library of St. John's College* [Cambridge, 1846], p. 71). In the 1631 edition of *De successionibus* the citation of Modena's *Riti* appears, as mentioned here, on p. 60 (with the first three words at the bottom of p. 59).

u. *the Digest*: Latin, *Pandectis* (the Pandects), syntactically in apposition to the phrase "Talmuds" above. The Pandects, or Digest of Roman laws organized according to subject matter, was the component of the *Corpus juris romani* closest in nature to the Talmud in Selden's conception (information courtesy of Anthony Grafton).

v. *compendium on the rites, life, and customs of the Jews*: Modena's *Riti*; see *The Life of Judah*, fol. 25a–b.

w. *William Boswell*: A fellow of Jesus College, Cambridge, theologian and Hebraist (d. 1649), who had traveled to Venice in his youth and had studied there with Modena. Boswell had been a member of the British Parliament in 1624–1625 and then served as secretary to Herbert of Cherbury and Dudley Carlton, who were ambassadors to Paris and the Hague. On September 6, 1628, Modena presented an inscribed manuscript copy of his *Riti* to Boswell. It was this copy to which Selden had referred in *De successionibus*.

x. *bishop of Lodève* . . . *extols me highly*: Jean Plantavit de la Pause (1576–1651) and his *Bibliotheca rabbinica*, a supplement to *Florilegium rabbinicus* (Lodève, 1645). Plantavit had studied with Modena in Florence in 1609 (see Howard Adelman's introductory essay). Shortly afterward he had offered Modena a position teaching Hebrew in Paris, but subsequently he and Modena were out of contact for about the next thirty years. In February 1639 the priest Ignatio Rundi of the Riformatori paid Modena a visit on behalf of Plantavit, now bishop of Lodève in France, and asked him to prepare some verses in honor of Plantavit's Hebrew book, *Neta' ha-gefen: Thesaurus synonymicarum hebreo-chaldaica rabbinicus* (Lodève, 1645), which was about to be published. Modena retrieved a poem he had written for Plantavit in 1611 and also wrote a new one for the book (*Divan*, nos. 48, 49). On December 10, 1639, Modena received a letter and some page proofs from Plantavit. In the letter Plantavit advised Modena that he had begun an alphabetical dictionary of Hebrew writers and had already accumulated seven hundred names, including Modena's with a reference to his *Midbar yehudah*. In his reply Modena mentioned that this task had been started by many, including himself, but finished by none, though he had collected five hundred names. To make sure that he would be well represented in Plantavit's listing, Modena sent him a list of his own published books, which, in addition to *Midbar yehudah*, included *Lev ha-aryeh*, *Galut yehudah*, *Tzemah tzaddik*, *Beit lehem yehudah*, and *Beit yehudah*. Missing from the list were *Sur meraʿ* and *Sod yesharim*, Modena's earliest books, which had been published anonymously. When Plantavit published his *Bibliotheca rabbinica*, however, he included among his entries only *Midbar yehudah*, *Sur meraʿ*, and *Sod yesharim*, as well as great praise for his former teacher, and attributed his knowledge of several other works to Modena. Isaac min Haleviim claimed that Plantavit had mentioned all Modena's books, but that does not appear to be the case; see Roth, "Leone da Modena and the Christian Hebraists," pp. 395–398; Kobler, *Letters*, vol. 2, pp. 423–426; Blau, "Plantavits Lehrer in Rabbinischen," pp. 113–120; Haleviim, introduction to *Magen ve-herev*, fol. 11b; Ancona 7, fols. 3a–4b for a bibliography of 355 works that Modena had listed; and historical notes to fol. 35a.

y. *Manasseh ben Israel*: 1604–1657, rabbi, scholar, writer, and publisher in Amsterdam who succeeded Isaac Uziel as preacher at the Neve Shalom congregation in 1622. He became most famous for his involvement in the negotiations during the 1650s with Oliver Cromwell for the return of the Jews to England. Interestingly, many of the arguments in Manasseh's *Humble Addresses* were taken from the *Discorso* of Simone Luzzatto, which was based on the experiences of the Jews of Venice. See B. Ravid, " 'How Profitable the Nation of the Jews Are': The *Humble Addresses* of Menasseh ben Israel and the *Discorso* of Simone Luzzatto," in *Mystics, Philosophers, and Politicians: Essays in Jewish Intellectual History in Honor of Alexander Altmann*, ed. J. Reinharz and D. Swetschinski (Durham, N.C., 1982), pp. 159–180. For an overview of Manasseh's life see C. Roth, *A Life of Menasseh ben Israel* (Philadelphia, 1934).

z. *Oral Confession*: In his *Divan* (no. 51) Modena preserved a poem he had written for a Latin book on the confessional by the priest Pietro Bel-Occhio, whom he had described as "good for the Jews," *tov le-yisrael*.

FOLIO 37a

a. *burden fit for a camel*: This expression is an allusion to the size of the Zohar, supposedly written by Shimon bar Yohai in a cave while hiding from the Romans. Modena discussed this assertion made by kabbalists in his critique of the Zohar; see *Ari nohem*, chap. 17.

b. *In a different generation . . . they would be more pleasing than many others*: Modena seems to be alluding to the tantalizing issue of the changing values

268

in the Jewish community as a result of the transition from Renaissance to Counter-Reformation and Baroque and the possibly related growing internal conservative reaction and spread of Kabbalah; see Howard Adelman's introductory essay, note 183.

c. *Simhah Luzzatto*: Simone Luzzatto (ca. 1585–1663) was younger than Modena and always signed rabbinic documents after him. Modena made many references to Luzzatto in his writings, reflecting both collegial cooperation and personal rivalry. Luzzatto became Modena's successor as the chief official translator of Hebrew documents for the Venetian government; see Simonsohn, *Ziknei*, pp. 45–46; M. Shulvass, "Rabbi simhah luzzatto," in the Hebrew translation of Luzzatto's *Discorso* by D. Lattes under the title of *Ma'amar 'al yehudei venetziah*, ed. A. Z. Aescoly (Jerusalem, 1950), pp. 9–26 (republished in Shulvass, *Bi-tzevat ha-dorot*, pp. 33–55); Ravid, *Economics and Toleration*, pp. 93–98; Luzzatto, "All'Illustre Dr. M. Steinschneider," p. 255; Haleviim, *Medabber*, p. 104.

d. *Nehemiah Saraval*: The son of Gaon Yehudah Leib Saraval, Nehemiah (d. 1646) received his title of *haver* from Samuel Judah Katzenellenbogen. Even though he was older than Simhah Luzzatto, he usually signed rabbinic documents after him; see Simonsohn, in *Ziknei*, p. 52.

e. *Shemaiah di Medina*: A native of Salonika, Medina was a Sephardic rabbi in Venice; see Benayahu, *Ha-yehasim*, pp. 197–202.

f. *Abraham H[aver] T[ov]*: See *The Life of Judah*, fol. 16a.

g. *Isaiah Nizza*: A Venetian rabbi and kabbalist (*Toledot gedolei yisrael*, p. 185, no. 113), possibly identical with the Isach(a) Nizza mentioned in Ancona, "Inventario," pp. 258, 264.

h. *and . . .* : Those who compiled the inventory of his books after he died but are not mentioned here include Gershom b. Solomon Alpron and Aaron b. Judah Volterra, who appraised his household effects; see Howard Adelman's introductory essay.

i. *Moses son of Judah Luzzattin*: His family name is a diminutive of Luzzatto. Simone Luzzatto had two nephews with the name Moses, one the son of Isaac and the other, of Judah (Haleviim, *Medabber*, s.v. index). Moses Luzzatto was also the name of Modena's landlord from 1642 to 1643 (*The Life of Judah*, fols. 27a, 27b). The posthumous inventory of Modena's Italian books was made by Moise Luzzatto (Ancona, "Inventario," p. 267).

j. *Solomon son of Mordecai Ashkenazi*: Ancona, "Inventario," lists a Salamon Todesco as a witness, pp. 258, 261. Presumably, again, he is the same person.

FOLIO 37b

k. *Magen ve-herev*: Modena's grandson Isaac related in the introduction to the manuscript copy he made of *Magen ve-herev* that Modena began this book three years before his death. On the relation between *Magen ve-herev* and *Ari nohem* in Modena's polemic against Christian Kabbalah and the interesting view on Jesus expressed in this work, his last, see Adelman, "Rabbi Leon Modena and the Christian Kabbalists." *Magen ve-herev* was published by S. Simonsohn (Jerusalem, 1960).

l. *my quarto-sized journal*: Modena had written his ideas for *Magen ve-herev*, often in the form of quotations from books he had read or selections from his own correspondence, in a journal he kept to help him prepare this book. This journal is still extant and shows the richness of the sources on Christianity that Modena had at his disposal; Ancona 7, described by Simonsohn, in *Ziknei*, p. 16.

m. *should be given to the haver Moses son of J[udah], mentioned before*: Moses gave a copy of the manuscript to Isaac min Haleviim with the stipulation that he not give a copy to anybody else. But in his account of his life, Isaac explains how Isaac Modena, his uncle, Leon Modena's son, intimidated him into giving him this copy of the book before he had a chance to copy it in its entirety. Moses Luzzattin considered this action a betrayal of his agreement with Isaac min Haleviim; see Haleviim, *Medabber*, pp. 90–91.

n. *Shabbat Shirah*: This Sabbath, which falls near the holiday of Tu Bishevat, is the one on which the portion Beshalah, Exodus 13:17–17:16, containing the Song (*shirah*) of the Sea (Exodus 15), is read.

o. *Shabbat Zakhor*: This Sabbath comes before Purim and is so called because of an association between Amalek and Haman. The reading, Deuteronomy 25:17–19, begins "Remember (*zakhor*) what Amalek did to you."

p. *Shabbat Hagadol*: Always preceding Passover, the Haftarah portion for this Sabbath, Malachi 3:4–24, contains an allusion to the "great day of the Lord."

q. *Sabbath before the 9th of Av*: Also called Shabbat Hazon. The Haftarah, Isaiah 1:1–27, begins with the word *hazon*, "vision," and deals with Israel's sins and with preparation for the commemoration of the destruction of the Temple.

r. *Nahamu*: Shabbat Nahamu follows the 9th of Av. The Haftarah, Isaiah 40:1–26, begins with words of comfort, *nahamu*.

s. *repentance*: (*Teshuvah*). This Sabbath, called Shabbat Shuvah, falls between Rosh Hashanah and Yom Kippur. The Haftarah, Hosea 14:2–10, begins with the word "return" (*shuvah*), from the same root as *teshuvah*.

t. *begging letters*: In Hebrew such a letter is called a *kibbutz*, literally a "collecting" letter. Modena wrote many of them on behalf of poor persons, usually for a fee, substantiating their claims of poverty and their need for assistance; see Boksenboim, *Iggerot*, nos. 352–365, 367, 369; Haleviim, *Medabber*, pp. 51, 57, 81.

u. *journals*: A journal with rough drafts of Modena's Italian and Hebrew works, including letters, responsa, poems, and some riddles that he wrote beginning in the autumn of 1638, is still extant; see BL Or. 5395. As he added his corrections and alterations to each piece he would leave instructions in Hebrew for a copyist or himself to transcribe at least two copies of it, one for one of his permanent collections of letters, poems, or responsa, and one for the recipient. This manuscript is one of Modena's least polished that has survived. Its rough state makes it particularly valuable because in addition to revealing how he worked it also includes random notes about people he met and about books he had lent or sold. Because he referred here to journals in the plural, it is reasonable to assume that there were similar ones for other periods in his life, though only one is extant.

v. *memorandum notes*: An example of Modena's notes is found in Ambrosiana Q 139 sup., where he recorded excerpts from *Sefer ha-mitzvot* of the Karaites, Elijah Delmedigo's *Behinat ha-dat, Yosippon*, and "an old book." Other examples of Modena's memorandum notes are reproduced in Boksenboim, *Iggerot*, pp. 343–351. See also excursus 2, "Who Wrote the Ambrosiana Manuscript of *Hayyei yehudah?*"

w. *Kuzari*: Modena prepared an index to this classic of medieval Jewish philosophy by Judah Halevi (1075–1141). This index is extant in at least two manuscripts; see JTSA 2285; Kaufmann 269 (Weisz, *Katalog*, no. 269).

x. *Kohen-Job*: The reference is apparently to the commentary on Job by Isaac b. Solomon Hakohen, printed in Constantinople in 1544/1545 (Benjacob, *Otzar ha-sefarim*, p. 644, no. 431). This commentary is mentioned in Modena's bibliographic list in Ancona 7, fol. 3a.

y. *Keli yakar*: Books with this title by two different authors were published during Modena's lifetime: (1) Samuel ben Abraham Laniado (d. 1605), a Syrian rabbi, Bible commentator, and preacher published a commentary on the former prophets in Venice in 1603. It was 564 pages long and only 190 copies were produced (Benayahu, *Ha-yehasim*, pp. 180–181); (2) Ephraim Solomon ben Aaron of Luntshits (1550–1619), a rabbi and preacher from eastern Europe, wrote a commentary on the Torah in a homiletical style. It was published in Lublin, 1602; Prague, 1608; Amsterdam, 1609; and subsequently in many editions of the rabbinic Bible.

z. *treating it as precious on account of the notes that I jotted down therein*: Marginal notes were an important aspect of Modena's research and thought. *Magen ve-herev* was based on his notes on Pietro Galatino's *De arcanis catholicae veritatis*. His views on Kabbalah, along with important autobiographical statements were written in the margins of Azariah de Rossi's *Me'or 'einayim*. Modena expressed some views against Christianity in the margins of the copy of *Sefer alfonso* by Abner of Burgos that he owned. A copy of *Sefer tashbetz* (Cremona, 1556), in the library of the Jewish community of Livorno, bears Modena's signature and at least one inscription in it; cf. C. Bernheimer, *Catalogue des manuscrits et livres rares hébraiques de la bibliothèque du talmud torah de Livourne* (Livorno, 1914), p. 173. Fortunately, many of these books are still extant, and further investigations may disclose others that Modena owned and annotated.

a. *Divrei shelomo*: The most likely book of this title that Modena could have owned was a collection of five sermons for each weekly Torah portion, along with sermons for the holidays by Solomon bar Isaac Leveit Halevi. It was published at Venice in 1596.

b. *'Akedah*: This work is *'Akedat yitzhak* by Isaac ben Moses Arama (ca. 1420–1494), a Spanish rabbi, preacher, and philosopher. *'Akedat yitzhak* consists of 105 sermons treating philosophical ideas in the light of biblical and rabbinic texts. It was published first at Salonika in 1522 and many times thereafter.

c. *Abravanel on the Torah*: This work is the commentary on the Torah by the Spanish statesman and philosopher, Don Isaac Abravanel (1437–1508). As mentioned previously, Modena had utilized it when preparing *Ben david*. Abravanel's commentary on the Torah was first published at Venice in 1579 and again there in 1604.

d. *my legal heir*: Modena's legal heir was his daughter Diana; see Howard Adelman's introductory essay.

FOLIO 38a

e. *Will*: This will of 1634 coincides with the point in the autobiography at which Modena begins to lament over his declining health and approaching death; see *The Life of Judah*, fol. 23a.

f. *instead of with a sloped top*: This request was a gesture of modesty because the sharp-pointed coffin was for men of note; see *Riti* (1637) 5.7.2.

g. *place only books I have written*: It was standard procedure to place books on the coffins of rabbis; see *Riti*, 5.8.2.

h. *Tokhahot*: A genre of Hebrew religious poetry that deals with the theme of confession and repentance for sins.

i. *Let them bury me*: The Jewish cemetery is on the Lido across the lagoon; see C. Boccato, *The Ancient Jewish Cemetery of San Nicolo on the Lido in Venice*, trans. L. Hertzberg (Venice, 1981).

j. *grandfather, and uncle*: His maternal grandfather, Johanan Halevi, and his mother's brother-in-law, Isaac Simhah.

k. *Let them march around my grave . . . custom of the Levantines*: Modena described this Levantine custom of circling the grave in *Riti* (1638) 5.7.4. It is interesting that an Italian rabbi desired to be buried in accordance with Levantine customs.

FOLIO 38b

l. *Kaddish*: A prayer extolling God recited as part of the regular worship service and also specifically in memory of relatives after their death.

m. *acquisition binding*: See textual note 21; *The Life of Judah*, fol. 10a and historical note y; I. Blumenfeld, "Schreiben des herrn Prof. Lelio della Torre an herrn Ignas Blumenfeld in Wien," and "Schriften des Dr. L. V. Cantarini an Pastor Ch. The. Unger," *Otzar nehmad* 1 (1856): 135–141.

n. *And this latter way seems right to me*: When he later rewrote this epitaph, he incorporated his own suggestions (*Divan*, no. 225). This version was the one that appears to have been in circulation during the 1800s and 1900s as the actual text, but neither version corresponds exactly to what appears on the tombstone:

> Words of the deceased
> Four cubits / of ground in this courtyard
> By making the acquisition / binding and eternal
> From above they have transferred to the possession of Judah Aryeh
> Modena now acquainted with Him and at Peace

> Died on the Holy Sabbath 27 Adar 1648

For a photograph of the tombstone at the time of its rediscovery in 1929, see A. Ottolenghi, "Leon da Modena spunti di vita ebraica del ghetto nel secolo XVII," *Rivista di Venezia* (July, 1929): 15–16.

In 1973 the cemetery was cleaned up again, and this time, unfortunately, another tombstone was placed at the base of Modena's, obscuring the bottom lines (see fig. 13). Entering the gate of the oldest cemetery, which faces the bay and abuts the rifle club, and walking toward the high monument in the middle, one finds Modena's tombstone about ten paces down, on the right, in the middle of the row. It is one of the lowest tombstones in the area and the upper lefthand corner appears almost to have been broken off.

o. *the Cigala place . . . "Cave of the Makhpelah"*: See *The Life of Judah*, fol. 27a.

p. *left the Luzzatto place . . . I[saac] O[badaiah]*: See *The Life of Judah*, fol. 27b.

q. *house of Cervo*: See *The Life of Judah*, fol. 28a, where the name of the landlord is given as Naftali Cohen Scocco.

r. *h[ouse] of M[oses] L[uzzatto]*: See *The Life of Judah*, fol. 28a.

s. *house of Baldoz*: See *The Life of Judah*, fol. 28a.

t. *Cannaregio*: See historical note to fol. 19a.

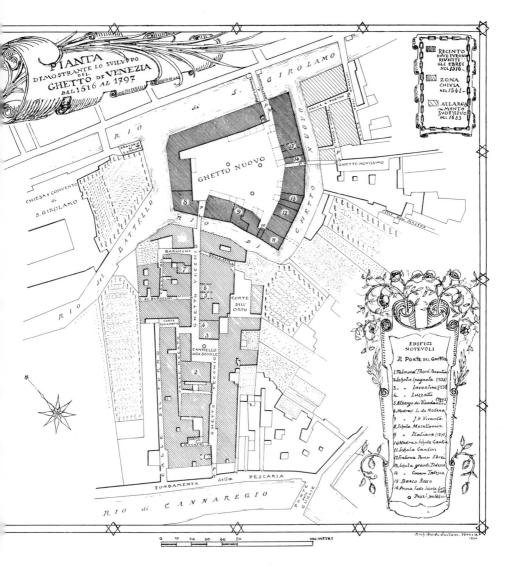

14. Plan of the Venetian ghetto, 1516–1797.

15. View of the Ponte di Ghetto Nuovissimo connecting the Ghetto Nuovo with the Ghetto Nuovissimo.

16 *(top)*. The square of the Ghetto Nuovo.
17 *(bottom)*. Main street of the Ghetto Vecchio, with the alleged midrash
(school) of Leon Modena in the foreground (first doorway on left) and the
Sephardi synagogue at the end (nos. 6 and 2, respectively, in fig. 14).

277

Excursus 1: The Venetian Ghetto
in Historical Perspective

BENJAMIN C. I. RAVID

FROM THEIR earliest diaspora days onward, Jews chose freely, for a variety of reasons, to live close together, as did many other groups residing in foreign lands. This tendency was strengthened in the eleventh and twelfth centuries, as the secular authorities, primarily in the Germanic lands and Reconquista Spain, offered Jews special quarters as an inducement to settle in their realms. These areas, often referred to as the Jewish quarter or street, were neither compulsory nor segregated. Jews continued to have contacts on all levels—economic, intellectual, and even physical—with their Christian neighbors. But the Catholic church, growing in strength, looked askance at these relationships, and in 1179, the Third Lateran Council stipulated that henceforth Christians should not dwell together with Jews. To become effective, this general policy statement had to be translated into legislation by the numerous European secular authorities. On the whole—with the exception of some places in France and the Germanic lands—only infrequently were laws confining the Jews to segregated quarters enacted in the Middle Ages, and sometimes these laws were not actually implemented. The few segregated Jewish quarters that were established, the best known of which is probably that of Frankfurt am Main dating from the 1460s, were never called ghettos because the term originated in Venice and came to be associated with the Jews only in the sixteenth century.

While the Venetian government permitted individual Jews to reside in the city of Venice in the later Middle Ages, it never officially authorized Jews to settle there as a group, with the exception of a brief period from 1392 to 1397. The government did, however, allow Jewish moneylenders to live on the mainland, across the lagoons at Mestre, and the terms of their charter allowed them to seek refuge in Venice in case of war, in order to safeguard loan pledges from Christians that were in their hands. Accordingly in 1509, during the war of the League of Cambrai, a severe conflict during the course of which the enemies of Venice advanced across the mainland toward the island city, the Jewish moneylenders of Mestre and other places on the mainland fled to Venice. Shortly afterward, the Venetian government recovered its territories and ordered all the refugees to return home. But soon it realized that allowing the Jews to stay in the city was doubly beneficial: first, they could be required to provide the hard-pressed treasury with substantial annual payments, and second, permitting them to engage in moneylending as pawnbrokers in the city itself would be convenient for the needy, whose numbers had been swelled by war. So the government issued a five-year charter that authorized the Jews to stay in the city and lend money in it.

Jewish moneylending was clearly very important. In addition to giving the government an additional source of revenue and assisting in promoting urban tranquility, it also had great significance in the religious sphere. Because both Jews and Christians adhered to the biblical commandment that forbade members of the same faith to lend money to each other at interest, the presence of Jewish pawnbrokers lending money on interest on loan pledges to the Christian poor rendered it unnecessary for Christians to engage in that activity in violation of the religious tradition. It also obviated the need to establish in Venice, as had been done elsewhere, a pawn-broking establishment under municipal or ecclesiastical supervision known as a *monte di pietà*, which could cause theological and political difficulties. Because the Jewish moneylenders thus not only helped to solve the socioeconomic problems of an increasingly urbanized economy but also prevented Christians from violating church law, the Venetian government periodically renewed the charters of the Jewish moneylenders until the Venetian Republic surrendered to Napoleon Bonaparte over two and a half centuries later, in 1797.

While the Venetian government tolerated the presence of the Jews in the city, the Catholic clergy—especially during the Easter season, when anti-Jewish sentiment tended to intensify—fulminated against them, against their residence in the city, and against their moneylending activities, and advocated their expulsion. Under clerical influence, on March 29, 1516, the Venetian Senate asserted that no God-fearing inhabitant of the city desired that the Jews should dwell spread out all over it, living in the same houses as Christians and going where they pleased day and night, and legislated that henceforth all Jews in the city were to go to live together on the island known as the Ghetto Nuovo (the new ghetto). Gates were to be erected on the two bridges leading out of it, and those gates were to be locked at sunset and only opened again at sunrise, with a substantial fine for any Jew caught outside after hours. The Christian inhabitants of the ghetto were required to leave, and as an incentive for landlords to comply, the Jews were required to pay a rent one-third higher, with that increase exempt from taxation.

Clearly, the word "ghetto" is of Venetian and not Jewish origin, as has sometimes been conjectured; it is encountered in Venetian sources from the fourteenth and fifteenth centuries, and today it is generally accepted that the name derives from the previous presence of foundries where artillery was cast (*il ghetto* or *il getto*, from the verb *gettare*, "to pour" or "to cast").

Despite the attempts by the Jews to ward off segregation in this new compulsory area, the Venetian government was adamant; while willing to compromise on a few administrative details, it was unwilling to make even minor concessions on the general principle that all the Jews in the city had to live in the ghetto. The presence of the Jews was necessary for economic reasons, and the ghetto was the institution that relegated them to their appropriate permanent position in Christian society.

Some twenty-five years later, in 1541, a group of visiting Jewish Levantine merchants complained to the Venetian government that there was not sufficient room for them and their merchandise in the ghetto and requested additional space. The government investigated, found their complaint to be valid, and, noting that the greater part of the imports from the Ottoman Balkans was handled by these Jewish merchants, granted their request. It ordered the area called the Ghetto Vecchio (the old ghetto), across the canal from the Ghetto Nuovo and connected to it by a bridge, walled up and joined to it and assigned to the Jewish merchants. Henceforth, Venice had not one ghetto but two, and they were to endure until the end of the republic.

The term "ghetto" soon spread beyond the city of Venice. In 1555, as part of the hostile attitude toward the Jews that was adopted by the Counter-Reformation, Pope Paul IV, shortly after his inauguration, issued a bull that severely restricted the Jews. Its first paragraph provided that henceforth in all places in the papal states, the Jews were to live separated from Christians on a single street—and should it not suffice, then on as many adjacent ones as necessary, with only one entrance and one exit. In compliance with this bull, that same year the Jews of Rome were required to move into a new compulsory segregated quarter, which was apparently called a ghetto for the first time seven years later in 1562.

Influenced by the papal example, many local Italian authorities instituted special compulsory, segregated quarters for the Jews. Following the Venetian and now also Roman precedents, these new areas were called ghettos already in the legislation that ordered their establishment in, for example, Florence, Siena, Padua, and Mantua.

Significantly, this new use of the word to mean a compulsory Jewish quarter came to be known also in Venice. In July 1630, the Jewish merchants in the city requested that the ghetto be enlarged for the sake of some additional Jewish families who, they claimed, would come to the city if they had suitable quarters. Very sharp objections were raised by both the Christian landlords who owned the buildings in the ghetto and those Jews who had built additional stories onto existing buildings, on the grounds that expanding the ghetto might lead to their own dwellings going unrented. Thereupon, to demonstrate that they did not seek the enlargement of the ghetto for their own sake but only for that of the newcomers, the Jewish merchants offered a guarantee of three thousand ducats, to be pro-rated according to the number of the anticipated twenty new families that did not actually arrive. The Senate, always concerned with attracting merchants to the city in order to enhance trade, and no doubt especially so after the plague of 1630–1631, accepted this offer and in March 1633 provided that an area containing twenty dwellings, located across from the Ghetto Nuovo in a direction almost opposite from the Ghetto Vecchio, be enclosed and joined to the Ghetto Nuovo by a footbridge over the canal. This area was not designated by any name in the Senate legislation of 1633, but a report issued by one of the magistracies of the government in 1636 referred to it as the Ghetto Nuovissimo, the newest ghetto. Obviously, this term did not refer to a "newest foundry" once in operation on that site, but rather to the newest compulsory, segregated, enclosed quarter of the Jews.

Subsequently, in a process that has not yet been traced, the word "ghetto" came to be used in a looser sense to refer to any area densely populated by Jews, even in places where they had freedom of residence and could and did live in the same districts and houses as Christians. Later still, it came to be the general designation for areas densely inhabited by members of any minority group, almost always for voluntary socio-economic reasons rather than for compulsory legal ones, as had been the case with the initial Jewish ghetto.

It must be noted that the varied usages of the word "ghetto" in different senses has created a certain blurring of the historical reality, especially when the word appears in phrases such as "the age of the ghetto," "out of the ghetto," and "ghetto mentality," so often applied to the Jewish experience in the Germanic lands and in eastern Europe in the seventeenth, eighteenth, and even nineteenth centuries. Actually, the word can be used in the Counter-Reformation Italian sense of a compulsory, segregated Jewish quarter only in connection with the Jewish experience in a few places in the Germanic lands, and certainly not at all with that in Poland–Russia. Although up to the Russian revolution of 1917 the Jews often lived in small towns and rural villages that were predominantly Jewish, they were never confined to specific segregated, walled-up quarters apart from their Christian neighbors. If the word "ghetto" is to be used in its original literal sense in connection with eastern Europe, then it must be asserted that the age of the ghetto arrived there only after the German invasions during the Second World War. But there was a basic difference: unlike those ghettos of earlier days, which were designed to provide the Jews with a clearly defined permanent place in Christian society, these ghettos rather constituted merely a temporary stage on the planned road to total liquidation.

Largely because of the word's negative connotations, the nature of Jewish life in the ghetto is often misunderstood. Clearly, the establishment of ghettos did not—as the autobiography of Leon Modena demonstrates—lead to the breaking off of previous Jewish contacts with the outside world on all levels, from the highest to the lowest, to the consternation of church and state alike. Additionally, apart from the question of whether the ghetto succeeded in fulfilling the expectations of those in the outside world who desired its establishment, from the internal Jewish perspective, many evaluations of the alleged impact of the ghetto on the Jewish mentality and on Jewish cultural and intellectual life require revision. For example, an investigation of the cultural life inside the ghetto of Venice and the extent to which external trends penetrated it—as attested by the writings of Leon Modena, Simone Luzzatto, and Sarra Copia Sullam—leads to a reevaluation of the alleged negative impact of the ghetto in the intellectual and cultural spheres. In general, the determining element in those spheres was not so much the circumstance of the Jews being required to live in a ghetto, but rather the nature of the outside environment and whether it offered an attractive supplement to traditional Jewish genres of intellectual activity. In all places, Jewish life and culture should be examined in the context of the environment, and developments—especially undesirable ones—should not merely be attributed to the alleged impact of the ghetto.

An extended investigation of why the word "ghetto" is used so loosely and imprecisely would reveal many complex motivations. The most common reason is no doubt merely a simple casual use of the word without any awareness of its origin and nature. Others, however, are somewhat less innocent and may involve a desire, proceeding from either religious, national, or psychological considerations, to portray the life of the Jews in the preemancipation European diaspora unfavorably. The shared element is, significantly, that the term has become a value concept with negative connotations, rather than a descriptive word indicating a particular system under which Jews lived. The result has been to blur the historical reality of one of the basic aspects of Jewish survival, the Jewish quarter, thus giving additional urgency to the need for its systematic examination.

FOR FURTHER details, see Salo W. Baron, *A Social and Religious History of the Jews*, 18 vols. to date (New York and Philadelphia, 1952–), vol. 9, pp. 32–36, vol. 11, pp. 87–96, vol. 14, pp. 114–120; Benjamin C. I. Ravid, "The Religious, Economic, and Social Background and Context of the Establishment of the Ghetti of Venice," in *Gli Ebrei e Venezia*, ed. Gaetano Cozzi (Milan, 1987), pp. 211–259; and idem, "The Establishment of the Ghetto Nuovissimo of Venice," to appear in the memorial volume for Umberto Cassuto.

Excursus 2: Who Wrote the Ambrosiana Manuscript of *Hayyei yehudah*?

MARK R. COHEN

S CHOLARS have long accepted, without systematic analysis, that the manuscript of *Hayyei yehudah* found in the 1960s at the Biblioteca Ambrosiana, Milan, is an autograph. After a careful study of the manuscript in preparation for this English translation, comparing its script with other specimens of Modena's handwriting and examining other significant details contained in it, I feel confident that this opinion is correct.

Description of the manuscript

The manuscript (shelfmark X 119 sup.) consists of several quires and a few loose pages bound in a small notebook with a cardboard cover. The binding is decorative, with a design in four colors (red, white, yellow, and gray). There are thirty-eight leaves between the covers of the notebook, and the watermarks are uniform. The pages measure 20.2 by 15.5 centimeters, and a full page of writing contains, usually, twenty-five closely written lines.

The manuscript is provided with a title page, as was customary even with unpublished works during this period. Folio 3b (the Arabic pagination is that added recently by the Biblioteca Ambrosiana) contains the words *Hayyei yehudah* centered on the page and surrounded above and below by a design of wavy lines (see fig. 3). Beginning on folio 4a, the first page of the narrative, and continuing through folio 27b, the manuscript bears an original pagination using Hebrew letters for numbers (*alef* through *mem-het* for pages 1 through 48). At the top of "page 1" (see fig. 4) there is an abbreviation of the motto "With God's help may we do this successfully, amen," superscribed by Modena with a similar decorative flourish representing the first letter, *b* (with), as in other manuscripts written in his hand. This prayer is followed by the opening words of the autobiography, "This is the life story of Judah Aryeh." This introduction is set off from the beginning of the narrative proper by its form: it is written in large, square letters and contrasts sharply with the rounded cursive that is used throughout the rest of the autobiography.

The text of the autobiography runs from folio 4a through folio 29b. Folios 30a through 34a (nine pages) are blank. Folios 34b and 35a contain a list of short, cryptic notes entitled "Miseries of my heart in brief." The section begins, "Apart from the banishments, the death of my sons, and the other matters recorded here," and lists disturbing episodes in Modena's life between 1601 and the death of his son-in-law, Jacob Motta, in the summer of 1645. These fragments of narrative are in the form of "memorandums"—*mazkeret* (plural *mazkarot*), sometimes called *reshimot le-zikkaron*, "memorandum notes"—that Modena often recorded in various places. Some but not all of the entries are elaborated with greater clarity in the main body of the discourse, and it is possible that many of them originated in jottings Modena made elsewhere from time to time as he thought of episodes he wanted to include in his autobiography. Natalie Davis's suggestion (see her introductory essay, note 38), however, that the section as it stands on folios 34b–35a, with its heading, "Miseries of my heart in brief," represents a topical rethinking of Modena's life around 1645 (perhaps inspired by a similar chapter in Girolamo Cardano's autobiography published in 1643) has great merit. It is also consistent with the view held here that Modena himself wrote the Ambrosiana manuscript of *Hayyei yehudah*.

Similar to the "Testimony of Illustrious Men Concerning Me" that Cardano included in his autobiography (see Natalie Davis's aforementioned note), on the penultimate pages of his own autobiographical notebook (fols. 35b–36a; see fig. 12), Modena recorded some commendations of his own work by noted authors. He copied a passage in Latin from *De successionibus*, a book on Jewish inheritance practices by the English Christian Hebraist, John Selden, indicating the author's indebtedness to Modena's book on the Jewish rites, and cited (in Hebrew) two other laudatory statements, one by a former Christian student, Jean de Plantavit de la Pause, bishop of Lodève, and the other by the Amsterdam rabbi Manasseh ben Israel.

Following another blank page (fol. 36b), the notebook ends with two versions of the author's last will and testament, one written in 1634 and the second in 1647–1648. The earlier will was copied, appropriately, on the *last* blank page of the notebook (fol. 38a–38b). Having suddenly begun in the spring of 1634 to feel old and infirm and to believe that his end was near, as he related in his autobiography (fol. 23a), Modena drew up his will at the end of May of that year and copied it, symbolically, on the *end* page of the notebook that contained his ongoing autobiography. Thirteen years later, however, intervening events in his life and other personal concerns, including a sudden, precipitous decline in his physical and psychological state, prompted him to write a new last will and testament, for which, now, only the penultimate pages in the notebook (fol. 37a–b) were available.

At the bottom of the last page of the notebook, following the will of 1634, there are some additional cryptic jottings about Modena's peregrinations from dwelling to dwelling between 1642 and 1647. These seem to fall into the category of the "memorandums" jotted down on folios 34b and 35a. Indeed, with one minor exception, all of the facts in this section are found in their place in greater detail in the autobiography proper.

Separated from this section by a line are five more short jottings on two lines. The facts in these lines do not have a counterpart in the autobiography. Their meaning remains a mystery.

Orthography, Inks, Catchwords, Interpolations, and Other Features

The orthography of the Ambrosiana manuscript of *Hayyei yehudah* matches samples of Modena's handwriting in other manuscripts. A case in point is Bodleian Library, Oxford, MS Canon Misc. 204. This is an unfinished commentary by Modena on the Torah. In 1601, as he relates in the autobiography, he received a commission from a wealthy Levantine Jewish merchant named Joseph Pardo to compile an anthology of Bible commentaries culled from twenty-seven different authors. Modena began work on the project in the summer of 1601, but the commission was retracted a few months later. Modena was left with a rough copy of the few sections of the Torah that he had completed. Thirty years later he returned to the project. In the summer of 1632 he directed his eleven-year-old grandson, Isaac—then living with him following the death of his own father, Modena's son-in-law Jacob Halevi, three years earlier—to make a legible copy of his rough draft. Isaac accomplished the task in a few months, and the results are preserved in Bodleian MS Canon Misc. 204. To the completed manuscript Modena added a preface of his own (fol. 170b; the manuscript was paginated by the library from back to front) in which he described the history of the project (omitting embarrassing details about the reasons for its cancellation, which he discloses quite candidly in *Hayyei yehudah*; see fol. 13b and the historical notes) and the circumstances leading him to have his grandson recopy his thirty-year-old illegible draft. Modena signed and dated this preface on the 12th of Shevat 5393 (January 23, 1633). The handwriting of this signed preface is unmistakably identical with that of the Ambrosiana manuscript of *Hayyei yehudah*.

Apart from the similarity of handwriting, the clearest evidence supporting the view that *Hayyei yehudah* is an autograph is internal. For instance, the last pages of the narrative, recording events of the 1640s, when Modena was tired, weak, and ailing, show intermittent lapses in the neat, stable handwriting that characterizes most of the previous part of the manuscript. The first sign of deterioration begins in the middle of folio 27b, corresponding to page *mem-het* (48), the last page in the notebook to bear a Hebrew number. This section, which closes at the end of the third line on folio 28a, relates events that occurred between the Jewish New Year of 5403 (September 1642) and the end of that Jewish year (September 1643). The deterioration in penmanship resumes on folio 29a–b, which contains the last recorded events of Modena's life between the summer of 1645, when his son-in-law Jacob Motta died, and the end of February 1648, just weeks before his own death on March 21.

The same deterioration in handwriting is revealed by the comparison of the two wills. That of 1634 is written in the vigorous script of the younger Modena, while that of 1647–1648 betrays the unstable hand of the sections of the autobiography, beginning on folio 27b, that were written in the 1640s. So do the last section of "Miseries of my heart in brief," listing tribulations from 1641 through 1645 (see fig. 11), and the cryptic notes at the bottom of folio 38b, the last page in the notebook, which were apparently jotted down in 1647.

Close examination of the manuscript yields additional clear indications that it is an autograph. Two colors of ink appear in the manuscript: black and reddish brown. The reddish brown apparently represents an inferior quality ink, which during the course of time changed color from its original black due to oxidation of its iron content. The black ink appears consistently between the first page and the bottom of folio 15a (p. 23 of the Hebrew pagination). The reddish-brown color appears for the first time at an entry for the year 1611 (top of fol. 15b, p. 24 of the Hebrew pagination), continues for the following five folios through a section recorded in April or May, 1621 (fol. 18b, p. 30 of the Hebrew pagination), and recurs intermittently thereafter.

The hitherto unremarked use of different inks and the intermittent alternation of inks in the second half of the autobiography correlates with the fact that Modena began writing the long first part of his family's history in 1618, following the death of his son Mordecai, and worked on it steadily until April 1621, when he finally reached the shattering event itself (see fol. 17a, note 2). This, in turn, correlates with another detail that has till now gone unnoted. The manuscript contains catchwords at the feet of verso pages, but only from the beginning up to and including folio 17b, page 28 of the Hebrew pagination, the very page on which Modena concludes his account of Mordecai's death. This fact suggests that the section covering the history of the family down to the crucial event that precipitated the writing of the autobiography was recorded on loose sheets of folded paper, with catchwords to preserve the order of the pages (the only place where a catchword is omitted is at the foot of folio 16b, page 26 of the Hebrew pagination, immediately preceding the first word in the account of Mordecai's demise at the top of folio 17a, page 27 of the Hebrew pagination). Then at some point—apparently in April or May 1621—Modena gathered what he had compiled thus far and bound the pages into a notebook along with additional blank quires and individual pages on which to record subsequent events in his life. The binding, of course, eliminated the need for further catchwords.

The pattern of catchwords in the Ambrosiana manuscript correlates with yet another significant detail. The first twenty-nine pages of the autobiography—the ones for which catchwords were provided—are relatively clean and neat, while from page 30 (fol. 18b) on, interpolations, both interlinear and marginal, lines separating entries, and other marks in the margin begin to appear frequently. It may well be that Modena recopied parts of the first section of the autobiography from drafts before incorporating them into the notebook, a hypothesis that would explain the relatively unmarred appearance of the first twenty-nine pages of the text. Whatever the case, the various interrelated physical features of the Ambrosiana manuscript discussed here are wholly consistent with the view that it is an autograph.

This opinion is strengthened when one considers the nature of the manuscript interpolations, which are clearly the result of revisions made by the author. Modena inserted comments and facts by writing above the line (often signaling the insertion with a caret), by adding words in the margin, and by squeezing in passages at the end of a line or at the bottom of a page. Some of these interpolations were clearly added as a result of subsequent reflection or in the light of new information. This authorial revision over time is sometimes confirmed by the appearance of the ink. Often the color of the interpolation contrasts with that of the original passage in the text, one black and the other reddish brown, indicating that different batches of ink were employed.

Frequently the author's own sense of what he should not omit from his autobiography led him to make interpolations. For example, Modena sometimes inserted negative comments about the behavior of individuals in his family, evidently having decided that it was important to transmit his "true" feelings in these cases to posterity. A fascinating interpolation having to do with people outside his family is his note, squeezed in at the bottom of a page after the year 1635, in which he rejoices over the deaths of two of the murderers of his son Zebulun in 1622, exclaiming, "may their bones be ground to dust in hell. They died in Livorno, the second of the two in 5395 [1634/1635]. Of the others, some died as a result of calamities, some became apostates, and of some not a trace remains. Blessed is he who has granted me revenge."

The additions motivated by Modena's sense of self to his "bibliography" clearly attest to the fact that the manuscript is in his own hand. This list of writings—books, poems, and prefaces, in both Hebrew and Italian—some already published, others completed in manuscript, and still others not yet finished, was originally begun in the wake of his aforementioned son's death in 1622. Later, as time passed and the autobiography progressed, he supplemented that list with newly published works, which he added above the line and in the right-hand margin (see fig. 6). These revisions clearly reflect the mentality of a proud writer, continuously updating his curriculum vitae, much like writers and scholars of our own day.

The same sense of self led to other interpolations in the manuscript, further supporting the view that it is an autograph. In the case of the list of twenty-six occupations that Modena engaged in during his lifetime, he highlighted his accomplishments by devoting a separate page in the notebook to it and by writing the names of the jobs in two parallel columns of equal length. The original list contained only twenty-three items. Later on, as in the updating of his bibliography, he added three more activities by squeezing them into the right-hand column. These interpolations are easily detectable both by observing the spacing between items and, if one consults the original at the Biblioteca Ambrosiana in Milan, by the fact that the original list of twenty-three is black while the added items are reddish brown in color, thus indicating that they were written in ink from a different batch (see fig. 9, which shows all the physical features except the contrasting color of the inks). The prominent layout given to this list and the addition of the three items omitted in the original enumeration, like other personal touches in the manuscript discussed in this excursus, add interesting sidelights to the larger picture of Leon Modena's self-centered personality that is so evident from the content of the autobiography and demonstrate unequivocally that the Ambrosiana manuscript was written by the author himself.

The Theory of Daniel Carpi

All this evidence—graphological and other—regarding the Ambrosiana manuscript of *Hayyei yehudah* seems to confirm beyond a reasonable doubt the previously untested hypothesis about its autographical nature. In his new Hebrew edition of the autobiography, however, Daniel Carpi rejects this view. He believes the Ambrosiana manuscript to be a copy of the original, which is now lost. He finds the handwriting too consistently uniform and neat to have been written by one person in installments over such a long period of time. Further, Carpi concludes on the basis of handwriting comparison that the manuscript is the handiwork of Modena's grandson, Isaac min Haleviim. The interlinear interpolations and additions in the margin are, according to Carpi, the work either of the "copyist" Isaac, who may have made some of the changes "during the Rabbi's lifetime and at his direction," or of a later "corrector" (*magiah*; see Carpi's introduction).

His argument, from internal paleographical evidence, that the manuscript is the work of someone other than the author is in large measure subjective and overlooks certain telling observations mentioned here. For one thing, the assertion about the neatness of the manuscript fails to take into account the fact noted above that only the first twenty-nine pages of the manuscript are actually clean and neat. Moreover, the claim about uniformity of penmanship ignores the deterioration near the end of the manuscript, where the sentences are written in a shaky hand. Carpi does recognize that there is a change of handwriting in the last part of the section entitled "Miseries of my heart in brief." While he does not attribute it to deterioration stemming from the writer's old age and infirmity, his suggestion that it was "copied by the same copyist but after a passage of years" generally confirms the assumption I have employed to buttress the view that the manuscript is an autograph. Furthermore, Carpi's suggestion about Modena's possible direct involvement in some of the interpolations supposedly copied by his grandson reflects a well-founded instinct about the authorial nature of so many of these revisions, based on the obvious fact that a copyist would have integrated them into the text. Finally, Carpi does not explain why a copyist would have left so many blank pages between the author's last words (on fol. 29b) and the brief notes, commendations, wills, and lists of peregrinations found between folio 34b and the end of the notebook.

There remains Carpi's argument from external paleographic evidence that the handwriting of the Ambrosiana manuscript of *Hayyei yehudah* is that of Isaac min Haleviim, as represented, for instance, by the latter's handwritten autobiography, *Medabber tahpukhot*, similarly preserved in the Biblioteca Ambrosiana (discussed in Carpi's edition of *Medabber* as well as in his introduction to *Hayyei yehudah*). To be sure, there is a tremendous similarity between Modena's handwriting and that of his grandson. This fact is not in itself surprising in view of the fact that Isaac's grandfather reared him in his home and taught him from the time he was eight years old. It is even true that Isaac copied other of his grandfather's works, such as the unfinished commentary on the Torah commissioned by Pardo. Nevertheless, these very manuscripts contain evidence that supports the view about *Hayyei yehudah* put forth here.

Particularly persuasive in this regard is a manuscript of a work by Mo-

18 *(on facing page)*. Page, in the handwriting of Modena's grandson, Isaac min Haleviim, showing part of Isaac's introduction to the copy he made of Modena's *Magen ve-herev*.

Discimus hec ex Leonis mutinensis Judei
qui Venetijs hodieq ut audio Archisinagogus est
compendio Italice conscripto de Ritibus, uita, &
moribus Hebreor, exemplar mecum pro sua hum=
nitate comunicauit F. & eruditissimaq Guilielmus
Boswelus qui ab eo autographum accepit eius.

Procemio Rabi Juda da modena

dena that Isaac copied in his mature years. In the year following his grand-father's death in 1648, when Isaac was in his late twenties, he made a copy of Modena's anti-Christian treatise, *Magen ve-herev*. That manuscript is also part of the Ambrosiana collection (Biblioteca Ambrosiana, MS Q 139 sup.). Close examination of Isaac's mature hand, coupled with other significant paleographical features of this manuscript, establish even more firmly the case for the autographical nature of the Ambrosiana *Hayyei ye-hudah*. Both in the specimen of Isaac's youthful script described previously and in the manuscript of *Magen ve-herev* that he copied when he was a young adult there are telling features that differentiate his hand from that of his grandfather. One major differentiating feature of Isaac's handwriting is the form of his block letters. In the two variants in which they appear, they contrast markedly with the block letters used at the beginning and end of *Hayyei yehudah*. Another telling graphological element is the cursive ligature '*l* (*alef lamed*). Whereas Modena's '*l* ligature typically slants far to the left, Isaac's typically stands erect—as can be seen in the facsimile of a page from his introduction to the Ambrosiana manuscript of *Magen ve-herev* (fig. 18). (To be sure, occasional examples of a slanting ligature, similar to that of his grandfather, can be found in manuscripts copied by Isaac.)

In addition to the contrasting features in the written Hebrew of grand-father and grandson, an overlooked but crucial piece of evidence regarding their respective vernacular scripts confirms that *Hayyei yehudah* was copied by Leon Modena himself rather than by Isaac min Haleviim. In Isaac's introduction to *Magen ve-herev* (printed by L. Geiger, *Leon da Modena: Rab-biner zu Venedig und seine Stellung zur Kabbalah, zum Thalmud, und zum Christenthume* [Breslau, 1856], Hebrew section, fols. 10b–11b), he repro-duced verbatim from *Hayyei yehudah* the passage by John Selden mention-ing the latter's debt to Modena and his book on the Jewish rites, the *Riti*. If the hypothesis that Isaac copied the Ambrosiana *Hayyei yehudah* were correct, we would expect to find complete congruence between the ver-nacular handwritings in the two manuscripts. On close examination, how-ever, of the facsimiles provided of the relevant pages in the respective man-uscripts of *Magen ve-herev* and *Hayyei yehudah* (figs. 18 and 12), the similarities are completely overshadowed by the differences. The letter *h*, as in *haec* and *hodieque*, and the letter *d*, as in *audio* and *compendio*, are sub-stantially dissimilar. So is the letter *l* in *exemplar*, *Gulielmus*, and *Boswellus*. Uppercase *I* in *Italice* and uppercase *B* in *Boswellus* (spelled correctly with two *l*s in *Hayyei yehudah* but with only one in *Magen ve-herev*) constitute additional telling contrasts. Both the form and the spelling of the word *Ebreorum* (*Hebreorum* in *Magen ve-herev*) diverge considerably. Anthony Grafton of Princeton, to whom I showed the two facsimiles and who con-curred with my judgment that the vernacular hands are substantially different, notes, in addition, that the spelling *Venetiis* with double *i* in *Hayyei yehudah* was more likely to have been employed by someone educated in the sixteenth century (like Leon Modena), while the spelling *Venetijs* in *Magen ve-herev* would have been regular for an individual (like Isaac min Haleviim) trained in the seventeenth century.

Finally, the vernacular handwriting in *Hayyei yehudah* can be verified as belonging to Leon Modena by comparison with other manuscripts. One example, notices of receipt of payment written by Modena in the expense ledger of the Italian synagogue, is shown in figure 10. Even the variants employed by him on the same page, in entries separated by but a few months, show how different his Roman script was from that of his grandson.

These graphological and paleographical data, combined with the weighty evidence provided here regarding the Hebrew handwriting of the manuscript, the pattern of interpolations, and other significant details (more of which are mentioned in the textual notes to the translation), confirm conclusively that the copyist of the Ambrosiana *Hayyei yehudah* was none other than the author himself.

Index

Note: References to pages from the text of the autobiography *Hayyei yehudah* (The Life of Judah) have been set in *italics*; references to textual notes appearing on these pages have been set roman.